THE CREW

DAVID PRICE's early interest in aviation was inspired by days exploring deserted RAF airfields in his native Cumbria. He has written for many newspapers and magazines on military aviation. He is the author of *A Bomber Crew Mystery: The Forgotten Heroes of 388th Bombardment Group* (2016).

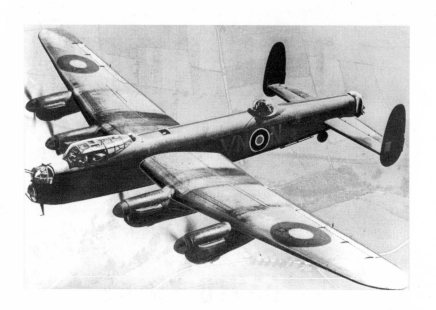

THE CREW

THE STORY OF A LANCASTER
BOMBER CREW

DAVID PRICE

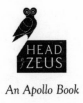

An Apollo Book

This is an Apollo book, first
published in the UK in 2020
by Head of Zeus Ltd

9 7 5 3 2 4 6 8

A catalogue record for this book is
available from the British Library.

ISBN (HB): 9781789542707
ISBN (E): 9781789542691

Typeset by Adrian McLaughlin
Maps by Jamie Whyte

Printed and bound in Great Britain
by CPI Group (UK) Ltd

Head of Zeus Ltd

5–8 Hardwick Street
London ECIR 4RG

WWW.HEADOFZEUS.COM

Endpapers
An Avro Lancaster heavy bomber
seen from above during a Second
World War bombing raid over
Hamburg, Germany.
(Science & Society Picture Library /
Getty Images)

Image Credits

Apic / Getty Images: p. ii; Author's
own photographs: pp. xv, 309, 348;
Central Press / Stringer / Getty
Images: p. xxv; Daily Herald
Archive / Getty Images: p. 124;
Hulton Archive / Stringer / Getty
Images: pp. 13, 17; IWM (CH 10403):
p. 95; IWM / Getty Images: pp. 111,
186; Popperfoto / Getty Images: p.
157; With permission from the Bowes
family: pp. 52, 233, 265, 288, 317,
342 (above and middle); With
permission from the Cook family:
pp. 30, 125; With permission from
the Cook, Bowes and Woollford
families: pp. 56; With permission
from Ken Cook: pp. 123, 334, 336,
337, 346, 364; With permission
from the Owens family: p. 293; With
permission from the Woollford family:
pp. 208, 342 (bottom); Public domain:
pp. xi, 34, 41, 58, 67, 69, 79, 120, 135,
151, 159, 191, 207, 223 (both), 229,
266, 298, 319, 339.

To Trish, long-suffering but ever supportive

Avro Lancaster
range and bomb load

Lincoln

with 22,000lbs

with 12,000lbs

with 7,000lbs

775 miles

865 miles

1265 miles

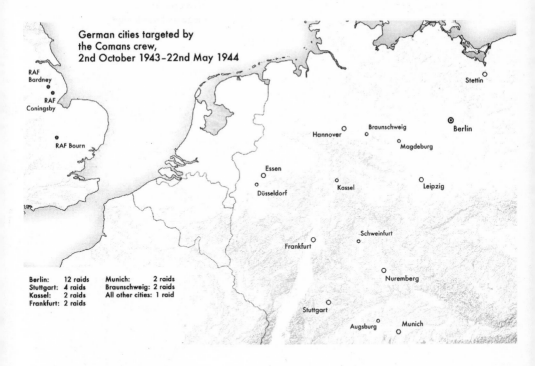

German cities targeted by
the Comans crew,
2nd October 1943–22nd May 1944

RAF Bardney
RAF Coningsby
RAF Bourn

Stettin
Hannover
Braunschweig
Berlin
Magdeburg
Essen
Düsseldorf
Kassel
Leipzig
Schweinfurt
Frankfurt
Nuremberg
Stuttgart
Augsburg
Munich

Berlin: 12 raids   Munich: 2 raids
Stuttgart: 4 raids   Braunschweig: 2 raids
Kassel: 2 raids   All other cities: 1 raid
Frankfurt: 2 raids

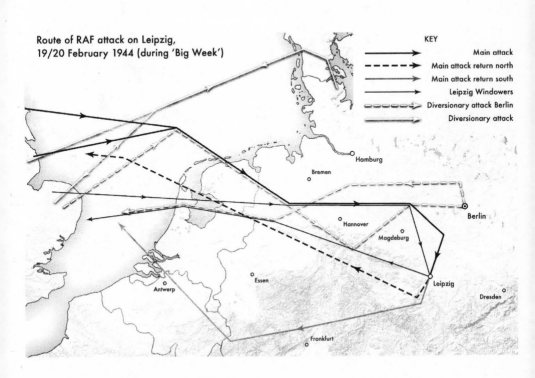

Route of RAF attack on Leipzig,
19/20 February 1944 (during 'Big Week')

KEY

Main attack
Main attack return north
Main attack return south
Leipzig Windowers
Diversionary attack Berlin
Diversionary attack

Hamburg
Bremen
Hannover
Magdeburg
Berlin
Essen
Leipzig
Antwerp
Dresden
Frankfurt

Contents

A Note from the Author

B omber Command drew young men from all over the Commonwealth, tens of thousands of them who thrilled at the thought of flying. They were trained thoroughly and then asked to perform extraordinary technical feats while packed into a flying metal tube. They were all volunteers who exposed themselves to extraordinary dangers. The lives of these men became intertwined in the formation of a crew, each with its own characteristics and unique personality. In examining one such crew, it was my desire to represent the thousands of others who served quietly and bravely throughout the Second World War. I wished the emphasis to be not on 'war heroes', whose exploits placed them head and shoulders above their comrades, but, rather, on ordinary men who did extraordinary things, and who have not previously attracted the attention of historians.

The plethora of books and films about Bomber Command has tended to focus on events that easily capture the imagination. Arguably, the most famous is the *The Dam Busters*, a beguiling story of British technology at its most ingenious. At its heart, it contained all the elements necessary for a successful book and film. An intrepid band of airmen overcame strong German defences to achieve what had seemed impossible. They were led by Guy Gibson, a figure who fulfilled the traditional heroic role of a successful military leader. Where real-life events did not quite match up to the cinematic demands for excitement, fictitious accounts like *633 Squadron* entertained the baby-boomer generation with a fast-paced storyline and stirring soundtrack.

The Crew is written at a time when we can look back on our wartime achievements with justifiable pride, but also view them through a lens of sometimes critical analysis. The Second World War was a vast and brutal conflict that has taken seventy-five years to come to terms with. The way we view – and portray – the men who fought in that conflict is more nuanced, and less romanticized, than it once was. We no longer require our Second World War soldiers to be Hollywood stars with perfect teeth, or stiff upper-lipped English gentlemen speaking in clipped public-school tones. Real warfare is anything but entertaining, but we can draw inspiration from those real-life individuals who passed through its extreme trials.

With any project, the formulation of an idea is often a gradual process. Some of the best stories grow from tiny seeds, almost by chance – but I am not a believer in chance, preferring to look for a natural order to events. The earliest inspiration for this book came from two black and white photographs. They appeared on an American website of the USAAF 388th Bomb Group that had been based at RAF Knettishall in Suffolk during the Second World War. I had been researching the 388th for another project but, among dozens of photographs of B-17 bombers, these two caught my eye. The grainy 'Box Brownie' pictures showed a Lancaster bomber with a collapsed port undercarriage. The squadron code by the roundel read 'OF-H', and with a few clicks of the mouse I found it was from 97 Squadron, Royal Air Force.

This Lancaster had been returning from a sortie to Rheine, not far from Germany's border with the Netherlands, west of Osnabrück. Although Rheine was a small town, a railway and the Dortmund–Ems Canal both passed through it, and it had been subjected to numerous raids. The weather on 6 November

1944 had been poor and the six returning aircraft of 97 Squadron diverted to different airfields instead of their home at RAF Coningsby in Lincolnshire. According to the 97 Squadron Operational Record Book, Flying Officer J. W. Greening in Lancaster ND692 landed safely at RAF Snetterton at 9.15 that evening. However, the photograph taken the next day shows ND692 at Knettishall, seven miles away, with a wingtip firmly planted in the asphalt. Whether Greening decided

Lancaster ND692 of No. 7 Squadron at RAF Knettishall, Suffolk, 7 November 1944.

to join the three other 97 Squadron Lancasters that diverted to Knettishall the next day or whether the undercarriage collapse happened on the night of the raid is unclear. Had Greening mistaken Snetterton for Knettishall when he completed his report? The incident remains one of the small mysteries that researchers love.

Once I had decided to write *The Crew*, the initial task of finding my subjects was eased by the crashed Lancaster at Knettishall. I had approached the 97 Squadron Association for more information and now it seemed natural to seek a crew who served with them. In January 2018 I asked for suggestions for a crew on the Squadron Association Facebook page. I received many responses and I noticed some repetition in the suggestions. A number proposed the crew of Bob Lasham, but Bob, the last member, had passed away shortly before my request. Another was that of Wing Commander Ken Cook, who was the Association chairman. He had been a bomb aimer on pilot Jim Comans' crew and a twenty-year-old flying officer at the time. This crew proved to be the right fit for the project and Ken provided me with first-hand accounts in a number of interviews. Although many of Ken's memories have faded or become disjointed after nearly seventy-five years, his contribution towards bringing this story alive has proved invaluable.

Of the other crews put forward, some were more difficult to consider than others. Many families wished to see a relative commemorated, but their service and lives had left too faint a trace to provide sufficient material for the historian. Like many servicemen of their generation, most of them were single men who experienced tragically short careers, bequeathed no enduring testimony to their wartime deeds and left no children to remember them. They are voices that can no longer be heard, their accounts, not least of their final flight, lost forever. This book is dedicated to them, for, had it not been for the fatal trajectory of an anti-aircraft shell, or the deadly aim of a night fighter in 1942–5, they themselves might have been the subject of this book.

97 Squadron was first formed on 1 December 1917 at RAF Waddington, serving through the rest of the First World War to 1920 when it was subsumed into 60 Squadron. Re-formed in 1935, it served in training roles and was briefly disbanded on two further occasions as the RAF reorganized its wartime forces. In 1941, after a sizeable donation to the British government by residents of the Malay Straits towards Avro Manchester bombers, the squadron was renamed 97 (Straits Settlement) Squadron and served under this identity until January 1956. For the purposes of this book I have shortened the squadron name to '97 Squadron' for convenience.

In *The Crew* I hope you will experience some of the demands of Lancaster crewmen, feel some of their claustrophobic moments in a cramped fuselage and an inkling of the terrors that prowled around their aircraft at high altitude. For months, this was their life, a daily routine of duty that carried with it the risk that this might be their last day. Although the Allied bombing campaign is still the subject of critical scrutiny, the gallantry of the men fulfilling the tasks given them remains undiminished. It is my hope that in recounting the events of this terrible war, we might learn from it and be inspired by the crews' tenacity and raw bravery.

PROLOGUE

The Right Stuff

Ken Cook, March 2018.

Protruding from the Avro Lancaster's nose, the curved Perspex glass bomb-aiming position is like a small greenhouse perched on a 20,000-foot precipice. The land beneath lies dark and formless, with every house blacked out. There are no street lights.

Out of the featureless expanse a German city slowly appears within its ring of probing searchlights. Flares cast their unearthly light, flak shells burst nearby. The percussion of bombs exploding four miles below creates deep, undulating rumbles along the aircraft.

It is a world of extreme danger, a world where a man can be scythed in two by shards of metal in a fraction of a second. Bomber Command crews hated this part of a mission. On final bombing runs they had to fly straight and true, accepting everything thrown at them.

The bomb aimer clutches his release button, eyes fixed to the bomb sight, watching the green flares below converge with his cross-hairs. A small movement of his thumb will determine the release of the bombs. But for the mission to be a success he must keep his nerve, silence the inner voices telling him to drop early.

Twenty-year-old Ken Cook is barely a man yet here he sits, high above the cauldron with six other airmen. Many RAF crews' lives end in this supremely dangerous moment, but the journey to and from the target is always costly. Should their Lancaster be hit by ground fire or by a German night fighter, some crew members will have to fight to save their crippled bomber – extinguishing fires, jettisoning bombs and equipment – before opening the hatches to entrust their lives to a large piece of sewed silk on strings. Others are vaporized in catastrophic explosions which light up the sky.

Franklin D. Roosevelt said: 'War is young men dying and old men talking.' Over the past seventy-five years the testimonies of the young men who flew with Bomber Command have provided a compelling record of their service and sacrifice. There are now very few living survivors of the brutal bombing war against Germany, which claimed the lives of 55,573 RAF airmen.

Ken Cook lives with his daughter and her husband near the village of Haltwhistle in Northumberland, on the high moors between Carlisle and Newcastle. The road up leads me into a landscape of low drystone walls, its muted colours blanketed by thick snow. Cherry Tree Cottage nestles in the corner of a quiet hamlet, an unassuming house with the rendered walls and stone surrounds typical of the region. Ken's daughter answers the door and leads me into the sitting room, where her father sits in a comfortable chair clasping an old RAF logbook. A large oil painting of Lancaster bombers flying into the sunset dominates the room.

The ninety-five-year-old fixes me with a steady gaze, weighing me up as he might a new recruit. Wing Commander Ken Cook has a natural authority about him, an inbuilt resolve and solidity, but as we talk his warmth and humour come through. For some airmen the trauma of conflict was impossible to shake off. Preferring to say nothing, they took their memories to the grave. For others war was terrible but exciting, to the point that no experience afterwards compared. Cook is a man who has looked death in the face and not been cowed. He has talked about his wartime experiences, given lectures and written a detailed account for his family. Though his short-term memory is now poorer, he becomes animated when he talks about the bombing war. For those familiar with the story of Bomber Command he is a well-known figure, and, as president of the 97 Squadron Association, he has attended scores of memorials. But at each event the number of chairs set aside for veterans grows smaller.

Second World War bomber crews faced a casualty rate far higher than the infantrymen of the First World War. A soldier enlisting in the British army in 1914 faced a 14.2 per cent chance of being killed. Of the aircrew who served in Bomber Command a staggering 44.4 per cent lost their lives. High-altitude flying was exhausting, a physical and mental marathon, and it wasn't uncommon for airmen to fly three missions a week. With the appalling losses among their fellows, many thought imminent death inevitable. A sanguine few believed they were immortal, but most airmen simply celebrated every safe return. For a crew to survive forty-five operational sorties, it might be assumed that a high proportion of its targets were easy ones. But the Comans crew, whose remarkable operational history forms the subject of this book, flew during the harshest phase of the air battle when Nazi Germany had greatly improved its defences.

Ken Cook is now the only surviving member of his crew and one of the very last witnesses of the Allied bombing campaign. He tells me about being hit by flak, the night-fighter attacks, the bombers blown up right next to them. He looks at me and shrugs: 'What could we do?' Through the sheer terror of it all, the crew simply flew on, always completing their missions.

Most Bomber Command operations were conducted at night. The initial daylight raids had assumed that bombers in numbers could defend themselves, a theory that was to be painfully disproved. But the RAF's early night bombing had been wildly inaccurate. Urgent solutions were required and the Pathfinder force was formed in 1942 to provide accurate target marking. Airmen wishing to join it had to demonstrate that they were of above average ability. Ken Cook joined the Pathfinders in December 1943.

Six men served alongside him in the Avro Lancaster, each tasked with a particular duty. The pilot, Flying Officer Jim Comans, was also their captain. Crews were always referred to by the pilot's name, so they became the 'Comans crew' and flew together for thirteen months – a period of their lives that would define them all. In common with many RAF crews they were recruited from across the Commonwealth. The Australian Comans had a Canadian, a Scotsman and four Englishmen under his command. Ken recalls their pilot as 'bluff, a straight-talking disciplinarian'. Older than the others, the thirty-one-year-old from Redfern, New South Wales, 'didn't suffer fools gladly', but he bonded with the men. The quiet Canadian George Widdis was 'not a man of the world'. Remembering him, a broad smile spreads across Cook's face and the memories flood in. In the mix of cultures, the crew forged their own identity. They did most things together on the base, believing that the closer they were the greater would be their chances of survival. But this was a professional relationship rather than the bonding of close friendship. Each of the seven young airmen displayed extraordinary courage and skill. Like the test pilots for the American space programme whose experiences were documented by Tom Wolfe, the Comans crew were 'The Right Stuff'.

As soon as he was eighteen in 1941, Ken Cook was eager to join the RAF. Becoming an airman had an element of romanticism about it. The Volunteer Reserve was the recruiting ground for future aircrew and he was sent to train as a pilot in an Elementary Flying Training School. In common with thousands of others he failed to make pilot but was offered and accepted the role of bomb aimer.

The pages of the small RAF logbook are yellowing but in good condition. Each entry is neatly transcribed in ink – black denoting flying activity, red for operational flying – a simple layout with columns showing the date, pilot, aircraft identity, destination and flying hours. Sparse though the details are, they chronicle the extraordinary story of one man's war. From the autumn of 1943 to the early summer of 1944 Cook's log lists forty-five missions, including sorties to Berlin, Karlsruhe, Schweinfurt, Essen and Nuremberg. The aim of the crew's final mission, to Châtellerault near Poitiers in western France, on 15 June 1944, was to bomb the railway to prevent fuel supplies reaching the Panzers in Normandy. After D-Day a week or so earlier the air war had changed from the nightly pounding of German cities to more fluid targeting. By summer 1944 the Comans crew had amassed 275 operational hours, with an average flying time of six hours per mission. In recognition of his service Ken Cook was awarded the Distinguished Flying Cross in July 1944.

Since 1945 fierce debates as to the morality of the bombing campaign have raged. Bomber crews have faced unfair criticism, much of it uninformed. By any reasonable assessment, there is a world of difference in the level of moral responsibility between the commanders giving orders in smoke-filled rooms in London and the seven anxious young crewmen aboard an Avro Lancaster who were charged with carrying them out.

The likelihood that you would be killed in action was very high. You fought at night against an invisible enemy. Most airmen never saw a single German throughout the conflict; many of them never even saw Germany in daylight. In the trauma of war, it wasn't the suffering of the enemy that they witnessed, but the sudden loss of one of their own. All too often fellow airmen disappeared without trace, their folded clothes taken from lockers, the empty beds made up for replacements.

Little was said because little was known, and only with the passage of time has it been possible to tell the stories of the men who flew and died in the thousands of operational sorties made by RAF Bomber Command between 1942 and 1945. The tales of Ken Cook and his six fellow crew members are as compelling as any of them.

PRELUDE

The Command of the Air

The ivory hue of the eastern sky promised another sweltering day. Ribbons of fine mist drifted over the pastures; birdsong filled the air. A line of Belgian troops straggled along the road and into the fields opposite. They had been there all night, heavy serge coats and trousers damp with dew. Fighting sleep, their dark conical hats kept dropping onto their Comblain rifles. The previous day the Imperial German Army had crossed the Meuse four miles away, throwing Belgium into crisis. As forward scouts, the Piottes expected an attack at any time; a row of bicycles rested in the lee of a hedge 50 yards away ready to make a swift getaway. One mile behind them sat the deep-dug concrete emplacement of Fort Fléron, one of a string of Liège siege forts.

The crack of artillery began at 4.30 a.m., German 77mm shells whistling overhead towards the fort. Crouching deep in the grass, the Belgian troops watched through their gunsights for any movement over the ridges of the fields. They saw nothing. Fort Fléron replied, lobbing shells in the direction of the German positions. The percussions rippled across the countryside, a wall of thundering echoes. Suddenly, at 5.30 a.m., the shelling stopped. A lone figure stepped onto the deserted road ahead of the men. He walked cautiously towards the Belgian line, his arms extended slightly in front of him. In one hand, he carried a short stick with a handkerchief attached. He was dressed in a black suit; his crisply pressed white shirt and polished shoes exuded importance. Identifying himself as a German diplomat, he asked to see the Belgian army commander of Liège as a matter of urgency. The German was blindfolded and taken first to the fort and then on to the Belgian army headquarters at rue Sainte-Foi, where he was received by General Leman. The message he brought was polite but firm: surrender Liège by 13.00 hours or it will be bombed by Zeppelin.

There was a terse exchange of telegrams between Liège and Brussels, but the final one was unequivocal: 'Broken diplomatic relations. Continue operations: 15th mixed brigade is ordered to strengthen you.' The ring of Liège forts had not been tested by the German attackers, so the Belgians were reluctant to surrender the city so cheaply, whatever the threat. The diplomat returned to the German positions and shelling recommenced.

Sixty miles away, an immaculately dressed Prussian army officer with trimmed moustache and beard surveyed the enormous airship straining on its tethers. At 140 metres long, she was as large as a battleship, a breathtaking Goliath of aerial supremacy. The thirty-eight-year-old Hauptmann Rudolph Kleinschmidt was proud to command her, but he knew – given that the majority of airships produced to date had been destroyed by strong winds, fires or crashes – that he faced a challenging task. Despite his apparent stoicism, Kleinschmidt was anxious, for added to the long list of hazards he faced was that of enemy action. His biggest fear was fire. If the helium sacks ignited, the ship would explode in a giant fireball, incinerating the crew in seconds. Fresh in his memory was the disaster at Johannisthal near Berlin on 17 October 1913, when Zeppelin L2 had exploded, killing twenty-eight passengers.

Sir Hugh Trenchard inspects cadets at the RAF college at Cranwell, Lincolnshire, December 1926.

That night, shortly after 1.00 a.m. on 6 August 1914, Zeppelin Z VI* slipped its moorings at Cologne and set course for Liège. The bombs she carried were artillery shells adapted with streamers made from horse blankets to give stability. Despite clear weather, it became apparent that the weighed-down Zeppelin was struggling to reach the desired altitude. At 3.00 a.m., Kleinschmidt made the decision to attack at a lower

* Z VI had a construction number of 'LZ21' to denote its operation by the German Imperial Navy.

altitude. Sailing over the roofs and spires of Liège, the huge cigar-shaped craft loomed dark in the pre-dawn sky. The defenders were waiting. The air whistled with the zip of bullets as riflemen in the streets below took aim, each with the ability to destroy the airship. With no time to spare, the Zeppelin crew manhandled the projectiles through a hatch in the gondola floor. As the last explosion rocked the city, the Zeppelin made her slow turn for home. Passing a fort, she was picked out by a searchlight. The clatter of rifle and anti-aircraft fire found their target, puncturing the gas sacks. Limping back and losing altitude, the Zeppelin clipped trees before ploughing into a wood near Bonn. Z VI was damaged irreparably. No men were lost, but Kleinschmidt was stretchered from the tangled wreckage of the gondola. He had been seriously injured and would spend many months in hospital recuperating.

The first air raid of the Great War claimed nine Belgian lives. It was an unsophisticated affair but showed that the German commanders believed terrorizing civilian populations might be an effective way of persuading their opponents to surrender. It was only the start of Belgium's suffering. Within days of crossing the border, the advancing German army massacred men, women and children in a ruthless hunt for guerrilla fighters. Some were shot or bayoneted out of hand, while others faced organized firing squads. Eight hundred and fifty civilians died in actions that shocked the world. That Germany had chosen to ignore the 1839 Treaty of London, guaranteeing Belgian neutrality, was a matter of consternation, but the manner in which it invaded Belgium was considered outrageous. In scenes reminiscent of medieval spoiling, the German army rampaged through Louvain. The library was torched, destroying 300,000 books. Two hundred and forty-eight residents were killed and 10,000 forcibly displaced.

Lurid tales of the killings filled English and French newspapers, announcing a new and brutal age of warfare. The deliberate targeting of non-military personnel, making the civilian an integral part of the war, was a new strategy. The occupation of tiny Belgium cost 23,700 civilian lives. In a chilling portent of the future suffering of Europe, Germany deported 100,000 Belgians as slave labourers and erected an electric fence on the Dutch border – the so-called 'wire of death' (*Dodendraad*) – which killed more than two thousand civilians.

*

From January 1915, Germany launched Zeppelins against Britain. Flying under cover of darkness and with no effective opposition, air attacks accounted for 1,413 killed, most of them in London. The Zeppelins were not the only bombers. Eight hundred and thirty people were killed in daylight raids by Gotha bombers – large twin-engined biplanes launched from Sint-Denijs-Westrem near Ghent. Some raids were brazen in their execution. On 7 July 1917 twenty-two Gothas from Kagohl 3,* the 'England squadron' of the Imperial German Flying Corps, had crossed the Channel and formed up over Epping Forest before striking at London. *The Times* reported the event in sporting terms:

> As a spectacle, the raid was the most thrilling that London has seen since the air attacks began. Every phase could be followed from points many miles away without the aid of glasses [i.e. binoculars or a telescope], and hundreds of thousands of people watched the approach of the squadron, the dropping of the bombs, the shelling of the German aeroplanes [by anti-aircraft guns] and the eventual retreat.

Dozens of British fighters were scrambled to oppose the raid.

---

* Kagohl 3 was an acronym for **Ka**mpf**g**eschwader der **O**bersten **H**eeres**l**eitung 3 ('Battle Squadron of the Supreme Army Command 3').

Swarming towards the ungainly bombers, the BE.2c biplanes were unable to reach the necessary altitude. Hundreds of anti-aircraft shells pocked the sky with small flashes, leaving puffs of white smoke. Only one Gotha was brought down, crashing in the sea off Ostend, but only after a long chase by British fighters.

Kagohl 3 had successfully dropped 4,475 kilos of bombs on docks and warehouses on the north side of the Thames between Charing Cross – the station was hit several times – and Tower Bridge. Fifty-seven civilians were killed, leading to demands that air raid precautions be better organized. As a result, police officers were given signs to put around their necks which read 'Police Notice. Take Cover'. All seventy-nine fire stations in London were equipped with warning rockets, often referred to as 'Sound Bombs', fired in threes to warn of an approaching raid. Open-topped police cars drove around with buglers on board, some of whom were Boy Scouts. The 'All Clear' was sounded on whistles. Alerted by these hastily arranged – almost comical – methods, some 300,000 Londoners found themselves ushered into eighty-six London Tube stations. It is estimated that a further 500,000 took shelter in basements and cellars in the capital.

Britain was slow to retaliate in kind. It was not until late 1917 that mounting public pressure produced promises of raids. Lord Rothermere, Air Minister, newspaper proprietor and founder of the *Daily Mail*, outlined his beliefs in December 1917:

> At the Air Board we are wholeheartedly in favour of air
> reprisals. It is our duty to avenge the murder of innocent
> women and children. As the enemy elects, so it will be the case
> of 'eye for an eye, and a tooth for a tooth,' and in this respect
> we shall slave for complete and satisfying retaliation... We
> are determined, in other words, that whatever outrages are
> committed on the civilian population of this country will be
> met by similar treatment on his own people.

Revenge may have been a matter of national pride, but it turned non-combatant civilians into military targets. Hugh Trenchard, Chief of the Air Staff, took a different view from Rothermere's. A career soldier, he believed that strategy was best formed by prioritizing military interests and not by public opinion. He clashed with Rothermere on numerous occasions, not least because he viewed the brash newspaper magnate with suspicion. Nevertheless, a bombing campaign against German cities began in June 1918, much later than its advocates had hoped for. Airco DH9 and Handley Page O/400s biplanes, not unlike the German Gothas, succeeded in dropping 660 tons of bombs on German industrial cities, despite struggling against headwinds that brought the bombers to a near standstill. The French were far less enthusiastic. The Germans launched their retaliation against their cities, not British ones.

These developments, however faltering they may appear to modern perception, had opened a terrifying new chapter in the history of warfare. German Zeppelin Corps Commander Peter Strasser was blunt in his appraisal: 'Nowadays there is no such animal as a non-combatant, modern warfare is total warfare.' Strasser lost his life in Germany's last airship raid on Great Britain, when his Zeppelin L70 was destroyed over the North Sea by a de Havilland D-4 bomber on 6 August 1918. His sentiments might well have found favour with another believer in the principle of 'total war', an Italian general and theorist of aerial warfare named Giulio Douhet. Already a passionate advocate of bombing during the First World War, Douhet crystallized his thinking in his treatise of 1921, *The Command of the Air*. Essential to Douhet's thinking was a belief in the power of a bombing war to break a nation's morale by destroying its centres of military power, industry and government. Critical to this process, argued the Italian general, was astute selection of bombing targets. Douhet's vision of the bomber as a potentially unstoppable weapon in future wars was the subject of debate in France, Germany and America in the interwar period. *The Command of the Air* was less influential in Britain (there is no evidence that Hugh Trenchard, a key British advocate of strategic bombing, had even read it), but a speech to the British Parliament, 'A Fear for the Future', made by former prime minister Stanley Baldwin in November 1932, seemed imbued with the spirit of Douhet:

> I think it is well also for the man in the street to realise that there is no power on earth that can protect him from being bombed. Whatever people may tell him, the bomber will always get through. The only defence is in offence, which means that you have to kill more women and children more quickly than the enemy if you want to save yourselves…

1.

Uncertain Years:
1919–1939

The narrow, dusty streets of Redfern, New South Wales, Australia, seemed a world away from the massive conflict about to engulf Western Europe in 1914. Founded a century earlier on land granted to William Redfern, a doctor and pardoned convict, the area soon became popular with settlers planting vegetable gardens to supply the burgeoning city of Sydney. The broad main streets gave way to alleys of packed balconied houses. A fresh influx of families came to work on the railway in the 1850s, many of them from Ireland, seeking a new life after the Great Famine. It was here, on 2 March 1912, that James Leopold Vincent Comans was born into an Irish Catholic family. He was destined to become a Lancaster bomber pilot, and he was the oldest member of the crew he would ultimately command.

Shortly after Jim Comans reached his fifth birthday, the March Revolution in Russia was sending shock waves across the world. In August, the 'Great Strike' in New South Wales saw thousands of tram and railway workers take to the streets. In a poor neighbourhood, the suspicion surrounding a new card system for tracking employees led 3,000 men at Eveleigh Railway Workshops in Redfern to down tools. There was already scepticism that the 'War to End all Wars' would do anything to improve working conditions.

Two and a half years earlier, in November 1914, the mood had been very different. Crowds packed the piers at Sydney to see thousands of young men on their way to join troopships at Albany, in Western Australia. As the ships slowly moved away from the harbourside, bands played 'Auld Lang Syne' and 'God Save the King'. Well-wishers cheered, waved and cried. Paper ribbons between soldiers and their loved ones were stretched, finally breaking to fall into the water. The men on board were excited, most of them never having left Australia before. This was a huge adventure whose allure was dimmed only by the prospect that the war might end before they could take part. Few had any inkling of the terrors that awaited them.

The grim harvest of Gallipoli ripped through the nation five months later. Columns of names appeared in newspapers, fine printed one-line entries for each man killed or wounded. Gifts given to soldiers on the quayside – pens, lockets and notebooks – were returned to Redfern as the personal effects of the dead. In keeping with regulations, bodies were not returned, compounding the grief that swept the community. Yet Australia had found its soul in the scorched trenches of the Dardanelles. The 'Diggers', always less than enthusiastic about British military discipline, went on to distinguish themselves on the Somme in the late summer of 1916 – at Pozières and in the mud-churned slaughter around Mouquet Farm. By the end of the war, no one doubted the tough, no-nonsense character of the Australian soldier.

In early 1918, Spanish influenza had broken out in Europe, spreading across the continent by the end of the year. With thousands of men flocking back to Australia on crowded troop-ships, impatient to reach home, the virus was transported to the other side of the world. Tragically, the population of Sydney, so far removed from the sufferings of Europe during the war, was to feel the full force of the outbreak. *The Byron Bay Record* of Saturday 15 February 1919 reported: 'A suspicious case reported from the *Argyllshire* troopship, on Saturday, was yesterday pronounced one of influenza. High indignation was expressed on Saturday by *Argyllshire* troops at having to stay in quarantine. They blamed the State Government and attributed their detention to jealousy of the Victorian Government.'

By June 1919, over 40 per cent of Sydney's population had contracted influenza. The Comans family feared for Jim's safety as newspapers reported daily on those succumbing to it. The very young and old were most at risk, but the pandemic was carrying away able-bodied people at an alarming rate. The strain of flu was so severe that a victim could feel well in the morning, but within hours experience fatigue, fever and headache that developed into pneumonia. By evening they could be struggling for breath to the point where they suffocated to death. The city ground to a halt. Owing to a shortage of trained medical staff, first-year medical students were enlisted as doctors, but there was little they could do. Six thousand died in New South Wales during the outbreak.

Jim Comans grew up in this gritty post-war community. He went to the Marist Brothers High School in Darlinghurst, a Catholic brotherhood. For a child, the imposing four-storey school on the corner of Liverpool Street seemed enormous. By the 1880s, the broad, planned streets closer to the city centre were becoming expensive. The brothers struggled to afford the plot, problems further compounded by a 20 per cent rise in building costs. Despite the rear of the school resembling a prison, the façade was pleasing to the eye, with horizontal white stone courses dressing the brickwork. The overall severity of design suggested that neither God, nor his representatives, were to be taken lightly.

At times, Jim was unsure who he should fear the most, the

Lord or the brothers. The teachers seemed to have an unending list of punishable offences, but in this stern and sometimes punitive environment many students flourished. Darlinghurst was performing well, a good number of its students going on to enter university. Jim's first appearance in print appeared in the Catholic press at the 1927 school prize-giving, commended as part of the Senior Cricket competition. Sport became a lifelong obsession for Jim, whether it was cricket, horse racing or rugby – he was fascinated by anything that moved.

*

In Britain, the immediate post-war period witnessed a series of chaotic events. The influenza pandemic carried away 228,000, strikes led to civil unrest and thousands of former soldiers struggled to find jobs. James Cook had been too old for war service. He had left the back-breaking labouring work at Stonehouse Brickworks near Stroud in Gloucestershire to find employment as a gardener. By the early 1920s he was working at Woodchester Mansion, a large unfinished house with sweeping gardens and long driveway. It suited James to be out of the dust and smoke of the brickyard. The Woodchester estate had been in financial peril for some time. Construction of the elegant Pugin-inspired house began in 1858, but was abandoned in 1870 on the death of the owner, William Leigh. Merchants from Cheshire, the Leigh family had worked their way through an inherited fortune. Owing to further poor investments by William Leigh's son, Willie, the funds needed to complete the house had all but dried up. Large portions of the structure remained a ghostly shell, its windows without glass, the interior without floors or ceilings. But the gardens still required attention, although members of the Leigh family themselves were reduced to living in the gardener's cottage.

The Cook family lived in Randwick, a small village just over a mile from Stroud. Its narrow streets, built into a steep hillside, were lined with weavers' cottages built of honey-coloured lime-stone brought down from nearby Colstone Hill. It was a quiet working village, unpretentious, but not poor. Matilda Cook was expecting her fifth child at forty-two years old, late for those times. Kenneth Cook was born in April 1923. The 'baby' of the family benefited from the attentions of his older siblings, including his eldest sister, Mabel, who was eighteen. All of them crammed into Yew Tree Cottage, a small two-bedroom rented terrace with an attic room. It was a rural upbringing away from the hustle and bustle of the cities. James kept the family supplied with vegetables from an allotment by the parish church. Ken and his brother Charles were members of the church choir and were photographed for the family album in their white surplices. In 1928 Ken began school at Randwick Church of England Primary School, a short walk from their house. It was a tight-knit village whose inhabitants lived cheek by jowl and little could be hidden from one's neighbours. With the children all at school, Ken's mother resumed her job in the laundry at Ebley, a bus ride away from Randwick.

Passing his eleven-plus exam, Ken was admitted to Marling Grammar School for Boys in Stroud, making the daily journey by bicycle. He had a passion for sport, playing football, cricket and rugby at school. Academically, he excelled in science subjects, a preparation that would benefit his later RAF career. At times, Ken would accompany his father to work, walking down to Cross Lanes to catch the bus. He spent hours walking on his own around the grounds of Woodchester. He sometimes watched the various craftsmen at work in the house, particularly captivated by the intricate work of the glaziers on the stained glass.

In the brief eleven years from Ken's birth until his entry to grammar school, Britain – and the world – had changed a great deal. The optimism of the 1920s had been lost in the rising tide of turmoil across Europe. By the time the young men of the future Avro Lancaster crew reached their teenage years in the mid-1930s international tensions were rising and an arms race had begun. The boys were too young to understand the minutiae – and the repercussions – of the Treaty of Versailles of 1919, but they could hardly have failed to notice that events in Germany, and in particular the rise to power of Adolf Hitler, were frequently front-page news.

*

The cessation of hostilities in 1918 allowed Britain to return to its primary concern, the governance of the Empire. British participation in the First World War was not solely about defending freedoms in Europe, but also about containing Germany's colonial aspirations. Post-war developments in aircraft design were geared not to facing an enemy with modern industrial capability, but to creating aeroplanes suitable for policing imperial outposts from Burma to Sierra Leone.

The dual task of post-war demobilization and establishing the Royal Air Force as an independent service fell to a former infantry officer named Hugh Trenchard. He had joined the army in 1893, serving in South Africa – where he lost a lung to a Boer bullet – and later in Nigeria, where he distinguished himself in expeditions mapping 10,000 miles of the interior of the country. He was appointed a temporary lieutenant colonel in 1908 and looked set to continue his career in Africa. However, in 1910 he suffered a liver abscess that forced his return to Britain. After recuperation he sought a new position in the army, but was unhappy with home assignments. A friend, Captain Eustace Loraine, knowing he was unsettled, suggested he learned to fly. Trenchard, almost the model of a *Boy's Own* hero in his colonial service, realized he had only three weeks to qualify before his fortieth birthday, the age limit for trainee pilots. By the time he reached Thomas Sopwith's flying school at Brooklands in Surrey, he had only ten days to complete a flying course. He succeeded in going solo after just sixty-four minutes in the air, gaining his Royal Aero Club certificate. His instructor was polite about his performance, calling Trenchard 'a model pupil', but it was clear the newly qualified pilot could not fly well. Part of Trenchard's problem was that he had only partial sight in one eye, which he kept a secret from his flying instructors. In later training, his deficiencies were discovered and, although he qualified as an instructor, he did not fulfil the role.

On the outbreak of war in 1914, as a senior officer with flying experience, his services were in demand. He became commander of the Royal Flying Corps in 1915 and Chief of Air Staff in November 1917. Seeing the conditions in which the armies fought in France and Belgium, he became convinced of the need for air power to play an enhanced role in future wars. He believed an air force independent of the army was an essential progression in command and strategy. Trenchard's unwavering conviction made him a pivotal figure in the formation of the RAF – as an amalgamation of the Royal Flying Corps and the Royal Naval Air Service – in April 1918.

By 1919, the British presence in the former Ottoman territories of the Middle East was complicated by a severe shortage of funds. The occupying army comprised 25,000 British and 80,000 Indian troops and shrinkage was inevitable. When Winston Churchill approached Trenchard as Chief of the Air Staff to explore whether it would be possible for the Royal Air Force to take on an 'aerial policing' role, Trenchard responded enthusiastically, sensing an opportunity to bolster the RAF and ensure its autonomy. Following the granting of Mesopotamia to Britain as a mandate in April 1920 and emboldened by British troop reductions in what is now Iraq, Kurdish and Arab rebels mounted a full-scale revolt utilizing weapons left by the Ottoman

Turks. The 1920 Iraqi Revolt was no tribal skirmish, but a major uprising that resulted in the deaths of 1,040 British soldiers and many thousands of Iraqis. The financial cost of putting down the revolt staggered British politicians: at £40 million, this was more than the funding for the Arab revolt against the Turks during the First World War.

Promising cheaper alternatives than a large garrison, Trenchard's RAF was placed in command of all British forces in Mesopotamia in 1922 – the 'Iraq Command'. Smaller ground forces were deployed with armoured cars, the idea being to strike where trouble flared rather than cover huge expanses of territory with troops. Even after the revolt had been put down, tribal conflict continued. Punishment of groups stepping out of line included the bombing of their villages. Sometimes populations received warnings to leave before bombing took place, but unannounced bombing raids proved that the British were willing to use strong-arm methods.

The new aircraft used by the RAF in Mesopotamia were upscaled First World War designs. The Vickers Vernon, for instance, which entered service in 1921, was a development of the Vickers Vimy bomber. Larger engines and fuselages allowed greater carrying capacity, but essentially a fabric-covered wooden frame formed the primary structures. The fixed undercarriage remained, as did the open pilot's cockpit. The Vernon was introduced as a transport aircraft, carrying its passengers in a bulbous fuselage. In February 1923, the RAF used the Vernon to transport 500 British troops to Kirkuk in Iraq to counter a threat by Kurdish forces. It was the first recorded movement of troops by air.

In May 1924, 45 (Bomber) Squadron was formed, using the Vernon as bombers. Its commanding officer, Squadron Leader Arthur Harris, supervised the fitting of bomb racks and aiming sights. Harris had been a fighter pilot in the First World War, flying the Sopwith Camel, but this was his first experiment with bombing. When tribal conflict flared in Iraq, RAF aircraft would fly over villages that supported the uprising, dropping warning notices and broadcasting on loudspeakers. Forty-eight hours' notice was given of the intention to bomb, in which time it was expected that local fighting should cease. The village would be bombed if the warning went unheeded. The scenario became a familiar one. Circling high above a mud-brick Kurdish village, the bombers dropped their bombs. The ground pulsed with explosions, obscuring the target with dust. Going in lower, the gunners sprayed the area with machine-gun fire. Within minutes, the village had been destroyed. But not only had it been rendered useless to the rebels, more significantly its obliteration had eroded their will to fight. Harris saw at first hand the effects of aerial bombardment, and took note.

Casually brutal though the tactic undoubtedly was, it drew little criticism at home in the 1920s. Moral boundaries began to shift and attacks without warning became more common. There was an assumption that the tribal chiefs knew the consequences of sedition, but this was no comfort to the civilian population targeted. Harris's experiences in Mesopotamia convinced him that strategic attacks on civilian targets could help subdue armed forces around them. He noted:

> They now know what real bombing means, in casualties
> and damage; they now know that within 45 minutes a full-
> sized village can be practically wiped out and a third of
> its inhabitants killed or injured by four or five machines
> which offer them no real target, no opportunity for glory
> as warriors, no effective means of escape.

The approach was akin to a public-school caning. Punishment must be rapid but meted out in a controlled fashion. Harris returned from Mesopotamia in 1924 to take command of 58 Squadron, Britain's first heavy bomber unit, equipped with the

Vickers Virginia, another development from the Vickers Vimy. His next posting was to the Army Staff College in Camberley, where he served from 1927 to 1929. He was unimpressed with the army, observing that their fixation with horses held them back from embracing new technology. He quipped that they would be happy with a tank as long as it 'ate hay and thereafter made noises like a horse'. He was equally scathing of naval officers, saying three things should not be allowed on a well-run yacht, 'a wheelbarrow, an umbrella and a naval officer'. One of the few army officers he got on with at Camberley was Bernard Montgomery.

Harris's loyalty to the Royal Air Force is telling. It is clear that he was entirely committed to the concept of an independent air force. But his criticisms of the other services were not solely to do with his RAF allegiance. Harris was developing as an independent thinker in both the development of bombing technology and strategy. His next command was of a flying boat squadron where he continued to develop night bombing techniques. Promoted to group captain in 1933, he further advanced his career in 1934, becoming Deputy Director of Plans in the Air Ministry. It was from this senior position that Harris was able to press the ministry for the creation of a heavy bomber force.

Many senior officers in place at the formation of Bomber Command in 1936 came with experiences of aerial policing in the Empire and believed that an enemy could be not only suppressed but defeated by air power alone. Harris's desire to see the RAF obtain the latest aircraft technology was not born out of personal ambition, but from the realization that Britain had fallen dangerously behind the Germans. Whitehall had failed to grasp the leap in innovation from the 1920s into the 1930s and still relied on First World War production ideas. With a cruising speed of 65 knots, aircraft like the Vickers Vernon were not fast, but were developed in the belief that they would not encounter an aerial threat from fighters. The simplicity of maintenance suited the RAF. Wood and canvas were easily obtained in any part of the world and the repair skills required were more basic than they would be with a metal design. 55 Squadron, which was also based in Iraq, soldiered on with the Airco DH9 biplane bomber until 1930. The Airco's replacement, the general-purpose Westland Wapiti, was still a biplane with fixed undercarriage. Even with the threat of war looming, the squadron were equipped with new Vickers Vincent light bombers in 1937, an open cockpit biplane with few concessions to modernity.

★

General Hans von Seeckt arrived by car in the courtyard of the Bendlerblock in the Tiergarten district of Berlin. The enormous headquarters had been built for the German Imperial Navy in 1914, but now, under the new Weimar Republic, it housed the Reichswehr, the post-war German army. An orderly clicked his heels stiffly as he opened the car door. Seeckt was familiar with this place – he had been Chief of Staff here for the past four months – and now, in late March 1920, he stepped from the gleaming black car as Commander in Chief. Faces peered down from dozens of windows around the central square to watch the new man arrive. Seeckt was fifty-four years old, slim and immaculately dressed in a uniform with a high braided collar, decorative epaulettes, riding breeches and fine polished calf-length boots. The American scholar Louis Snyder wrote of von Seekt: 'Trim, precise, almost dainty in his well-tailored uniform, he became known as the Sphinx with the monocle.'

The Bendlerblock had been rocked for six days by the Kapp Putsch, a revolt inspired by Dr Wolfgang Kapp, a Prussian civil servant and vehement critic of the Treaty of Versailles, which had imposed on Germany a heavy burden of reparations. The putsch was an early right-wing attempt to depose the government of the Weimar Republic and replace it with an autocratic regime of the far right. When soldiers of General Walther von Lüttwitz, Commander in Chief of the Reichswehr, accompanied by groups of *Freikorps*, occupied the Reich Chancellery on 13 March, ministers fled the capital. Seeckt would not be drawn into the intrigue, but also refused appeals from the government to put down the putsch by force. 'Reichswehr do not fire on Reichswehr,' he told them. After thousands of civilians took to the streets, the movement collapsed, with Lüttwitz fleeing to Hungary on a false passport.

The dilemma for the Weimar government was how to placate a restless army. Still 350,000 strong, its officers were deeply unhappy at the signing of the Versailles Treaty, whose provisions would reduce it to 100,000. The notion of the 'Dolchstoss' (which loosely translates as 'stab in the back'), based on the myth that cowardly politicians had betrayed a potentially victorious German army, was gathering adherents in right-wing circles. Reichspräsident Friedrich Ebert had told returning troops in 1919, 'no enemy has vanquished you'.

The answer seemed to lie in the elevation of Seeckt, a solid but unexciting officer whose level-headed outlook would hopefully keep the peace. To allay suspicions of future interference by the army, Seeckt in March 1921 set out the Defence Law. 'Soldiers may not engage in political activity. While on duty such activity is also forbidden to military officials. Soldiers are forbidden to belong to political clubs or to participate in political meetings.' In setting out his stall so clearly, he avoided parliamentary scrutiny. Politicians were uninterested in what he did with his military budget, knowing the task of rebuilding the army within the confines of Versailles would be difficult enough.

This was not to suggest that Seeckt agreed with Versailles; on the contrary, he had vociferously voiced his opposition to its terms. However, he was a pragmatist who set quietly to work

In the aftermath of the First World War, a row of German planes awaits destruction by the Inter-Allied Aeronautical Commission of Control, under the terms of the Treaty of Versailles.

undermining the terms of the treaty, not by pushing soldiers onto the streets in rebellion, but by sleight of hand. He would appear to be dismantling the German armed forces as Versailles demanded, but he would covertly rebuild them into a new force. He was convinced that a future war was inevitable: 'My own training in history prevents me from seeing the idea of permanent peace as anything more than a dream, whereby it remains an open question whether one can consider it.'

From his marble-corridored headquarters, there was little Seeckt could do but watch as the treaty terms were imposed. While he could conceal details of the precise number of troops he had, hardware could not be hidden. The Imperial German Air Service (*Luftstreitkräfte*) fell under the axe of the Allies and was completely dismantled. Germany was obliged to surrender all her aircraft and was forbidden from importing or manufacturing replacements. In 1920, 15,000 aircraft were handed over along with 27,000 aero engines. Most were unceremoniously chopped up and stacked in large piles to be used as firewood. Only civilian aircraft production would be allowed. Here, Seeckt saw a chance to build new aircraft and train pilots ready for a time when restrictions on military flying were lifted.

In 1920, Seeckt secretly dispatched the former Turkish Minister of Defence, Enver Pasha, to Soviet Russia to test the waters for a formal alliance with Germany. Pasha was in hiding, having fled Turkey after being charged with various wartime crimes, including the forced deportation of Armenians, so was in no position to decline the request. As in the plot of any good spy story, Pasha's plane crash-landed in Lithuania and he was detained carrying papers that could incriminate the Germans. He was sprung from prison by a junior German officer – thus sparing the embarrassment of Seeckt. Not to be deterred, a nervous Pasha was dispatched once again, this time successfully returning with an optimistic report. 'Today I spoke with Trotsky. With him there's a faction that has real power, and also includes that party that stands for an understanding with Germany. That party would be willing to acknowledge the old German borders of 1914.'

The Treaty of Rapallo between Germany and Soviet Russia followed in 1922, striking a blow at the Versailles order. Germany was once again beginning to flex its muscles, peeling Russia away from its alliance with France and Britain. Although the agreement stated that Germany and Russia would 'co-operate in a spirit of mutual goodwill in meeting the economic needs of both countries', a secret understanding was the use of German 'black funds' hidden from the Allies to pour into Russian industry. In effect, even under close supervision of the Soviets, German companies took over factories capable of producing weapons – including aircraft.

The German businessman Hugo Junkers took advantage of this new accord. He was offered use of a former car factory at Fili on the outskirts of Moscow to establish a huge aircraft plant. Junkers was a congenial man, at heart a pacifist who had not turned his hand to aircraft design until he was fifty years old. His earlier achievements included patenting a tankless gas boiler for filling baths, the forerunner of today's combination boiler. He was a pioneer in the use of metals in aeroplane design rather than wood and canvas, producing the world's first all-metal mono-plane, the Junkers D1, in 1918. Junkers correctly predicted the future in using a lightweight aluminium alloy, Duralumin, produced in the Ruhr. The plumbing engineer had become an aviation innovator, but in his deal with the Soviets to produce 300 aircraft per year he had failed to recognize the financial and political difficulties of operating a thousand miles from Berlin. It was an expensive arrangement that disappointed both sides, with far fewer aircraft being produced than anticipated.

Junkers also built a large factory at Dessau, north of Leipzig, which later fuelled suspicions that the grants he received from the Soviets were not fully spent in Russia. Other manufacturers were just as industrious. In 1922 Ernst Heinkel built a plant at Warnemünde on the Baltic, Claude Dornier a factory in Italy, and, in 1923, Heinrich Focke and George Wulf formed the Focke-Wulf company in Bremen. The Bavarian Aircraft Company was taken over by Messerschmitt in 1925 to produce 'sporting' aircraft. The full effect of Seeckt's secret investments is unknown, but the rapid expansion of production suggests the new companies were well funded. In comparison, Britain's air-craft companies were still struggling to cope with the rapid drop in orders after the First World War.

Within the expanse of corridors and offices in the east wing of the Bendlerblock, Seeckt was able to conceal his plans for a new German air force. He gathered a small group of officers together in the Defence Ministry. Helmuth Felmy, Hugo Sperrle, Walther Wever, Albert Kesselring and Hans-Jurgen Stumpff all joined in the early 1920s and went on to become leading officers in the Luftwaffe. Seeckt's influence led to the appointment of his nominee Captain Brandenburg to the burgeoning Civil Aviation Department, coupling military and civil resources. Brandenburg had commanded the Gothas of Kagohl 3 on their raids on London, but in the days when many retired military pilots had civilian positions, the appointment of the former bomber commander did not seem unusual. With the foundation in 1926 of Deutsche Luft Hansa AG, a large number of men were trained as pilots in preparation for a time when military flying could commence once again. Within the swirling political intrigues of post-war Germany, however, Seeckt had made enemies. He was forced to resign in October 1926 after Prince Wilhelm, the grandson of the former emperor, was seen attending army manoeuvres on the invitation of Seeckt.

Under Seeckt's tenure, the foundations of the new Luftwaffe were set in place, albeit through a number of secret organizations. Seeckt died in retirement in 1936 at the age of seventy; he was found at home still clutching an English novel after suffering a fatal heart attack. Hitler and Goering, who attended his funeral, poured praise on Seeckt's achievements, although whether this admiration would have been reciprocated is debatable. Most senior army officers were cautious of 'the Corporal', considering Hitler a man beneath their social standing. For all Seeckt's achievements, he was despised by the Nazis – not least because his wife was Jewish.

★

Britain's technological time lag in the aerial arms race was not lost on Members of Parliament. Through the 1930s, the government was frequently questioned about the size of Germany's recruiting programme and their lead in aircraft production. Sir Philip Sassoon, Under-Secretary of State for Air from 1931 to 1937, dealt with such matters with the straightest of straight bats. In November 1934, the Conservative MP Borras Whiteside asked

Sassoon how large the German Air Sports Association* was, and whether it received central funding. Sassoon replied that its membership stood at 60,000. He continued, 'I have no information as to the financial or other assistance given to the association by the German Government, apart from a grant of 1,230,000 R.Mks. for gliding and some small grants for prizes and free ballooning.' Unconvinced by this reply, Cecil Pike, another Conservative,

Hermann Goering, the future Supreme Commander of the Luftwaffe, c. 1925.

asked, 'Could the Under-Secretary say to what extent this association is under the control of the German Government?' To which Sassoon simply stated, 'I could not say'.

It was a reply that circumnavigated the unpleasant truth that Germany had been allowed to build a huge air force-in-waiting. Although Hitler and Goering are often given credit for the formal creation of the Luftwaffe in 1935, in reality it was well established through the early work of Seeckt and others.

The British government had chosen carefully in their elevation of Sassoon. He was a man whose credentials satisfied the traditionalists, having entered Parliament as long ago as 1912, and served as private secretary to Field Marshal Haig from 1915 to

* The *Deutscher Luftsportverband* was founded in March 1933 by the Nazi Party to train military pilots.

1918. He had been a parliamentarian since 1912. But beyond the staid bounds of politics, he was a man of considerable wealth whose ostentatious parties at his home, Trent Park, became legendary. His hospitality furthered his influence: leading names in politics and the arts were pampered by white-coated footmen, while Sassoon himself flitted from one group to another. He became a keen aviator, flying his own Percival Petrel, a 1937 twin-engined aircraft finished in exquisite red leather. In the 1930s he became Honorary Commanding Officer of No. 601 (County of London) Squadron, which fielded six millionaire members. Openly homosexual at a time when homosexuality was illegal, Sassoon's wealth and connections enabled him to move effortlessly through society – charming yet supremely resourceful. It is unsurprising that Sassoon was hard to pin down when it came to the difficult questions of expenditure on the Royal Air Force. He shielded the government from scrutiny, sidestepping the thorny issue of underinvestment. As the country slid towards conflict, spending was increased, but the years of prevarication had taken their toll.

By the early 1930s the 'Treaty of Peace between the Allied and Associated Powers and Germany of 1919' was dead. Through the clandestine actions of men like General Hans von Seeckt, the seeds of resistance planted in the 1920s had germinated into open rebellion with the rise of Hitler. While France built the Maginot Line and recruited over 2 million men to their army, the British appeared, both literally and metaphorically, to be still sipping tea and playing croquet on the lawns of their stately homes. Germany's rearmament was no secret, yet in the British tradition of military spending decisions were left until the last moment. Winston Churchill, often considered too hawkish in his outlook, warned as early as November 1934 that the Germans were rearming with the '... new lamentable weapon of the air, against which our navy is no defence, and before which

women and children, the weak and frail, the pacifist and the
jingo, the warrior and the civilian, the front line trenches and
the cottage home, all lie in equal and impartial peril'.

★

At Randwick in Gloucestershire, an audible sign of the growing
pace of the aerial arms race was the change in tone of aircraft
engines. The gentle buzz of the training biplane was replaced with
the deeper growl of the Rolls-Royce Merlin. In 1938 the former
First World War airfield at Minchinhampton was reopened.
Following concerns raised by well-heeled villagers that house
prices might be affected, the airfield was renamed RAF Aston
Down. Soon the Hawker Hurricanes of 5 Operational Training
Unit were criss-crossing the skies above rural Gloucestershire
and firing the imaginations of young men such as Ken Cook. As
a boy, Ken was no stranger to aeroplanes. Cycling through the
lanes to Minchinhampton airfield, he would watch aircraft like
the de Havilland Cirrus Moth or new Miles monoplanes cruising
around the circuit. Recreational flying was becoming the pastime
of upper-middle-class enthusiasts who wore tailored leather flying
jackets over flannels or pleated skirts. In a new Edwardian era of
wicker picnic baskets, dainty sandwiches and fine wine, affluent
flyers toured the country by air, dropping in on other flying clubs.
In the wider world, legendary aviators such as Charles Lindbergh,
Amelia Earhart and Amy Johnson dominated the newsreels with
epic, record-breaking flights. In Germany, aviation continued
to assume a more overtly political hue: flying clubs held parades
and adopted military uniforms with swastika insignia.

Few people in Britain had any experience of air travel. For
many, the opportunity to catch their first flight arrived in the
early 1930s, when Sir Alan Cobham inaugurated his 'National
Aviation Day' displays. With the slogan 'Make the Skyways

Britain's Highways,' his Flying Circus toured Britain, visiting nearly every town between 1931 and 1935. The shows included pleasure flights, aerobatics and stunts. Gliding, parachuting and wing walking were all staples of the displays, captivating onlookers with feats of daring. Thousands enjoyed their first giddying experience of flying in five-minute joy rides for seven shillings and sixpence, many from an open cockpit. In the mid-1930s, during the flying season, one of Cobham's shows would be playing in a town somewhere in Britain. Ken Cook recalls seeing the 'Flying Circus' near Stroud, a large marquee set up in preparation for thousands of visitors. Most pilots were former First World War airmen flying machines not dissimilar to their combat aircraft. But a new generation of civilian pilots were making their mark, including women. The *Chester-le-Street Chronicle* of 28 June 1935 reported: 'Miss Joan Meakin describes her evolutions by radio-telephony while performing aerobatics in her new "Wolf" glider. Miss Meakin is the first woman to loop a glider and her machine is the first engineless aircraft to be equipped with wireless transmission.'

Accidents and even deaths were commonplace. Alan Cobham recalled a distressing incident in his 1978 biography:

Finally, just before we closed down for good on 30 September 1935, we suffered the appalling tragedy of a mid-air collision over Blackpool. A pilot named Carruthers was waiting for the others to join him so that our arrival could be announced by the usual formation flight, when he suddenly felt a violent impact from below… Carruthers managed to land his aircraft in one piece without hurting anybody, but the pilot of the machine that had flown into him from below – Stewart by name – was killed, as were his two girl passengers and the blind man on whose house they fell. It was a terrible thing.

As the clouds of war gathered, the flow of exciting new

aeroplane designs was constant. Newspapers, while careful not to divulge secret information, were enthusiastic about the new breed of aircraft racing across Britain's skies. The Bristol Blenheim, Fairey Battle and Handley Page Hampden were sweeping the outmoded 'stringbags' before them. The new Supermarine Spitfire was beginning to turn heads. It suited the government to promote these new arrivals to head off criticism that they still lagged far behind Germany in numbers. In some cases, the test of combat would prove British aircraft to be an unsuitable match for their German opponents. The Germans had already honed their designs through their involvement in the Spanish Civil War. After the launch of a right-wing coup in July 1936, Hitler received a request for help from General Francisco Franco to help move his Spanish Army of Africa, based in Morocco, to mainland Spain. An initial group of twenty-two Junkers 52 transport aircraft flown by Luft Hansa pilots were granted. Germany's involvement quickly increased to form the Condor Legion in October, a Luftwaffe unit that provided Franco's Nationalists with air support. Goering was keen to flex the muscles of his new air force, seeing the opportunity to use the Spanish conflict as a testing ground. Thus the Messerschmitt Bf 109 and Junkers 87 Stuka made their combat debut in Spain. The bombing of the Basque market town of Guernica on 26 April 1937 by German and Italian aircraft was without precedent as a targeted attack on a civilian population by an air force, and outraged European public opinion. By the time the civil war ended on 1 April 1939, the Luftwaffe had not only more advanced aircraft than the RAF, but a key advantage: battle experience.

★

In Australia, Jim Comans gained entry to the University of Sydney to study law. Much of his free time was given over to rugby league, which form of the game the students had adopted in 1919, in the face of considerable hostility from the traditionalists of the University Sports Association. Refusing to be browbeaten, the students formed a team to play in the League Premiership. Jim joined the university side when he was still a teenager, playing first-class games from 1932 to 1936. These were years marked by disappointment, as time and time again he saw his team soundly beaten. In 1937, the university side pulled out of the Premiership having won only 44 games out of 226. It had become clear that the students could not hold their own against the older professional players. But Jim had made his mark, and was referred to as the 'thinking man's forward'.

In the formation of character of the bomber pilot, Comans' experiences on the pitch played their part. In both war and rugby, the odds were stacked against him. When put in a difficult position he had a sharp mind and quick reflexes – important attributes for a man who would fly Lancasters. Faced with a dangerous situation brought about by nothing other than bad luck, many men panicked and were lost. The key to survival lay in the speed of the pilot's reaction in the critical few seconds after the incident took place.

In line with Britain, Australia declared war on Germany on 3 September 1939. Australia was already, by the terms of the Statute of Westminster of 1931, an independent sovereign nation, but chose to follow the 'mother country' in matters of foreign policy. Only after 1942, when Australia adopted the Statute, would she assume the right to pursue her own diplomatic course. Prime Minister Robert Menzies broadcast to the nation on all radio stations at 9.15 that evening: 'Fellow Australians, it is my melancholy duty to inform you officially, that in consequence of a persistence by Germany in her invasion of Poland, Great Britain has declared war upon her and that, as a result, Australia is also at war. No harder task can fall to the lot of a democratic leader than to make such an announcement.'

Jim Comans was twenty-seven years old and in his first legal practice as an articled law clerk in Rose Bay. Australia was at no immediate risk from the new war in Europe, although Japan's war in China was cause for concern. The Royal Australian Air Force was small, with only 246 aircraft, but would grow to more than 6,000 by the war's end. Although others were volunteering, Jim held back. Older men who had fought in the Great War advised him to think carefully before leaving a promising career in law. It would be nearly two years before Jim enlisted at No.2 Recruiting Centre in Sydney, but he already knew he wanted to fly.

★

After leaving school, Ken Cook started work in the laboratory of a plastics manufacturer at Lightpill Mill, a former cloth mill in Stroud. The Stroud woollen mills had declined, leaving space for other industries to take over their buildings. Lightpill Mill produced Casein, trademarked 'Erinoid', which could be dyed and was useful for making beads, buttons and other items. When an American firm, Sperry, set up a new plant at Bond's Mill to make gyroscopes and aircraft instruments in 1938, Ken took up a new job with them. Not only did he become familiar with the instruments he would later see daily in RAF service, he also got to know a girl named Muriel Davis who worked in the same office. This early romance blossomed. The pair would often be seen walking out together at the end of the working day, Ken pushing his bicycle with one hand as they talked.

Don Bowes, destined to be a navigator with the Lancaster crew, was born two months after Ken Cook, in County Durham, in June 1923. He, too, came from a working-class background: his father Hugh was a miner at the nearby pit. The family lived in Eldon Lane, near Bishop Auckland, where they occupied a brick-built terraced house of a kind similar to thousands of working-class homes of the time. It had no bathroom and the toilet was outside, at the end of a narrow-walled yard. Standing against the wall was a galvanized steel bathtub, which was brought inside and filled with hot water when the need arose. It was placed close to the fire to keep it warm. At the end of the terrace was a washhouse with a coal-fired boiling tub, the copper serving a number of families.

Rationing during the First World War had begun only in 1918, and restrictions on most foods had been lifted by 1920. Families in the 1920s had enough to eat and conditions were tolerable, although few in these working-class communities would have described themselves as well off.

While Germany began its inexorable slide towards the nationalist right during this period, Britain enjoyed its first experience of moderate socialism under Ramsay MacDonald, who became prime minister of the first – minority – Labour government in 1924. Hugh Bowes' days as a miner were numbered. Known as a union man, he found it hard to keep down a job in his native County Durham. In the early 1930s, Hugh seems to have been charged with the theft of a turnip. Whether this apparently heavy-handed application of the law was a shot across the bows of a potential left-wing troublemaker, or arose from a simple misunderstanding, is not known – Hugh always maintained he found the turnip on the road after the harvest – but this trivial incident may have had some bearing on the family's move to Castleford in the West Riding of Yorkshire in 1934. The pits there were also reluctant to give Hugh a position, so he settled for work with the local council as a bricklayer and labourer. As a result of his family's relocation, Don had missed the chance to sit the eleven-plus examination, but after persistent efforts on his mother's part, he eventually gained a place at The King's School in Pontefract.

The contrast between the conditions in which Hugh Bowes worked and those of his German counterparts could not have been sharper. While Hugh had suffered discrimination in the pits for his union views, his trade union membership was not illegal in the eyes of the state. In Germany, however, Hitler forcibly dissolved all trade unions within months of taking power. Characteristically, the move came overnight on 2 May 1933 as police raided trade union offices, arrested officials and confiscated funds. In their place Hitler created a National Socialist labour organization, the German Labour Front (*Deutsche Arbeitsfront*), which took over the representation of the working class. Strikes, a frequent occurrence in German industry, were banned in 1934, but as production figures rose, accompanied by extravagant promises of future prosperity, opposition was forced underground. Those supporting the idea of unions were branded Communists. Hitler hated Communists almost as much as he hated Jews. A former union man was likely not only to suffer discrimination, but to fall under the suspicion of the Gestapo. Some individuals were executed without trial, while others were sent to be 're-educated' by hard labour in the concentration camps.

Hugh Bowes, a middle-aged man with a glass eye who enjoyed playing the organ at his local Methodist church, would have made an unlikely enemy of the state. However, had the Nazis occupied Britain, as a trade unionist he would have lived in fear of the secret police. When war broke out in September 1939, Don took work at Castleford Town Hall as a clerk. He was still too young to volunteer, although it was only a matter of months before he would enlist.

In the spring of 1940 Ken Cook awoke to hear a new noise high above Yew Tree Cottage. The deep throb of German bombers was to become a familiar sound. At times, Ken could hear the thump of anti-aircraft guns at Bristol, a distant unnatural thunder breaking the still air of Randwick. Throughout that summer and autumn, Swansea, Cardiff and Bristol were all hit by the Luftwaffe. The war had arrived on Ken's doorstep. Newspapers carried pictures of a dozen wrecked towns and cities. All manner of RAF aircraft filled the daytime skies, training becoming more intense after the evacuation from Dunkirk in late May and early June. The Hurricane pilots who had learned their trade over the rolling hills and ancient villages of the Cotswolds gained glory in the Battle of Britain, fought from July to October. Ken was certain that when the time came for him to enlist he wanted to be a pilot. He had joined the newly formed Air Defence Cadet Corps, later renamed the Air Training Corps, while he was still at school. This early introduction to the Royal Air Force paved the way for Ken to join the RAF Volunteer Reserve in 1941. He confesses that it seemed a natural thing to do – at no point did he consider joining the army or navy.

The war was about to throw together a group of men from many different backgrounds. Roy Woollford, destined to be the crew's radio operator, was born in Lambeth in 1922. His father, Claude, worked at Woolwich Arsenal, in a position that not only engaged him in a job, but also made him part of a close community. With the demand for weapons greatly reduced after the First World War, the family faced an uncertain future as redundancies took hold. Nevertheless, the arsenal remained a major employer with 19,200 employees in 1920. Roy was to lose his father to tuberculosis when he was just five years old. Jack Hadden, a family friend who had once worked with Claude at the arsenal, drew closer to the Woollfords after Claude's death, offering the family solace in bereavement. Hadden now lived in Luton, where he had opened a number of successful cobbler's shops. In due course Roy's mother married 'Uncle' Jack and the entire family moved to Luton. When Roy left school, he began an apprenticeship at the electrical firm Snowdens, connected to the Vauxhall car factory at Luton. Vauxhall had invested heavily in their new 10-4 model, launched in 1937, a small but desirable family car developed with their German subsidiary partners,

Opel. Within the company the 10-4 was known as their 'first million pound' car.

The outbreak of war brought rapid changes at Vauxhall. The Luton plant shelved their precious 10-4 model for the duration, production not starting again until 1946. In its place, the line was turned over to the manufacture of the A22 Infantry Tank Mark IV, later known as the 'Churchill'. It was a rushed design that turned out to be underpowered, unreliable and, in its 2lb gun, poorly armed. Churchill remarked in jest that they named it after him 'once they discovered it was no good'. Britain lagged five years behind Germany in tank production. The Henschel vehicle plant in Kassel, which Roy would hear about in due course, had been turned over to Panzer production as early as 1935.

Roy knew what it was like to be caught in an air raid, and the terrible consequences of aerial bombing. At the height of the Battle of Britain, at 4.50 p.m. on 30 August 1940, twelve German bombers approached Luton. As people stopped in the street to gaze up at the formation, local boy Fred Morrad climbed on top of a coal bunker to get a better view. The bombers had appeared in the haze of a beautiful late summer's afternoon, 10,000 feet above the Bedfordshire town. There were no air raid sirens. In the effort to protect airfields further south, Luton had been left open to attack. RAF Biggin Hill in Kent had been bombed as waves of German bombers stretched the resources of Fighter Command to the limit, flying 1,310 sorties against them in a single day. In the tangle of twisting vapour trails across the South of England, the bombers had slipped through the net and headed for Luton. Fred remembers fighters engaging the Germans as they arrived overhead, the rattle of machine guns sounding far above. One bomber fell away, but it was too late.

Tiny dots appeared from the aircraft as they released their bombs, 194 in less than a minute, whistling and shrieking as they fell. Watching crowds scattered as blasts ripped through the town, throwing palls of smoke and dust high into the summer sky. Thick black plumes of smoke rose from the Vauxhall plant followed by the percussive force of a large explosion. Fifty-nine were killed in Luton, of whom thirty-eight were employees at the Vauxhall factory. The works gasometer had been hit, blasting the surrounding buildings.

There had been no warning for Roy Woollford and the workers at Snowdens close to the Vauxhall factory that late Friday afternoon. The windows shattered from the force of the bomb blasts, sending workers sprawling to the floor to avoid the thousands of lethal shards of glass. The ground shook and heaved as if massive hammers were pounding the factory. They ran to hide in cupboards, under tables and staircases. When it fell silent, the survivors ventured out into the concrete yard, the drone of the raiders receding into the distance. There was glass everywhere, and pieces of wood and roofing were scattered over a wide area. Casualties staggered out, many of them bleeding heavily from cuts. Helpers rushed inside to bring out cloths to be ripped up to bind the wounds. Others stood motionless, eyes wide in shock, hardly able to believe what had happened. Some reached instinctively for a cigarette to calm their nerves, only to hear shouts of warning about gas. What Roy experienced that day is unclear, but his family recalled that he was shocked to the core, suffering a stress-related illness for weeks afterwards.

Under these circumstances, it is remarkable that Roy volunteered for Bomber Command. Of all the members of the Lancaster crew, it was the radio operator – huddled over his table in the fuselage of the bomber – who saw the least. While some men joined the Royal Air Force out of excitement or a sense of duty, Roy knew what bombs could do. His choice to serve was probably the most informed of his group. Most of his generation were too young to understand what war was, but they were led by men who knew only too well the misfortune that could befall them.

2.

The Adventure

The broad platform at Paddington Station echoed with the sound of thousands of footsteps. Steaming gently, a Castle class engine rested at the buffers as passengers hurried from the carriages. Pulling his suitcase from the rack above him, Ken Cook stepped down into the river of people heading for the gates. He was struck by the towering expanse of the roof, huge spans of curved iron giving way to soot-blackened glass. Many of the swarming crowd were in uniform – everyone, except Ken, seemed to know where they were going. Porters pulling large trolleys stacked with suitcases and trunks shouted to one another, their voices lost in the melee. The cavernous station was filled with sound – slamming doors, whistles and hissing steam valves.

Ken had never been to London before. Following the flow out onto the street he caught his breath at the height of the Great Western Royal Hotel. Statues gazed down from the high façade, impassively watching the bustle of the taxi rank. Riding the black cab to Lord's cricket ground, Ken was struck by the scars of a city at war. The skeletons of bombed buildings scattered his route, large rubble-filled gaps in ornate terraces. Some streets were blocked off by barriers guarded by men in

The young Ken Cook in training, early 1940s.

steel helmets. Walls of sand-bags protected entrances – small wooden signs pointing to air raid shelters.

The RAF had commandeered Lord's as an aircrew reception centre in 1940, handling 115,000 new recruits throughout the war. Ken's arrival was a puzzling experience. Hundreds of men filled the stands or queued on the pitch. Ken was ushered into a section of other men standing with their suitcases at their feet. A barrage balloon hung low over the nursery ground next door, its rear fins sagging lazily. For the next few days they filled in forms, were prodded in medical examinations, interviewed and given uniforms. They slept in the stands the first couple of nights, but afterwards they were accommodated in luxurious apartments on the north side of Regent's Park. Ken could not understand why these flats, still filled with furniture and oil paintings, had been vacated. At the start of the Blitz in 1940, many owners of means left their fine London apartments. Some owned other residences outside the city, others chose to rent in a safer area. Subsequently, the RAF requisitioned empty properties around St John's Wood to use as accommodation for their recruitment centre.

For a young man from the country, London was the beginning of a long journey, both physically and emotionally. After three weeks of initiation, Ken was transferred to Scarborough College in North Yorkshire for basic training. The pupils of the public school had made way for the RAF, which established an Initial Training Wing here. The autumn days were filled with kit inspections, marching and exercises on the beach, including runs on the headlands. There was no sign of an aeroplane at Scarborough.

Finally, after weeks of instruction in military life, at RAF Booker, in Buckinghamshire, Ken Cook came face to face with an aircraft he was expected to fly – the de Havilland Tiger Moth. At first glance the biplane seemed to be all struts and wire. Most of the recruits had never seen an aeroplane at close quarters, but Ken recognized the design from his trips to Minchinhampton. The lower fuselage and wings were bright yellow with green and brown camouflage on the upper surfaces. There weren't many instruments in the cockpit, but the mysterious dials filled with numbers would take time for a student flyer to master. The joystick, a plain tubular piece of metal with a rubber hand-grip, projected from the floor. The equally plain metal bucket seats looked uncomfortable. Located in the upper wing above the student's head, a fuel tank fed the carburettor via a tube that looked thin enough to cut with a pair of scissors. The 130-horsepower Gypsy Major engine powered a wooden twin-bladed propeller. Running their hands along the side, the students could feel the canvas stretched taut over the ribs of the frame. Mechanically, everything was simple to understand; many of the parts were similar to those of a car or motorbike.

As a basic trainer, the 1932 Tiger Moth had few faults. The undercarriage was fixed, the top speed of 75 knots hardly rapid, yet for those brave enough it could reach 18,000 feet. It wasn't without some imperfections, but it could handle most mistakes presented by a student pilot.

Ken was placed in the front seat for his first flight, the instructor in the rear, enjoying a better view behind the wings. On command, a ground crewman swung the prop and stepped back smartly as the engine spluttered into life. The sudden blast of air was caught by the small glass windshield. As the breeze increased Ken checked his goggles. The noise of the engine seemed deafening as the vibration travelled through every part of the aeroplane. After a few words through the intercom, the instructor taxied over the grass to the marked-out runway. Pausing for only a few seconds, he opened the throttles, allowing the biplane to bump and wallow over the grass strip as it picked up speed. The tail slowly lifted and, seeing the horizon over the nose of the aircraft for the first time, Ken wondered for a second if the propeller would strike the ground on the next bump. At 40mph the Tiger Moth gracefully parted company with the ground. The small hangars of the pre-war airfield disappeared as the patchwork of countryside beneath them grew smaller. The needles of the dials moved slowly as they gained altitude.

'You have control.'

Ken was already gripping the joystick firmly, in anticipation of the instructor's words, his feet lightly resting on the rudder pedals. For the next few minutes Ken made some gentle port and starboard turns, each time levelling the aircraft back onto the horizon. The voice of the instructor was calm in his earphones. Trying to master the odd sensation of flight was like learning to ride a bicycle. Ken was more than a little frightened by this collection of parts from a hardware drawer. In the elation of flying for the first time, each student was aware that unless they learned quickly they would fail and be moved to another RAF role. They knew that only two out of five made it all the way through flying training to front-line service. Many had not even made it this far, refused on grounds of eyesight or some other physical condition – including not being tall enough.

The instructor brought the aircraft in to land. Swinging deftly into line with the grass strip, he cut the engine, letting the Tiger Moth glide in quietly. Touching down with a gentle bump, the wheels settled, squeaking and rumbling before the engine was throttled up again to taxi in.

Over the next few weeks Ken learned to love the Tiger Moth. After five hours' flying, the instructor changed places so that Ken had a better view in the rear cockpit. From here he could identify the small villages around High Wycombe, which helped him with navigation. Despite his growing confidence, Ken made more than the odd rough landing. When he bounced the aircraft in a series of kangaroo hops, the language in his headset turned colourful. Nevertheless, the students all admired their instructors – it took real guts to get into the cockpit each day and allow boys to place their lives at risk. Some accidents were inevitable, and the flimsy biplane offered little protection in the event of a crash-landing. The wood and canvas fuselage would twist and snap as the heavy engine planted itself in the ground. The trainees heard stories of aircraft failing to recover from a spin, flipping uncontrollably to earth and taking pupil and instructor with them. Thankfully, most such incidents occurred at slow speeds and, with a stall speed of 25 knots, the Tiger Moth was not easily upset.

*

Having enlisted in August 1941, Jim Comans was following a similar route. After basic training at RAAF Bradfield Park, not far from Jim's Sydney home, he was sent to 4 Elementary Flying Training School (EFTS) in the nearby suburb of Mascot. The Tiger Moths here, so far from the enemy, had no need of camouflage. Their all-silver finish gleamed in the sun against the landscape beneath them. The airfield was modest and, like RAF Booker, had only a few hangars. On the roof of one of them the word 'Mascot' was painted in large letters to help identification – something that was impossible in Luftwaffe-targeted Britain. Since the training course was held at the height of the Australian summer, student pilots did not have to worry about changing weather – an ever-present factor in rainy, cloudy Britain. RAAF Mascot (now Sydney International Airport) lay to the south of

Jim Comans' Australian identity photo. The band on his cap indicates that he is a trainee pilot.

the city, still within reasonable distance of Jim's home. Comans was streamed to be a bomber pilot. Decisions on whether pilots would fly fighters or bombers might be based on their flying style, but sometimes it was simply a matter of fulfilling quotas. After fifty hours on the Tiger Moth Jim moved to RAAF Mallala, north of Adelaide, to train on Airspeed Oxfords and Avro Ansons.*

Although these aircraft did not exhibit the flying style of fighters, they presented a new level of sophistication to the students. Both Anson and Oxford were twin-engined with a retractable undercarriage. Far more powerful than the basic trainers, they could prove a handful if mishandled. After flying much simpler machines, it was easier to make a mistake with these more complicated aircraft. Solo pilots often forgot to lower the landing gear on approach, only being reminded of the omission when they saw an emergency flare fired from the Watch Office. The larger complement of levers and switches in the Oxfords and Ansons could cause temporary confusion in the mind of a trainee, and even a few seconds of indecision were enough to provoke a stall.

* These Airspeed Oxfords and Avro Ansons were built in Britain and transported to Australia by ship. In Canada, 1,500 British-built Ansons for the RCAF were supplemented by a further 1,822 planes built by Victory Aircraft in Toronto.

★

Having successfully completed his Tiger Moth course in May 1942, Ken Cook found himself posted to Canada and the United States for further flying training. But one important matter required Ken's attention before he travelled to Scotland to join the ship that would take him across the Atlantic: absence from Muriel Davis had made his heart grow fonder, and he returned to Stroud to marry her.

The train north took Ken through the highest mountains he had ever seen. Before climbing the slopes of Shap Fell in Cumberland, the train had stopped to have a second bank engine added. Heaving upwards, it was soon over the crest before running down to Carlisle and on through the lowlands of Scotland. Having arrived on the Clyde as instructed, Ken joined a large crowd of servicemen waiting on the dockside to board ship. The SS *Letitia* loomed above them, a liner-turned-troopship.

The rails and decks were already filled with servicemen peering down at the new arrivals. The mood was light-hearted – men cheering a stumble on the gangplank or a dropped kit bag. A single-funnelled 13,500-ton steamship, *Letitia* normally carried some 1,600 people but packed in more than 2,300 troops on these long wartime sea crossings. As well as filling the cabins, bigger spaces like the ballroom were filled with paillasses. At 15 knots she was hardly a transatlantic hare, unlike Blue Riband-winning ships like the *Queen Mary* or *Elizabeth*, which could turn 28 knots. A submerged U-boat could maintain only 7.6 knots, so the early spotting of a target and positioning to meet it was key to their success. SS *Letitia* normally stayed within the confines of a zigzagging convoy. She had been armed with eight six-inch guns to act as a convoy protection vessel, but the Admiralty decided in 1941 that her role was impractical. She became a troopship.

Ken found his bunk in a cabin with five others in the enlisted men's section of the ship. Ahead lay a nine-day voyage to Halifax, Nova Scotia. Unknown to the men, *Letitia* would be sailing alone. Convoy CT17 had left three days before them, and even the captain did not know the reason for their timing; it was in the hands of the Admiralty. During the Battle of the Atlantic as many as 3,500 Allied merchantmen and 175 warships were sunk. Sending *Letitia* alone was a calculated risk. Most U-boat operations in recent weeks had been closer to North American ports and not mid-Atlantic. Until 1 February 1942, the codebreakers at Bletchley Park, Buckinghamshire, had been able to crack German admiralty codes. Particularly precious were the transmissions from surfaced U-boats sending reports and receiving orders. However, Allied ships now faced a fresh challenge in the form of a new version of the Enigma machines used to relay ciphered messages to and from the German U-boats. The new Enigma machine, the M4, included an added rotary code dial. It would take Bletchley Park a further ten months to crack the code, and during that time U-boats took an increasingly heavy toll of Allied shipping.

As *Letitia* sailed along the Firth of Clyde, Ken was struck by the beauty of the hills and inlets of Argyllshire on the starboard bow. The Isle of Arran and then the Mull of Kintyre slipped past as they turned north to head out into the Atlantic against a head wind. As the initial excitement of this expenses-paid cruise to Canada subsided, there was little to do on board but play cards and walk the decks. The men had four weeks' advance pay in their pockets ready to be plucked from them by experienced poker players. Carrying a tin mug around helped beat the tea queues, although it seemed odd using it for servings of warm beer. As it crossed the North Atlantic, the liner made frequent course changes, in order to outwit any lurking U-boat. The smoke from the funnel painted a long dark brown streak across the clear June sky, advertising their position for miles around. The lookouts kept constant watch for the trail of a periscope. The long days somehow felt safer than the nights, although the chances of being observed were higher. Once the light finally faded, the dimly lit decks throbbed to the pulse of the engines, seeming louder to the men lying in their bunks. When a big wave swept across the bow, the ship juddered and pitched before settling back into the thudding pattern once again. On they went, occasionally seeing smoke from ships in the distance, but normally the sea and sky were empty.

Ken was aware of the dangers of the U-boats. He spent time working out an escape route from his cabin, reassured by being in the upper portion of the liner. He remembers thinking to himself, 'I'm going to be careful here and not take anything for granted'. After several days the upper decks were littered with the seasick. Unable to cope with stuffy mess decks, they had dragged themselves topsides, wrapped in blankets. Some lay motionless, curled against a bulkhead, others sat in lines like beggars. The ship's doctors regularly checked them, cajoling some to return to their bunks, but many, pale and incoherent, were deaf to their attentions.

On their final day at sea, a thin strip of land appeared on the horizon. As the word spread, men sauntered up the stairwells to catch their first sight of North America. A Lockheed Hudson appeared high overhead, its twin radial engines rumbling above the sound of the ship. Banking gently in a wide arc, it made several passes, a signal light flickering. They felt safer closer to Halifax, yet ironically, it was here that they were most in danger from submarines. The Germans had launched Operation *Paukenschlag* ('Drumbeat') in January, sending individual submarines to penetrate the Saint Lawrence River. Their captains were given permission by the Kriegsmarine to roam and strike targets at will. Other than through occasional position reports, it was much harder for Allied codebreakers to anticipate the U-boats' intentions. By April 1942 they had sunk 198 ships in the area; by September, they had rendered the river unusable.

Letitia made it to Halifax without incident, nonetheless. Once the ship had docked, everyone was more than ready to disembark. The scene at the railway station was chaotic, as thousands of men milled around, trying to work out where they should go. Ken Cook's itinerary would take him east to Moncton, New Brunswick, before he embarked on a two-day onward journey to his eventual destination, Albany in Georgia. For a young man who until a few months previously had never even visited London, the epic train journey taking in the whole of the eastern United States left a lasting impression.

Ken's training in the United States was part of the 'Arnold Scheme', an initiative created before America entered the war. In April 1941 General 'Hap' Arnold, Chief of the USAAF, flew to London to meet RAF officers at the Air Ministry. He offered to train 4,000 pilots alongside American cadets – an offer enthusiastically accepted by the British government. In the months before Pearl Harbor, RAF recruits were instructed to change from uniform to civilian clothes as they entered the still-neutral United States. Between June 1941 and March 1943, 7,785 men entered the scheme, of whom 3,392 failed to reach the required standard for pilots. This high rate of failure was typical of pilot training throughout the war on both sides of the Atlantic. The perception, therefore, that pilots were barely trained before entering combat is illusory: most had spent two years in training before reaching a front-line squadron. By 1943, an RAF pilot averaged 335 hours flying in training, twice as many as his Luftwaffe counterpart and close to that of a modern fast jet pilot. The loss of so many RAF crews in early bombing missions illustrates the terrible waste of human resources.

To the bemusement of the new arrivals at Turner Field, Albany, they were required to undergo a month-long acclimatization course in army procedure, which included learning American drill. The discipline could be irksome, not least owing to the presence of 'Upperclassmen' – Americans on the course above who would enforce strict rules. These included the practice of insisting their subordinates ate 'square meals', the American military tradition of sitting bolt upright with arms at right angles, so forming a square shape. Other peculiarities included reporting others for minor infractions – with an expectation that individuals who realized they had broken the rules should report themselves. Some servicemen relate stories of bloodied noses when scores were settled later in the course. Not all RAF personnel were ready to tolerate a culture they saw as petty and vindictive, even if, by openly opposing it, they ran the risk of being removed from the course. The daily drone of training aircraft above reminded the recruits why they were there.

The Britons arrived still wearing their blue flannel uniforms and sweltered in the heat and humidity of July in the Deep South. To their relief, the Americans equipped them with a looser-fitting uniform, which, with the sleeves rolled up, made the 34° heat bearable. The airfield at Turner was larger than anything the cadets had seen in Britain. Numerous runways intersected each other, allowing more than one aircraft to take off and land at the same time. The aircraft used on the advanced flying courses hosted by Turner included twin-engined trainers like the Curtiss AT-9, a slick all-metal aircraft that looked very modern.

The locals welcomed the British warmly during their time at Turner Field. The Southern drawl was different from the accents the men were familiar with from Hollywood films, the ex-Confederates still referring to northerners as 'Damyankees'. Ken remembers the Georgians as uncomplicated in their outlook, many of them unsure where Britain was and puzzled as to how to get there. They were eager to introduce the airmen to the food and culture of the South, but also to the jitterbug, a dance that was sweeping America.

After a month of tedious drill, the British trainees were released to nearby Darr Aero Tech, an airfield that had been a civilian flying field before the war. There was some friction over the proximity of the two airfields, particularly after a collision some months earlier between a Darr Aero Tech trainer and a twin from Turner Field, which resulted in the deaths of a student and instructor.

Neat lines of Boeing Stearman trainers greeted them at Darr Aero Tech. Resplendent with bright blue fuselage and yellow wings, the aircraft had a robust, no-nonsense look about them. The Boeing Stearman, like the Tiger Moth, was a biplane with a fixed undercarriage, but it was larger than the British aircraft. The open Lycoming radial engine, with exposed finned cylinders, looked rudimentary, and the Stearman had a coarser engine tone than the Britons were accustomed to. Despite the aircraft's basic appearance, the Stearman's engine produced over 250 horsepower – twice that of the Tiger Moth. In flight the wooden propellers made a rasping sound, the engine driving the propellers so fast that their tips broke the sound barrier.

The flying instructors at Darr were civilians, disarming the students with their tendency to call everyone 'buddy' rather than using surnames, as was standard practice in RAF training. This term might be used casually, or, should the need arise, in stern intervention. The instructors were amused by the British mix of stuffiness and self-deprecating humour. The 'Limeys' had a way about them, but, at times, the exact meaning of their words escaped the Americans. In flying, the instructors wanted their students to gain an instinctive feel for their aircraft. One of them, 'Kinky' Gunn, had enjoyed a career as a Hollywood stunt pilot and made a point of taking his students up and flinging the aeroplane around in aerobatics. The point was to illustrate that they should learn to fly by the 'seat of their pants', although most felt too ill to fully appreciate the lesson.

Supervising the course, gruff Major Knight of the US Army Air Corps tried to keep a tight rein on his excitable and sun-burned trainees. He was a man who did not entertain any form

Instructors at Darr Aero Tech, Albany Field, Georgia.

of humour, and at times he despaired of the British, who seemed incapable of tight discipline. He would send a man back to Canada for the smallest violation of army rules. Drinking was forbidden and the mere suggestion of moral indiscretion would produce an explosion of volcanic proportions. Wearing the straight-brimmed hat of a West Point officer, he was nicknamed 'the Boy Scout' by his British charges.

Ken Cook was more than ready to clamber into the cockpit of the Stearman. It seemed too long since he had flown; he hoped he had not forgotten too much. To avoid the heat of the day, flying started early in the mornings. Among many differences between the American trainer and the Tiger Moth was the fact that the Stearman's seat had to be adjusted to the right height, otherwise seeing out of the cockpit could be difficult. Many students took off with the seat too low, much to their later embarrassment. When the pilot looked out over the engine, the movement of the propeller and the resulting heat formed a shimmering haze that made it difficult to see the horizon. Ken found the Stearman had a life of its own, testing his nerves. At take-off the torque of the engine tended to pull the biplane to port. Rudder technique was essential in keeping her straight. If he was too heavy on the rudder the aircraft would twitch back and forth, producing mutterings from the instructor. The Stearman was not a fast aeroplane – her cruising speed was just 90mph – but when the throttles were opened she produced a surge of power. Soon the students were learning the feel of the aeroplane, getting used to its whistling wires and creaking wings.

Although he was settling into the flying, there was one element that frightened Ken above all other manoeuvres. Landing was proving to be very stressful. Unlike the gentler Tiger Moth, the Stearman's stall speed of 55mph meant the biplane needed to be flown all the way to touchdown. A good landing involved judging the stall speed correctly. Too much height and the aircraft would hurtle towards the runway and bounce ferociously. All too often Ken stressed the landing gear as he fought to keep control, giving his bewildered instructor an experience akin to a fast descent in an elevator. Even once the wheels touched the ground the Stearman seemed to dig in, propelling it from one side of the runway to the other in a series of chaotic lurches. If all went well, the terrified pilot would eventually gain control, sweating and shaking as the aircraft subserviently rolled to a halt as if nothing untoward had happened.*

* A pilot with 3,000 hours of flying experience in the Stearman, Tom Lowe still experiences the anxiety that the 'beast within' will manifest itself. '… to this day, every landing on a hard surfaced runway is preceded by a feeling of apprehension, a dry mouth, a tightening of the sphincter muscle which induces an advanced case of "pucker" that leaves me wondering if this will be the Stearman landing that will finally jump up and grab me.'

After twenty-seven hours of flying, ten of which had been solo, Ken learned that he had not made the grade. He confesses that he never mastered the Stearman – it made him nervous, and with this lack of confidence he lost the ability to fly well. He was informed that he would be returned to Trenton, Ontario, to await further pilot training. Ken knew he had 'washed out', but he still hoped that he could get on a future course.

On 21 September 1942, Ken began the two-day train journey north to Canada, which gave him plenty of time to think about his future. Up until then, everything had gone well for him, but suddenly the dream of being a pilot seemed to be slipping away. At Trenton he was informed that all future pilots' courses were full. Few who failed got a second chance; the system was pushing hundreds of men into the conveyor belt of pilot training. For those who fell off, there were plenty of other roles to fill – the RAF needed six crew members for every bomber pilot. Ken confesses he felt miserable as he returned to the barrack-room routine of parades and kit cleaning. There was nothing much to do. Thousands of miles from home, he felt in limbo. After some weeks of despondency, he was offered a position on an air gunnery course for RAF bomber crews. He refused firmly but politely. 'Not bloody likely,' he said later. A second offer sounded more attractive. Would he be interested in training for the new position of 'air bomber'? This would involve training in navigation as well as more conventional bomb aiming. He would also train as an air gunner, but this was a secondary role. This time, Ken accepted the offer. If he could not fly as a pilot, a position in aircrew would have to do.

Taganrog, southern Russia, November 1941

Günther Rall checked the straps of his harness, shuffling a little in his seat. It was a tight fit, his shoulders rubbing against the sides of the cockpit. After a couple of attempts the Daimler Benz 603 engine burst into life. It was a bitterly cold late November day in 1941, the temperature tens of degrees below freezing. The outside of the cockpit was frosted, making the handle slippery as he reached up to close the canopy. He waved across to his wingman, signalling that he was beginning to taxi. The two Messerschmitt Bf 109s moved slowly over the deeply frozen ground, weaving from side to side so that the pilots could see over the long snouts of their fighters. Fully armed and fuelled, they lifted off from Taganrog, 200 miles east of the Crimea. Their sweep headed towards Rostov-on-Don, where palls of thick smoke were rising from a ferocious battle. The Germans had taken the town only six days earlier, but now a large Russian counter-attack was driving them out. Little did they realize that this was the first successful operation of many that would eventually turn the tide against them.

The light was fading when they spotted a group of Russian fighters below them, dark green with red stars on their wings. In the chill air, exhausts streamed telltale white ribbons. Turning quickly towards them, the Russian group broke; they had seen the Messerschmitts. Günther was not too concerned: he had been in this position a dozen times. When it came to a dogfight, the Me 109 could out-turn a Russian every time. He was one of the highest scoring aces on the Eastern Front, supremely confident in both his aircraft and his abilities. He set to work closing in on his prey, like an expert stalker keeping downwind of his victim. After a couple of minutes' twisting and turning he planted himself on the tail of a Russian. He fired a brief burst, his two 13mm machine guns and single 20mm cannon ripping into the fighter. Engulfed in flames, the aircraft tumbled from the sky in front of him. Whether it was the cold, the fading light or just a momentary lapse, Günther could not recall. Flying straight and level as he watched the tumbling fireball of his latest victim, he paid for his few seconds of complacency. A Soviet fighter pounced on him, bullets slashing through the thin aluminium skin, killing the engine dead.

Günther reacted immediately, breaking and diving – but his power was gone. The prop slowed to a flutter. He had to hope that the Russian would not follow him down to finish the job. He also knew he was over Russian positions – not that the front here was fixed. In the half-light he made out some German Panzers and decided to belly-land as close to them as possible. His approach was too fast, and, noticing a small ravine spanning his landing area, he struck the ground hard before sailing over the gap and churning the aircraft into the field opposite. He remembers a wall coming to meet him before he was knocked unconscious.

His wingman circled above, watching but unable to help. Günther's wings and engine were torn off in the crash, but there was no fire. Hanging in the wreckage, he was cut out by a tank crew and taken back to a burned-out school in Taganrog. There was no medical aid available, but eventually he was evacuated to Romania, his back broken in three places and paralysed on his right side. Doctors were sceptical about a recovery, falling silent when he told them he wanted to fly again. After months in hospital his determination paid off, and he returned to flying duties on the Eastern Front in August 1942. He was to survive the war as a high-scoring ace, but he was shot down eight times, on the last occasion losing his thumb to a P-47 Thunderbolt.

Günther Rall's first dogfights had been over the English Channel in 1940. Ordered to close escort Junkers 87 Stuka dive bombers, all advantage of the speed of the Me 109 was lost. Spitfires and Hurricanes tore into their formations with devastating effect. He had great respect for the RAF pilots and their aircraft, but he knew that Luftwaffe strategy in the Battle of Britain had been poor. When he moved to the Eastern Front, his dogfights with the Russians resembled a turkey shoot, but what the Russians lacked in skill or technology they made up for in numbers. Günther lost many colleagues, experienced men the Luftwaffe could ill afford to lose.

That a man of Günther Rall's ability ended up 1,700 miles from Calais demonstrates the folly of Hitler's wild leap into Russia in the summer of 1941. It was a strategic blunder that enabled RAF Bomber Command to build a force capable of attacking Germany's cities. After the end of the Blitz in May 1941, Britain's airfields and aircraft manufacturing capacity had been left alone to flourish. Thus it was that when the RAF announced its Area Bombing Directive of February 1942, it possessed the planes and weapons it needed to implement the lethally effective strategy of targeting Germany's cities and industrial centres. While Günther languished in a full body cast in hospital, large raids on Germany began in earnest. The first major attack was against Lübeck in late March 1942, and created a firestorm that severely damaged the Baltic city.

Reichsmarschall Hermann Goering had won Hitler's confidence as head of the pre-war *Sturmabteilung*, the SA, in the early 1920s. He had reorganized the body 'from a rabble', as Hitler enthused, but his leadership of the Luftwaffe as its Supreme Commander from 1935 was vacuous. Much of the strength of the Luftwaffe came from the services of officers recruited under Seeckt's secretive direction in the 1920s. Goering, addicted to morphine after a 1923 injury, retreated into a pampered world of fine clothes and looted artworks. Günther Rall's opinion of Goering was typical of most Luftwaffe officers. 'At the time I became acquainted with him, I was cold to him. He was a big fat man, a very pompous man, and not only I but my comrades felt that he was out of touch with reality. He was certainly not respected as an air force leader.'

That Goering lacked experience in directing a coherent air

strategy is unsurprising. His pandering relationship with Hitler prevented informed opinion from reaching the ears of the Führer. Generalfeldmarschall Erhard Milch, former head of Luft Hansa and Goering's immediate subordinate from 1933, pleaded with him to prevent the 'madness' of a Russian invasion, but Goering forbade him any contact with Hitler. Milch was correct in believing that the Russian front would lose Germany the war. By late 1942, the Luftwaffe, although sustaining great losses, still managed to maintain a force of 2,500 aircraft on the Eastern Front. Had these resources been available to attack Britain in 1941, it is unlikely that the manufacture of the Lancaster and Halifax could have taken place in such numbers. Airfield attacks would have limited the building-up of Bomber Command forces and kept Britain firmly on the back foot. One significant problem would have remained, however: the flow of trained pilots from Australia, South Africa, Canada and America. The men enjoying the adventure of a lifetime under untroubled skies abroad were the slow-burning fuse of a demolition charge.

*

Embarking on his second career in the Royal Air Force Volunteer Reserve, Ken Cook made the thirty-five-mile journey from Trenton to Picton, Ontario. He found himself on another large airfield – 31 Bombing and Gunnery School. The huge expanses of flat land around the airfield were filled with low scrub and trees. Viewed from the air, the landscape defined itself as a patchwork of thousands of fields, stretching in wide bands along the shores of Lake Ontario all the way to Toronto and beyond to Lake Huron. The lakes were huge, yet navigators needed to be careful not to cross the invisible line of the US border mid-lake twenty-five miles south of Picton. To the north, the land was uncultivated and wild, extending some five hundred miles across Quebec and Ontario to Hudson Bay. It was not uncommon for crews to become lost – sometimes hopelessly – in the Canadian wilderness. On 30 October 1942 an Avro Anson flying out of Patricia Bay in British Columbia went missing with four crew on board. The crashed aircraft was not discovered until October 2013 by logging workers on Vancouver Island, finally allowing recovery of the bodies.

The skies above North America seemed much bigger than at home, but the baking sun of Albany had long since set. It was October 1942 and chill winds were beginning to whip across the airfield at Picton. Gradually, the rich hues of autumn faded, a portent of the harsh Canadian winter. Rows of H-shaped, shingle-clad huts filled the site, their red corrugated iron roofs ready for the coming snowfall. The site was well planned, with tarmac roads connecting the accommodation blocks. Trainees lived in dormitories with shared bathroom facilities. In front, six cavernous hangars dominated the view, providing shelter for the training aircraft and space for classroom work. Although a white steel security fence topped with barbed wire secured the boundaries, the risk posed by spies or saboteurs was slight. Life for servicemen was spartan, but when leave was taken it was possible to travel as far as New York City to see the sights.

Ground training was supplemented by flights in the Avro Anson – 'Faithful Annie' or the 'Flying Greenhouse', as it was affectionately known. Designed as a light bomber, it fulfilled many roles throughout the Empire, mostly in training and light transport.

Through the deep-snowed months of December and January, Ken trained with 33 Air Navigation School at Mount Hope, near Hamilton. The Fairey Battle, an aircraft introduced in 1937 but considered obsolete less than three years later, served as their principal trainer. Too large and underpowered for its single engine, the Battles were hopelessly outclassed in the battle for France in 1940. They flew 100mph slower than the Me 109s they were pitched against. Flying over a featureless white landscape presented problems for trainee navigators as they sought out waypoints for course changes. Snow showers often limited their visibility, leaving them reliant on dead reckoning. When the dark strip of Mount Pleasant's runway appeared in front of the nose, there was a feeling of relief. But the pilots still had slippery concrete to contend with, capable of depositing the unwary into the large snowbanks along the edges of the runway.

Ken Cook completed his bombing and gunnery courses successfully, also receiving his commission as pilot officer.* Soon he was homeward bound on RMS *Empress of Canada*, but this time in the officers' quarters. Although the opulence of the ocean liner was somewhat diminished by the presence of thousands of troops on board, some areas still carried the refinement of their pre-war days. The wooden-panelled upper-class cabins with brass wall lights and patterned carpets were a reminder of an age of peace-time cruising. *Empress of Canada* would not enjoy such carefree times again. She was torpedoed three weeks later off the west coast of Africa by the Italian submarine *Leonardo da Vinci*. Of 1,800 passengers, 392 were lost, over half of them Italian prisoners of war.

After home leave and the chance to spend some time with Muriel, Ken was posted to RAF Wigtown on the Dumfries and Galloway coast. He made acquaintance with the Blackburn Botha, a light bomber that, like the Fairey Battle, had failed to live up to expectations. Despite its underwhelming performance, Ken enjoyed his time dropping sticks of practice bombs and firing machine guns. Although very small compared to the Lancaster, Ken remembers the Blackburn Botha as a 'real' aeroplane. As in Canada, life for the trainee airmen was simple and

* The rank of pilot officer was held by all receiving a commission in the RAF and did not necessarily denote that they were a pilot.

uncomplicated. There were opportunities for the pilots to vary their flights, to drop in on airfields that offered hospitality or interesting flying. The Isle of Man, Scottish Isles and Lake District peaks all offered excellent sightseeing opportunities, although the Botha's near-allergic reaction to climbing had to be kept in mind. This was to be Ken's last posting to an isolated unit; hereon he would be thrust into the culture of Bomber Command. The business of war became serious. Training apart, an airman needed to prepare himself for action and the close proximity of death.

★

In early June 1943 the men were ushered into the large flat-ceilinged crew room at RAF Cottesmore in Rutland. Most had arrived only a few days before, found a bed with an upright locker next to it and deposited their kit. They knew that the next milestone in their training was to be 'crewed up'. Around one hundred men assembled for the first time, glancing around at the mass of unfamiliar faces. The instructions were simple – they were to organize themselves into crews. Crews would form around the pilots and, other than ensuring that there were the right number of men for each position in the room, there was no further interference by senior RAF officers. It was a process that resembled a Christmas party game, but the act of self-selection created a psychological bond that locked the crew together. They had all volunteered for aircrew, but most decisions after this had been taken for them. But now, for a brief moment in their military career, they took back control. The choices they made in that crowded room would define their destinies.

The crews gathered at RAF Cottesmore were brought together by the exigencies of wartime and drawn from all parts of the British Empire: there were Australians, New Zealanders, Canadians and South Africans. Whether each individual lived or died in the future might depend on the personal connections they made in the next ten minutes – a brief conversation, a first impression of a pilot, a sympathetic engagement with another trainee. Henceforth they would be bound to their new colleagues as interdependent members of a team. Except for the interruptions of illness, injury or death, most crew members would remain together for the duration of their tour of duty. In numerous cases, the men would share not only the day-to-day rhythms of each other's lives, but also their final moments. Many of the men who crewed up that day lie together in lines of white headstones in cemeteries from Utrecht to Berlin.

Ken Cook remembers being one of the first to meet Jim Comans. They talked only briefly, but Ken was impressed by the Australian. They 'struck it off' immediately, although Ken later felt Comans remained somewhat aloof in his relationship with the crew. Comans, too, had married in 1942, but being eleven years older he had an air of authority about him. Navigator Don Bowes was also an officer and, like Ken, 'washed out' from pilot training school in the USA. George Widdis, the Canadian upper gunner, had likewise made the journey from Ontario across the Atlantic in early 1943. The new crew was completed by tail gunner 'Jock' Bolland from Scotland, flight engineer Ken Randle from Birmingham and the Luton man Roy Woollford as radio operator. All were in their early twenties. The room was filled with the babble of conversations. This was it: after nearly two years in the Royal Air Force they were finally part of a crew. Even at this early stage, it was possible to read their characters. Three were quiet, unassuming men, one gregarious, and the other three, all officers, shared a more phlegmatic approach – but with a twinkle in their eyes.

RAF Cottesmore was a busy airfield. Day and night the air was filled with the roar of aircraft taking off and landing. Gone was the slower pace of the Empire training grounds; 14 Operational

Don Bowes, the Crew's future navigator (kneeling), with three of his fellow trainees, Canada, early 1940s.

Training Unit (14 OTU) was in a state of perpetual motion, feeding replacement aircrew, as needed, to the front-line squadrons. Losses were mounting, but the bomber force was continuing to expand. The crew knew they had four months of intensive training before they were posted to an operational squadron. For the first time they were close to 'Bomber Country' with its many air-fields, stretching from North Yorkshire to East Anglia. The spectacle of gathering bomber streams fascinated them. As twilight fell on the long June evenings, the 'heavies' began their rumbling climbs over the countryside. Halifaxes, Lancasters and Stirlings rose like gnats in the distance, soon visible only as tiny dots against the deepening blue skies.

The month before the crew formed at 14 OTU, the Dam Busters raid of 16/17 May had enthralled the country. Suddenly, bombers had captured the imagination of the public in a way that the Spitfire and Hurricane pilots had done in the summer of 1940. Although the activities of Bomber Command were reported in newspapers or in the clipped tones of BBC announcers, there had been nothing as exciting as this since the Augsburg raid of April 1942. The newspaper headlines were dramatic – 'Dambusters', 'Heart of Ruhr Flooded', '100 miles wave' – and stories of the raid occupied many column inches for days afterwards. Photographs of the breached dams pouring water were more arresting than blurry, high-level images of smoking factories. A new hero, Wing Commander Guy Gibson, was born, a *Boy's Own* figure who had already enjoyed an illustrious RAF career. He had been posted to Cottesmore with 14 OTU for two brief weeks in 1940, but he was unhappy and successfully lobbied to be moved. A pre-war pilot, Gibson was thrown against the enemy in the ill-equipped and inexperienced bomber force that found itself struggling in France in May and June 1940. He had survived by luck, but in the years following he became an outstanding pilot.

The crew's first flights together were from a satellite training airfield, RAF Saltby, a seven-mile drive in a blue RAF bus. The Vickers Wellington was a far bigger aircraft than the men had flown in before. Squat and menacing, it carried two Bristol Pegasus radial engines in bulbous housings close to the wing root. Its 64-foot wingspan did not match the Lancaster's 102 feet, but in length the fuselage was only five feet shorter. A prodding finger revealed that its fuselage was canvas stretched over a complicated Duralumin frame. Introduced in 1936, the Wellington had been the RAF's most modern bomber, yet with the massive increase in wartime production its use had declined, Bomber Command favouring the new Halifax and Lancaster. Although the Wellington's role as a long-distance bomber had diminished by 1943, it continued to serve Coastal Command in the Battle of the Atlantic as well as serving in training units.

While German designers flung themselves determinedly into the all-metal aeroplane, old habits died hard in Britain. Designers did not fully trust the new technology. The Hawker Hurricane, a hugely successful fighter, still had a wooden-ribbed, canvas-covered rear fuselage. Part of the problem was engine capability, and arguably the Germans at the start of the war were still ahead in power output. The Wellington was still capable of comfortable speeds for a bomber at 235mph, but 40mph slower than the Heinkel He 111, a similar-sized aircraft carrying the same bomb load.

The Wellington might not have been the latest bomber, but to the crew it was a technological marvel. Jim Comans had already been taught how to fly the Wellington; the next step was to see how he could command a group of men crewing it. Climbing the short yellow ladder in the nose of the aircraft, the crew were struck by the complexity of the geodesic structure with its thousands of interlocked diamond shapes. Designed by Barnes Wallis, the geodesic airframe – which bore some similarity to a Zeppelin – comprised a latticework of criss-crossing metal struts, creating a fuselage that was light but extremely strong. Wellingtons had survived many attacks over Germany, returning with canvas burned off and large punctures in the fuselage. Apart from the cramped turrets, it was far roomier than other aircraft the crew had flown in. However, the Wellington was far from luxurious, offering little head height. Some consideration had been given to allowing natural light into the fuselage, via a long strip of windows over the wing root. The crew were familiar with the equipment it carried – the radios, navigation aids and cockpit instruments were the same as in other trainers.

Ken Cook's first flight with the new crew took place on 11 June 1943. He took off at 11.00 hours, and the flight lasted 2 hours 55 minutes: 'familiarisation with aircraft & crew', he wrote in his logbook. Like the Avro Anson, Ken's regular training companion, the Wellington had a canvas-covered fuselage which offered no protection from the deafening noise of the aircraft's engines. The tips of the propellers seemed to spin inches away from the cockpit. Despite some shortcomings, the Wellington, or 'Wimpy', was a well-loved and reliable aeroplane, which continued in production until 1945.

The crew was beginning its airborne training, but getting to know the detached voices from the intercom began in the bar, at dances, pubs and cinema showings. All bomber aircrew held a minimum rank of sergeant, a social standing that enabled the men to mix more freely with the officers. Aircrew had their own set of rules regarding rank when they were in the air. It was common for a flight sergeant to be a pilot and have commissioned officers in the crew, yet as skipper he had command over them. The promotion to sergeant allowed higher rates of pay in recognition of the training undertaken, but it also ensured better treatment in the event of the individual becoming a prisoner of war. The Germans still maintained a strict military code of honour in dealing with downed airmen: non-commissioned officers were treated with greater deference than men of lower rank.

The crew flew most days, dodging the rainstorms and thunder of an unsettled month. The Wellington, often lightly loaded, proved powerful and agile in the air. The men had taken Jim Comans' piloting abilities on trust when they first met, but nothing that had happened since had dimmed their confidence in him. As they talked with other crews, however, it was clear that not all pilots were made of the same stuff. Rough landings were a common complaint. Tales of poor handling and muddled thinking were swapped around the bar. In these respects, Comans caused little concern. Not only was he a good pilot, his air of command inspired confidence.

Incidents and accidents were commonplace, a constant reminder that flying was a hazardous occupation. On the day of the crew's first flight from RAF Saltby, a Wellington of 14 OTU crash-landed on the Chatsworth estate in Derbyshire, injuring some of the crew. Engine problems had caused a loss of power and F/O Leo Patkin was forced to perform a wheels-up landing, writing off the aircraft. Simple errors could prove fatal, as in the case of Sergeant Wilford Collins, who raised his flaps instead of the undercarriage on the night of 6 December 1942 and was killed when his Wellington ploughed into a field not far from the end of the runway. By the war's end, eighty-nine servicemen were buried in Cottesmore's village cemetery extension. Nationally, Operational Training Units lost 558 aircraft in 1943, only a small fraction of them to enemy activity.

In August 1943 the crew were deemed fit to move to the next stage of their training. Excitement and apprehension mounted as they were posted to 1661 Heavy Conversion Unit (HCU) at RAF Winthorpe, near Newark. Most of the men had experience of five or six different aircraft types, but now they came face to face with a career-defining leviathan, the Avro Lancaster. The aircraft seemed very high compared to the low-slung Wellington. The tyres were bigger than any they had seen, and the capacious wheel bay seemed large enough to hold a small car. A huge bomb bay ran from the nose to beyond the rear of the wing, open doors revealing the mounting points and control mechanisms. The skin was all metal, finely riveted in squares, giving a sleek but robust look.

The ground crew were proud of their aircraft and devoted time to introducing the new arrivals to every area of the bomber. Four in-line Rolls-Royce Merlin engines protruded from the leading edge, their smooth cowlings meeting the propeller hubs. Even the exhaust stubs were designed for speed – angled rearwards, as in the Spitfire, to give a few added miles per hour. They had seen the Lancaster in flight, the Rolls-Royce Merlin engines sounding smoother and more melodious than the radials of the Wellingtons. In daylight the cockpit was light and airy, with the canopy extending rearwards towards the navigator's table.

The Lancaster Mark 1s of 1661 HCU had already seen squadron service. Battle damage repairs on the skin were noticeable; they were veterans, yet still examples of one of the most advanced aircraft of the war to date. Another emotion stirred the crew as they looked around the Lancaster for the first time. It was the feeling of receiving a special gift, perhaps akin to buying a first car. The Lancaster was inspiring, frightening and engaging, all at the same time.

The Crew, photographed with Lancaster W4113 of 1661 Heavy Conversion Unit, RAF Winthorpe, Nottinghamshire, 7 September 1943. Back row, left to right: George Widdis, Don Bowes, Jim Comans, Ken Cook and Ken Randle. Front row: Roy Woollford and Daniel 'Jock' Bolland.

The next few weeks were filled with exercises and classroom work. Most of the flying was done at night. Radio operator Roy Woollford had only flown nineteen hours in darkness, but within three weeks his total had risen to sixty. Despite the intensity of the training, questions began to gnaw at the pits of their stomachs. How would they cope in action? Would their nerves hold? The gunners knew the speed a fighter could fly at them. In daylight, they appeared as specks closing in quickly. The target appeared in the gunsight for only a few seconds before whipping away above or underneath them with incredible speed. In the dark, the sudden movement was unnerving. In training, on several occasions friendly fighters had appeared so quickly that there was not time to aim. More frighteningly, there were times when neither gunner saw them until the snarl of the fighter's engine overhead made them duck.

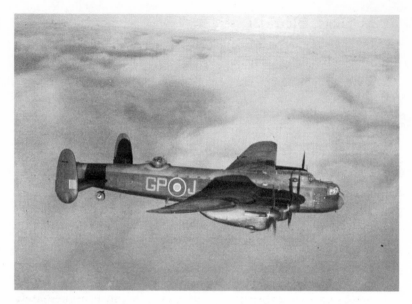

Lancaster W4113 in flight.

Occasionally, a damaged aircraft would drop in to RAF Winthorpe, its fuselage holed with fist-sized puncture wounds, its sides and wings peppered with smaller flak shards. This dark intimation of what lay ahead could not be dwelt on; there were daily hazards in training to overcome. In their third week at Winthorpe, Lancaster W4929 did not return from a night navigation exercise. All eight of its crew died when it crashed high in the Black Mountain near Fan Foel in the Brecon Beacons. The accident was a stark reminder that flying was inherently dangerous. The Comans crew flew the next day, practising evasion manoeuvres under the supervision of Squadron Leader Pattinson. After one and three-quarter hours of being flung about the sky, including numerous corkscrew manoeuvres, they were grateful to land safely.

The men of the crew had changed over the last two years. Most had left their local railway station with a thousand thoughts packed into a small suitcase. Some had dreamed of becoming fighter pilots, effortlessly sailing through cloud-drifting skies like Douglas Bader or Bob Tuck. Gradually, they had been drawn into a darker world of black-painted bombers. 1661 HCU was introducing them to their new nocturnal world, technicians in a piece of complex machinery. Their training prepared them for the worst: treating injuries, how to use survival equipment, parachutes and evasion techniques. They had all watched the films *Target for Tonight and One of Our Aircraft Is Missing*, both of which centred on the experiences of Wellington bomber crews. They were drawn to the men's heroism and intrigued by the bombers they flew in. However, as the moment approached when they themselves would have to undertake operational flying, the future began to appear less romantic. There were also wives and sweethearts to consider, but more immediately the wellbeing of their comrades.

Roy Woollford carried with him the memory of the Luftwaffe's bombing of Luton in the late summer of 1940. At least now he would be able to strike back at an enemy that had destroyed the Vauxhall factory, killing young girls on the shop floor in a deadly shower of flying glass. The attack had affected him deeply, the events of 30 August 1940 never far from his thoughts. But now he was in love. A chance decision by the crew to go for lunch in nearby Newark led to Roy meeting a local girl, Phyllis Brewer. They had much in common. She, too, had experienced the effects of a factory bombing raid. Her father worked at the Ransome and Marles ball-bearing plant in Newark. It was attacked on 7 March 1941 by two German bombers, a raid in which forty-one were killed. Her grandfather had ridden to the factory on his bicycle, anxious for news of his son, who worked in the tool room. He was stopped at the gates by policemen. The wrecked roofs and rising smoke told the story all too clearly. Happily, Phyllis's father was safe, although shaken.

As the wheels of Lancaster F-Freddie touched down after

their final training flight on 23 September 1943, the crew knew their own 'phoney war' was over. After two years of training, the RAF had given them just twenty-three hours' night flying time in the Lancaster. Only one training session had lasted as long as an actual raid. Now they were to be propelled into the real world of a bomber crew. Their operational posting appeared on the noticeboard: they were going to No. 9 Squadron, based at RAF Bardney in Lincolnshire.

3.

Lancaster

Wearing the attire of an early aviator, the figure stands gazing in admiration at a model of a Wright biplane held in the hands of his outstretched arms. His high boots, loose-fitting jacket and flat cap with open-face balaclava beneath mark him as an explorer. The bronze statue in Agincourt Square, Monmouth, was erected in memory of an aviation pioneer who lost his life in pursuit of his passion. Charles Rolls was educated at Eton before going up to Cambridge University in 1895, but he was soon consumed with a love of early motor cars. 'Dirty Rolls' always seemed to have his hands stained with oil. At the age of eighteen he bought his first car in Paris, a Peugeot Phaeton, and joined the Automobile Club of France. It was the first car resident in Cambridge, and only the third in Wales. In 1903 he established a world land speed record of 93mph in a French Mors car in Dublin. A year later he met Frederick Royce and created one of the most iconic of all manufacturing brands, Rolls-Royce. Within months, they had produced their first car.

Rolls was also a keen balloonist and, as the aeroplane began to make its presence felt, his interest in aviation led him to purchase a French-built Wright biplane. In appearance it did not differ greatly from the model that had skimmed the flats of Kitty Hawk,

North Carolina, but it had a new tail assembly with a rudder. As a founder member, Rolls became licence holder No. 2 of the Royal Aeronautical Society. On 2 June 1910 he successfully completed a double crossing of the English Channel without landing, starting and ending at Dover, an event also commemorated with a statue of Rolls on the town's esplanade. Town councillors at Monmouth, a few miles from the Rolls' country seat at Llangattock, immediately proposed a statue be erected in Charles's honour. Their enthusiasm was no doubt spurred by the realization that the town lacked famous sons. Henry V had been born in the castle and Lord Horatio Nelson paid a brief visit in 1802. Monmouth badly needed a hero.

Sadly, within weeks of the council's proposal, Charles was dead, killed during a show at Bournemouth on 12 July when the newly designed tail sheared off his biplane. Horrified spectators saw the aircraft lift, twist in the air and plunge to the ground. Charles fell only 20 feet, but without head protection he succumbed to his injuries. *The Times* stated, 'he is the first Englishman who has sacrificed his life in the cause of modern aviation'. The statue, unveiled in October 1911, is a poignant reminder of the heavy price paid by the early pioneers of aviation. Royce continued with the Rolls-Royce company, finding success with luxury cars and aero engines. Had Rolls lived, he would have seen his company expand beyond all expectations. Henry Royce died in 1933, but not before designing his enduring legacy, the Rolls-Royce Merlin engine, which entered production in 1935. The 12-cylinder, 27-litre engine was to become a war winner and, like other great inventions, was updated and modified during its period of production. It had the ability to transform an unremarkable aircraft design into a class leader. The story of the Avro 683 Lancaster, an aircraft renamed after its meeting with the Rolls-Royce Merlin, is one of success, but the original aircraft, the Avro 679 Manchester, proved to be a misadventure.

★

Avro's chief designer Roy Chadwick had been with the company for twenty years. As he stood by the runway at Ringway near Manchester on 24 July 1939, he made polite conversation with visiting dignitaries from the Air Ministry but hoped this test flight would not be delayed much longer. Neatly dressed in suit and tie, his hair was closely combed down and pencil moustache carefully trimmed. He was part of the management, but his heart lay in hours of painstaking work at the drawing board. Like his mentor and early employer A. V. Roe, he was one of the new breed of aviation pioneers. Unlike Charles Rolls, who had poured his wealth into the new sport of flying, he was not a child of the landed aristocracy but was born on a farm, the son of a mechanical engineer.

His latest brainchild had taken years of development. Winning the tender for the Air Ministry's Specification P13/36 had been an exciting prospect. The project was to deliver a new medium bomber for the RAF capable of carrying 6,000lb of bombs at 275mph over a range of 1,000 miles. P13/36 envisaged it would be a twin-engined bomber that would require catapult-assisted take-off, an idea so outlandish it was not pursued in the final design. The '36' in the specification denoted the year, 1936, and even before their current bombers like the Wellington, Whitley and Hampden had seen action, planners were looking ahead to the next generation of aircraft. Of the companies tendering, two designs were chosen, the Avro 679 and Handley Page HP.56 (later named the Halifax) as reserve. The award of the primary contract would lead to significant orders, initially mooted at 1,500 units.

The Avro team were accustomed to maiden flights, but the Avro 679 had drawn a larger crowd of company and Air Ministry officials than normal. Workers gathered in small knots outside the Avro hangars to watch the new aircraft. It promised to be the most technologically advanced aircraft in the world. Many functions were hydraulic, and the new Rolls-Royce Vulture engine promised 1,750 horsepower, approaching twice the output of the recent Merlin. It had been an unseasonably wet day, and the test flight was held back until 6.30 in the evening. The 679, now named the 'Manchester', lined up on the runway, pausing for permission to take off. The buzz of anticipation was interrupted by the swell of the engines. Gradually gathering speed, the proto-type Manchester L7246 accelerated past the watchers, lifting off above the fine mist of water from the runway. The take-off run took much longer than anticipated. The Manchester, with chief test pilot 'Sam' Brown at the helm, disappeared from view. With no radio fitted, the waiting officials were left in suspense. Overhead the Manchester rumbled unseen above the low cloud, eventually breaking through the grey overcast sky to land seven-teen minutes later. As L7246 trundled onto the taxiway, Brown gave the thumbs up through the open cockpit window to Chadwick and Roy Dobson, Avro's managing director.

The early optimism was punctured, however, when Brown made his post-flight report. Both hydraulic pump shafts had broken and the engines had run very hot. Brown had to nurse the Manchester home watching engine temperatures. It handled heavily, requiring considerable physical strength to keep control. In the period leading to the test flight, Chadwick had become increasingly anxious about the weight changes of the design. It seemed each month saw additions to the concept. Unlike the early designs of Chadwick's youth, for which nearly every component was built on site, the Manchester was an amalgam of equipment built by other manufacturers. The new bomber was a carrying platform for ordinance, powered turrets, radio, navigation and bomb-aiming equipment. Further flights revealed that the air-craft was slower than specified, at times struggling even without loading. The problems were not all of Avro's making. Key to the success of the aircraft were the new Rolls-Royce Vulture engines. They were not performing well, producing 300 horse-power under Rolls-Royce's promised performance.

Two Manchester prototypes were tested throughout August and September 1939, revealing a catalogue of issues, most connected to the engines and hydraulics. Rolls-Royce were optimistic, believing they could iron out teething problems with the Vulture.

'Sam' Brown found plenty of challenges on each flight. On Sunday 11 October he took off from Ringway for a forty-five-minute flight. It was the ninth test flight and, to date, every one had experienced a technical failure of some description. Bringing the Manchester round onto approach, Brown had just fixed his eyes on the runway when an explosive judder threw the aircraft off balance. The port engine had blown up, forcing pistons and conrods through the crankcase. The aircraft yawed as power was lost, and Brown fought to keep control. Losing precious altitude at an alarming rate, he kept the nose straight ahead and abandoned any attempt to reach the runway. After two nerve-testing minutes he was relieved to see the airfield boundary fence slip beneath him. He set the aircraft down firmly on the grass, bouncing on the Dunlop balloon tyres, and rolled safely to a stop. He confessed in his diary that he had 'rather a shaky time getting her down'.

With both engines replaced and work to the propellers and hydraulics, Brown flew a week later, but reported the aircraft 'very difficult to control'. Only after a further five days of intensive work at Avro, during which Roy Dobson turned the screws on his overburdened staff, was Brown able to make his first trouble-free flight. However, once the gremlins had found a home, they aimed to raise a family. It seemed that at almost every turn the Manchester was jinxed. After a small number of successful flights, it was time to hand the aircraft over to the testing establishment, A&AEE Boscombe Down in Wiltshire.*

On Tuesday 28 November Avro test pilots Brown and Thorn took off in L7246 to make the flight from Ringway, but after only ten minutes both engines stopped. Side-slipping into an open park at Charnes Hall near Stoke-on-Trent, the pilots managed to land safely. Only then did they discover – to their embarrassment – that they had failed to open the fuel cocks to the main petrol tanks. After discussions with the owner of the property, it was agreed that with the felling of several trees the Manchester could take off again to return to Ringway for checks. The Avro team had to emphasize to the reluctant owner the importance of this new secret aircraft and that there was 'a war on'.

Finally, twelve days later than planned, the Manchester was handed over to Boscombe Down. Test pilot Collins conducted the first extended flight on 20 December 1939, but not without drama. He experienced a hydraulic failure and trouble opening and shutting the bomb doors. To round off his difficulties, he was attacked over the South Downs by RAF fighters who failed to recognize the unusual aircraft as British. To Collins' credit, he flung the Manchester around enough to shake off the over-enthusiastic attackers. On the next flight three days later, L7246 crash-landed in a field of cabbages after the port engine failed. The second prototype sent in replacement subjected test pilots to a constant stream of problems. With twenty airframes already on the production line at Avro's Woodford factory, the project was in crisis.

To compound the anxiety of Chadwick and Dobson, competitors Handley Page were closing fast in the race to provide a bomber. Their concept had been developed as a backup to Avro's

---

* A&AEE stands for 'Aeroplane and Armament Experimental Establishment'.

Avro Manchester L7247 at Ringway Airport. This, the Manchester's second prototype, first flew in May 1940.

as the Air Ministry's safety net. Handley Page had abandoned the idea of a two-engined aircraft in favour of four engines early in their design process. Their pragmatic approach relied on proven engine performance and not promises given on a new and untested power plant. The Halifax took to the air three months after the Manchester, but immediately became the front runner. Avro were floundering. It was not the first time that Handley Page had beaten Avro in a design competition; it seemed history was repeating itself. With little expectation that the Air Ministry would commit to an extensive order, the Manchester was threatening to be a costly debacle.

★

The lineage of the Avro Lancaster can be traced to a stable in West Hill, Putney, belonging to the brother of Alliot Roe. While in the Merchant Navy, Alliot had become fascinated with aeroplanes and on his return from sea devoted himself to the new enthusiasm around flight. The passion of the young men involved in pioneering British aviation knew no bounds and many took risks that led to their eventual deaths. Alliot appears to have been headstrong, but not reckless, although his ability to fall out with others typified a pioneer. Alliot was accepted for the post of Secretary at the Royal Aero Club in 1906 after an interview with Charles Rolls, but he was soon lured away to work on a new seaplane project with G. L. O. Davidson that enjoyed the backing of Sir William Armstrong (of the later Armstrong Whitworth company). The aeroplane was being built in Denver, Colorado, and Roe relocated to work on the project. However, disagreements over the design and tensions over his salary led to his returning home after a short period of time.

Alliot turned to model-making to test his aeronautical ideas. The science of plane making was new, and although mathematicians were already getting to grips with the algorithms of flight, for the pioneer discovery was a far more practical process of trial and error. Unlike some others who rushed into building their own aeroplanes, Alliot did not have deep pockets. Those who were wise learned to fly by keeping company with leaders like Blériot and Wright, but many others were self-taught. There was no legislation governing pilots until the 1920s, although the use of airspace for international travel was under discussion much earlier.

It was only when Roe won £75 in a *Daily Mail* flying model competition in 1907 that funds became available to build his own full-sized aircraft. The free tenancy of stables in Putney gave Alliot the space he needed to build his *Roe I* biplane.

Roe's first successful attempt at flight was at Brooklands in June 1908, an occasion he claimed was the first combination of a British aircraft and British pilot. These early forays were a series of short hops rather than sustained flights, leading John Moore-Brabazon to claim the crown as the first Briton to achieve powered flight in a heavier-than-air machine in 1909. At times Roe was so short of money he resorted to using paper to cover parts of the aeroplane rather than canvas. His temperament seems to have led to disagreements with the management at Brooklands and he left to set up a new workshop under a railway arch in Walthamstow Marshes.

With further help from his brother, Humphrey, who was persuaded to put up funds, A. V. Roe & Company came into existence in January 1910 in rented space at Brownfield Mill in Manchester. It forged a partnership with the region that would last nearly eighty years. Alliot learned his craft quickly and, as the threat of European conflict gathered pace, his fledgling company produced the Avro 500 biplane in 1913. It displayed at Hendon, the global shop window for designers, particularly those who recognized the importance of military contracts. The Avro 500 wooed the crowds with its speed and manoeuvrability, but, just as importantly, it impressed the aviation correspondents. The *Daily Telegraph* wrote in high praise: 'The spectators at Hendon were given a remarkable demonstration of the wonderful qualities of this fine Avro biplane, whose splendid performances stamped it as one of the finest aeroplanes ever designed, if not indeed the finest of all.'

Much of Roe's success can be traced to Roy Chadwick, who, as

Avro 500 biplane, 1913. The Avro 500 was mostly used as a training aircraft in the early years of the First World War.

an eighteen-year-old, joined Roe in 1911 as a personal assistant. He was Roe's foil, quieter by nature and, as a draughtsman, more practical in translating Roe's shifting ideas to paper. By 1918, Chadwick was appointed Avro's chief designer, a young man whose wide-ranging abilities would lead to myriad Avro creations over the next thirty years. Conflict had brought a tidal wave of funding into aviation throughout Europe. For many aeroplane companies the First World War catapulted their businesses from backstreet enterprises to large-scale manufacturers. Companies were formed that later became the backbone of the British aviation industry through to the 1960s. Avro, Blackburn, Bristol and Sopwith all flourished during the war, with Sopwith's fortunes being revived by its incorporation with Hawker in 1920. By 1918, Roy Chadwick's office was filled with more than a hundred draughtsmen, many of whom had not been previously involved in aircraft design. It was a thrilling time for an aircraft creator, for after years of penny pinching, the government had pumped huge amounts of money into aviation.

Avro's runaway success in the First World War was the 504 biplane. Originally produced as a fighter, it quickly became the mainstay of pilot training. More Avro 504s were manufactured than any other type of aircraft during the war – 8,970 being produced in total. Success brought with it unwelcome constraints. Although the design office worked on fifteen different aircraft types, it seemed Avro were destined to provide only trainers. Proposals for fighters and even large bombers like the Avro Pike did not get beyond prototype stage. It seemed that competitors Handley Page had a near monopoly on producing bombers, a reputation that stifled all attempts by Avro to break through.

The end of the First World War caused immediate financial problems for the inflated aircraft industry. Suddenly, order numbers dropped and all firms needed to shrink or face bankruptcy. The success of the Avro 504 alone was not enough to counter the inevitable contraction. The solution was to sell 68 per cent of shares to Crossley Motors, who utilized spare production facilities. In the inter-war period Avro continued to supply training aircraft, with another big seller, the Avro Tutor, proving to be their most successful design of the era. The Tutor was a biplane known as the Type 621 and became a mainstay of pilot training with the RAF until 1939.

The story of Avro is one of a small number of successful designs that outsold their competitors by a considerable margin. As the 1930s dawned, Avro still lacked a successful bomber in its catalogue. The Avro Anson of 1935 was to be another boon aircraft. Intended for maritime reconnaissance, the Anson was used as a light bomber, but excelled in transport and training roles. Avro produced 8,138 Ansons with a further 2,882 produced under licence in Canada. The Anson remained in RAF service until 1968.

The Air Ministry produced a confusing number of specifications for new aircraft in the years leading up to the Second World War. As Germany forged ahead with new aeroplanes, most of them of all-metal construction, Britain's response was woefully inadequate. The Handley Page Heyford appeared in squadron service in 1934, a huge biplane with fixed undercarriage and spats. The cockpit was open, with the front gunner perched in the tip of the nose, obscuring the pilot's view. Life was no better for the rear gunner, who sat hunched in the slipstream halfway down the wood and canvas fuselage. This lumbering leviathan could reach 115mph, a whisper of the 217mph top speed of the Dornier 17 that flew later that year. The government fought off probing questions, insisting, even as late as 1938, that the Royal Air Force could adequately match the Luftwaffe, even though home strength was 1,750 aircraft to the Germans' 3,700.

Winning the 1936 P13/36 bomber contract propelled Avro into a new arena of bomber design. The direction of the company had changed in 1928 when Alliot Roe sold his interest in Avro to Armstrong Siddeley. Roe had not abandoned his aircraft pioneering interests, forming the Saunders Roe company in Southampton to build flying boats, but he left Roy Chadwick behind at Avro. Vickers had bought into Armstrong Whitworth in 1927 to improve its standing in heavy engineering and, in turn, sold the aircraft arm of the company to J. D. Siddeley.

Chadwick and the design team could see that crew positions in the new Handley Page Hampden or Armstrong Whitworth Whitley were cramped. The Hampden was particularly small (nicknamed 'the flying suitcase') although the Whitley provided an outlay that, when scaled upwards, gave Avro ideas for their Manchester. The company association with the makers of the Whitley also helped in the transfer of technical knowledge; arguably the Manchester carried many of the design elements of the Whitley. The protruding 'jaw line' of the forward section, twin tail and crew stations were similar. The Whitley was powered by two Rolls-Royce Merlin engines.

Some of the design specifications of P13/36 were very strict, others were open to interpretation. 'The pilot's seat. If not in the centre of the fuselage, is to be on the port side, and is to be adjustable in flight through a 4-inch vertical range; arm rests are to be provided.'

In the materials section: '22. All parts of the aeroplane that contribute to its final strength in flight are to be of metal.'

'23. With any form of fabric covering wing or tail plane, the leading edge shall be metal covered.'

Certain principles had been established as good practice by other manufacturers. The new bomber would have powered turrets rather than hand-held machine guns on mounts, even though P13/36 specified the latter. It was a concept that the British correctly anticipated would be more effective. The Germans chose to equip their aircraft with standard mounts, with the gunners holding the stock of the machine gun. While there were many cases of pursuing fighters being shot down, results were patchy. The effects of recoil and movement on the mount meant accurate aiming was difficult, the gun tending to spray bullets over a wide area.

The Battle of Britain proved that German bombers could not defend themselves adequately with hand-aimed guns. Fighters had to be employed to fly in close support, often disadvantaging themselves in height and speed. Powered turrets gave gunners a stable platform to fire from, but the British still relied on the Browning .303 machine gun, which fired a small-calibre bullet. In some senses, British developers were locked into the idea that the higher fire rate of the smaller round produced more chances of damaging an enemy aircraft. The Germans, using two 7.92mm wing machine guns and a single 20mm cannon firing through the spinner of their Messerschmitt Me 109, proved the case for higher calibre weapons. A small number of Spitfires were fitted with 20mm cannon during the Battle of Britain (19 Squadron) but they proved problematic. Fighter Command had its wishes granted in November 1940 with new Spitfires built with the stronger 'C' wing capable of carrying cannon.

Despite the proven advantages of the 20mm cannon, Bomber Command was not given access to them, despite Air Marshal Harris's requests. Even the larger .5-inch gun was denied until late on in the bomber war. Some of the problems came in persuading the Air Ministry that the .5-inch was better; they believed the effective range was too similar to the .303 to be an advantage. The reality of experience showed that a German fighter could stand off and hit an RAF bomber with its cannon before closing into the .303 Browning's range. Although the technical arguments were explored in the Air Ministry, a very British form of bureaucracy stayed their hand. The .303 round had been introduced into the British army in 1889 and, after the First World War, Britain held millions in stock. Some estimates placed the stock available at the start of the Second World War as enough for 100 years of use.* One of the first questions asked within the Ministries in arming a new aircraft was, 'will it use the .303?'.

In the United States, Boeing were developing their B-17 'Flying Fortress'. It was designed on the principle that flying in formation with cross-covering fire from other aircraft would provide a strong defence. Using a combination of powered turrets and side-mounted machine guns, the Fortress looked invincible on paper. The downside was that it operated with a ten-man crew, a lot of extra weight in guns, ammunition and gunners. This restricted its climb speed and bomb load.

When the B-17 appeared over Europe from July 1942, German fighter pilots spent time studying the arc of fire of the B-17s, even using models to teach where the weaker defensive points were. The result was the high-angle beam attack. Striking from above, German fighters dived through formations hitting the B-17s in a near-collision course with devastating effects.

The projected bomb load of the new Manchester, at 8,000lb, was four times the size of Germany's leading bomber, the Heinkel He 111. Chadwick's enormous bomb bay, running much of the length of the fuselage, was a feature that enabled a constant development in bomb technology. Wing loading set the Manchester and later Lancaster apart from nearly every other bomber of the Second World War.

The design of the large spar running through the fuselage was an inconvenience for the crew, who had to slide over it to reach the rear of the fuselage, but it was incredibly strong. It allowed innovators like Barnes Wallis to dream up new weapons, the bouncing bomb or the gigantic 12,000lb 'Tallboy'. In attempting

---

* The Ministry of Defence only disposed of its last stocks of .303 ammunition in 2005.

to solve the problem of the intrusive wing spar, the Consolidated B-24 Liberator, an American heavy bomber, slung its fuselage under a high wing. Although a very competent bomber, the B-24 had a tendency for the wings to fold if damaged near the wing root, with terrifying consequences. Fellow Americans on B-17s considered their aircraft far safer, pitying the B-24 'Flying Boxcar' crews in daylight raids. It seemed German fighters would always head for the B-24s first.

The new generation of wider-fuselage aircraft was necessary not only for crew accommodation, but the increasing amount of equipment for navigation and bomb aiming. Little consideration, however, was given to the comfort of the crew members who were integral to the correct functioning of this machinery. The war would be a radar-led conflict, and the wider body of the Manchester design allowed for a multitude of black featureless boxes to be mounted. Both the British and Germans were developing long-range radio beams that enabled bombers to follow a course to the target. The Germans expanded the *Lorenz* radio device that had been invented to guide Luft Hansa aircraft. The advent of *Knickebein** aerials allowed bombers to fly along a single radio beam and find a transecting beam close to their target. Countermeasures including jamming or misdirecting beams began in earnest in 1939 under R. V. Jones at the Air Ministry. Britain's answer was longer in development. Oboe, a system using a transponder to measure distances to the transmitting station, did not start operating until December 1941. Its improved cousin, Gee, came into service in March 1942.

The introduction into Bomber Command of the world's first airborne radar in February 1943 changed the parameters of the bombing war. With H2S, the first airborne, ground-scanning

---

* *Knickebein* means 'crooked leg', a reference to the shape of the transmitters.

radar system, a bomber could navigate independently of ground devices, plotting its own course.

Unfortunately, the technology was discovered by the Germans almost immediately, when a Vickers Wellington carrying the device was shot down just two days after it was introduced. However, countering the effectiveness of H2S was a huge challenge. The generation of British heavy bombers developed at the start of the war all had the important factor of space available for future developments. Eventually radar dishes were slung underneath bombers in oval bulges.

The RAF could not countenance ten-man crews; even a co-pilot was a luxury in the eyes of the Air Ministry. Pilot training was being increased, but the Manchester could only have one pilot. For all the striking innovation of the Manchester's fuselage, one problem dominated, namely its lack of engine power. To improve handling, Chadwick needed to extend the wings to 90 feet on the prototypes. Avro were walking a tightrope. It seemed their innovation would be wasted unless Rolls-Royce could provide a solution. The Vulture engine was the result of development of another successful engine, the Peregrine, which had a standard V-form cylinder bank like the Merlin. By adding a second cylinder bank to make an X formation, it was hoped to double the power output. The idea of two engines instead of four seemed a sensible proposal, but in practice the Vulture was a step too far.

By early 1940, the confidence of the Air Ministry was badly shaken. With the country at war, the need for new aircraft was urgent, yet the Manchester was failing to live up to expectations. The Ministry had already committed to introducing the Manchester, although the decision to go ahead smacked of desperation to increase bomber production rather than prudence in matters of design. After a conference of thirty-seven senior officers, ministers and civil servants at the Air Ministry in April, it was agreed to push ahead with the production of the Manchester, even though Roy Chadwick had plans to dramatically change the aircraft. He proposed to lengthen the wing and fit four Rolls-Royce Merlin engines. Chadwick still believed in the layout of the bomber fuselage and wing shape, and the redesigned fuselage looked similar to the original. Chadwick told the Air Ministry that the improved model would bear a different number, the Avro 683, and a new name, the Lancaster.

In hindsight, Chadwick achieved the near-impossible feat of creating brilliance from tawdriness. The Lancaster was the silk purse created from a sow's ear. In the new bomber, Chadwick found power, agility and payload ability that outstripped anything in service to date. On 9 January 1941 'Sam' Brown opened the throttles on the prototype Lancaster BT308 at Ringway and was catapulted into the sky with such ease and confidence that he could hardly believe the difference. It was immediately apparent that the Lancaster handled well – she turned quickly, responding to the gentlest of touches. 'Marvellous – easy to fly and light on the controls,' Brown reported ecstatically. Unlike his experiences with the prototype Manchester, there was no downside to his report.

As news of the Lancaster's success reached the Air Ministry, it was decided to upgrade the production lines, principally at Avro's works at Chadderton near Oldham to convert to the new aeroplane. The other option was to scrap the project completely and convert the production lines to the Handley Page Halifax. The Lancaster upgrade seemed to make more sense. While the new Lancaster was built, 193 Avro Manchesters were pushed out to front-line squadrons. They flew 1,269 sorties but lost 78 aircraft to enemy action and a further 45 to technical failures. Their retirement to training roles was swift once the new Lancaster was available.

With limits on production space, the Lancaster was eventually produced by five other companies, Armstrong Whitworth, Austin, Metropolitan-Vickers and Vickers Armstrong. In Canada a special aircraft company – the Victory Aircraft company in Ontario – was created to produce the Lancaster.

★

Squadron Leader John 'Flap' Sherwood of 97 Squadron at RAF Woodhall Spa, south-east of Lincoln, received orders to pull seven of his Lancasters from operations for special training. It was April 1942 and the aircraft had been with them for only a few weeks. The target would remain secret, but the training orders were clear; long-distance flights were to be undertaken in daylight at low level. The Lancasters were to be grouped in two triangular 'vic' formations of three with a spare aircraft following in case of technical failures. Taking off from RAF Woodhall Spa for the first time, the aircraft closed up before flying in loose formation and creeping slowly down to acclimatize themselves to low level. Every part of the pilot's instinct was to gain altitude, but, as Sherwood levelled out at 200 feet, the Lancaster was pleasingly stable. Looking across to his left and right he saw the other Lancasters take up station. They were unaccustomed to formation flying, so at first kept a cautious distance.

As their speed built up, each crew member experienced the exhilaration of thundering across open fields. Trees and houses flitted past the bomb aimer's domed Perspex viewpoint. It seemed at times they flew close enough to grab branches as they passed. As they pressed lower, people on roads stopped in their tracks, open-mouthed. Some, caught unawares, ducked or threw themselves to the ground. As tail gunners watched the prone figures recover themselves, they were already too far away to see the furious reactions. What impressed the crews was how ably the Lancaster handled. When they encountered buffeting caused by rough air in a valley, the bomber bobbed a little, but in a split second the pilot had corrected, continuing their hurtling journey.

They had a week to train, gradually increasing their flying times. Threading their way north, they avoided towns and dodged chimneys, church spires and radio transmitters before launching a mock attack on Inverness. Squadron Leader John Nettleton from 44 Squadron at RAF Waddington – a dozen or so miles west of Woodhall Spa – was also part of the training exercise with seven of his Lancasters. He was to lead the operation. Wherever its target was, the crews were not unduly worried. They believed they were flying too low for flak to reach them and with the combined gunnery of three Lancasters together, fighters could be driven off. The confidence of the crews was mirrored higher up in the chain of command. The Lancaster was their wonder aircraft, but in the elation, they were about to ignore hard-won lessons. The early days of the war demonstrated that sending in bombers in daylight was potentially costly. Only when close

Squadron Leader John Nettleton practises low-level flying in preparation for the Augsburg raid, April 1942.

fighter support was provided did the heavier aircraft stand much chance of getting through.

When the briefing room map was revealed on the morning of 17 April 1942, the crews at Woodhall Spa erupted into laughter. Someone had moved the ribbons to create a course that seemed to cover most of Europe, a practical joke that eased some of the nervous tension. Wing Commander Collier walked to the front to begin the briefing as the room came to order. 'Well, gentlemen, now you know where the target is.' Puzzled silence. Had he not noticed someone had interfered with the map? Gradually, it dawned on the crews that the blob that lay at the end of the ribbons, marking the Bavarian city of Augsburg, was indeed the real target. As Collier continued, they had to suspend their disbelief. They were to fly 500 miles each way in broad daylight over occupied Europe. It was beyond their comprehension that such a flight could be possible, even given the outstanding handling of the Lancaster.

The target was the MAN diesel works in Augsburg, which made U-boat engines. The submarine threat worried Churchill. Two hundred and fifty-three ships had been lost in the first quarter of the year and without strikes on submarine production, there seemed little way of staunching the haemorrhage of merchant shipping. Seeing an opportunity to demonstrate how Bomber Command could change the fortunes of war, Air Marshal Harris authorized the attack on Augsburg. It was somewhat out of character for Harris, who generally much preferred to concentrate his forces against larger targets, but his options were limited by the fact that the Lancaster was still arriving at squadrons in small numbers. It was a bold gesture. If the bombers were successful, it would improve the reputation of the RAF and perhaps further the perception that air power could defeat the Germans without the need for a major land invasion.

Even the most optimistic planner knew that getting the

Lancasters through the defensive belt of northern France would require stealth and not inconsiderable luck. At low level, the aircraft had the best chance of ducking German radar, which was still primitive, but was still very capable of detecting raiders in the clear space of the English Channel. By avoiding towns, they could reduce the risk of anti-aircraft fire, but if they were attacked by fighters their chances of escape were limited. The plan was to draw Luftwaffe fighters away in a series of air raids on the Pas-de-Calais by Boston bombers supported by 100 Spitfires. The hope was that the German fighters would have landed to refuel just as the Lancasters swept across the region.

The mood was sombre as ashen-faced airmen returned to their quarters to write their final letters to loved ones. These were propped up in their lockers with other personal items they wished their families to receive. It was a convention played out before every raid, yet that day the stakes seemed higher than ever before.

At RAF Woodhall Spa and Waddington, the fourteen Lancasters were filled to the brim with petrol. Lancaster fuel tanks were lined with layers of rubber, a self-sealing device that reduced the risk of fire. Even with this innovation, the crews knew they would be flying what were, in effect, massive Molotov cocktails. Each carried four 1,000lb bombs with time delays of eleven seconds to enable the bombers to be clear of the target before they exploded. The briefing had included detailed maps and photographs revealing the area of the MAN factory they were to hit, which was no bigger than two football pitches. With an attack height of 50 feet it would take every ounce of skill to plant the bombs in the right place. Take-off was timed so that the attack in the late afternoon allowed for the cover of falling darkness on the return leg.

Sherwood of 97 Squadron was the first to take off from Woodhall Spa. His Lancaster's wings bowed under the weight of the bombs and fuel load, but he cleared the boundary fence safely. One by one the others followed, the pounding tone of the Rolls-Royce Merlins filling the airfield. At start-up, the squadron's reserve aircraft flown by Ernest 'Rod' Rodley was called forward as an engine malfunctioned on another bomber. It seemed the whole base had turned out to see the squadron off: airmen and WAAFs* lined the runway, waving as each Lancaster lumbered past. In the cockpit and gunners' positions, hands waved back, fleeting glimpses of faces that would not be seen there again. At Waddington, the scene was much the same as 44 Squadron took off and formed up over the station before heading south.

Reducing their height, both formations converged at Selsey Bill on the Sussex coast. 44 Squadron's spare aircraft turned for home, wishing the others well. With throttles open the Lancasters dashed across the Channel at low level. The 'tail-end Charlies' kept watch for telltale changes on the wave tops that would warn them they were too low. At this level, the mesmerizing pattern of the sea could trick the eye of the pilot. Sherwood noticed Nettleton was taking a course north of their planned route. As the two formations opened out, Sherwood decided to pursue the original course. Since the plan had been for the two elements to separate closer to the target, he concluded that Nettleton's change would make no difference. The formations pulled up sharply over the cliffs near Le Havre before planting the Lancasters firmly down to 50 feet again as the French landscape rushed beneath them.

The diversionary attack by the Bostons was forty minutes early, and as Nettleton's formation passed close to the airfield at Beaumont-le-Roger near Évreux, German fighters were returning to base. It was Nettleton's second vic piloted by Sandford,

---

* Members of the Women's Auxiliary Air Force, whose numbers would reach a peak strength of 180,000 in 1943.

Crum and Beckett that first spotted the dots of German fighters in the sky. There was still hope they might not be seen. The closest fighter was on its approach to the airfield, wheels down, sinking lower towards the hedgerows. In profile it moved lazily towards the ground. In a few seconds they would be obscured from view. Sandford held his breath; they would shortly cross the nose of the fighter, their distant silhouette a giveaway. Crum and Beckett closed up to Sandford, the grass of the fields whipping wildly as the Lancasters sank as low as they dared. The fighter suddenly pitched upwards, its wheels popping back into the wings. For a time, it looked like it might turn again for the airfield as it flew parallel to them. They could sense the indecision in the pilot's course. What were these strange aircraft? Other fighters began to power down towards them, and, with a twitch, the first fighter banked to attack.

The Germans had never seen a Lancaster before and, as the turrets of the three bombers started pouring tracer rounds towards them, they approached cautiously. Realizing the defensive machine guns were .303s, they launched their attacks from the beam. Closing quickly to 700 yards they opened fire, breaking off before getting into the range of the lighter machine guns carried by the Lancasters. By now, two waves of fighters, Messerschmitt Bf 109s and Focke-Wulf Fw 190s, had joined the chase, thirty aircraft weaving in pursuit of the fleeing bombers. Crum was injured in the first attack as shells ripped through the canopy, showering him with shards of Perspex. Dedman, Crum's navigator, was concerned to see blood running down Crum's face, but was relieved when the pilot waved him away with a smile. Beckett was also hit, and flames began streaming from the wings. The crews could see cannon shells thudding into the fields and buildings around them, sending up plumes of earth and shattered rock. Beckett fell back, as the other crews watched helplessly. His Lancaster, engulfed in flames, hit a tree and exploded.

Crum was also in trouble. He ordered the bombs to be jettisoned, knowing the delayed action timers would allow him to fly clear. Mindful that pulling up or banking would expose him to even greater strength of attack, he knew that whatever he decided to do needed to be on the present course. As cannon shells tore repeatedly through his aircraft, the end had to come. Throttling back, Crum ploughed his bomber into a wheat field, clipping the heads before wallowing to a halt in among the crops. Scrambling out, the crew attacked the fuel tanks with fire axes before setting fire to the Lancaster.

Sandford's was now the sole remaining aircraft of his vic. The man who always flew wearing pyjamas under his uniform for luck had an impossible fight on his hands. He steered his Lancaster under power lines to try to shake off his pursuers, but all four of his engines were ablaze and he hit the ground in a ferocious explosion of flame.

Nettleton, Garwell and Rhodes looked on, knowing they were now in the firing line. The fighters closed on them. Rhodes fell next, guns jammed and turrets out of action, his cannon-raked aircraft transformed into an inferno. Rising suddenly, the Lancaster's nose pitched for the sky before stalling and falling to earth. A wheel broke free of the fireball, bounding across the fields as if it was chasing the other Lancasters. Nettleton and Garwell pressed on through the attacks, chunks of their aircraft being blown away, their guns broken and useless. But the Germans had reached the extent of their range. The fighters melted away leaving the two Lancasters to continue their wild flight. Despite instructions that if one member of the vic were lost, the remainder should abort the mission, they pressed on.

Further south, 'Flap' Sherwood's two vics of three passed unmolested. In the distance they could see a number of burning aircraft fall to the ground but assumed this was from the diversionary raid by the Bostons. They pressed on for hundreds of miles, flashing scenes of daily life below them clearly visible. A French farmer in a large field doffed his cap and bowed to them as they passed. A parade ground full of German soldiers scattered as the gunners gave them a quick burst. Turning to fly down Lake Constance, they passed a white steamer serenely cutting a gentle wave in the water. On the stern, a German officer pulled out his Luger and fired at them; they could see the smoke rising from the barrel. Ten miles south of the target at Lake Ammer, a Bavarian duck hunter fired his shotgun at them. Other than this, they met no resistance.

German controllers were aware of the bombers. The telephones kept ringing as reports came in giving the position of the low-flying intruders. They were convinced the target would be Munich and scrambled fighters to search for the oncoming aircraft, but puzzlingly, there seemed no sign of them.

Nettleton and Garwell were still ahead of Sherwood's aircraft as they crossed a ridge and saw Augsburg spread out before them. It was late afternoon and Augsburg had been enjoying a festival. Food stands filled the streets and a funfair with a Ferris wheel entertained children as crowds began to wander home for their evening meal. Some, not realizing the bombers were British, waved enthusiastically. Crossing the Munich railway line, the two Lancasters burst across the city. Gunners in flak towers and rooftop machine-gun posts began firing a steady stream of tracer towards them. Incredulously, they saw the 88mm batteries* firing shells from levelled barrels hitting buildings around them as they flew. As the British airmen saw the turn in the river, the sheds of the MAN works came into view. A lone machine-gun post on top of the factory roof fired into

* The 88mm anti-aircraft gun was one of the most feared German weapons of the Second World War. It was also deployed very effectively as an anti-tank gun.

them at point-blank range. Dropping their bombs, they swung away, watching the sides of the factory suddenly crumple as the delayed action bombs exploded.

Garwell was on fire. The whole of his fuselage, rear of the cockpit, was an unstoppable roar of flames. With no time to consider pulling up to parachute out, he decided to crash-land. Looking across to Nettleton, he gave him a two-finger salute before banking towards fields on the outskirts. Blinded by smoke, the wireless operator, Flight Sergeant Robert Flux, banged out the top hatch above the navigator's table, momentarily clearing the choking fumes enough for Garwell to flop the Lancaster down in a field at 80mph. Jumping clear, the crew realized they could not reach two of the crew trapped in the inferno of the fuselage. Flux, whose actions probably saved the crew, had been flung from the aircraft through the hatch and killed, his body pinned under an engine.

By the time Sherwood's 97 Squadron vic reached Augsburg, they could see the smoke rising from the damaged factory. The German gunners were expecting them and poured fire into the approaching Lancasters. In the first section Sherwood, Rodley and Hallows bombed successfully, but a plume of white haze on Sherwood's wing burst into flame. The fuel tanks were holed. As the others turned away, Sherwood's plane struck the ground at full speed in an enormous explosion. The second section of Penman, Deverill and Mycock bore down on the corridor of intense fire. Releasing their bombs, all the aircraft were badly hit. Mycock's plane blew up shortly afterwards. All the crew were lost.

Of the twelve raiders only five returned, all of them badly damaged. Forty-nine aircrew had died. Shortly after landing, Penman called on Sherwood's wife, who lived on station at RAF Woodhall Spa. Having seen the squadron leader's aircraft destroyed on the ground, he felt it was his duty to inform her of her husband's fate. However, she assured Penman that he was still alive and that she would know if he had been lost. This sense of telepathy – not uncommon in the wives of aircrew – was all too often inaccurate, but not on this occasion. Remarkably, six weeks later, news was received that Sherwood had survived. Catapulted from the Lancaster still strapped to his seat, he had landed in trees, suffering only minor burns. The rest of his crew had died.

The Augsburg raid was one of the most daring and, some might say, foolhardy missions of the war. It was born of over-confidence in the abilities of the Lancaster, yet it performed very well given the hand it had been dealt. The tooling area of the MAN factory was hit but there was little disruption to its engine-making capacity.

The Royal Air Force did not abandon low-level daylight raiding, but they realized that the Lancaster was not the aircraft to undertake such raids. In the checks and balances in the intro-duction of the Lancaster, Augsburg served as a reminder that the heavy bomber was vulnerable in daylight. It confirmed, albeit through tragic loss, that night operations were the only realistic options for the RAF bombers. Had the Air Ministry maintained that the Lancaster should not be used in action before all trials were complete, the Augsburg raid might not have taken place. On 24 April 1942, exactly a week after Augsburg, a Lancaster undertook tactical trials at the Air Fighting Development Unit at RAF Duxford in Cambridgeshire. To test its flying and defensive characteristics, the Lancaster was pitted against three Spitfires. Report 47 stated, 'Fighter affiliation… has proved that if a formation of Lancasters simply relied on low flying, it will always provide an easy target for fighters… It cannot be over-emphasized that flying at ground level is not in itself an adequate form of evasion when attacked.'

Nettleton was to receive the Victoria Cross for his actions in the Augsburg raid, later touring the Avro factory at Woodford with Chadwick and Dobson for a Pathé newsreel. Sherwood, although recommended for the VC, received a Distinguished Service Order. Air Marshal Harris saw the Augsburg operation as a key tool in promoting the work of the Royal Air Force. Despite glowing articles in newspapers, few in government were convinced by the RAF's performance in the field of bombing. Action by Fairey Battles on 12 May 1940 over the Albert Canal in Belgium had won two Victoria Crosses, but the aircraft was too slow to be a credible bomber. Daylight raids over the Kiel Canal in the Battle of Heligoland Bight in December 1939 had pitched Hampdens and Wellingtons against the latest German fighters. Despite exciting newspaper headlines, the *Daily Mail* reporting 'RAF Bomb Nazi Fleet', 'Direct hits scored on battleships: attack a success – official', little damage was done and the RAF suffered unsustainable losses. A sharp lesson had been learned, and daylight operations for heavy bombers were suspended. Night bombing was the only strategic option that would work. At a time when Harris needed victories, the Augsburg raid looked like a costly mistake that ignored the lessons of 1939 and 1940. However, for all the failures of what many saw as a 'stunt' on Harris's part, at its operational heart was an aircraft that he knew would stand up to scrutiny.

In the Lancaster, Harris had not only a highly effective bomber, but a star worthy of adulation. Like the Spitfire, the Lancaster was aesthetically pleasing, and while this quality alone could not guarantee its success, it went a long way towards impressing informed correspondents. *The Engineer* magazine was invited to inspect the new Lancaster in August 1942. After Augsburg, the Air Ministry was already talking about the bomber being a 'war winner'. The magazine liked the look of the Lancaster, finding it had 'particularly graceful lines and a pleasing appearance, perhaps rarely seen in large military aircraft'. The modular design meant the Lancaster could be built in different sections and even transported to different sites for final assembly. This *The Engineer* liked, too: 'The design, the makers claim, lends itself to rapid and relatively cheap production, as the entire machine is built up of numbers of components which are manufactured largely as separate and self-contained units, and are easy to transport and to assemble.'

Although it would be unlikely for a magazine to publish a negative review of a new military aircraft, there is a sense that the statements made were not the chaff of propaganda. An attractive aeroplane could prove to be its downfall. Reichsmarschall Hermann Goering promoted the Messerschmitt Bf 110 as a fighter purely on the basis that he liked the look of it. Lacking the manoeuvrability to withstand attacks by RAF fighters, it suffered unnecessary losses in the Battle of Britain. Unlike under the Nazi regime, where key strategic decisions could be steered by a small number of men, Harris had the Air Ministry and politicians to contend with. Members of Parliament had free rein to ask questions of the prime minister, and even suggest their own solutions in strategic matters. On 27 May 1941, the day of the sinking of the battleship *Bismarck*, Arthur Woodburn, MP for Clackmannan and Eastern Stirlingshire, had put the following question to the prime minister: 'Would the right hon. Gentleman consider the dropping of weeping gas bombs on the "Bismarck" to see whether she could not be captured?' While such impractical suggestions did not bother Harris, it was vital for him to keep the prime minister on side. Churchill himself was quite capable of putting forward operational ideas of his own, some of which exhausted his aides in their eccentricity. A further strength of the Lancaster was that its capabilities not only fulfilled the wishes of the strategists, but also created new possibilities for weapons designers.

The Lancaster that entered service through the summer of 1942 soon won the confidence of its new crews. In addition to being more powerful than anything they had been equipped with to date, it flew with ease, showing an ability to manoeuvre well if the need arose. And in Squadron Leader John Nettleton VC, the Lancaster crews had a courageous role model. Most new aircraft types appeared in publications like *Aeroplane* or *Hutchinson's Pictorial History of the War*. The serviceman often saw photographs and read descriptions of new aircraft before they flew them. In many cases, the glowing reports as to their capabilities did not match their flying experience. Aircraft like the Blackburn Botha made their limitations known immediately; others – like the Fairey Battle – promised great things until they were put to the test in the air. The Lancaster was rare in that it lived up to the expectations of the prospective crews. Arguably, the Handley Page Halifax performed equally well, but the Lancaster had the blend of style and quality the RAF needed in the arena of public relations.

On 13 July 1943 John Nettleton was lost on an operation to Turin. Because of the short summer nights and the distances involved, the bomber force had to take a longer route home from northern Italy. As day broke, Nettleton's Lancaster was caught by day fighters in the Bay of Biscay and shot down. His body was never recovered. But by now the Lancaster had a new hero. Wing Commander Guy Gibson had led an audacious raid on the dams of the Ruhr Valley using Barnes Wallis's 'bouncing bomb' on 16–17 May 1943. His Lancasters had been modified by cutting out the bomb doors and narrowing the depth of the fuselage where the weapons were carried. Such major surgery on an airframe attested to the Lancaster's burgeoning repu-tation as a rugged bomber. After the Avro Manchester debacle, the success of the Lancaster is made more remarkable by its continued development and also, more fundamentally, to its remarkable ability to adapt and develop. Many front-line aircraft proved too difficult to improve. The Vickers Wellington served admirably, but its design could not be stretched far beyond its original structural parameters. The Lancaster was different. It evolved continually throughout the war. More powerful engines, changes to bomb-carrying configurations and more sophisticated radar installations continued to keep the Lancaster at the forefront of service.

Although the purpose and fitting out of the Lancasters changed, few structural modifications were made throughout the war.* The first B I models differed little from the later B III marks. A stop-gap B II model was equipped with Bristol Hercules radial engines instead of the Rolls-Royce Merlin as the former was in short supply owing to the demands of fighter production. The long-term answer lay in the United States and the Packard Motor Car Company. The Packard V-1650-1, a licence-built Merlin 28, produced 1,350 horsepower. Through the war Packard produced over 55,000 units, providing engines for the Lancaster B III and P51 Mustang.

By the time the Jim Comans crew flew their first Lancaster at 1661 HCU at RAF Winthorpe in August 1943, many of the Lancaster B Is in use at the airfield had already been operational aircraft but were now withdrawn to training duties. The standard aircraft in service, and the version the crew encountered as they began flying with 9 Squadron, was the B III. It was a thoroughly

---

* Roy Chadwick's design lived on after the war in the form of the Avro Lincoln. Introduced in 1945, it soldiered on in RAF service through the jet age until 1963. The Avro York was a wartime development that sported a wider body for Transport Command duties. The Avro Shackleton developed from the Lincoln remained in service until 1985, an aircraft that used the Rolls-Royce Griffin engine, essentially an improved Merlin. Sadly, Roy Chadwick's greatest creations were to outlive him. His final months were spent working on designs for the Avro Vulcan and the Avro Tudor, a new civilian transport aircraft. On 23 August 1947, Roy Chadwick was killed in a crash at Avro's Woodford works after the test Tudor failed to get airborne. The loss of a man not only of outstanding ability, but a humble and likeable figure in the industry, was keenly felt throughout the company.

tested and very reliable aircraft – one that inspired the confidence of its crew. Most of them agreed that, if they were to risk their lives, they couldn't think of a better aircraft in which to do so than the Lancaster.

4.

Bardney

Jim Comans was off Tamarama Beach, floating on his back looking up at an azure sky. He felt the waves lifting and dropping him gently, the warm sun bringing a welcome drowsiness. But all was not well in this brief picture-perfect dream. Moments later he was in his RAF uniform, sodden and cold, the sun that had been so bright a moment ago giving way to a chill darkness. A rush of panic filled his mind, everything dimmed as featureless faces appeared out of the gloom. His eyes focused, and he recalled where he was. The sleep of exhaustion had overcome him for only a few minutes.

This was not how James Vincent Leopold Comans imagined his war would end, adrift in the North Sea with six strangers in a yellow life raft. The dank smell of stale seawater, petrol and vomit brought him back to reality. They had been there some hours, carried along by a stiff breeze. He could feel the surge of the waves pulling at the underneath of the J-Type dinghy. Seeing no horizon, the movement of the sea against an overcast sky was their only reference point. There should have been eight of them in the raft, but two were missing. They had taken it in turns to be sick over the inflated walls of the pitching raft. Now, with knees drawn up and backs pushed firmly into the sides, each of them fought the pervasive nausea. Their world had shrunk. An oval red box containing a Very pistol and three red flares was a precious possession. They had agreed that there was no point firing them all in the dark; a rescue boat would still struggle to find them.

Their hopes were pinned on the BC778 'Gibson Girl' distress transmitter. Shortly after they had clambered aboard the small circular dinghy, they had deployed the radio antenna, a box kite on a 200-foot wire hurled skywards on a rocket. The transmitter was a yellow hour-glass-shaped box with a winding handle on top. Taking it in turns, they placed it between their legs, cranking the handle to send a Morse SOS signal. It gave them something to do, but there was no way of knowing if it was working. All they could do was wait for the morning and hope that the wind and tide would not drag them out further into the North Sea.

The day had started with mixed feelings of excitement and apprehension. Jim Comans' name was on the noticeboard to fly that night. His last training flight had been five days before. At last, after many months, he was to fly his first combat sortie. He would be a guest aboard Flight Lieutenant Leonard Hadland's Lancaster, the 'spare bod', an eighth man on an experienced crew. It was standard practice to send a new pilot on his first sortie with another crew. After the briefest of introductions, Comans joined the crew for the briefing. They were heading for Bochum, a city in the Ruhr between Essen and Dortmund known for its coal and steel production. Although Comans had spent time studying maps of Western Europe to familiarize himself with likely targets, Bochum was not a name that had imprinted itself on his mind. This would not be a 'milk run' – the Ruhr was heavily defended. But Bochum was only sixty miles from the Dutch border, so it would be safer than some of the flights that penetrated deeper into Germany.

The 28th of September 1943 was a typical autumn day – grey, cloudy and breezy. RAF Bardney, ten miles east of Lincoln, was

Squadron Leader A. M. Hobbs and crew board Lancaster ED831 at RAF Bardney for a raid on the V-2 rocket facility of the Zeppelin works at Friedrichshafen, 20 June 1943. Six days later crew and aircraft were lost returning from a raid on Gelsenkirchen.

home to the Avro Lancasters of 9 Squadron. The base had opened five months earlier and, in some respects, it felt like an unfinished campsite. 9 Squadron had made it their own and would remain there throughout the war. A bus dropped the Hadland crew off by the nose of Lancaster ED648, which bore the squadron code 'WS-D' painted in big dark red letters along the side. All 9 Squadron aircraft carried the code 'WS', the RAF roundel and the identification letter, in this case, D for Delta. Today they would benefit from a daylight take-off, a luxury few would enjoy during the coming winter of 1943/4. The Lancaster had no second pilot station, and Jim stood in the cockpit as Hadland and flight engineer Sgt Ken Taylor went about their pre-flight checks.

They were airborne at 6.20 p.m. and, as they began the climb up towards the assembly area, Taylor gave up the flip-down seat to Comans, in so doing unwittingly surrendering his life. Within a minute of take-off, they were in cloud, but breaking through, they arrived in the orange rays of the setting sun. Other Lancasters were rising out of the cloud into the dusk, twinkling Perspex catching the light. Their black undersides glowed as if tongues of fire were playing off the curves. Comans had flown in exercises before, but he had never seen this many bombers together. More dark dots were rising to join the stream from other airfields, the air alive with activity. As the light receded, the rich dark-blue dome above enveloped them, and the Lancasters slowly faded into the night. It was too beautiful an evening to be at war, yet their pent-up anxiety forced their minds back to the task. The course set was a series of jinks and turns to try to outwit German radar. If all went well, they would be back on the ground around eleven that night, and Jim would have completed his first operation.

From what Comans could observe, the journey to the target went well. As they approached the Ruhr, he could see the searchlights of Dortmund to the left and those of Essen to the right. There was a lot of cloud beneath, and, as they drew closer to Bochum, Jim leaned over to look down as far as he could see. Flak was exploding below them, creeping its way higher until, at 20,000 feet, it began to burst around them, momentarily producing dazzling flashes. Through the buffeting air of the anti-aircraft fire he could see marker flares directing their way in. The bomb aimer was calling that he could see the target markers, and at 8.51 p.m. the bombs were away. Hadland's crew seemed unflappable; they had done it all before. With its load lightened, the Lancaster wanted to soar upward, but Hadland deftly banked her at the end of the bombing run. The compass moved steadily as the navigator called out the new course. Jim found the experience of sitting as a passenger a little unnerving, his hands and feet subconsciously flying the Lancaster.

Weather conditions deteriorated on the return leg. Lancaster ED648 rocked and dropped in strong gusts, straining against a headwind. The buffeting sounded like a giant fist punching the sides of the alloy fuselage. The windscreen ran with water, forming tiny streams before spraying off the canopy frame. Hadland began his descent over the North Sea, hoping to gain better visibility beneath the cloud base. Despite recommendations that they should not descend below 7,000 before landfall, the pilot pushed on. They were not more than twenty minutes to touchdown, but there still was nothing to see. Not even a glimmer of light marked the horizon. As the pilot let down through the cloud, the altimeter began to sink – 7,000 feet, 6,000 feet, gently downwards – but all remained dark outside.

Suddenly Comans was jolted powerfully against his seat straps and flung towards the instrument panel. A deafening explosion ripped through the aircraft, accompanied by rushing and tearing sounds. Jim sat stunned for an instant. He was immediately aware that the engines had stopped, the canopy engulfed in spray. The horrible reality dawned: they had crashed into the sea. Water began to gush up from the shattered nose. The next few minutes were a haze. Somehow, whether through guidance or instinct, Comans was propelled through the top hatch and found himself squatting on the wing root against the curve of the upper fuselage. Dark shapes moved around him as the crew tried to deploy the dinghy. Jim noticed that the propellers were bent, the engines hissing furiously as plumes of steam were forced upwards. The Lancaster wallowed in the water as waves started to break over the upper wing surfaces. With her nose dipping and tail rising, she would sink before long. Comans clambered into the now inflated raft from the trailing edge of the wing. Shapes were being pulled from the water; gasping and shaking, they plunged headlong into the middle of the raft, lying there for a few seconds in relief.

'Who's in?' a voice asked repeatedly.

The Lancaster's twin tails protruded above sea level, like dark flags against the gloom. Gradually, between the wave tops, they slipped lower. And then they were gone. The crew broke out the paddles and started to manoeuvre the raft as best they could, calling out the names of missing men. Within a couple of minutes all they could see was the falling and rising of the nearest wave. Taylor and Beames, the flight engineer and bomb aimer, were gone. Hadland speculated that the altimeter must have been faulty, that they had hit the water as he dropped to 1,000 feet. Comans, however, suspected he had misread the altimeter. As a solicitor, it was in his nature to question. He was frustrated that he had not been watching the altimeter at the point of impact. But there was nothing that could be proved, either way: ED648 was on its way to the bottom of the North Sea and, in all probability, two good men had gone down with her.

Above them, the deep musical note of the returning bomber stream filled the sky, reminding them of their perilous position. They had taken the passage over sea for granted on many occasions, but now, in the swell, they wished they could hear the drop of the undercarriage and the skid of tyres on the asphalt beneath them. Soon the aircraft overhead were gone, leaving only the sound of lapping waves around the raft.

After the longest night of their lives, the growing light of dawn revealed the occasional glimpse of a dark strip of land on the horizon. They paddled towards it, but struggled to make headway with blades that seemed little bigger than a child's seaside spade. Somewhere in the middle distance was movement. A white trail bigger than a wave; surely a boat? Hadland stood up uneasily, pitching the dinghy from side to side. They fired a flare and watched the hissing trail of smoke soar into the air above them. It exploded with a pleasingly loud crack above their heads. The fierce red glow of the dropping star looked unmissable, and, more than anything so far, filled them with optimism. They could now hear the drone of an engine, the noise getting closer with each second. It had not occurred to them until now that a rescuer might be German and not British, so it was a relief to see the dark-blue hull of an RAF rescue launch with the familiar roundel on the side. The launch was soon upon them. Cutting its engines, it drifted gently the last few yards alongside the dinghy. Outstretched arms reached down as ropes were thrown towards them.

They knew they had been very lucky. On the deck, blankets were flung around their shoulders as they were ushered down the steps onto bench seats in the cabin. Tea had never tasted so good as they warmed their hands on the sides of the tin mugs. They had barely sat down before the boat's powerful engines swelled and they began powering towards the shore. The launch from 22 Air Sea Rescue Unit landed the crew at Grimsby.

Such launches patrolled constantly after a raid, or when a report of any missing aircraft was received. In all, they rescued 13,000 British airmen throughout the war, but the hostile environment of the North Sea reduced airmen's chances considerably. Had it been winter, they knew that rescuers might have been pulling their frozen bodies from the raft. They had been adrift for eight and a half hours, but they still hoped Taylor and Beames might be found. Sadly, this was not to be. Kenneth Taylor's body was recovered from the sea over two weeks later, on 16 October. Kenneth Beames was never found.

Shortly after breakfast, news reached the Comans crew at RAF Bardney that Jim had not returned. The term 'missing' covered many possibilities. It was a catch-all word that could remain on a man's record for many weeks before 'missing presumed dead' would be applied. If Comans had been shot down on his first mission, it would have been poor luck, but not unheard of. There was nothing to do but hang around waiting for news to come through. It was too soon to discuss their futures. Each man knew that without a pilot they would be split up to fill vacancies in other crews as the need arose. After months together, it would be a bumpy ride adjusting to a new skipper.

Comans arrived back at camp from Grimsby later that day. He wanted to sleep and, respecting his wishes, the crew left him alone to do so, although there were a thousand questions they wanted to ask him. When the time came to talk, exhaustion had turned to indignation. Comans aired the opinion that Hadland's story about a faulty altimeter was dubious, and that he had flown the Lancaster into the sea by mistake. But in this criticism, bluntly put, there still needed to be deference to seniority. Hadland was 'A' Flight Commander. In fairness to Hadland, an instrument reading mistake seems unlikely as he was an experienced pilot with many flights under his belt. To be hundreds of feet adrift with a dual needle altimeter would have been a schoolboy error. The RAF Court of Enquiry convened to look into the incident also took the view that an altimeter fault was the only possible explanation. Whether Comans' testimony contradicted Hadland's is unknown, but it seems unlikely, given Comans' legal training, that he would have proffered his theory without hard evidence.

On 1 October 1943 the Comans crew were together again for a training flight in DV284, G-George. It was the first 9 Squadron aircraft they had got their hands on, a modern Mark III Lancaster and not the slightly worn Mark I they were familiar with on 1661 HCU. They had a slot booked at the bombing range at Wainfleet on the northern side of The Wash to conduct several high-level bombing passes. Ken Cook had flown there before, the ribbon of coast giving way to brown mudflats that stretched for miles. On a clear day it was possible to see the Humber estuary to the north and the coast of East Anglia sloping away to the south. The day was sullen and overcast, so bomb aimers would use H2S radar to determine their position rather than the optical bomb sight. They climbed to above 10,000 feet. Over the range their timing had to be perfect or their slot would be taken by other aircraft – and this was their last chance to practise-bomb before they flew against Germany. Navigator Don Bowes fed forward their position, and, once the range controller had called them in, they began their bombing run. They completed four attacks, each time dropping a single bomb. The voice of the range controller crackled over the radio; to their relief, the results were satisfactory. All the crew had admiration for the men on the ground, for they knew that misguided bombs, even practice bombs, could cause damage. Their flight had only lasted an hour, but it was an important confidence-building trip, reassuring the crew that Comans had not been too shaken by his recent North Sea excursion.

2 October 1943, Munich

It is often believed that a crew were allocated their own aircraft for the duration of their combat flying. Although a crew might settle in to using an individual Lancaster, there was no guarantee it would be available to them on every trip. Ken Cook's logbook appears to show they completed ten flights in G-George, of which three were on missions. However, the practice of recoding replacement aircraft reveals that DV284 was lost halfway through the Comans crew's tour, and that her place was taken by a new aircraft, also coded 'G'.

After 205 hours of flying training, of which eighty-eight had been at night, Ken Cook boarded Lancaster EE188 and readied himself for his first mission. As he did so the question at the forefront of his mind was: 'what *have* I got myself into?' The road to this, his first operational flight, had been a long one, taking him from RAF Booker to Lord's cricket ground and then to Georgia and back, dodging U-boats as he crossed the Atlantic. Their target tonight was to be Munich, a city that was not only a target of military importance, but also the heartland of Nazi ideology. Hitler's failed Beer Hall Putsch here in 1923 led to his imprisonment in Landsberg jail, to the west of the city, where he wrote *Mein Kampf*. In the pseudo-religious fervour of the Nazis, Munich was a place of temples and meeting places. If Nazism had a holy city, this was it. But Munich lay at the furthest reaches of the Lancaster's range. The longest the crew had flown at night was five hours and ten minutes. Munich was to stretch them by a further three hours. They were being thrown in at the deep end.

What Ken remembers most vividly was the effect of anxiety on their bowels. It was to be a lingering problem throughout the flight. Once they were in position, the chances of relieving themselves were limited. Ken describes this first mission as an 'SOB' flight; an acronym that did not carry the meaning usually represented by these letters in American English, but rather meant *'Shit or Bust'*. In this earthy description, the reality of the bomber crew is far different from the dashing heroism portrayed by actors like Richard Todd in *The Dam Busters*. A good mission in Ken's eyes was one from which he returned with dry underwear.

Munich's geographical location, only 200 kilometres (130 miles) from the Swiss border, raised the possibility of some interesting escape routes in the event of an emergency. Throughout the war 250 Allied aircraft crashed or made emergency landings in Switzerland, after which their crews were interned. Although their treatment was generally good, some American servicemen testified to rough treatment from their captors. It seemed there was a measure of pro-German sentiment on the part of some of their Swiss prison guards. American aircrew with German ancestry tended to suffer more than others.

Should their aircraft be hit, the prospect of flying a crippled Lancaster home across 700 miles of Nazi-controlled northern Europe was a daunting one. The icy North Sea presented a final challenge to a crew losing height. Even if they survived a ditching, they had only a few minutes in the water before the onset of hypothermia. Some chose an alternative route to try to avoid captivity. The decision ultimately rested with the pilot as he assessed how badly damaged his aircraft was. Nearly all airmen hated the idea of the parachute, in many cases preferring to stay with their stricken craft until it was absolutely essential to bail out.

With escape kits including maps, rations and a photograph that could be used in false civilian papers, those who parachuted to safety over eastern France could choose to head west and south, in the hope of making contact with a resistance group. By early 1943 the ranks of the resistance had been swelled by ever more repressive German policies. A new regulation decreed that all Frenchmen between the ages of twenty and twenty-two must serve two years working in Germany. The promised good wages failed to materialize, and it became clear that these French migrant workers were slave labourers in all but name. Knowing the conditions that awaited them in Germany, many young Frenchmen chose to leave their homes, and obtained forged papers to avoid deportation. The resistance movement they joined began to devise more sophisticated escape routes for downed airmen, taking them through Vichy France to the Spanish border and eventual repatriation via Gibraltar.

By now the swell of the engines of a Lancaster was a familiar sound. Each crew member tensed a little as the fully laden bomber picked up speed down the runway. They would never feel relaxed until the wheels had come up and the engines settled into the long climb away. As the Comans crew took off, they hoped for an uneventful trip. No amount of training could fully prepare them for the experiences that lay ahead. Statistically, they faced much higher odds of loss or injury in their early sorties. Ken Cook was determined to keep his head down and do his job to the best of his ability; it was his way of controlling his feelings of fear. In the close confines of the Lancaster each man was directly connected to the aircraft by his oxygen supply. The black rubber corrugated hose from their face mask connected to the panel close by with a brass bayonet fitting. Within minutes of connecting up, they had forgotten about the rubbery smell as they got on with the early tasks of the flight. Their world had become the enclosed space around them; the small plotting desk, the dimly lit instruments or the globe of a gun turret. On a long flight like this one, their progress seemed slow. They knew they were flying at nearly 200mph, but at this altitude, with little light outside, they sensed only the vibration and noise of the engines. Most could not see anything but their own station in the Lancaster.

The flight seemed to be 'going everywhere', Ken recalls, straying east into Austria before turning west again towards Munich. They could sense Jim Comans putting the aircraft into the turns, a gentle bank that seemed to accentuate the heaviness of the loaded bomber. After three hours' flying, the lakes around Munich came into sight, the towering, snow-capped peaks of the Alps dominating the view from Ken's bombing position. In the clear night he glimpsed the lights of neutral Switzerland twinkling across the border. It seemed strange that life there was going on as normal, while the rest of Europe was embroiled in war. A curtain of hundreds of searchlights created a white wall rising above Munich. There was no choice but to fly through it and hope that their matt-black underside would hamper the view of German observers.

Flak rose from Munich, travelling upwards almost lazily – far more slowly than they had imagined. Other than Comans, no one on the crew had seen flak before. The novelty of these peculiar fireworks soon began to wear thin. Ahead Ken could see the target markers were clearly visible, intense glowing lights far below. Picking up the Würmsee* as the start of the bombing run, they turned towards the city centre and began their nerve-jangling straight and level flight. Ken released the bombs from 17,000 feet. Eleven Lancasters had been dispatched from 9 Squadron, and all of them dropped their bombs within five minutes of each other, shortly after 22.30 hours. The attack was deemed a success, the squadron report reading: 'Bombing was concentrated around the T.I.s (Target Indicators) and many bomb bursts were seen. Several large fires were left burning.' Flight Sergeant James Argent, pilot of JA690, reported that the glow from the fires could be seen in Strasbourg, 175 miles away.

Far beyond Munich, the vast German Reich stretched deep into Central and Eastern Europe. That same day, 500 miles away, near Kraków, German Governor-General Hans Frank issued an edict to attempt to legitimize the mass killings taking place in occupied Poland. Far removed from day-to-day life in his quarters and offices at the palatial Wawel Castle, Frank's reign of terror was gathering momentum: 'Non-Germans who violate laws, decrees, official regulations or orders with the intention of hampering or interfering with German construction work in the Government General will be punished by death.' In the days following, prisoners from Warsaw jails were dragged into the streets and shot by firing squad. Their mouths filled with cement or taped over to prevent them shouting final patriotic words, they were killed in groups of up to two hundred at a time. Those laying flowers at the sites afterwards were fired at indiscriminately.

Shortly after landing at RAF Bardney, the crews gathered around small tables for debriefing, sipping tea and smoking as

---

* The Würmsee changed its name to Starnberger See in 1962.

intelligence officers plied them with questions. It was an interesting relationship, because it was not in a crew's interest to
report their failings. If they had dropped short or in the wrong
place, it would be better to blame failing equipment or the
shortcomings of the Pathfinders. Although the official report
credited 9 Squadron with accurate bombing on their 2 October
mission, the individual reports mention 'creep back' – bombs
falling short of the target. By the time the crew made it to their
bunks, it was past four in the morning. For some, sleep was
easy to come by, but others lay awake for some time playing the
night's events through their mind. In their half-sleep, they were
still flying, the bunk vibrating to the hum of the Lancaster's
engines.

As they slept, orders for the day were received and crews
allocated. They would be flying another raid that night. Bomber
Command took advantage of the cycles of the moon, using the
darkest nights to launch their raids. If the weather permitted it,
crews would find themselves flying almost daily at some times
of the month.

3 October 1943, Kassel

The medieval city that was home to the brothers Grimm had
developed over the centuries as capital of the region of Hesse.
Located on the Fulda River, Kassel was a natural crossing
point, bringing trade and prosperity to the whole region. As
the railways developed through the industrial revolution, the
city became home to the Henschel works, a locomotive manufacturer. The engine works moved to tank building in 1935.
Henschel constructed the Panzer I and III, the factory expanding
throughout the war and using as many as 8,000 workers, many
of whom were forced labourers. Like dozens of other industrial

towns and cities across Germany, Hitler's arms race had made it a prime target for Bomber Command.

From 1 August 1942, Henschel were the sole producers of the Tiger, the most sophisticated and feared tank of the war. During Operation Barbarossa the realization that Soviet tanks were superior to anything available to the Germans had come as a shock. Designer Erwin Aders' solution was a robust over-engineered heavyweight – 50 tonnes with 120mm armoured plate in places. The Tiger's 8.8cm gun packed a punch that was hard to defend against. Despite huge advantages over its lighter opponents, the Tiger's price tag limited production. Some in the Wehrmacht were scathing of the monster, dismissing it as an impracticality, an expensive tin can.

The RAF had hit Kassel on three previous occasions, the last attack on the Henschel factory having taken place in late August 1942. Given Kassel's importance, its one-year escape from the attentions of the bombers is remarkable. All this was to change from 3 October 1943. It was the start of a series of devastating attacks on the city, which was to be obliterated in a further seventeen raids before the war's end.

The Comans crew were once again allocated EE188. Although they had flown only one mission in her, the feeling of continuity was comforting. Few Lancasters on the squadron were considered old. EE188 had rolled off the production line at Chatterdon, near Manchester, less than a year ago. She had joined 9 Squadron three months earlier, but even that apparently brief period of survival made her a lucky aircraft. It was enough time for the paint to flatten and lighten, and for greasy marks to appear around handles and engine panels. Newer paint, some of it carrying brush marks over the factory-sprayed finish, marked where the aircraft's skin had been patched to repair flak damage. In daylight, the older warriors had a weather-worn look, wearing their scars like campaign medals. Sometimes whole panels several feet square had been re-skinned, at other times smaller holes were patched with plates, each corner curved with a close-riveted perimeter.*

Kassel would be another daylight take-off at around 6.30 p.m., and a much shorter flight, five hours rather than the eight to Munich. On the map Kassel looked like a short hop over the Dutch border, but no aircrew was naive enough to believe this could be easy. This part of north-western Europe was one of the most intensely defended areas in the world. Pathfinders would mark the target first and 9 Squadron were among the workhorses following in their wake. As the bombers took off, they formed into a stream of 547 aircraft: 223 Halifaxes, 204 Lancasters, 113 Stirlings and 7 Mosquitos. The Mosquitos were equipped with Serrate radar detection and homing devices for night-fighter duties. Their task was to defend the bomber stream and attack Luftwaffe fighter airfields. The Stirling was the poorer cousin of the Lancaster and Halifax, flying more slowly and more conspicuously than the others. The four Bristol Hercules radial engines produced circular glowing exhaust rings that could be easily visible from a distance, leading many pilots to question the wisdom of sending the Stirling into action. By December of that year the Stirling was relegated to a training role, leaving front-line service almost exclusively to the Halifax and Lancaster.

With numbers came the certainty of air attack as the bomber stream entered the hornet's nest of German fighter defence. As the sun set golden on the rim of the horizon, the numbing cold penetrated the thick layers of clothing. None were more uncomfortable than tail gunner 'Jock' Bolland, cramped into his Perspex and metal booth. At least he had an electrically

---

* Unlike preserved examples in museums, the operational Lancaster was rarely repainted in its entirety. There were neither the facilities nor the time available to respray the aircraft.

heated suit, but many turned them off in the knowledge that drowsiness could kill them more quickly than the cold. Gunners had complained that the curved panel immediately above their head reflected light, and that night fighters approaching from above were being missed. Some began to break or remove the upper panel, preferring to endure the icy, 200mph blast than risk missing an attacker. Orders were received that the panels were to be immediately replaced, but, in a stand-off, the gunners won the day. The turret remained open to the elements. Bob Pearson, then a nineteen-year-old tail gunner, remembers:

> My face was exposed to the slipstream – the temperature of which plummeted the higher we went – but it was better to freeze than not to see the enemy. Some rear gunners greased their cheeks with lanolin to ward off the effects; we were often exposed to temperatures of minus thirty or minus forty degrees. My breath froze into an icicle in front of me. I waited until it was three or four inches long before breaking it off with my hands; they, at least, were warm thanks to the four pairs of gloves I had on.

As the crew crossed the border into Germany the attacks commenced. Fires could be seen in the sky as bombers were hit by fighters. Trails of tracer rounds could be seen curving through the sky, thin flashes of light marking machine-gun fire. At Minden, not far across the German border, a Junkers 88 with upward firing guns began to stalk EE188. He had seen a contact on his radar screen, a blip of light moving at the right speed for a bomber. Unseen, the night fighter moved in the cover of the dark landscape below. Lining up onto the silhouette of the Lancaster above, he fired a burst from his two upward-mounted 20mm cannon. Ken Cook was checking the bomb bay as the fierce crack of shells whistled past. Tracer shot by close to the starboard wing, alerting Comans to a near miss. A split second later 20mm cannon shells ripped through the floor of the cockpit, leaving the smell of cordite lingering in the air, detectable even with oxygen masks on. Air roared up from the shattered Perspex nose. Shouting a warning, rear gunner 'Jock' Bolland reacted immediately, swinging his turret towards the attacker, but the Junkers was still invisible to him. Pushing the nose down, Comans turned sharply to port, turning on his wingtip into the corkscrew. Flung against their seat straps, the crew clung instinctively to the nearest support. Anything loose in the aircraft – pencils, maps, and bottles containing urine – ricocheted around the sides of the fuselage. Counting on the agility of the Lancaster to confuse the aim of the fighter, Comans bottomed off the sweeping manoeuvre before heading into a climb. They were now flying against the flow of the bomber stream, and it was essential they turned again onto their original position. As he had hoped, the fighter had overshot them and disappeared.

After the suddenness of the attack, Comans was aware that the sound of the engines had changed. Looking to his right, he saw the starboard inner engine streaming smoke. Flames flickered around the panels by the exhaust stubs. Instructing flight engineer Ken Randle to activate the engine fire extinguishers, Comans shoved the throttle lever of the damaged engine back to the stop and reached for the kill switch. Randle moved quickly. Flipping the spring-loaded cover on the 'fire' button, he paused for a moment to double-check he had identified the correct engine before pressing. Watching the airspeed stabilize in the climb, they waited for the extinguishers in the engine nacelle to kill the flames. It was a tense few minutes. Not only could the fire have ignited the main fuel tanks, but, had it spread, the torch of flame from the engine would have signalled their position for miles around.

There was no question in Comans' mind of their continuing the mission. They were at the wrong altitude and position in among a stream of hundreds of other bombers. If they weren't picked off by fighters, they might collide with another aircraft. The voices over the intercom were clear and strong. Everyone was shaken, but unhurt. Comans ordered Ken Cook to jettison the bomb load. They were heading home. It was a risk to leave the bomber stream. Lone targets on enemy radar were fair game for the prowling night fighters. With the weight of bombs

gone, the three-engined aircraft seemed to be sprightly enough, and, as the minutes passed, confidence rose that they would make it home. With no other bombing duties, Ken took up position in the front turret to keep watch. Secondary problems needed to be overcome, not least that the pneumatic system was fed from the shutdown engine. Initially, this was not an issue: the pneumatic system recharged an air bottle, feeding wheel brakes and radiator shutters. As long as 80lb per square inch remained from 300lb, the brakes would operate. Another factor that influenced the decision to abandon the bombing run was

The bomb bay of an Avro Lancaster of No. 9 Squadron RAF at Bardney, Lincolnshire, loaded with 1,000lb bombs before a night raid on Stettin, 5 January 1944. A camera can be seen forward right of the bomb bay.

the lack of vacuum pressure to the bomb sight. While there was a vacuum pump on both inner engines, and pressure could be transferred, a single pump could supply the flying instruments, but not the bomb sight as well. With only three engines it might be necessary to throttle back at times to stabilize the engine temperatures, so Comans relied on flight engineer Ken Randle to keep careful watch.

Comans allowed their altitude to slip away on the home leg. Below 10,000 feet, their oxygen masks could come off. It was a relief to breathe without them, although the chilly air tended to set off bouts of coughing. At last, as they dropped below cloud level, they saw the Lincolnshire coast pass beneath them, but even here they needed to be vigilant. Enemy fighters could be lurking, ready to attach themselves to the incoming stream. It was not unknown for aircraft to be shot down on their final approach.

Over the intercom, upper gunner George Widdis began to sing, and soon the whole crew joined in. This communal singing of popular numbers became a tradition as they approached base. Each time it was George who started it, his accent adding a touch of North American glamour. Wireless operator Roy Woollford was also a keen singer – he would enjoy performing in amateur opera after the war. A sense of euphoric relief swept the aircraft as they touched down, thirty minutes ahead of the rest of the returning force, the first to land back at RAF Bardney. It was one minute past midnight. The crew always relished the few minutes it took to taxi to their dispersal, savouring the rumble of the tyres beneath them. Opening the bomb bay doors, they swung off the peri-track onto the circular dispersal area assigned to them. They were home.

As they shut down and left EE188, the ground crew were already playing torches on the damaged engine. Oil and fuel were dripping from holes, splashing dark onto the light grey concrete beneath. The wing had been sprayed with machine-gun bullets, but the calibre told them it was not German cannon fire from underneath. Rounds from a German fighter would normally produce large, ugly holes in the aluminium, gashes that were several inches long. But these were neat punched holes smaller than the width of a little finger caused by bullets fired from a Browning machine gun. EE188 had been hit by fire from another Lancaster during the fighter attack. Ironically, it might have been this fire that saved them. Had the Junkers 88 had time to refine his aim, his cannon would have hit the central fuel tanks, destroying the Lancaster in a huge fireball. Such damage was an occupational hazard. Since the Browning .303s used as turret guns in the Lancaster had an effective range of as much as 1,500 yards, incidents of friendly fire were common.

Further forward, the damage to the nose was clear: a series of larger holes recorded the German 20mm cannon hits. Only a few feet further back and the shells would have entered the bomb bay, with disastrous results. Instead, and seemingly by a miracle, everyone in the cockpit had remained unscathed. 'We were lucky, very lucky, on that occasion,' recalls Ken Cook. The ground crew carried over a large wooden stepladder ready to turn the securing catches to take off the engine side panels. At the very least, it looked likely they would have to make an engine change. And, with hangar space limited, they would need to do it here in the open and begin now.

The deep rumble of approaching engines announced the return of the main force. Eleven Lancasters gradually joined the circuit, feeling their way down to the runway at Bardney. It was clear that fighters had been the biggest threat on this mission and although no aircraft had been lost from the squadron, damage was apparent. At the start of the bombing run, a Focke-Wulf 190 had pounced on Lancaster ED654, flown by Pilot Officer Walkup. Cannon shells ripped through the fuselage, killing the upper gunner, Sergeant J. Leslie. The tail gunner, Sergeant Mullet, was injured, but reported the Fw 190 destroyed in the attack. The intercom and oxygen connection to the rear of the Lancaster was inoperative and the fuselage holed. For ground crews, seeing their bomber return with damage was disturbing, but nothing was more distressing than removing dead or injured comrades. Evacuation would be carried out immediately the aircraft had rolled to a stop on the nearest piece of peri-track to the runway. Vehicles rushed to the scene, eager hands gently lifting injured crewmen out of the Lancaster's rear door onto a stretcher. Once the ambulances had left, the ground crew would bring a tractor and tow the Lancaster to its dispersal point using a towing arm attached to the rear wheel. The task of cleaning blood from an aircraft was a grim one; those on the ground also carried a heavy burden.

Walkup did not fly again for two weeks, but his next flight proved the hazards of flying the Lancaster with one pilot. Sent to Hanover on the night of 18 October, the crew reported: 'No target attacked. When aircraft at 53.20N and 03.50S crew noticed that Captain was unwell and not in complete control of the aircraft. It was decided to return to base. Captain just managed to land the aircraft at base and immediately thereafter became unconscious and was taken to hospital.'

The nature of Walkup's illness is not recorded, but he was removed from flying duties.

★

Away from the dangers and challenges of flying missions over Germany, the crew's accommodation at Bardney was hardly luxurious. The Nissen huts tended to be slightly damp, and, as autumn took hold, decidedly chilly. In the wee small hours, they didn't care; pulling the coarse woollen blankets further round their shoulders, they were soon asleep. They didn't stir when the orderly came in at seven o'clock rattling the pot-bellied stove. He might receive the odd grunt of thanks, but little more.

At times through that autumn they awoke to find neigh-bouring beds vacant, tidily made up, lockers emptied ready for replacement airmen. It was as if invisible hosts had spirited away every trace of the previous crew. Nothing was said, but they knew that the previous occupants of these beds were missing and not expected to return. There were no expressions of grief or gestures of remembrance in the huts. The new men would arrive as quickly as fresh sheets appeared on their beds.

In these early weeks of their operational career, the Comans crew were learning the harsh realities of combat. In training, it had been possible to beat off a fighter attack, claiming that since the guns had loosed off a few hundred blank rounds, their defence had been successful. Fighter affiliation pilots* were scathing of reports of their supposed downfall. Some of them had fought in the Battle of Britain and derided the idea that they were easily shot down. For all the rigours of training, it could never prepare a pilot for the reality of battle damage and the peculiar problems it caused. Once on a mission, it was as if the pilot's operating notes had been thrown to the wind with only a few scattered pages remaining for reference. For the crew, it was a matter of making it up as they went along, of trying to work out whether technical failures were simple or complex. Fear was perhaps the most corrosive element. When an incident occurred, there were specific drills that the crew were trained to follow, but in the eye of the storm, terror could all too easily take hold again. A crew's mental toughness would dictate its success or failure – and its chances of survival in the future. The incident of Walkup's illness illustrates the courage and dedication of the crew. Although parachuting out of a Lancaster entailed considerable risks, it would arguably have been more sensible to abandon the aircraft than to entrust its landing to a semi-conscious pilot.

---

* Pilots who played the 'enemy' in dummy attacks during training.

22 October 1943, Kassel

The Comans crew had unfinished business at Kassel, as did Bomber Command, once they discovered that most of the bombs dropped in the first raid had fallen well short of the target. Damage was reported as far as fifteen miles away. With the Henschel plant still in full operation, the USAAF returned in daylight four days later, hitting the plant with 122 B-24 bombers. Kassel had reached the top of the list for targets requiring a 'knock-out' blow. The largest raid of the war so far was scheduled to be launched against the town on the night of 22 October 1943.

The bomb load chosen was a mix of high explosives and thousands of 4lb incendiaries. The aim was to create a firestorm in the city centre. It was a brutal and merciless strategy, and one that has attracted much controversy and criticism since. But it was entirely in keeping with the Allied strategy of seeking to disrupt German war production. The bombing of Hamburg three months earlier, in July 1943, had been deemed a success. Operation Gomorrah, which consisted of eight days of attacks that left 42,600 civilians dead and 37,000 wounded, had produced the most destructive outcome of any Allied raids to date. Its impact was believed to be so terrible that Nazi Germany would succumb rather than see similar destruction. It was a calculation that proved to be incorrect, although supporters of the area bombing campaign noted how effectively Hamburg had been neutralized as a centre of industry. It was a logic that, at the time, was hard to argue against. With hindsight, strategists have spent much time exploring theoretical alternatives to area bombing. However, with no Allied soldier yet landed on French beaches, the pressing task was to degrade the German war effort to a critical point before invasion.

The crew briefing for Kassel detailed the approach to the target area, a deceptive feint towards Frankfurt before turning sharply onto the target. Taking off at 18.00 hours, the city was already burning fiercely when the crew arrived three hours later. Ken Cook reported that they attacked at 21.08 from 20,500 feet, dropping their bombs on the south-east corner of the fire. Almost simultaneously, another large fire took hold four miles away and, as the crew turned for home, they could see enormous black clouds of smoke rising.

Pilot Officer Manning's crew reported seeing the fires joining up into one massive conflagration. Only minutes later, Manning was hit by a concerted fighter attack involving four aircraft, at least three of which were Junkers 88s. With the upper gunner killed and tail gunner injured, his Lancaster suffered extensive damage in the six-minute action. Remarkably, Manning limped back home. His Lancaster was EE188, the aircraft that had taken the Comans crew successfully to Munich and scraped back from Kassel on their first aborted mission. She had been repaired in a matter of days after the first Kassel attack, but now she faced more in-depth repair. She would return to combat operations nineteen days later.

Her luck finally ran out on the night of 16 December with Pilot Officer Ian Black and crew on the return from Berlin. RAF Bardney received a radio transmission from her minutes before the end, but no more was heard. EE188 crashed near Salzbergen close to the Dutch border, 250 miles from Berlin, killing everyone on board. Black had been caught by night-fighter ace Major Egmont Prinz zur Lippe-Weissenfeld flying a Bf 110 G-4 from Twente airfield in Holland, less than twenty miles away.*

---

* Twenty-five-year-old Lippe-Weissenfeld came from the royal household of Lippe, one of the German provinces that lost its monarchy in the new republic of 1919. He had originally enlisted in the Austrian army but transferred to the German Luftwaffe in 1939. In August 1943 he was awarded the Knight's Cross, having been credited with forty-five aerial victories, nearly all of them at night. Three months after his successful interception of Pilot Officer Black in EE188, Lippe-Weissenfeld was killed in a flying accident on 12 March 1944.

Even from far above the city, the effect of the raid on Kassel was terrifying. Few at 9 Squadron had seen anything as destructive. While large fires were seen on many raids, the scale of damage inflicted on this city was new to them. As at Hamburg, the intensity of burning buildings, many of them wooden-framed medieval structures, created a firestorm. One hundred mile-an-hour winds took hold, spreading flames, but dragging in oxygen to feed them. Many were suffocated as they took refuge in shelters and basements. Others, attempting to flee, were dragged back towards the inferno. High-explosive bombs had ruptured water mains, making firefighting all but impossible. Fires burned for a week after the attack as rescuers fought desperately to save buried survivors. As in Operation Gomorrah, the destruction was of biblical proportions. The death toll rose to over 10,000, and made a further 150,000 homeless, many of whom chose to become refugees rather than risk staying.

*

Although dry weather had helped the fires of Kassel, further west strong winds, lashing rain and low cloud limited operations. 'Harry Clampers', days when flying was near impossible, were common. These were typical English autumn days when Bardney disappeared in a fine mist of dampness, obscuring dispersals and flattening the mood of the ground crew. Even with waterproofs, it was hard to keep dry. By the end of October, the Comans crew had flown five combat missions, all to cities in Germany. They had been diverted to different airfields because of damage or bad weather on two occasions out of the five. They were beginning to fight the long battle of winter. While planners were happy with the onset of longer nights, the crews realized their life was perilous enough without bad weather to contend with. Despite night flying training, Jim Comans had never flown in such conditions.

Another idea was forming in Jim Comans' mind, perhaps born out of his competitive sporting nature, or perhaps from the need to be a leader rather than a follower. The idea was to volunteer for the Pathfinders. Another 9 Squadron crew, led by Jack Anstee, had volunteered and waxed lyrical about their 'promotion'. Ken Cook remembers how any decision to volunteer had to be unanimous, but he adds: 'We were young and always looking for a challenge. Besides that, we were good at our job, and we knew it.' Nevertheless, a meeting was held with the Squadron Commander – its mood appropriately serious, given the perils of the course the crew were contemplating. Each member of the Comans crew was asked whether he was happy to join the Pathfinders. No one demurred. There was a price to pay for their enthusiasm, however. A normal tour of duty lasted thirty missions, after which a period of leave was offered. A second tour of twenty missions could be undertaken, but this was at an individual airman's discretion. Pathfinders would normally end their operational flying after forty-five missions. Having flown ten missions with 9 Squadron, the crew were to begin their tour of operations with the Pathfinders immediately. They were not to be offered a break or a period of leave until they had flown another thirty-five missions.

18 November–16 December 1943, Berlin

Arthur 'Bomber' Harris, Air Officer Commanding-in-Chief RAF Bomber Command, directed operations from a large leather-topped desk at RAF High Wycombe. The brutally successful attacks on Hamburg and Kassel had whetted his appetite for intensifying the attacks on Berlin. If Germany was to capitulate under the weight of Allied bomber attacks, it had to be during the winter of 1943/4. Harris had a huge force at his disposal.

Air Chief Marshal Sir Arthur Harris, at his desk at Bomber Command HQ, High Wycombe, April 1944.

He knew the weight resting on his shoulders. The air armada he commanded was comparable to any of the great fleets of history and infinitely more powerful than Nelson's at Trafalgar. Nobody could predict the outcome of such force, but it seemed sensible to assume it must bring about the end of the war. Harris knew that once spring came the invasion of north-west Europe would change priorities, taking the momentum away from his strategy. Having seen the horrors of the trenches at first hand, there was no doubt in his mind that a land war would be cruel and costly. Harris concluded the only way Hitler could be shaken was to pulverize Berlin, destroying Nazi governmental structures and disrupting communications.

Harris wrote to Churchill on 3 November 1943, urging American cooperation with his plans:

> We must get the USAAF to wade in with greater force… We can wreck Berlin from end to end if the USAAF will come in on it. It will cost between us 400–500 aircraft. It will cost Germany the war.

The USAAF, however, badly burned by heavy losses sustained in the Schweinfurt–Regensburg mission of August 1943, would not join Harris's assault on Germany's capital, and Bomber Command would embark on the Battle of Berlin on its own. The start of the operation against the German capital was planned for 18 November 1943. By December, with the aid of early damage reports, Harris was touting the view to the Air Ministry that Berlin would be so damaged it would be in 'a state of devastation in which surrender is inevitable'.

Such optimism was not shared by the Lancaster crews at RAF Bardney, for whom each target presented a fresh challenge. After a brief but successful mission to Düsseldorf in early November, the Comans crew prepared for their first trip to Berlin – and the first raid in Harris's master plan. Those who had flown there before tended to suck air through their teeth when Berlin was mentioned. Others were more guarded in giving an opinion, but all agreed Berlin was a difficult target. Tonight, it would be important not to hang about, as the rising moon was still strong enough to betray them. But the raid was not to be for the Comans crew.

Less than an hour out from Bardney and only minutes after the navigator had uttered the words 'Enemy coast ahead!', the starboard inner engine began to splutter. They were still climbing, or trying to, but it was clear that the ill-performing engine was impeding their progress. Their Lancaster, ED532, was fully loaded, the wings bending perceptibly with the weight. Fuel for such a long trip was a fine balance, and the increased huffing and puffing from the starboard inner was a problem. Comans asked Don Bowes for a return leg course to take them over the bomb jettisoning area – only a fool would consider bringing back a bombed-up Lancaster in these circumstances. The jettisoning area was marked on maps as a triangular zone at sea, and maritime and air traffic was warned off using it.

They had been flying for only one and a half hours when they touched down at RAF East Kirkby, only thirteen miles from Bardney. Another faulty Lancaster, W5011, was on the inbound leg to Bardney, so it is likely that Comans was directed to East Kirkby instead. Lancaster W5011 made a dramatic arrival back at Bardney fifteen minutes later, ploughing across the runway in a wheels-up landing. The reason for return was a sick navigator and a port engine playing up. Why the undercarriage did not function is not clear, nor did it concern the flustered ground crews who needed to remove W5011 as quickly as possible and sweep the runway free of debris. Fortunately, there were no further early returns, leaving the runway clear for the main arrivals, but two squadron aircraft were lost that night. Despite two Lancasters from 9 Squadron being detailed to fly a North Sea dinghy search the next day, nothing was found.

Although early returns were commonplace, there would always be an examination of the facts by the Flight Commander to make sure the aircraft had not returned under flimsy pretences. One of the first indicators of pilot or crew fatigue was the return rate. Although pilots were always cautious about embarking on long flights with any form of technical failure, the return rate for missions with tough targets was higher. Conversely, crews did not like to return early and risk suspicion of LMF – 'lack of moral fibre', an offence that would see them removed from the squadron with haste. There was little doubt in this case that ED532 *was* sick. She required two days in repairs before Comans could take her back to Bardney – just hours before he would embark with her once again for Berlin.

Two Lancasters had failed to return from the 18 November raid on Berlin. One was DV284, G-George, the first 9 Squadron Lancaster the Comans crew had flown seven weeks before on that grey morning over the Wainfleet ranges. She wasn't 'their' aircraft – they had not been flying long enough to develop a relationship with a particular Lancaster – but she was one of their regulars. Only the day before they had flown G-George on a practice bomb mission. On DV284's last, ill-fated journey, she was flown by Pilot Officer Gordon Graham and crew. With them was Pilot Officer John McComb on his first acclimatization mission before piloting his own crew. McComb was the

Date	Hour	Aircraft Type and No.	Pilot	Duty	Remarks (Including results of bombing, gunnery, exercises, etc.)	Day	Night
							4·45
3-10-43		Lancaster C	F/O. Comans	Air Bomber	Op. DUSSELDORF		
5-11-43		Lancaster C	F/O Comans	" "	PRACTICE BOMBING	1·05	
6-11-43		Lancaster B	F/O Comans	-	PRACTICE BOMBING	1·20	
8-11-43		Lancaster J	F/O Comans	" "	AIR TEST	·50	
12-11-43		Lancaster G	F/O Comans	" "	PRACTICE BOMBING.	1·30	
17-11-43		Lancaster H	F/O Comans	" "	PRACTICE BOMBING	1·35	
18-11-43		Lancaster C	F/O Comans	" "	Ops BERLIN S'bound near U/S		1·30
22-11-43		Lancaster C	F/O Comans	-	EAST KIRBY - BASE	·15	
22-11-43		Lancaster B	F/O Comans	" "	Ops. BERLIN		6·45
23-11-43		Lancaster S	F/O Comans	" "	Ops. BERLIN		6·45
25-11-43		Lancaster D	F/O Comans	" "	N.F.T.	·25	
26-11-43		Lancaster S	F/O Comans	" "	Ops. BERLIN DIVERTED LECONFIELD.		7·24
28-11-43		Lancaster	F/O Comans	-	LECONFIELD - BASE	·35	

SUMMARY FOR NOVEMBER 1943
DAY 6·55 hrs.
NIGHT 27·09 hrs.
TOTAL OPS HRS. 58·39 hrs.

J. G. A. Hadson F/LT
O.C. "A" FLT.

Pages from Ken Cook's 9 Squadron logbook for November 1943. His total operational hours for the month were an impressive 58 hours 39 minutes.

son of a labourer from the tightly knit terraces of the Shankill area of Belfast. His father, James, had married Liza Young at the imposing Townsend Street Presbyterian Church in 1919. They were very proud of John as their eldest son; not only had he succeeded in pilot training, but a month before this flight had been promoted to pilot officer. It was a rise in social status they could hardly have imagined before the war. But all their hopes for John would be cruelly swept away when DV284 was caught by flak ninety-five miles south-west of Berlin. It looks likely she was caught in the flak belt of Leipzig, crashing near the small town of Burgwerben. Although he would have been a face among the crowd of some 140 men in the briefing room at RAF Bardney, it is unlikely that Ken Cook met John McComb. He was new, had probably been on base for less than a week, and was lost

RAF men, in jovial mood, assess a range of potential destinations, c. *1943.*
Lancaster crews in fact dreaded the long flights to Berlin, Europe's most
heavily defended city.

too soon to feature in the memoirs and stories of the squadron. After the war the crew of DV284 were reinterred together at the Berlin 1939–1945 War Cemetery at Charlottenburg close to the shores of Lake Havel. They lie together in the city they could not escape.

The bomber crews had no idea of the target strategy of their superiors. However, it became very apparent that Berlin had become a central focus for Bomber Command. After the technical issues and aborted mission of 18 November, the Comans crew flew against Berlin on 22, 23 and 26 of that month. It was a level of combat flying they could hardly have imagined as they were pottering around Britain in Avro Ansons a year earlier. Berlin would be the most frightening ride of their lives, hundreds of aircraft converging on the city night after night. As they jostled for position over the burning maelstrom below, they could see Lancasters to each side of them and, most disturbingly, underneath them on the bombing run. The planners had hoped each element of the stream would arrive on time at altitudes that would avoid such crossovers, but the reality was far more chaotic. Even if each crew had managed to navigate successfully, the effects of headwind and occasional avoidance measures meant that timings were fluid. To the credit of 9 Squadron, most aircraft embarked on their bombing run within minutes of each other after the 600-mile outbound journey. However, once the bombers approached the searchlight and flak belts, it was every man for himself.

Ken Cook recalls the shock of a near miss over Berlin on the final run into target. As they concentrated on flying straight and level, a roar like an express train pounded their aircraft. A Lancaster passed

Ken Cook photographed just before he joined the Pathfinders. The 'B' insignia below his left lapel stands for 'Bombardier'.

above them, missing by only a few feet. George Widdis stared wide-eyed from his upper gunner's position at the huge dark underside of the aircraft as it swept over them. The downdraught swung their Lancaster, juddering Comans' controls for a second as their unwelcome friend disappeared to starboard. It happened on more than one occasion, and for a crew already tensed for the possibility of fighter or flak, this sudden interference reduced their chances of returning home with unsoiled underwear.

Another 9 Squadron Lancaster, EM361, flown by Flying Officer Reid, experienced a terrifying stall spin when trying to avoid a collision with another bomber at 21,000 feet. Reid estimated the spin lasted over thirty seconds as the aircraft plummeted 7,000 feet before he regained control. Had the design of the Lancaster not been so sturdy, undoubtedly the wings would have folded under the enormous strain.

In these desperate late November nights over Berlin, it was clear an uneventful mission was an impossibility. The squadron were losing one bomber per trip, sometimes two, with many reports of near misses, accidents or unpleasant incidents. The return flight of 23 November was marred by poor weather conditions, with some crews reporting electrical storms and torrential rain. Flight Lieutenant Hadland described his last 100 miles as 'bumpy indeed' with the cloud base down to less than 1,000 feet. After his extensive 'swim' in the North Sea, he knew all too well the consequences of losing too much altitude. The Comans crew reported the last 100 miles to be 'very unpleasant', heavy rain hampering their progress. Others did not make safe landings. After overshooting when their undercarriage indicator lights failed to show, Pilot Officer Ward and crew in DV327 suffered a sudden drop on their next approach, causing the Lancaster to slip starboard, crashing short of the airfield. They were lucky: all walked away from the accident unhurt. Another crew from 9 Squadron in Lancaster ED656, flown by Pilot Officer N. G. Robinson, were not, the bomber crashing ten miles north of Bardney and killing all but two of its crew.

The losses of 9 Squadron were typical of these operations. Loss rates were running at over 3 per cent of the force sent, but at this early stage in the battle Harris was not too concerned. Later the rate would rise, with some raids losing over 7 per cent of their bombers, figures close to disastrous.

When the crew returned from their mission of 26 November, the third they had made to Berlin in five days, it is apparent they were in good spirits. The raid had gone well for them, the target marking had been tight and Ken Cook felt the bombing to be smack on point. Their entry in squadron records is concise: 'Primary attacked. 21,000ft. Concentrations of fires seen east and west of AP [aiming point]. Green flares dropped in centre of concentrations. Attack concentrated. Best of three this week.'

Meanwhile, word had come through that they had been accepted to join the Pathfinders. Their posting was to be to 97 Squadron at RAF Bourn, close to Cambridge. But before then, and immediately after Christmas, they were to be sent on a navigation course to RAF Upwood, south of Peterborough.

The Comans crew's last mission with 9 Squadron was to Berlin on the night of 16 December 1943, a date that would become infamous within Bomber Command: 'Black Thursday', a raid in which dozens of bombers were lost. The enemy on this night was thick fog, which made landing extremely hazardous. The Comans crew returned safely to land at RAF Leconfield, north of Bardney, in the East Riding of Yorkshire, after feeling their way home through intensely thick mist. Bombers were scattered all over the eastern region, but 97 Squadron suffered the most, losing some of their most experienced crews in crashes.

★

Across Europe, for most people Christmas 1943 brought little to celebrate. In Berlin, the floor of a large gymnasium was filled with the victims of Bomber Command's deadly sorties. Christmas trees lined the walls as undertakers brought in hundreds of coffins. Despite generous sprinklings of disinfectant among the contorted shapes, the smell in this makeshift morgue was appalling. There would no respite for Berlin amid the smoking ruins and shattered roads of the city. Bomber Command would return with redoubled ferocity in the New Year.

In southern Italy, near Ortona on the coast of Abruzzo, Allied troops celebrated in their forward positions, a little disgruntled that the Germans appeared to have the luxury of a church service across the valley. The battle for Ortona raged throughout the Christmas period, a fierce close-combat battle likened to Stalingrad by those who fought there. At Carthage in North Africa, Churchill had been dangerously ill with pneumonia and heart problems. Suffering a fever that lasted six days, even Churchill was unsure of his chances of survival. He told his daughter Sarah not to worry, '… it doesn't matter if I die now, the plans for victory have been laid, it is only a matter of time'. By Christmas Day he had recovered enough to meet with General Eisenhower, although he was still in his dressing gown.

For many, not able to leave the confines of barracks and air bases, Glenn Miller's live broadcast performance from the Halloran General Hospital in Staten Island brightened their day, but few could forget it was a Christmas at war. In England, the Pathfinder navigation course began at RAF Upwood on 27 December, setting the Comans crew on the next leg of their adventure.

5.

Bourn: The Road to
Black Thursday

April 1941

Skimming just below the dull base of the clouds, the German pilot kept the Junkers Ju88C low and fast as his navigator checked their bearings. If a night fighter appeared, he would pull up into the overcast. The rooftops of a large town appeared ahead. He steered to port, keeping Cambridge on his right. Easing the aircraft gently upwards, they spotted the St Neots road running ahead of them and their target appeared as marked on their map. The smooth runways caught the light, a new moon revealing just enough to guide the Junkers to them. In a broad sweeping turn, the aircraft lined up along the centre line of the runway. It was impossible to miss, being longer and wider than most the men had seen in Germany or France. He bore down across the base of the runway and, as the broadness of the new asphalt filled the pilot's view, he knew this was an easy target. Speeding past the first intersection of the runways, the crew could hear the muffled explosions of their bombs behind them.

The Junkers crew expected anti-aircraft fire to streak towards them, but there was no sign of opposition. Going around again the pilot flew towards the network of low buildings until their mass was in his gunsight. He pressed his trigger, feeling the pounding of the guns in the aircraft's nose. He pulled up sharply, tipping the Junkers on one wing as his rear gunner fired a few rounds towards the target. Enough. They knew they would have awoken every defence for a hundred miles around. Getting the Junkers down towards the hedgerows, they sped homeward.

It was first light before a party of men set out to look at the damage at RAF Bourn. They had been warned that going out in the dark was dangerous in case the raider had sown butterfly bombs. At little over 18 inches long, these small grenades had spring-loaded arms that shot out of the body to arm them. If they were touched on the ground they would go off. Thankfully, this morning, there was no sign of the devices. This had been a standard lone intruder attack typical of dozens the Luftwaffe launched across Britain. Curious foremen gathered around the depressions of the bomb craters – many of them had never seen one before. They agreed they were a nuisance but could be repaired soon; most of the debris could be shovelled back into the holes and packed down before new concrete was poured and asphalt relaid on top. Happily, the raid caused no deaths or injuries; the airfield was unfinished and there were, therefore, few men around the site. Nor were there any aircraft at Bourn that April day – they would not be arriving for some time.

★

For centuries these fields had been farmed without disturbance. Crops had been planted, grown and harvested here, across the many years of change from the Norman conquest to the Napoleonic Wars. Little broke the quietness around the small villages of Bourn, Little Gransden and Hardwick. They prospered as Cambridge, their sophisticated neighbour eight miles to the east, grew in size and importance. In the nineteenth century, more affluent visitors discovered the villages and began the rural escape, building handsome houses with gardens. Girls from the villages found work as servants, cooking and cleaning for their wealthier neighbours. Most workers were employed on the land, but the Great Depression reduced Bourn's population to less than six hundred. The motor car brought new visitors, dodging horses and alerting walkers with noisy horns. Carefree students, picnics in their rucksacks, roamed the narrow lanes on bicycles on sunny Sunday afternoons. The gentle pace of life had changed little until the day, in the summer of 1939, when a car arrived in the yard at Grange Farm. Men in suits and trilbies stepped out, accompanied by an RAF officer.

There had been word for some time around the farmers' markets that land was being bought up for airfields. RAF Oakington, four miles to the north-east, had already displaced its tenants to begin construction. The strangers at Grange Farm walked out into the fields carrying stands and theodolites. They paused to hold windspeed-measuring devices above their heads, noting measurements on clipboards. There weren't too many gradients to survey, they could see that most of the surrounding land was flat, both south of the St Neots road and around the lane that led west to Bourn village. On the eastern boundary the settlement of Highfields Caldecote presented a slight challenge with its lines of houses, long gardens and smallholdings. Still, they felt there was enough room to fit the three transecting runways. Ancient hedgerows and trees would have to go, but there was no question of protest delaying the work.

The farmer watched their progress with growing apprehension. The men had spent hours in his fields, so he knew that the interest of the Air Ministry was not a passing whim. As the delegation packed the boot of their car, they refused to be drawn on the nature of their work. They had four more farms to visit, after which the farmers would be informed in writing. Land surveys were taking place throughout the region, and in some cases nothing further was heard. Perhaps this, too, was just another contingency plan to be stored away in a manila file in the depths of Whitehall? But for landowners around Bourn, the answer was swift. Letters arrived from the Air Ministry stating which fields were to be requisitioned. Financial compensation would be provided, but this offered little comfort to those who were losing land that had been in their families for generations.

Complaints were widespread, the Rutland branch of the National Farmers' Union reporting that 'in 99 cases out of 100 RAF officers had no idea about farming'. Even furious interventions by local politicians had little effect; there was a 'war on', they were told. The novelist E. M. Forster warned: 'The fighting services are bound to become serious enemies of what is left of England. Wherever they see a tract of wild, unspoiled country they naturally want it for camps, artillery practice, bomb dropping or poison gas tests.'

If Forster's intervention seems a little melodramatic, it is worth recording that, by 1944, as much as 11 million acres – 20 per cent of Britain's land surface – was under some form of military control. Directions issued by the War Office in May 1940 regarding the acquisition of farming land instructed that the military had 'absolute discretion to override any such objections'. Complainants would not be permitted to seek redress in the courts, and there was to be no public enquiry or further consultation; the landowner was powerless to stand against the will of the war ministries.

The land for RAF Bourn was acquired in early 1940 with 400 acres taken from Grange Farm in the south, Great Common Farm in the west and Highfield Farm. Grange Farm was so reduced that it ceased to exist. In common with many others whose acres were requisitioned for defence use during the Second World War, the owners were unable to recover their land after the end of the conflict. The site of the farmhouse and buildings fell within the river of new concrete that formed the runways. Once they were swept away they were gone forever. One wooden-clad barn survived to be used for motor vehicle garaging, a forlorn memory in the featureless expanse of runway and grass.

Local children remember the first signs of change came with the felling of trees. Soon afterwards an army of men and bulldozers moved in to clear away any encumbrance to the new airfield. From dawn until dusk the fields reverberated to the groaning of tracked vehicles crashing through the bases of the hedgerows. Convoys of lorries transported large quantities of earth as diggers began cutting a network of channels in the soil, in which workers laid miles of drainage pipes. The size of the task amazed the villagers, who gazed across the new landscape stretching far into the distance. Thousands of tons of crushed stone were brought from quarries in a stream of dumper lorries, trailing dust clouds in their wake. When the time came to lay the runways, men stripped to the waist to toil over large steel frames as machines pounded the soft concrete slurry flat. An average airfield took 18,000 tons of cement and 90,000 tons of aggregate. Many said it was the hardest work they had done in their lives.

It soon became apparent that one of the roads from Bourn would have to be rerouted as it crossed the airfield's planned accommodation area. A small village of green Nissen huts appeared in the fields. Invented by the American-born army officer Peter Nissen in 1916, the curved-roofed huts were easily built in sections and required only a concrete pad to sit on. Accommodation blocks, washrooms, offices and briefing rooms all clustered around narrow paths. The Nissens were supplemented with concrete sectional buildings brought onto the site and bolted together. The simplicity of the buildings belied the extraordinary effort required to support them. Drainage, sewers, pump stations, water pipes, fire hydrants and miles of electrical and telephone cables had to be installed and laid. Had RAF Bourn been one of only a few airfields built, it would still have counted as an engineering wonder, but it was one of hundreds of airfields that were constructed around the country at the same time. The enormity and ambition of this building programme is little short of awe-inspiring. Only four miles away to the north-east, its sister airfield at Little Gransden was also under construction. Before the war's end, the RAF had more than eight hundred bases in use, from radar sites to small backwoods flying fields, scattered the length and breadth of Britain. Bomber Command had 103 operational bases stretching from North Yorkshire to Suffolk, each averaging 2,000 staff.

Although it was originally proposed as a satellite airfield for RAF Oakington, Bourn soon took on a life of its own. Even as the lone Junkers 88 attacked in April 1941, plans were in place for the nearly completed airfield to be upgraded. The new specifications meant that the runways would be lengthened and widened to take the expected new generation of heavy bombers. Finally, in February 1942, it welcomed its first operational aircraft, 101 Squadron flying Vickers Wellingtons. Local boys stood wide-eyed in wonder as the bombers flew into RAF Bourn. It was a sight they would become familiar with, but each remembered the first time they saw the Wellingtons enter the circuit before landing. Approaching slowly, the sound of engines seemed to fill the sky. The outline of their dark bulbous fuselage would change shape as the wheels dropped. Lining up on the runway two miles away, their landing lights appeared, shining brightly against the grey sky. The shape of their wings grew larger as others filed in behind them ready to land. Sweeping over the hedges of the nearby fields, they sank onto the runway with a distant screech of tyres. The boys pedalled furiously along the lanes to get a better view.

The arrival of the Wellingtons had been the last piece in the giant jigsaw puzzle. The site was now packed with airmen,

A royal visit to RAF Bourn, 1942: Prince George, Duke of Kent, younger brother of King George VI, is third from left. He was to die, along with fourteen others, in an air crash in north-eastern Scotland on 25 August 1942.

1,805 men and 276 women. The invasion was not unwelcome. Local businesses, not least the pubs, prospered and while some still considered the destruction of the farms to be an act of vandalism, others saw the new airfield as a business opportunity. For the next few years the buses into Cambridge were fuller and more frequent. The university, however, was quieter, as many undergraduates chose to break their studies to serve in the forces. The regular 'town and gown' population was boosted by numbers of blue-uniformed airmen collected from a dozen or more local airfields in the evening rush for cinemas and dances. The influx of Americans had not yet got underway in early 1942 and the Royal Air Force men still had the pick of the ladies, although they were frequently in competition with soldiers.

The pace of flights around Bourn became constant. Through the day Wellingtons would take off for test flights and navigation exercises. With other airfields nearby, it seemed the drone of aircraft was constant. In the early evenings the Wellingtons hung low after take-off. Everyone in the area got to know the straining sound of Bristol Pegasus radial engines at full power. Sometimes they circled the airfield as they gained altitude, before breaking into a loose formation to fly east. At this early point in the war, 101 Squadron was only fielding eight to ten aircraft per raid, sometimes fewer. The dots of the bombers had finally disappeared into the gathering darkness. Several hours later the noise of the returning Wellingtons would once again fill the quiet lanes and gardens of Bourn. But under the cloak of darkness the villagers could not see how many came back.

Sometimes, inevitably, bombers that took off safely failed to return. Their losses affected other communities, hundreds of miles away, in Holland, Belgium and France. Wellington R1703 of 101 Squadron, stationed at RAF Oakington, crashed at Boxbergheide near Genk in Belgium on 31 August 1941, killing three of its crew. The Germans buried the bodies of twenty-two-year-old Pilot Officer Frederick Ashton, navigator Sergeant Ernest Lane and wireless operator Sergeant John Redden on barren heathland near the village. The graves soon became a symbol of resistance with flowers and stones laid around them. When they were desecrated by German sympathizers, local children continued to restore the graves. A wooden cross made by Polish labourers was put up, but was repeatedly torn down. A more substantial concrete cross was constructed in secret at the nearby Winterslag coal mine in 1943 and erected with a firm foundation. This became known as the '*Heidekruise*' (the 'cross on the heather'), and would lead to the building – after the war – of a larger monument to 139 RAF aircrew who had lost their lives in the region. The cross began a tradition of remembrance, with children laying flowers every second Tuesday in September.

★

Bomber Command's onslaught on German cities in the early months of 1942 produced many angry protests from the Nazi propaganda machine, but little in the way of retaliation. The Luftwaffe had its hands full in Russia, and lacked the bombers to attack airfields like RAF Bourn. The Germans knew precisely where the bombers were flying from and which squadrons were based at each airfield. Special holding and interrogation centres, *Dulag Luft*,* were set up by the Luftwaffe for the growing stream of shot-down airmen, the principal camp located at Oberursel near Frankfurt. In addition to interrogations, much information had been gleaned from high-level photography. Now that the British had good radar cover and integrated fighter units, the Germans knew that launching raids was a trickier proposition than it had been in 1940–41, when the skies had been comparatively open. However, some response was required.

On 12 September 1942, high above the English Channel in a Junkers 86R-2, Sergeant Horst Götz could clearly make out the French and English coasts far beneath. His crew sat in a pressurized cabin, to their knowledge untouchable from interference by enemy fighters. At 42,000 feet their nitrous oxide-injected diesel engines purred, powering two four-bladed props slicing the thin air. This was one of Hitler's secret weapons, a reconnaissance plane that was clearly visible to British radar but flying 20,000 feet above the ceiling of a Spitfire. From their eagle's eye, the Germans used banks of cameras to photograph large swathes of England, plotting every airfield. Suddenly, a flash of sunlight to the rear of the Ju86 formed into an unmistakable shape. The navigator alerted Götz that he had seen a fighter. But how could this be? Götz had watched Spitfires try to close on him before.

---

* *Durchgangslager der Luftwaffe* ('air force transit camp'). Captured Allied airmen spent time at the *Dulag* before being housed permanently in a *Stalag* (*Stammlager*, or 'main camp').

Their distinctive shapes and slim noses pointed upwards had always failed to reach his altitude. This time, disbelief turned to alarm as the Spitfire closed in, firing at the Junkers. Cannon shells whipped past, flashes of bright light, zipping and cracking over the cockpit. The fighter dropped away after its first attack but was not for giving in. For the next forty-five minutes, Junkers and Spitfire engaged in the highest dogfight of the Second World War, as Götz tried to slip and turn his slow bomber away from the sleek blue fighter. When a heavy thump resounded through his aircraft, the German knew he had been hit. Götz finally managed to make his escape, turning for home in the knowledge that the Ju86 had lost its invulnerability.

The Junkers 86 had first appeared high in the skies of Britain in 1940 and, for a brief period, flew without challenge. Strangely, the Junkers 86 was not the product of an extensive scientific programme, but a remodel of a redundant design. The early 86, supposedly designed as a civilian passenger plane, was in fact a bomber. It had flown in the 1930s during the Spanish Civil War, when Nazi Germany supported Franco's Nationalists in Spain with the Condor Legion, but it was found to be too slow. The bomb load was small and by the outbreak of the Second World War the Junkers 86 was pushed into the reserves. When Junkers answered the call to provide a high-level reconnaissance aircraft, they chose to modify the 86 rather than create a completely new aeroplane.

The new re-engined aircraft were still slow and were unarmed, but they propelled the crew to heights considered to be the realm of spacemen. During 1940 they were untouchable but did not drop bombs. The RAF had enough to contend with trying to deal with high-flying reconnaissance aircraft of more conventional design. Flying at 20,000 feet, these aircraft, such as the Junkers 88 and 188, were within the reach of RAF fighters but were often successful in outwitting their pursuers.

The extent to which the Luftwaffe mapped Britain was not fully appreciated until after the war. In 1963 a group of German industrialists flew into Silloth on the north Cumbrian coast to visit local factories. RAF Silloth had been a Coastal Command station and considered relatively isolated from Luftwaffe interference. It had suffered the attentions of a few lone raiders, but nothing of significance. When the welcoming committee greeted the Germans, one announced he had been to Silloth before. He pulled a folded reconnaissance photograph of the airfield from his jacket pocket and presented it to his surprised hosts. The detail of the airfield had been labelled in German – hangars, fuel dumps and fire station were all clearly marked.

Before the RAF could deal with the Junkers 86s in 1940, they had disappeared. Withdrawn to the Russian front in 1941, only small numbers were available; Britain was left untroubled by their prying eyes. Despite this, Junkers continued to improve their design, particularly increasing engine power. In Britain the Air Ministry were also working on designs for high-level aircraft, but with the threat diminished, progress was slow. When the Junkers 86 reappeared in 1942, it came as a bomber in an attempt to avenge the nightly RAF onslaught. Although they never flew in more than twos and could carry only one 551lb bomb each, their unreachable nature created a considerable threat. A bomb dropped in the centre of Bristol during the morning commute on 28 August 1942 killed forty-eight civilians. Near-panic ensued in the Air Ministry.

Fred Plum, manager of the Experimental Section at de Havilland, called an urgent shop-floor meeting. Instructing the men to move their prototype pressurized Mosquito, a plane intended to fly at high altitude, into the hangar, he stood on a soap box to address them. Explaining the situation, he said that work needed to start immediately to fit a new nose on the aircraft to house guns. Pausing for a second, he viewed the crowd before exclaiming, 'You aren't listening to what I'm saying. I said that we are starting straight away – hasn't anyone got a saw?' A carpenter rushed off to find tools and, after being instructed where to cut, began slicing through the plywood nose. Fred Plumb continued his address, interrupted only by the sound of the nose crashing to the floor.

Supermarine were also answering the call to arms in the form of a flight of specially adapted Spitfires at RAF Croydon. All excess weight was stripped back, new wooden lightweight propellers were fitted, and pilots trained in high-altitude physiology. On 12 September 1942, as we have seen, Pilot Officer Emanuel Galitzine, flying his high-altitude Spitfire, successfully intercepted the Junkers 86 of Horst Götz. Despite only hitting the aircraft with one cannon shell before his guns froze, it was enough to persuade the Germans that the Junkers was now vulnerable. Overflights of Britain by the Ju86 were suspended.

Three days earlier, the peace of RAF Bourn had been shattered by another night raider. The Stirlings of 15 Squadron had been at Bourn for under a month, yet it seemed the Luftwaffe already knew where they were. The few bombs scattered by the Dornier Do217 did little damage, however. The raider was caught almost immediately afterwards by a Mosquito night fighter, crashing five miles away near the village of Orwell with the loss of all four crew.

★

On 18 April 1943 the sight of heavy bombers circling Bourn announced the arrival of 97 (Straits Settlement) Squadron. Word quickly spread in the village that Avro Lancasters were arriving. The aircraft had gained a reputation in the press for both its effectiveness and aesthetics. As part of the newly formed Pathfinders, the squadron regulars did not welcome the move to Cambridgeshire. Until now, 97 Squadron had remained in a knot of Lincolnshire bases: RAF Waddington, Coningsby and Woodhall Spa. The established social life of Lincolnshire provided well-known pubs, frequent dances and opportunities for liaisons with the opposite sex. The officers' mess at Woodhall Spa was based in the palatial Petwood Hotel, arguably the most luxurious posting in the Royal Air Force. Petwood, a sprawling Tudorbethan building, had been built by a wealthy heiress, Baroness Grace von Eckardstein, using her favourite wood ('pet wood'), and she later turned the house into a hotel, which was requisitioned by the RAF when war came. Life between raids might include a stroll around the manicured gardens or a drink in the bar. For 97 Squadron, coming to Bourn with its temporary buildings and soggy footpaths was a shock. The Comans crew, however, arrived at Bourn in December 1943 from RAF Bardney in Lincolnshire, a similarly spartan and mud-laden camp. So for them, Bourn was less of a jolt to the system.

Three crews did not follow 97 Squadron to Bourn. Pilots John Maltby, Joe McCarthy and Les Munro slipped away to serve in a new secret squadron. They had little clue that their next operation would rank as one of the most famous of the war. Maltby had only just returned to operations with a new crew in early March 1943. McCarthy and Munro were just completing their tour of operations when they received the telephone call from Squadron Leader Guy Gibson inviting them to join the mysterious 'X' Squadron, later known as 617. In the frequent movement of crews, the transfer went unnoticed. It was not until after the Dam Busters raid two months later that their names became better known.

The numbers of air accidents around Bourn decreased with the arrival of the Lancasters, although for some village residents the impact of the aircraft was more disturbing than others. When the wind changed its prevailing course, the villages of Highfield and Hardwick were on the flight path of one of the runways, the shortest of the three. A local man, Bob Plane, recalled Lancasters labouring to gain height as they flew directly overhead. 'They used to come over the tops of the houses, laden with bombs, and one would think "Please God, let them get over." You would be sitting there with a cup of tea, and when they had gone over the saucer was full of tea and the cup was only half full because of the vibrations.'

Life on the bustling RAF station filtered down into the community. Local girls introduced young men to their parents over Sunday tea, women took in washing for officers and aircrew became known in local pubs. The goings-on at the airfield were a topic of daily village conversation, but never with strangers. When word spread of men failing to return from a mission, their losses were keenly felt in these rural Cambridgeshire villages.

97 Squadron spent exactly twelve months at Bourn as Pathfinders with 8 Group. Their operational career had begun two years earlier on 9 April 1941, when four aircraft were dispatched to Kiel to attack naval facilities. In the words of the Australian Associated Press report:

> The Air Ministry announced to-day that planes of the Bomber
> Command heavily and successfully attacked the important
> naval port of Kiel last night in perfect weather. Great fires
> raged in the town, while hundreds of tons of the most powerful
> bombs caused destruction to the submarine building yards
> and docks.

An examination of statistics reveals that whether the bombers flew in small or large numbers, loss rates were still high. In the first two years 97 Squadron was operational, it had lost thirty-eight aircraft, but numbers dispatched on each raid through 1941 averaged less than five. On a number of occasions, a single bomber was the only contribution to the combined force. As the rate of aircraft production gained momentum, the numbers of aircraft sent on raids by 97 Squadron rose, and by the time of their arrival at RAF Bourn they were frequently sending as many as ten aircraft per raid. Numbers continued to rise in the first half of 1943, reaching their full complement of aircraft with the twenty-one Lancasters sent to Hamburg in July. 97 Squadron were to lose fifty-nine aircraft in 467 sorties from Bourn during their twelve-month tenancy.

Bad weather hampered operations soon after 97 Squadron arrived at Bourn, and it was not until 26 April 1943 that eight Lancasters set off for Duisburg in the Rhineland, the world's largest inland port. Although the Pathfinder force claimed to have marked the target accurately, it was clear by daylight reconnaissance that they had marked the north-east part of the city rather than the area of dockland at the confluence of the rivers Ruhr and Rhine. Although Bourn's aircraft all returned, Sergeant Anthony Reilly landed with flak damage after being caught over the target by searchlights. One of a crew's worst nightmares was to be 'coned'. After one searchlight had fastened onto an aircraft, four or five others might quickly do the same, creating 'interlocking' beams and thereby illuminating the bomber for the AA guns on the ground. To be found by one searchlight was uncomfortable, but once others joined it it was very difficult to escape into the safety of darkness. Reilly had used every trick he could think of in jinking and diving his Lancaster. When the flak hit, everything became a blur of bright light and confusion. Giving the command to jettison the aircraft's bomb load, he successfully dived free of the lights, all too aware as he did so that he was placing his aircraft at greater risk of collision with the other bombers.

97 Squadron again escaped losses during a raid on Essen four days later. Was Bourn proving to be a lucky station? Any such hopes would be dashed by an incident on the return from the next raid, to Dortmund, on 4 May. Once again, Anthony Reilly's

crew were caught in a drama as they returned in bad weather. Diverting to RAF Waterbeach just north of Cambridge, Reilly overshot the landing and collided with a parked Stirling bomber. Reilly was killed and three other crew suffered multiple injuries. This, 97 Squadron's first loss during its time at Bourn, proved that the weather could be as dangerous an enemy as the guns of the German night fighters. Reilly had barely begun his operational career. Having arrived fresh from training on 8 March, he and his crew were on only their sixth sortie.

16/17 December 1943

One night would cast a long shadow over RAF Bourn. Black Thursday is noted for heavy losses throughout Bomber Command, but it proved to be especially costly for 97 Squadron. Following a raid on Berlin, the returning force was informed that thick fog had formed around the whole north-eastern part of Britain. As many as 483 Lancasters and ten Mosquitos were airborne at the time. Concern on the ground mounted – the fog seemed so thick as to be impenetrable. It was past midnight when the Lancasters began their approach to home on the darkest of nights and with the ground beneath them completely obscured. As the pilots let down through the banks of swirling mist, they watched their altimeters wind down, alarmed there was no sign of breaking through the cloud base. The controllers at Bourn radioed each aircraft, holding them in a pattern 500 feet apart in altitude. The drone of Lancasters circling resounded in the gloom. Even with their landing lights on, the ground crews could see only a fleeting glow as an aircraft passed overhead. When called in to attempt a landing, the pilots used a blind-landing radio navigation system known as SBA, Standard Beam Approach, to locate the runway. On the night of 16/17 December, the pilots' approaches were entirely blind, with visibility reduced to less than 100 yards on the ground. SBA transmitted a series of bleeps and, as it fell silent, the pilot would tune in to the next marker. However, following the SBA was not a complete solution: to land safely they still needed to see the ground lights. For most of the Lancaster crews, the conditions that night were the worst they had ever experienced.

Elsewhere, the situation was little better with the cloud base as low as 500 feet. In North Yorkshire, Flying Officer Russell Clark in Lancaster DS737 of 408 Squadron was attempting to return to RAF Linton-on-Ouse, but was advised that the fog was too thick. He was redirected to RAF Topcliffe, and then RAF Leeming, but conditions there were no better. Lost and short of fuel, Clark's Lancaster struck high ground between the villages of Boltby and Hawnby near Thirsk. Clark, a Canadian, survived the initial crash along with two other members of the seven-man crew, but died of his injuries on 21 December. Other aircraft diverted to airfields in Lincolnshire and Norfolk where a system known as FIDO, 'Fog Investigation Dispersal Operation', was used. Rows of pipes and burners running along either side of the runway enabled fuel to be lit in jets, providing a wall of flame to disperse fog. The closest FIDO-equipped airfield to Bourn was at RAF Graveley, six miles to the north-west, but landing there was still immensely difficult. Even with jets of flame illuminating the runway, the airfield was hard to find.

With fuel becoming critical, the controllers at Bourn called in the Lancasters of 97 Squadron one at a time from their holding positions. Descending through the thick mist, the pilots were desperate to glimpse the runway flare path. The pinging of the SBA tones in their ears told them they should be very close. However, a fleeting vision of the runway lights to one side of them told them they had missed and, powering up the Merlins, they pulled back on the yoke. Gradually, amid the chaos of missed approaches, false hopes and sheer terror, aircraft began to land. The first crash on the airfield boundary at Bourn shocked everyone. Through the fog, the burning wreck served as a terrible beacon.

Flight Lieutenant Charles Owen in JB-671 had reached the end of his patience. His instruments were failing, fuel was low and he was not prepared to hold any longer. The deceptively matter-of-fact account he entered in his diary hardly begins to capture the tension and anxiety that must have attended his landing:

> Trip was generally quieter than usual. 10/10 cloud over the target and rather less flak than usual. W/T and 'Y' and 'G' packed up on the way home, so homed across the North Sea on D/F Loop, which luckily was not jammed. Homed onto the Base on SBA beam, breaking cloud at 250 feet to find fog, rain and visibility about 300 yards and deteriorating. R/T then packed up, so after circling for 10 minutes at 200ft landed without permission in appalling conditions.

An account of the landing by Tom Leake, the Owen crew bomb aimer, in an interview recorded in his later years, provides a little more in the way of colour:

> So, he [Owen] said, 'Well, look, lads, I'm going to land'. The navigator [Bill Shires] got very concerned and said, 'If you land without permission, this could be a Court-Martial.' 'Yes, and if we don't try to land it could be a coffin for us.' So the navigator called out again, he said, 'But the runway's not clear, there's an aircraft still on the runway.' 'Oh well,' Charles Owen said, 'we'll have to take that chance.' Meanwhile, all the other aircraft were circling around and he came down low and we could just see 1 or 2 of the perimeter lights at a time, but it was very difficult to see much. He came in and the flight engineer helped him to try and pick out the flare path, and we landed

with a terrific bump and shot up in the air, but it was the best landing we ever made.

Eight Lancasters landed at Bourn despite the difficult conditions, but a further five ran out of fuel and crashed in the vicinity of Bourn, Graveley and Gransden. Although pilots struggled to make out the runways, the fires from crashed aircraft were clearly and unnervingly visible. Twenty-eight men were killed that night, and a further seven injured – all of them experienced men who formed the backbone of the squadron. Two crews led by pilots Smith and Mooney diverted further north, but still failed to find an airfield to take them. They resorted to their parachutes and landed safely, their aircraft crashing near Ely and Wyton. Together with one aircraft missing in action, the squadron had lost eight Lancasters: nearly half of their operational strength and their single largest loss of their war.

It was perhaps the losses of 97 Squadron on Black Thursday that led to the Comans crew being assigned to the squadron two weeks later, on 2 January 1944. They, too, had flown the Berlin mission on the fateful night of 16/17 December with 9 Squadron from RAF Bardney, but Ken Cook's logbook gives no inkling of the drama of the thick fog. His entry in red ink simply states 'Berlin' and records the flying time as '7.30'. Nevertheless, the conditions at Bardney were poor. Another crew who were part of 9 Squadron, under pilot Bob Lasham, became lost on what was only their fourth mission. With little hope of finding their way back to Bardney, they put out a 'Darky' distress call using a specific radio frequency. They were directed to RAF Donna Nook, a small grass-strip airfield close to the coast near Cleethorpes. A searchlight was turned on to guide them in, and, despite it not being a bomber base, they landed safely. Their friendly reception at Donna Nook included the following amusing conversation.

'How often have you had to divert to a different airfield?' a member of the Donna Nook ground staff asked Bob Lasham.

'Four,' he replied.

'How many Ops have you done so far?'

'Four,' admitted Bob sheepishly.

The disaster that unfolded throughout the east of England on Black Thursday was a stark reminder of the dangers facing bomber crews. There were those who judged the fog over England to have been more deadly than the flak fired by their German enemies. In total, twenty-five Lancasters were lost in the Berlin operation, but a further thirty-one aircraft crashed owing to the fog. In all, 327 men were killed and seventy aircraft lost in Bomber Command operations that day. Proportionately, 97 Squadron had suffered the worst.

Tom Leake, interviewed in the 1980s, described the briefing the next day at Bourn.

> We lost crew we knew personally, it was very upsetting, and there was a great deal of indignation in the Squadron. Next day they assembled us all together and the Commanding Officer (acting C/O, Squadron Leader Dunnicliffe) came in with a very serious face and did a lot of straight talking. He said, 'Well, men, I know how you are feeling about the events that happened and you've lost colleagues, and it was very unfortunate that the weather changed as it did and brought such tragedy'. He said, 'No doubt you feel indignant about it, you feel like going out and talking about it', but he warned us that that was the very thing the enemy would want to know, the tragedy that had happened. We were told that it was a very serious matter and that if anyone spoke about this to the public, they were liable to a Court-Martial. It took some time to get over this, such a great loss and a great upset, but life on the Squadron had to go on of course, and 4 days later we set off on another trip.

The ramifications of the loss were not limited to the bases affected. Churchill sent a note to Harris urging future caution: 'I am not pressing you to fight the weather as well as the Germans, never forget that.'

The Comans crew arrived at Bourn two weeks later, to find a squadron still in deep mourning for the losses of Black Thursday.

6.

Berlin

ong before dawn revealed the Lancasters parked out on their dispersals, the ground crews trudged along the darkened, narrow paths between huts at RAF Bourn. Lines of bomb trolleys were being assembled, before starting their snaking journey to the dump pulled by Fordson tractors. The drone of lorries joined in as bowsers drove across the airfield, each with a painted sign above the windscreen. 'Popeye' and 'Big Ben' were

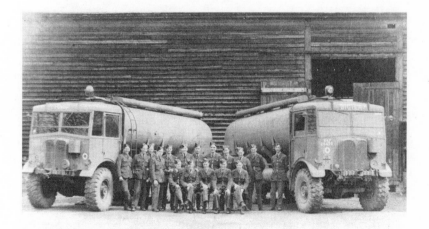

The refuelling lorries 'Popeye' and 'Big Ben' outside the old barn of Grange Farm at RAF Bourn.

on the move and would soon begin taking on the 150-octane petrol at Bourn's fuel farm. Each Lancaster could carry 2,154 gallons and fuelling 97 Squadron's twenty aircraft for tonight's raid would take well into mid-afternoon. In the hangar, fitters manhandled metal inspection platforms, the sounds echoing off corrugated sheet walls. Groaning on its runners, the huge door was pushed open to reveal Lancaster 'P-Papa'. Two days before she had returned from Berlin with a port outer engine fire and badly holed airframe. The engine had been removed, exposing internal fire damage and distorted panels across her wing. An acrid smell lingered in the hangar.

It was 1 January 1944, but RAF Bourn's New Year celebrations had been muted. There'd been a few raised glasses but no wild dances requiring clandestine returns to base. It wasn't a day to sport a thick head, particularly if you were an armourer, and as they were transported to the bomb dump in the freezing cold, memories of early summer mornings riding the trolleys seemed distant. Bourn's dump was a series of crude, earth-banked enclosures with rows of bombs stacked four high like giant sausages. They required careful preparation and, as the light improved, small cranes lifted them onto cradles. Where necessary they were guided down by hand. The metal was freezing to the touch and men needed to keep their hands warm to unshackle them. The loaded trolleys were then pushed into nearby Nissen huts for armourers to fit the bombs with rear fins and arm them.

Bomb technology had become more sophisticated as the war progressed. The Germans had led the way, introducing delayed action bombs in 1940. Their ZUS-40 anti-handling mechanism sat under a conventional fuse. Together with a 'tremble' sensor, which triggered if the bomb was moved, these devices had already killed 580 bomb disposal men, mostly Royal Engineers. Seeing how fiendishly effective such delayed action bombs were, both Britain and the USA developed their own versions. Although the bombs they created contained no electronic parts, they could be programmed by mechanical triggers to suit a variety of purposes. A delay of 0.5 seconds enabled a bomb to penetrate a building before exploding; instantaneous fuses inflicted more collateral damage. Others were timed to cause death, injury and disruption, with delays varying from fifteen minutes to 144 hours. In theory, bombs were relatively safe until they were dropped; they were activated by pulling out safety pins attached to fixed cables. Some were instant-detonation devices, which exploded via a nose percussion cap; others were armed via fans on the tail or nose. Despite the fail-safes, accidents happened. Later in 1944 ten armourers from 207 Squadron would be killed at RAF Spilsby when a fused 1,000lb delayed action bomb exploded. The Station Record Book recorded: 'It was nothing short of a miracle that the entire personnel working in the bomb dump at the time were not all killed as they were nearly all within a twenty-yard radius of the scene of the incident.'

That the RAF's largest bombs were still stored out in the open bears testament to how ill-prepared Britain had been for war. The resources available to build underground bomb stores on airfields were sparse, since the Air Ministry was under constant pressure to provide deep facilities at main bomb depots. In 1936 it had estimated that it required storage for 98,000 tons of bombs. The Ministry's initial pre-war order was for only 48,000 tons of bombs, which meagre stock was rapidly exhausted after war broke out. By October 1941, depot facilities for 632,000 tons were required. However, whether the bombs lay in open airfield bunkers or in deep repositories, human error was always the greatest danger. The largest explosion ever to occur in Britain occurred at RAF Fauld in Staffordshire on 27 November 1944, when 4,000 tons of bombs exploded in the deep repository, killing seventy workers and creating an immense crater. Investigations suggested an Italian prisoner of war had tried to remove a detonator with a brass hammer instead of the prescribed block of wood, but a definitive conclusion could not be reached owing to little evidence at the point of explosion.

Though early morning shifts provided the impetus for a new day, Bourn was operational at all hours. Orders for that night's target were typically received by 07.00. Security around the information was always tight, but it was necessary the squadron be fuelled and bombed in readiness. As soon as a target was known the process of preparing maps and charts for crew briefing began. Gathered under conical steel lights, the meteorologists spread their charts over broad trestle tables. Saturday 1 January 1944 was forecast to be frost-free and cloudy with strong winds. Ideal take-off time would be late afternoon, but a weather front was pushing across southern England, threatening rain. A meteorologist's job was purely to advise crews about the weather. All operational decisions were made further up the command chain.

In the armoury the 160 Browning .303 machine guns required for tonight's operation were being checked, the clicking of bolts and trigger mechanisms signalling final inspection. Guns sitting in the 'serviceable' racks had undergone a thorough process of scrutiny. In cases of prolonged action, barrels could bend and in some cases rupture. Though the recommended fire rate was a few seconds per burst, with enemy aircraft bearing down longer bursts were inevitable. Once they had been approved, the Brownings and their boxes of .303 ammunition belts were then carefully loaded onto Bedford lorries.

Across the road from the main airfield a team of WAAFs were checking parachutes, minutely examining the stitching and cords. Given the number of aircraft that sustained damage from enemy fire or were afflicted by mechanical failure during their missions, there was a strong likelihood that some would be used. Perhaps it was as well the WAAFs did not know just how heavily the odds were stacked against the bomber crews. That month alone 97 Squadron would lose eleven Lancasters, and of their crew only seven men would succeed in parachuting into captivity. Every WAAF took extreme pride in the job: 'I saw every parachute as a person,' one of them recalls. The largest parachute packing centre was at Ringway in Cheshire (now Manchester Airport), which supported the parachute training establishment at nearby Tatton Park. Here WAAFs packed a total of 497,000 parachutes throughout the duration of the war. Remarkable to relate, only one parachuting fatality would be attributed to human error on the part of these packers. The airmen found it comforting that their chutes were prepared by women. WAAFs were more empathetic than their male counterparts. If an airman wished to exchange a parachute – for reasons of instinct or superstition – a WAAF would undertake to do so without question.

1/2 January 1944, Berlin

Awaiting their first operation as Pathfinders, Flying Officer Jim Comans and his crew were newcomers to 97 Squadron. Since arriving at Bourn they had flown navigational exercises and completed ten hours of additional training. They were expecting to fly that day and at 9.30 a.m. checked their names on the crew list noticeboard. The seven airmen looked smart – hair combed, everything in place. It wouldn't do to appear slapdash on a new posting, even if the older hands looked a bit frayed around the edges.

There was little to occupy them before the midday briefing. Comans' men hadn't yet established a rapport with other crews. On a Second World War airbase, friendships established with one's fellow airmen were inevitably clouded by uncertainty over how long they would last. Officers and non-commissioned men socialized in the Crew Room and in warm weather chairs were pulled outside so that they could relax in the sun. These were young men struggling to create a veneer of normality under the most abnormal and stressful of conditions. The Comans crew may have been new to Bourn but they were not alone in their desire to fit in. The stream of heavy losses among aircrews on the base, combined with the departure of those fortunate enough to have reached their end-of-tour thirty missions, meant that faces in the squadron were constantly changing. Though few airmen were impolite to new crews, the latter found their peers distinctly guarded in manner. Only if they survived their first five operations did they become accepted squadron regulars.

The hours dragged before the midday briefing. Not knowing what the night's mission would be instilled a kind of listlessness in the crew. Bomb aimer Ken Cook recalls the early part of an operational day was the most trying: 'In my opinion the worst part… was the waiting around. We'd try and do something like take a walk. But the waiting was terrible.' Reading or writing letters might occupy part of the morning, but it was easy for a sense of foreboding to descend. Airmen who had already undertaken hazardous missions could be found sitting in a cloud of cigarette smoke wrestling with their thoughts. Others played cards or took exercise. At lunchtime, few had much of an appetite for the food they were served.

In a bomber crew that comprised differing personalities, bonding was essential. The quiet Canadian upper gunner George Widdis and gregarious Scottish tail gunner 'Jock' Bolland had to spend a lot of time together. There was no place here for the individualists of Fighter Command. Though personal space was important, they all watched out for a crew member who was spending too much time alone. 'We were all afraid,' Ken Cook recalls. 'How each man handled fear varied. Some would be loud, others would go quiet, but we knew if someone was struggling.

Waiting for take-off: a Lancaster crew prepares to depart on a raid to Berlin, 1944.

Nobody let us down though.' Rear gunner Gordon Cottrill of 35 Squadron vividly depicted the internal struggle:

> My overwhelming memory is of the fear and the comradeship of the air crews. When you were flying there was an intense feeling. You were part of a crew and you were afraid, but you could never show it and you should never let each other down. If you did you were branded LMF (lack of moral fibre) and you were straight off station, your stripes were gone and you were put on menial duties.

By mid-morning the Lancasters were running up, filling the airfield with a deep melodious hum. With the whine of the starter, propellers would begin turning – a notchy, uneven movement – until the cylinders fired, followed by pops and bangs and fumes from the exhaust stubs. Within seconds the props were spinning, the engines settling into the familiar roar of Rolls-Royce Merlins. Ground engineers had ensured that the brakes were on, chocks firmly in place. Every part of a bomber was checked over by the ground crews. Chief engineers – 'Chiefies'– oversaw all operations and they knew their Lancasters inside out. Though airmen flew the missions, the ground crew felt that the aircraft was their possession.

Before lunch the Comans crew had managed to fit in a fifteen-minute navigation exercise flight in Lancaster JB300 D-Delta. She wouldn't be on operations that night and the men relieved some of their tension in the short flight. Word then came through that due to a poor weather forecast the day's briefing would be delayed until 4 p.m. The mission would have a late take-off or, possibly, even be postponed.

*

After the hours of inactivity, anxiety and relief swept through the briefing room. The clattering of chairs subsided and all eyes were fixed on an easel supporting a large map covered by a cloth. Small talk ceased as the briefing officer walked to the front and removed it.

Berlin.

Groans and whistles echoed around the room. It was hardly as if the crews expected less, Berlin had been their focus for weeks. And they were Pathfinders, elite volunteers at the forefront of raids. Everyone dreaded being sent on missions to Europe's most heavily defended city, but each man could now begin plotting his survival. Instead of inactivity they were now engaged in preparation. During the briefing, ribbons were pinned showing routes in and out of the target. With hundreds of bombers in the stream, avoiding defences and collisions was vital. Survival depended on force of numbers. Those on the edges stood less chance.

With most of Europe shrouded in low cloud, opportunities for visual navigation would be scarce. Getting lost or drawn off course could result in fuel running out. They would have to rely on the ghostly green images of the H2S radar sets to identify their position close to Berlin. Between navigator Don Bowes and bomb aimer Ken Cook there would be intense pressure to get this right. As a recently arrived crew on squadron, they were to carry a standard bomb load of one 4,000lb 'Cookie' and four 1,000lb bombs. Other crews would indicate the position of the target using the sky marking method, or 'Wanganui', which was used in conditions of minimal visibility and involved dropping parachute flares to highlight the clouds above the target area with a coloured glow.

Many of the airmen gathered at the briefing had fought their way to Berlin only two days before. Long raids required enormous physical stamina and mental resilience. For several, the 30 December raid had been a brush with catastrophe. Aircraft had been badly holed by heavy flak and suffered a series of failures. The Wilson crew experienced a bomb failing to drop, a 'hang-up' in the bay. Hanging bombs could dislodge on landing

The Lancaster's ground-scanning H2S radar set – situated immediately behind the cockpit – helped Don Bowes and Ken Cook locate their targets on the foulest of winter nights.

and blow up the aircraft. In this instance a bomb had dropped off the rack on the return leg over France. Bombs couldn't be left to roll around inside the aircraft, and Wilson rapidly opened the bomb bay doors. To the crew's immense relief, the offending bomb fell away. But it was the Roberts crew who had the closest call of any members of 97 Squadron on this mission, losing their starboard wingtip in a collision with another Lancaster 20,000 feet over the target.

Four hundred and twenty-one bombers were amassing for the raid. Bomber Command's preferred approach to Berlin hooked over the North Sea and the base of Denmark before swinging south-east, but tonight they would have to take the more direct course over Holland. It wasn't an option the crews would have chosen but, objectively, there was no easy route to the Reich's capital. The return leg would also take them over mainland Europe. Exposed to night fighters and flak concentrations, it would be a long haul back across Germany and the Low Countries.

97 Squadron was but a small cog in the larger war strategy. The offensive against Berlin had started six weeks earlier. Air Marshal 'Bomber' Harris believed in the concept of the 'knock-out blow', a series of raids so devastating it would force the Nazis to the negotiating table. Speaking in 1942 he had declared: 'There are a lot of people who say that bombing cannot win the war. My reply to that is that it has never been tried... and we shall see.' The invasion of Europe was still months away and Harris believed he could force Germany into capitulation through bombing. Importantly, he had the backing of Winston Churchill and the War Cabinet. The scale of the bombing offensive was increasing dramatically: 226,500 tons of bombs had been dropped on Europe by Allied forces in 1943; 1944 would see 1,188,000 tons delivered, over half the total number used in the war.

Occupied Europe witnessed a constant flow of bombing

operations. The daylight skies were streaked by the vapour trails of the USAAF heading towards Germany, while the nights reverberated to the sound of RAF heavy bombers. Those living in cities heard the flak batteries and, high above, the stuttering of cannon and machine guns. Those willing to break curfew often saw the meteor trails of bombers in their death dives. The morning after a raid, local police would visit farmers to inform them that wreckage had fallen on their land. Sometimes large parts of an aeroplane were found, crumpled beyond recognition. It was common to find bodies scattered among the crops or on roads, even embedded in roofs. Those living in rural areas heard of downed airmen knocking on doors in the small hours. The shock led some to slam doors while others risked their lives to offer shelter.

In Germany there was no hiding the onslaught of Allied bombers. With Berlin living under a near-constant pall of smoke, even Nazi propaganda had been forced to admit the effects of the bombing. Reich Minister Joseph Goebbels' New Year's Eve radio broadcast offered a familiar message:

Suffering brought strength… what worked for the enemy
in the First World War will fail him in the Second World
War. There is no point in even speaking about it. Our people
survived so brilliantly the test of enemy air terror during the
year 1943 that the enemy can bury the hopes he had for it.
The nights of bombing have indeed made us poorer, but also
harder. The misery of air terror is to some degree the mortar
that holds us together as a nation in the midst of all dangers.
Our people have not fallen apart during the nightly fire storms
as our enemies hoped and wished, but rather has become a
firm and unshakable community.

This tawdry script had served the Nazis well. Betrayed by weak leaders in the First War, a humiliated Germany had risen again and remained unbowed on its path to victory. When the Wehrmacht swept through Western Europe in the heady days of 1940, Hitler could do no wrong. But now, with the Soviets advancing on the Eastern Front, and the Wehrmacht fighting desperately to stem Anglo-American gains in southern Italy, and the remorseless daily bombing of German cities, the mood was changing.

However, despite the intensity of the bombing campaign, Harris's longed-for collapse of the Nazi state had failed to materialize. Writing in 2002, the German historian Jörg Friedrich argued that the raids 'didn't provoke anything more insurrectionary than the craving for a bowl of hot soup... there was an overriding need for sleep and absolutely no desire to overthrow Hitler'. The journalist Ursula von Kardorff (who would later be at the margins of the July 1944 plot to assassinate Hitler) was more forthright. Her diary entry for New Year's Day 1944 is unambiguous:

> 1943. The worst year of my life. Jürgen's death, the raids,
> people rendered homeless by bombing, so that the Germans
> now wander around as homeless as the Jews, loaded down with
> the same kinds of sacks and bundles. At least it relieves one
> of some of one's guilt, and that is a comfort. 'This must be a
> better year'. I write that down again in my diary as a motto.
> If only the war could end this year and we could be freed from
> that monster Hitler I should never ask for another thing for
> the rest of my life.

In the late evening at Bourn, the crews, weighed down by kit, clambered onto buses taking them to their dispersals. They had spent the last few hours studying maps, calculating bomb and fuel loads, picking their parachutes and donning flying clothing. To combat the intense cold, airmen relied on multiple layers of underclothing beneath the standard RAF uniform. In the cramped conditions of the tail turret, the gunners wore Irvin leather sheepskin-lined jackets and trousers. Everyone wore fur-lined boots and carried yellow Mae West inflatable life jackets. Those who parachuted to safety over enemy territory faced the problem of making their clothing practical for escaping. One solution was the introduction in 1943 of 'escape boots', whose fur-lined uppers could be removed with a knife to render them less conspicuous. Few evaded capture in the clothes they bailed out in. Successful escapees were far more likely to have been hidden by the resistance before being reclothed and given false identities.

Bourn's taxiways and dispersals were ground-lit. Though this made the station vulnerable to Luftwaffe raiders, the risk of aircraft colliding in the dark was deemed greater. Lancaster JB353's internal lights were on as the seven airmen were greeted at the dispersal by their ground crew. Comans signed 'Form 700', which recorded the bomber's serviceability and fuel load. As they climbed the short ladder into the plane, the crew were greeted by the familiar musty smell – a mixture of oil, metal and damp canvas. The main door lay at the rear so, apart from the tail and mid-upper gunners, airmen had to clamber over the wing spar, which passed through the fuselage. Before the crew commenced the pre-flight checks there were rituals to perform. Some boarded as quickly as possible, others adhered to superstitions like walking around the aircraft, patting the panels or urinating against a wheel. Survival was a matter of luck, not character. Good people died with the same frequency as those who were considered less so. Ken Cook recalls that everyone had a lucky charm or tradition. He always carried a wallet with money inside it, giving him a feeling of preparedness. For others their mascots were essential. A crew from 106 Squadron carried a stuffed animal toy named 'Mr Fox', complete with red coat and jodhpurs, who accompanied them on all thirty-six missions, each successful operation being carefully recorded in ink on Mr Fox's leg. 'Lucky scarves' were common, some airmen even checking each other's to ensure that they were worn exactly as on previous missions. Anxiety levels generally subsided once everyone had boarded the aircraft.

One airman flying with Jim Comans that night wasn't part of the regular crew. Flight Sergeant Terry Smith had joined as flight engineer in place of Ken Randle, who was on leave after his wedding. Smith normally flew with the Wilson crew, who had experienced the bomb hang-up two days before. It wasn't uncommon for personnel to stand in for different crews (the replacement was referred to as the 'spare bod'). But in the case of Smith, the tragic coincidences of war link him forever with Lancaster JB353. Twenty-eight days later, on a raid to Berlin in this same aircraft, the Wilson crew – including Smith – went missing. The fate of their final flight remains a mystery. Most probably they were lost over the sea, though the gruesome possibility that aircraft and crew were obliterated in a mid-air explosion cannot be ruled out. Their names are recorded on the Runnymede Memorial at Englefield Green in Surrey, commemorating the 20,286 British and Commonwealth airmen who have no known grave.

Settling into the cockpit, Comans scanned his surroundings. There were few comforts in Lancaster seats, the base of which resembled a broad-rimmed metal tray. The back was padded and there were pull-down leather armrests, but they were a far cry from the generously sprung seats of American DC-3s. Comans' parachute was integrated into his harness and seat cushion – he was the only crew member who was actually attached to his means of escape from the aircraft. Some pilots preferred the clip-on chest parachutes used by other crew members, but in an emergency these had to be retrieved from the nearby stowage point and attached to the front of their harness. In the event of the aircraft going into an uncontrolled dive or spin, the inability of crew members to move – strapped as they were in their seats – accounted for high casualty rates in stricken Lancasters. Unable to reach their parachute through the flames, some airmen flung themselves out of the aircraft, considering it better to fall than to burn. The sight of falling men traumatized those who witnessed it.

Beside Comans on the flip-down seat, Smith read out the list of pre-flight checks:

- Adjust rudder pedals to suit length of leg and ensure pedals are adjusted evenly.
- Test that full rudder to port and starboard can be applied from normal sitting position without extending legs fully.
- Test all controls for full movement and put automatic pilot 'IN'.

There were fourteen instructions in all, each followed by an action and Comans' response of 'Check'.

The Lancaster's instrument panels were bathed in a soft orange glow from small lights, the black dials featuring luminous numbers and lines. In the small, convex Perspex nose below the cockpit, bomb aimer Ken Cook was checking a rectangular box set in a tubular frame. The Lancaster Mark XIV A bomb sight computer calculated variables of height and speed during bomb runs. When Cook had finished, he checked the front turret, which he would occupy in an emergency, before taking up his position behind the pilot on the enlarged navigator's desk.

Flying Officer Don Bowes had his maps spread out on a desk behind the pilot with guidance instruments to the front. The use of radio signal devices like Gee-H* could keep them on track but it was important not to neglect the practice of skilled calculation. A degree off course would put them many miles from a turn point or target. An additional navigational aid, the H2S ground-scanning radar set, which consisted of a row of knobs and a small round screen, had recently been fitted to the Lancaster.

---

* Introduced in October 1943 as an upgrade of the original 'Gee' system.

Flight Sergeant Roy Woollford was positioned further back, but still close to the cockpit in the wireless operator's position. The radio sets were mounted against a forward-facing bulkhead and Woollford sat at a small table with a Morse key attached. Although radio was important, Morse played an integral part in RAF communications, messages being kept to a strict minimum. An Aldis lamp, kept close to the wireless operator's position, was frequently used to communicate with other aircraft and shipping. Woollford's position was the most 'buried' in the fuselage. Earlier Lancaster models incorporated a small window at the wireless station but these were soon painted over and, on later Lancaster models, dispensed with altogether. Unlike some crew members, who had to remain at their stations throughout the flight, Woollford was required to carry out a number of tasks, some of which took him away from his table. One of these was to dump 'Window' – bundles of foil chaff – through a chute to confuse German radar.

Flight Sergeant George Widdis climbed into the Nash & Thompson-designed* mid-turret position, his upper body in the domed Perspex structure that housed the two Browning .303 machine guns, his legs protruding into the fuselage. From here he could survey the Lancaster's upper surfaces and the night sky. In his mini-observatory Widdis would be constantly looking out for any untoward movement in the darkness, having to decide in a split second whether it was another bomber straying too close or a German fighter.

Flight Sergeant 'Jock' Bolland made his way to the tail turret, accessible through two small sliding doors. It was a tight squeeze and there was no question of wearing a parachute, which was

---

* Nash & Thompson was an engineering firm, founded in 1929 by Archibald Frazer-Nash and Esmonde Grattan Thompson, which designed hydraulically operated gun turrets for aircraft.

clipped up inside the turret. Holding on to the handrails above his head, Bolland swung into the turret, coming to rest on the small bench seat. The doors had a robust catch – earlier versions had had a tendency to open unexpectedly, causing gunners to fall back into the fuselage. Despite this, some gunners propped the doors to stop them closing completely, their fear of the doors jamming and trapping them easily outweighing the inconvenience of a backwards tumble into the body of the aircraft. The 'tail-end Charlie' occupied the Lancaster's loneliest position; once the doors closed he would be separated from the crew. Running through his drill, Bolland switched on the gunsight, unlocked the turret by pulling up a knob and tested the power controls. In front of him were four Browning guns and ammunition feeds, which now needed priming. Using a wire with a loop on the end, he pulled the first round of the belt into the breeches and shut the covers. Using another wire tool, the bolts were pulled back and the Brownings cocked. Bolland was careful to ensure the metal slider to his right, which prevented the guns firing on the ground, was set to safety and checked the cranking handle, which could move the turret if power was lost. By revolving the turret to its furthest extent, he would be able to bail out backwards through the doors should he have no other alternative. Fat Bakelite jack-plugs were plugged into sockets and, once Comans had finished his own pre-flight list, he called up crew members on the intercom. As their position was named, each had to respond correctly in a prescribed routine.

'Bomb aimer.'

'Photo leads OK. Camera isolation Switch "ON". Bomb selectors Numbers. OK. Feed Clear, Oxygen Connected. I/C* OK when turret rotated.'

'Navigator.'

* Intercom.

'Instruments and lights OK. "GEE" set "OFF". Oxygen connected.'

'Mid Upper Gunner.'

'Turret elevation and rotations OK. Feed clear. Oxygen connected. Heated clothing OK. I/C OK when turret rotated.'

The crew members silently awaited their turn. Outside they could hear a small generator thudding away on top of a 'Trolley acc', a trailer containing rows of batteries upon which, until the engines started, the Lancaster relied for power. There was no heat in the aircraft and condensation fogged the Perspex. Oxygen system tests were essential before any flight – at high altitude even a short time without it could lead to hypoxia. When airmen moved from their stations, they always carried portable oxygen bottles. There was no internal lining in the fuselage or insulation, the dull green interior paint only broken by black boxes and protruding brackets with equipment attached. The handrails and grips were painted yellow, emergency knobs and release levers red. Looms of unprotected wire passed through the fuselage and the cockpit was a dense tangle of gauges, switches and levers. Apart from a sheet of armour plate on the pilot's seat there was no protection either for crew or equipment. Shards of flak or bullets ripping through the fuselage created lethal storms of splintered metal.

It was 12.10 a.m. and somewhere out in the darkness a first engine barked into life. Starting, taxiing and take-off were carefully choreographed to conserve fuel. More engines joined in the chorus. Comans fired the engines one by one and JB353 vibrated to the whir of twelve Hamilton Standard* propeller blades. The Lancaster wasn't noted for warmth – there were too many spaces where wind came through, particularly around the

---

* An American company that allowed its propellers to be built in the UK under licence by de Havilland.

turret fairings and slits – but the air that now began coursing through the vents was pleasantly musty.

Another Lancaster glided past their nose and Comans slid open the pilot's cockpit panel to signal 'chocks away'. The ground crew on either side grabbed ropes attached to the triangular ply boxes and pulled them clear of the wheels. A torch flash signalled that it was safe to move forward. The four throttle levers were grouped together, allowing the pilot to move them gently forward with one hand. The brakes came off and JB353 began to move, engines straining against the weight of the aircraft. With the Lancaster's tail still on the ground, Comans' view over the nose was limited and he used the fairing above the front turret as a centre line, careful to keep the bomber correctly positioned on the centre of the taxiway. If he veered to one side and got the wheels bogged down in the grass, he would delay everyone behind. The first Lancaster had reached the base of the asphalt-topped runway and a green light flashed in the darkness. The aircraft's four Rolls-Royce Merlin engines, now at full power, were singing at high pitch, pulsating in the night air. Squadron Leader Peter de Wesselow took his feet off the toe brakes and ND355 gathered pace. Roaring past the controller's small chequered caravan, he thundered into the darkness. It was 00.18 and the waiting was over. A highly experienced master bomber, de Wesselow would go on to lead the second wave on Dresden on 13 February 1945. The polyglot son of a White Russian surgeon, he had remustered to Bomber Command from the Brigade of Guards. Awarded the DFC only a month before, he went on to get a bar to his DFC and a DSO in 1945. De Wesselow was a man to inspire confidence, precisely what the squadron needed on this long and arduous mission.

The Lancasters took off at two-minute intervals to avoid the effects of 'vortexes' – swirling pockets of air created by departing aircraft – and reduce the likelihood of collision. The Comans crew's turn came twenty minutes after de Wesselow at the half-way point in the dispatch order. With the throttle levers pushed fully forward, engineer Terry Smith placed his hand behind them to ensure they remained fully open. As the take-off roll began, each man tensed. This was one of the danger points in a mission. If the aircraft failed to get airborne a crash was almost inevitable, and few could hope to survive it. The tail lifted, but the Lancaster was still wallowing on its huge Dunlop tyres. Every yard seemed like a mile. Then, just as margins were evaporating, JB353 was airborne. As their speed increased Comans selected the 'wheels up' position and, with a whir and a clank, the undercarriage stowed itself into the engine nacelles.

The Comans crew entered the large bank of cloud just ahead with apprehension. Flying blind, they could easily collide with another bomber. After what seemed an eternity the clouds fell away and night sky and stars appeared. Bolland spun his tail turret from side to side, lowering and raising the Brownings to ensure everything worked. The Lancaster settled into its reassuring hum, but would take time to reach its cruising altitude of 20,000 feet. The inhabitants of East Anglia were disturbed by the boom of climbing bombers. Many learned to sleep through the nightly orchestra, others put the kettle on.

Radio operator Woollford tuned his set to track pre-arranged radio frequencies. Once he had detected them, navigator Bowes moved the loop aerial above his head, enabling him to follow broadcasts. He was able to check his calculated position against them and instruct the pilot if directional changes were neces-sary. The crew set course for their first leg. Clearing the English coastline at Aldeburgh, Comans instructed his gunners to 'test guns'. Three short bursts followed and the smell of cordite filled the Lancaster. Ahead and to either side Comans glimpsed the blue navigation lights of other bombers. This was the safest part of the journey, but halfway across the North Sea all lights were switched off. The immense bomber stream headed towards the coast of German-occupied Europe.

As they approached enemy territory, the broad funnel of aircraft narrowed. At this point there was a real danger of collisions taking place, even though pilots tried to maintain height separations. Comans strained to detect darker shapes around. When JB353 strayed uncomfortably close to the bomber ahead, everyone felt its slipstream. Before landfall it was prudent to empty one's bladder, a far from easy business, particularly for the tail gunner. Cans, bottles and other containers were employed. Performing this while wearing thermals was challenging and exposed the airmen to extreme cold. Located in the rear fuselage, the Elsan toilet was a metal barrel with clips, which, in theory, held the lid down. One airman recalled:

> It doesn't take much imagination to picture what it was like trying to combat fear and airsickness while struggling to remove enough gear in cramped quarters and at the same time trying to use the bloody Elsan. If it wasn't an invention of the devil, it certainly must have been one foisted on us by the enemy. When seated in frigid cold amid the cacophony of roaring engines and whistling air, the occupant had a chance to fully ponder the miserable condition of his life.

Ken Cook remembers: 'There was a time when I needed to use the Elsan and found that I had become frozen to the seat. Comans was calling me on the intercom telling me to get myself back as we were approaching the target. It took some time to get myself free.'

Unlike in the First World War, when a pilot's eyes and skill were crucial, this air conflict was a clash of technology unimaginable twenty-five years before. Even as the crews were in their first minutes of flight the hunt had started. The sea, bastion of Britain's defence for centuries, was no longer impregnable.

Radar enabled the Germans to see over miles of airspace. Though the display of information on the radar screens of the 1940s was rudimentary and required skilled interpretation, the system overall was effective. In the right atmospheric conditions operators in Holland could see right up to the English coast, the telltale blurs and dots of bombers soon becoming visible. On the night of 1/2 January 1944, Luftwaffe operators were staring into their cathode tube screens for signs of an incoming raid. Thus far the screens had been blank. Many times they'd watched raids developing in the early evening but now it was past midnight and their thoughts were turning to ersatz coffee to help them through the small hours.

When it was introduced in 1939, the radar system known as *Freya* had so impressed German command that over a thousand sites would eventually be built. Each *Freya* consisted of a square aerial mounted on a base and was linked to a network of regional command centres. Some *Freyas* remained in fixed positions while others were mobile. By January 1944 *Freya* could be linked to other gun and searchlight radar sites, including the dish-shaped Würzburg gun-laying radar, which had entered service with the Wehrmacht and Luftwaffe in 1940. Controllers scanning the North Sea could see to a range of 120 miles but calculating a raid's altitude was difficult. It was far from easy to ascertain the precise course of a Lancaster bomber that was closing in at 200mph as well as making changes of direction in its flight path.

RAF bombers often turned out to sea to evade German radar but tonight the time for course changes was limited. As the bomber stream formed up, measures were being taken to block *Freya* frequencies. The RAF had developed a radar-jamming device with the codename 'Mandrel', which was mounted in aircraft noses. By deploying nine suitably equipped aircraft to circle fifty miles out at sea, Bomber Command could jam a 200-mile coastal area. Another measure taken by the RAF to counter

German radar was the formation in November 1943 of 100 (Bomber Support) Group. De Havilland Mosquitos were fitted with on-board devices that enabled them to detect radar-equipped German night fighters, with the purpose of shooting them down or disrupting their operations against Allied bombers. In addition, Lancasters from 101 Squadron were tasked to sow confusion by transmitting radio messages on the same frequencies as the German night fighters. They often flew with German speakers on board, issuing fake instructions and reports.

Once German operators had a fix on a raid's direction, night fighters were scrambled and placed into a 'box' in front of the bomber force. The Germans' *Zahme Sau* ('Tame Boar') intercept tactic, devised by the Luftwaffe ace Viktor von Loßberg, grouped night fighters around radio directional masts, ready to infiltrate the bomber stream. On-board radar enabled fighters to hunt individual aircraft. The Allies had been relatively successful in jamming early German radar, but by late 1943 the Luftwaffe had introduced the SN-2 Lichtenstein set, which used a lower frequency. Alongside *Zahme Sau* was *Wilde Sau* ('Wild Boar'), which used smaller fighters, such as the potent Focke-Wulf 190, to identify targets visually. Lurking beneath the bomber stream and using the darkness of the ground as cover, Luftwaffe pilots knew that the bombers had limited downward view and little defence against attacks from below. The most effective version of the Junkers Ju88 had upward-firing guns mounted in the fuselage behind the cockpit, an arrangement known as *Schräge Musik* (literally 'slanted music'). Sneaking in, skilled pilots could position themselves beneath a bomber and gently rise to close the distance. Flares dropped by fighters far above enabled the Fw 190s (which were not equipped with radar) to see the bombers and attack conventionally, and also allowed lurking Ju88s to see their silhouetted quarry. A brief press of the gun button would send 20mm cannon shells into the wing tanks and bomb bay.

Accurate shots could cause a bomber to explode instantly but the resulting shock wave could also take a Ju88 with it.

The Comans crew had passed the point of relative safety in the North Sea. Now their lives would depend on constant wariness. The intercom had been filled with chat, but the pilot reined it in. There were breaks in the cloud cover over the Dutch coast and probing searchlights. Comans swung the Lancaster from side to side, allowing the tail and mid-upper gunners to search for fighters. The crew awaited the announcement that they were crossing the enemy coast and, as they made landfall, anxiety mounted. Ken Cook recalls the tension: 'We knew the Germans could probably see us and were preparing to strike. We were resigned to it; what would be would be, so we chose to just get on with the job and try not to think about it. That's what we were there for.'

JB353 was still an hour away from Berlin to the east, sixty long minutes to evade the fighters and flak. Bolland and Widdis were staring into the void, moving their turrets in the prescribed pattern. A glaring white flare appeared high above, illuminating the cockpit and creating sharp shadows. Everything turned grey. With his night vision impaired, Bolland swore colourfully over the intercom.

Unknown to the Lancaster crews, a feint attack launched by Mosquitos on Hamburg had failed to distract the German defence controllers and, early in the operation, they directed night fighters into the bomber stream. Sixteen aircraft were lost en route to Berlin, of which eight were Pathfinders – 10 per cent of that night's Pathfinder force. Among the stalking night fighters was twenty-seven-year-old Major Heinrich Prinz zu Sayn-Wittgenstein, a former bomber pilot now flying a Ju88. The square-jawed aristocrat was everything the Luftwaffe craved in an air ace. Appointed *Geschwaderkommodore* only that morning, Sayn-Wittgenstein had all the instincts necessary for a successful fighter pilot and top-scoring air ace. He was adept at ensuring that he, rather than another pilot, was in the best position to engage with the incoming bombers. Lauded in propaganda films, Wittgenstein would eventually amass eighty-three aerial victories. It was deeply unfortunate for the Allied raid that it ran into a German pilot of such cold efficiency and implacable sense of purpose.

With his predilection for strategic meddling, Hitler had ordered fighters to concentrate their attacks over the Fatherland. He wanted bombers falling where the population could see them, visible proof that the Luftwaffe was beating the bombing offensive. The Germans were therefore narrowing the front and, though many bombers were shot down, most reached their targets. Conversely, the Luftwaffe's concentrated packs of fighters were more easily identified by the RAF's Beaufighters* and Mosquitos.

They were now less than a hundred miles from Berlin. Relocated to the Perspex nose, Ken Cook faced his busiest time of the night. Working with the navigator and pilot, the trio plotted how they would launch their attack. As Cook entered wind speed into the bombing computer, Bowes examined the green H2S display for ground features. Berlin was too big to miss and the navigator soon detected echoes of the city and land breaks around the Havel lakes, but because of cloud cover there would be little chance to observe the ground. Comans listened intently to the intercom as they made the final bomb run into target, all the while geared for evasive action to avoid fighters. He gripped the control yolk, ready to hurl twenty tons of Avro Lancaster into a wild dive.

The sky ahead was studded with flak. From the bomb-aiming

---

* The Bristol Beaufighter was a multi-role aircraft introduced in July 1940, during the Battle of Britain. It would prove to be a highly effective night fighter.

position Ken Cook saw the glow in the clouds increasing. Other Pathfinders were marking and dropping their bombs. So far the thunder of the Merlins had filled the aircraft but now they could hear and feel deep, percussive rumblings. The reports of flak shells sounded uncomfortably close. It was small comfort to them that their presence in the flak field made them safer from the attentions of German night fighters. The glow from fires and probing searchlights cast an ethereal light on Cook's station in the Perspex nose. Twenty thousand feet below several locations were burning, but he knew that he could not assume these were the correct targets for the bombs he was about to drop. Flak crackled and sparked around, and the pungent smell of explosives filled the Lancaster.

'Bomb doors open.'

Running straight and level, JB353 slowed as buffets of air within the open bomb bay took hold. Watching his airspeed indicator, Comans pushed the throttles a notch forward. Other Pathfinders were dropping their flares, the red and green Wanganuis disappearing beneath the clouds, diffusing light into wide patches. Bowes calmly called out the H2S readings as Cook directed the pilot in order to bring his cross-hairs onto the brightest light.

The bomb aimer pressed the trigger mechanism in his palm.

'Bombs gone.'

JB353 reared up as eight tons of bombs departed on their four-mile descent. In the mid-turret Widdis heard the clank of the bomb bay doors closing and saw the horizon moving under the sweep of wings as the Lancaster began its long starboard bank. As junior Pathfinder members they could now turn for home, while others of greater experience loitered to observe the results of the raid, re-marking the target if necessary. On leaving Berlin's flak fields they could easily be bounced by fighters and Comans kept to a pattern of swinging the aircraft from side to side and allowing downward views. Bomber Command had deemed the manoeuvre unnecessary, but few pilots agreed. Ground experts could make their pronouncements but in the air every pilot relied on instinct.

As the main body of the raid arrived the accuracy of Bomber Command's attack drifted, most bombs dropping on Berlin's southern outskirts or the wooded Grunewald region to the west. For an operation of this size the final tally of twenty-one houses and one industrial facility hit was paltry. Ken Cook attributes the drift not to inaccurate marking but differing wind speeds causing miscalculation at high altitude. In Berlin the casualties amounted to seventy-nine killed, twenty-five of them in a panicked crush at the Neukölln shelter. Owing to the late sounding of sirens, bombs were already falling as Berliners fled the streets.

Gerda Kernchen was a fourteen-year-old machine shop worker who sewed military uniforms. When air raids threatened, she, along with thousands of others, took shelter in one of the city's large concrete bunkers. As the raids became more frequent, Kernchen took to sleeping overnight in them:

> My parents and little sister stayed home. They listened to
> the radio, and when they heard the warning, they made it to
> the bunker just as the first bombs fell. When the final alarm
> sounded, you could already see Christmas trees – the coloured
> flares dropped by the Pathfinders to mark the target. You could
> see the searchlights streaming up from the ground, searching
> for aircraft. The city was surrounded by a ring of white light.
> Outside the bunker, you could hear the bombs whistling as
> they fell through the air, and then the explosions when they
> struck, and then see the fireballs rising. Inside the bunker, we
> could hear the explosions. Once the bunker almost got hit, and
> we felt it move. We knew if there was a direct hit from a big
> bomb, we would all die. The only people inside were women
> and children and old men. During a raid everyone was terrified.
> The mothers were hugging their children, and the children

were hugging their mothers. People were crying and praying aloud.

Twenty thousand feet above there was no escaping the tough-ness of the return leg. Ahead of JB353 lay a dozen or more industrial centres, each with significant flak batteries. Straying close to a major centre such as Cologne could prove fatal. Even provincial towns maintained 88s. Outside of flak belts the biggest risk was from fighters. As Berlin faded into the horizon, they had seen nothing of their bombing but, a few minutes behind them, another 97 Squadron crew piloted by F/O Wheble reported smoke rising to 10,000 feet. Avoiding Cologne, Comans pushed further south, bringing them closer to Aachen and its barrage. Soon they would be over Belgium. Every mile covered saw an improvement in prospects.

At what point flight engineer Smith became concerned about fuel consumption is unclear, but the Lancaster's gauges were dropping faster than normal. Had the fuel tanks been holed? Was there a leak, or were the gauges simply malfunctioning? They had to assume flak damage was causing fuel loss. Comans needed to make a decision – either find a landing somewhere on the south coast of England or carry on to Bourn. They had altitude in their favour and the engines were running well, so a push for home didn't seem reckless. But when the needles became critical how long could they have? Would the engines cut immediately, or might there be a grace period? Comans gave a situation report to the crew. Though little was said, each man checked his parachute.

The Owen crew in JB671 had left Bourn four minutes before Comans and were now enduring significant problems, their flight back marked by the whistling from a fuselage peppered with bullet holes. With a wounded tail gunner, they issued an emergency call and were directed towards RAF Tangmere, east of Chichester. Approaching the runway, they fired two red flares to signify an injured crewman on board. On hitting the asphalt they discovered that a main wheel tyre had been damaged and, with a shower of sparks and grinding of metal, the undercarriage collapsed as Owen wrestled to keep the aircraft in a straight line. When they finally ground to a halt, vehicles rushed towards them and Sergeant Thomas was lifted into an ambulance. It had been a very narrow escape, but the Lancaster was wrecked.

Ahead of the drama unfolding at Tangmere, JB353's fuel problems were now severe. But they were nearly home. Smith had tried pumping fuel from tank to tank but no amount of wishful thinking could summon up enough petrol to keep the Merlins running. The first engine stopped and Comans feathered the propeller, turning the blades to present least resistance. Then a second came to a halt and, in short order, the remaining engines fell silent. The bomber whistled and creaked in the air flow, a heart-stopping moment the airmen never forgot, but it was testament to the Lancaster's design that it could glide so well. Comans held her nose down to keep up speed. Though he could see Bourn's flare path ahead, he decided to land three miles away at RAF Gransden. Radio operator Roy Woollford sent a distress call to control. There was no time left.

Their worst fear was encountering another aircraft on the approach to the runway. There would only be one chance to land successfully, and any evasive action taken would result in a crash. Though Comans had left himself more altitude than normal, every foot was a precious commodity. Finally, the wheels of JB353 touched down and, as Comans pushed the brakes, he was exhilarated to feel the Lancaster slowing. Letting the speed bleed off, he left enough momentum to clear Gransden's runway and coast onto the taxiway. The airmen sat in the silence, their nerves pushed to the edge. They had survived another operation.

Equipment was shut down, safety harnesses unclipped, equipment stowed and Comans made his way rearwards. The crew door lay open and he descended the short ladder into the dawn light. After their eight-hour flight the ground felt unsteady. Cigarettes were lit, tension broken, the veneer of bravado returned. Blinkered lights weaved across the taxiway and a Hillman Tilly* materialized in the gloom. Debriefing, breakfast and sleep awaited them. It was not until later that it was discovered that flight engineer Smith had inadvertently closed the fuel cocks, starving the engines in the final minutes. Whether the unfamiliarity of the crew had made him nervous, or whether an uncharacteristic lapse of attention had caused near disaster is unknown.†

Other Lancasters were returning to Bourn, emerging from the darkness into the soft light of the runway. While some made textbook touchdowns, engines throttled back, hovering above the concrete, other damaged aircraft thudded down. Ground personnel waited at the dispersals for their Lancasters to taxi in, sharing the intense relief of safe returns. The last bomber landed at 07.45 and, as the clock ticked on, it became apparent that three dispersals lay empty. This wasn't yet a matter of grave concern since diversions to other airfields were common. Word came in of the Comans and Owen crews' safe landing but Flying Officer Robert Mooney's Lancaster JA960 was now long overdue. The complete story would not be discovered until after the war but after departure from Bourn nothing had been heard of the Mooney crew and they were posted as missing. It is now known that they reached Berlin but were hit by flak on the return leg near

---

* 'Tillies' (the name comes from 'utility' vehicle) were produced during the Second World War and based on existing car designs. The Ministry of Supply asked Austin, Morris, Standard and Hillman to produce military utility versions of their medium-sized saloon cars. The Hillman Tilly was based on the Hillman Minx.

† Mistakes made by aircrew were commonplace and would rarely lead to formal disciplinary proceedings. The pilot would often admonish the crewman involved if the mistake was of a serious nature, but not refer it higher.

Aachen, crashing into a hill near the village of Neu-Moresnet close to the German–Belgian border. The crash site's proximity to Aachen suggests that descent was very rapid with no controlled flight. Mooney and his crew were buried six days later in Aachen and after the war were reinterred in the Commonwealth War Graves Commission cemetery at Rheinberg, north of Cologne, along with other British and Commonwealth airmen who died on bombing missions to Germany. They are also commemorated by a small, neatly kept memorial in Neu-Moresnet.

Six of the bombers lost on 1/2 January 1944 were shot down by Sayn-Wittgenstein. But the battle had not been completely one-sided. The Luftwaffe lost six planes, with seven crew killed and four wounded. Though the figure appears insignificant by the grim standards of 1944, every loss of an experienced man counted. Twenty days later Sayn-Wittgenstein would himself die, shot down by a Mosquito near Berlin. He was posthumously awarded the Knight's Cross of the Iron Cross with Oak Leaves and Swords, one of Nazi Germany's highest military awards.

Such was the pace of Bomber Command's offensive that the mission of 1/2 January 1944 is barely a footnote in the wider ongoing onslaught on Germany. Other than maintaining pressure on Berlin, it had achieved little. Another similar operation would be mounted later that day, with many crews who had flown the previous night returning to the German capital.

Thirty-one aircraft, 7 per cent of that night's bomber force, had been lost, but they would soon be replaced. The delivery of new Lancasters was now averaging sixty per week. With Handley Page producing similar numbers of Halifaxes there was no shortage of available aircraft, or of freshly trained crews. The deaths of 183 RAF airmen in the raid of 1/2 January inflicted enormous suffering on their families, but Bomber Command considered the losses acceptable. A further thirty-three airmen would spend the rest of the war as POWs, with only one evading capture.

At RAF Bourn the pressing demand to have aeroplanes and crews available for future missions left little time to consider the dead. Empty spaces in the squadron were filled within days. Life – and the bombing war – went on.

7.

Pathfinders

30 August 1932, Munich

In the late summer of the year 1932, Winston Churchill and his party were just finishing dinner in the opulent dining room of the Grand Continental Hotel in Munich. But on this evening their attention was not drawn to the high ornate plaster ceilings and tall, arched windows. They were engaged in a detailed discussion of German politics, which were in deep crisis. Hitler's Nazi Party had made significant gains in elections the previous month and was now the largest single party in the Reichstag. The hopelessly fragmented opposition to Hitler – in the form of Communists and Social Democrats – would facilitate the Führer's accession to power the following year. Churchill had been touring Europe to research his biography of his ancestor the Duke of Marlborough, accompanied by his wife, Clementine, his twenty-one-year-old son, Randolph, and seventeen-year-old daughter Sarah. At Churchill's elbow was his closest associate, Frederick Lindemann, a German-born scientist who had moved to the United Kingdom as a young child. An eminent scientist and keen tennis player, Lindemann joined the Royal Aircraft Establishment in 1915 and learned to fly, an activity Clementine had persuaded her husband to abandon, much to Winston's chagrin. He liked Lindemann immensely and admired his scientific knowledge, delivered in a precise and clipped German accent.

Joining them at the table was Ernst 'Putzi' Hanfstaengl,* Hitler's foreign press secretary. Like Churchill, he had an American mother and had lived in the USA for more than a decade, attending Harvard and working for the US arm of his father's art publishing business. Returning to Germany in the 1920s, Hanfstaengl became close to Hitler and introduced the Führer to members of Munich's high society. He had landed in the Bavarian city earlier in the day in the company of Hitler and received a message from Randolph Churchill asking if they would join them for dinner. Hitler was dismissive. 'What on earth would I talk to him about?' he said to Hanfstaengl. Churchill had resigned from the shadow cabinet a year earlier. He held no position of authority and was in the period of his political career often referred to as the 'wilderness years'. Hitler had plenty of opportunities to meet fading European politicians. Churchill did not interest him.

Hanfstaengl came alone to dinner but left the table before coffee and found Hitler outside his apartment finishing a conversation with a Dutchman. 'Do you realise the Churchills are in the restaurant?' he asked him. Would he join them for coffee? Dressed in a dirty white raincoat, Hitler replied he had not shaved and had too much to do. Hitler and Churchill thus never met, although historians have long dreamed of what might

---

* Ernst 'Putzi' Hanfstaengl was to fall out of favour with Hitler after disputes with propaganda minister Joseph Goebbels. He fled Germany in 1937 to Britain but was imprisoned when war broke out. Subsequently transferred to a camp in Canada, he was handed over to the Americans in 1942 to work on President Roosevelt's 'S-Project', revealing information on approximately four hundred Nazi leaders. He was returned to Britain after the war and repatriated to Germany.

have been. Arguably, it was Frederick Lindemann whom Hitler needed to impress more than Churchill. During his tour of 1932, Churchill himself gained a clear view of Germany's rearmament, but Lindemann, with his deep knowledge of German culture, was able to provide him with insights into the current state of the country, and the threat of National Socialism in particular. Both men hated Nazism, Lindemann perhaps even more than Churchill. He would later turn his technically accomplished mind to the absolute destruction of the Nazis, and became convinced that the most extreme actions against Germany might well be necessary.

In the 1930s and throughout the war, Lindemann (Baron Cherwell from July 1941) would often be found in Churchill's company. When Churchill became prime minister in May 1940, he made Lindemann the government's chief scientific adviser, with a seat in cabinet. His self-assurance and abrupt manner upset many civil servants, but Lindemann's abilities transcended his unwillingness to engage in social niceties. In 1939 he had set up a group of academic economists known as S Branch, which would provide the wartime government with accurate statistics and supply Churchill with essential information on matters as diverse as military capability and food stocks. In 1941 Lindemann turned his attention to the bombing war.

When concerns were raised in Parliament about the accuracy of the bombs dropped by the RAF, Churchill asked Lindemann to look into the matter. The work he carried out would change Britain's bombing strategy and hasten the creation of the Pathfinders. Turning his finely tuned statistical mind to Bomber Command, Lindemann determined to obtain an accurate picture, not through observation reports, but by scientific research. With many bombers fitted with cameras, it was possible to audit targets. Analysis of 633 photographs taken in June and July 1941 revealed that fewer than two out of five bombers were getting

Left to right: Frederick Lindemann (Lord Cherwell), Air Chief Marshal Sir Charles Portal, Admiral of the Fleet Sir Dudley Pound and Winston Churchill attend a display of anti-aircraft gunnery, June 1941. Lindemann was an enthusiastic proponent of the carpet-bombing of German cities.

to within five miles of the target. Moonlit nights produced the best results, but even under these conditions only 45 per cent of bombs were landing near the target. On dark, moonless nights results dipped as low as 6 per cent. The full report issued in August 1941 by David Bensusan-Butt, a cabinet civil servant and private secretary to Lindemann, sent shock waves through Westminster. The conclusions were contested by some senior Royal Air Force officers, including Chief of the Air Staff Charles Portal, who believed the sample of June and July 1941 to be too narrow. However, even allowing for some margin of error, there was no contesting the fact that the quality of RAF bombing had been revealed to be inadequate.

Churchill called for urgent action and the response created two converging paths. Firstly, the introduction of more accurate bombing aids became a priority and an intensive debate began as to how such aids could be best used. Secondly, it was decided that bombing strategy should be widened. If the RAF could not hit the targets they were being given, it was time to give them something they could hit. In a memorandum to Churchill on 30 March 1942, Lindemann proposed that the way to cripple German industry was to 'de-house' its workers by carpet-bombing industrial towns and cities. This strategy was different from the 'knockout blow' theory propounded by newly appointed Air Marshal Harris, although in practice was the same in terms of bombing technique. Churchill's thinking moved strongly in favour of a new area bombing strategy.

Lindemann maintained that civilians would emerge from air raid shelters to find not only their factories flattened, but their homes, too. This would tie the German authorities into diverting precious resources into housing and feeding civilians. That civilians would die in the raids was not a primary objective, but in Lindemann's mind, in order to bring about the defeat of the Nazis, no price was too high.

It took six months for the conclusions of the Butt Report to be fully digested. On 14 February 1942 General Directive No. 5 was issued by the Air Ministry, which changed the focus from attacks on French industrial targets to area bombing of Germany. The directive's stated aim was: 'To focus attacks on the morale of the enemy civil population and in particular the industrial workers. In the case of Berlin harassing attacks to maintain fear of raids and to impose A. R. P. measures.'

*

In 1941 one of Britain's most urgent needs was for a better bomb sight. Since the outbreak of war, the RAF had been keen to acquire the American Norden bomb sight, which promised considerably enhanced levels of accuracy. Churchill pressed the Americans but encountered significant resistance on their part to the idea of sharing their 'wonder weapon'. Until the Japanese swept out of the December sky over Pearl Harbor, US foreign policy was in a state of profound ambivalence. At the same time as supplying Britain with ships and aircraft, and even training its airmen, it tiptoed around the matter of Nazi Germany and its expansionist policies, seemingly anxious to avoid war at all costs, yet by its actions the USA was clearly supporting Germany's enemies. The reluctance to share the Norden bomb sight was not solely to do with maintaining this tenuous neutrality. The Americans had poured vast amounts of resources into the project, seeing it as an expression of their technological supremacy.

Dutch émigré Carl Norden had lived in Germany and trained in Switzerland at a machine shop before entering Zurich Federal Polytechnic School. In America he worked for the Sperry Corporation, specializing in gyroscopes for stabilizing ships. Setting up his own company, Norden became convinced he could develop a highly accurate bomb sight, and from 1921 he poured all his efforts into the project. The American military took to the concept with enthusiasm. Although at first Norden appeared a quiet man, his contemporaries described him as 'self-centred, impatient, domineering, driven, abrasive, a perfectionist... and of the highest ethical standards'.

Norden's device calculated height, speed and wind conditions using a complicated series of gyroscopes and pullies, connected to an analogue computing device. Norden claimed he could 'hit a pickle barrel at 20,000 feet' and in some initial tests it performed well, but on balance, his masterpiece proved far less efficient than claimed. In some cases, only 10 per cent of bombs hit the target. The US government, convinced that such a device was a war winner, spent over $1.5 billion on the project between 1927 and 1945. To put this in context, it was more than half the amount spent on the Manhattan Project, the US programme to develop a nuclear weapon. Early Norden models were accompanied to the aircraft by guards and contained explosive devices to destroy them in the event of possible capture. Norden shied away from publicity, selling the patent to the US government for just $1. Nonetheless, during the war years he would always be accompanied by two bodyguards as a security measure. Before the war, however, Norden had spoken freely of the essential principles of his device to a visiting German delegation, and these conversations enabled the Germans to create their own bomb sight.

Gradually, Churchill's pressure on the United States bore fruit, and the principles of Norden were shared with British scientists. However, American cooperation did not extend to manufacturing the bomb sights for the British, not least because they required their production facilities to fulfil USAAF demands. Instead the British had to produce their own version of the Norden bomb sight, based on the technical specifications provided. The physicist Patrick Blackett at the Royal Aircraft Establishment at Farnborough made a major contribution to the design of the Mark XIV sight,* which was introduced in June 1941. One problem with Norden's 'pickle barrel' concept was that the bomb aimer needed to visually identify the target. If he couldn't see the barrel, accuracy became a theoretical nonsense. The unpredictability of northern European weather meant that the only way of locating a target with any degree of accuracy would be with the help of radio and radar devices.

* The Mark XIV sight is also known as the Blackett sight, after its primary inventor.

*

The Pathfinders were born at a moment when revolutionary new technology was being introduced to the bomber force. Every bomber could carry a bomb sight, but with H2S radar now available a small number of aircraft could be equipped with this state-of-the-art bombing aid. The Americans had already implemented their own system of 'Master' bombers – these being the leading aircraft in daylight raids whose job was to guide the formation to the target. As soon as they arrived in Britain in spring 1943, American heavy bomber formations were prescribed a fixed pattern in which every aircraft knew its place within a Bomb Group. Equipping the leading, target-marking aircraft with radar was a natural step for the USAAF, as it was for RAF Bomber Command.

Air Marshal Harris strongly approved of the principle of embedding target-marking pilots in existing squadrons, arguing that they should feature in *every* squadron. It was Group Captain Sidney Bufton, Deputy Director of Bombing Operations at the Air Ministry, who first proposed the formation of special Pathfinder squadrons in early summer 1942. Harris opposed the idea, convinced that the existence of a separate, elite force would give rise to jealousy and damage morale. But Bomber Command's C-in-C faced the challenge of ensuring that his aircraft could reach their targets successfully in night-time conditions. With the advantage of operating in daylight, American bombers could follow in formation visually. If they lost their lead aircraft, a formation could simply tag on to another one. In the case of the RAF's bombers, the radio signal navigation guide Gee could get them to the vicinity of the target, but at night each bomber in the stream needed to have the ability to act autonomously. In time, each Lancaster or Halifax would need its own radar set, or at least have aircraft in front of them that could accurately mark the target in advance. The question facing Bomber Command and the Air Ministry was whether Pathfinders within individual squadrons would be as effective as a dedicated target-marking force.

The Air Ministry, including Chief of the Air Staff Charles Portal, agreed with Bufton and forced the matter with Harris. However, Harris vetoed the suggestion that Basil Embry, a distinguished fighter pilot and Commander of RAF No. 2 Group, take up the reins of the Pathfinders. Considering Embry to be too like himself in character, in July 1942 Harris appointed Don Bennett, a plain-speaking Australian who before the war had pioneered long-distance flying with Imperial Airways. Throughout 1940 Bennett had commanded the transatlantic ferry operation bringing thousands of aircraft from the United States. Volunteering as a bomber pilot, he served in Whitleys and Halifaxes and was shot down on a raid on the *Tirpitz* in April 1942. Together with other members of his crew he successfully evaded capture, returning home via Sweden. Harris described

Air Vice Marshal Don Bennett (right), Air Officer Commanding No. 8 Group (the Pathfinders), accompanied by Group Captain John Searby, leaves the Headquarters of Air Defence of Great Britain, Bentley Priory, Middlesex.

him as 'one of the best airmen I know'. Bennett's career to date had not following the traditional route of promotion through staff positions. At just thirty-one, he was youngest of the Group commanders, and was unwavering in his belief in the Pathfinder strategy. Despite glowing praise from his chief, Bennett was not a man who was afraid to ruffle feathers. Aloof and humourless in his demeanour, he made few friends. He was to collide spectacularly with Ralph Cochrane, commander of 5 Group, on a number of occasions.

The Pathfinder Force (PFF) came into being in August 1942, taking a squadron from each of the five bomber groups. The squadrons in question were 156 Squadron from No. 1 Group (flying Wellingtons); 109 Squadron from No. 2 Group (Wellingtons and Mosquitos); 7 Squadron from No. 3 Group (Stirlings); 35 Squadron from No. 4 Group (Halifaxes); and 83 Squadron from No. 5 Group (Lancasters). The Pathfinders flew for the first time on the night of 18/19 August 1942, providing the first thirty-two of 118 bombers sent against Flensburg on the Baltic, but the mission was an abject failure. A mission to Frankfurt a week later was also disappointing, but a raid on Kassel on 27/28 August wreaked considerable damage on the town and on its military installations, for the loss of thirty-one out of the 306 bombers on the mission. Successful attacks on Nuremberg, Saarbrücken, Karlsruhe and Bremen followed, and technical improvements would further enhance performance over the coming months. In January 1943, the expanded Pathfinders became a new Group in their own right – No. 8 Group (PFF).

These early months of 1943 were a key time in the fortunes of Bomber Command. The Allies were failing to provide the much talked-of western invasion so important to the Russians. Stalin was suspicious, accusing the West of plotting the destruction of Communism by failing to aid him adequately. It was not an altogether unreasonable argument, but the truth was that, for all their promises, the Allies were not ready to launch their invasion in 1943. Stalin had sent a memorandum to Churchill and President Roosevelt on 13 August 1942 pressing them for an invasion of France. In his reply the following day, Churchill explained that the Allies could not launch an invasion that year, but he strongly implied that they *would* do so in 1943. An invasion in 1942, Churchill said, '... would... be far more a running sore for us than for the enemy and would use up wastefully and wantonly the key men and the landing craft required for real action in 1943'.

The delay during 1943 provided Air Marshal Harris with an opportunity to explore his theory that air power alone could defeat Germany. The prize would be victory without putting the lives of hundreds of thousands of Allied troops at risk. For this, he would need accurate target marking and decisive strikes. The Pathfinders were to be his key in the lock. At last, after the struggle to build Bomber Command, he had the resources to pour into the battle.

Post-Dunkirk, strategic leadership was essential, and this needed to come as much from politicians as from military planners. In a memorandum to the cabinet on 3 September 1940, Churchill had spelled out his thinking:

> The Navy can lose us the war, but only the Air Force can
> win it. Therefore, our supreme effort must be to gain
> overwhelming mastery in the Air. The fighters are our
> salvation... but the bombers alone provide the means of
> victory. We must therefore develop the power to carry an
> increasing volume of explosives to Germany, so as to
> pulverize the entire industry and scientific structure on
> which the war effort and economic life of the enemy depend,
> whilst holding him at arm's length from our island. In no
> other way at present visible can we hope to overcome the
> immense military power of Germany.

5 January 1944, Stettin

Jim Comans sat impassively through the briefing taking notes, his officer's peaked cap perched at an angle, the way he always wore it. The target tonight would be Stettin,* eighty miles north of Berlin and connected to the Baltic coast via a waterway. The crew were feeling a tumble of emotions. At least it wasn't Berlin, but it was close. They were still in their first week as Pathfinders, after narrowly scraping back to RAF Gransden three days earlier with stopped engines. There was no denying that the efforts of the last few months had taken their toll. Feelings of pent-up anxiety were inescapable. They still didn't know any of the other crews apart from Jack Anstee's, who were sitting a few tables away from them. The Anstee crew had also transferred from 9 Squadron, arriving two weeks before Comans'. Stettin would be a lengthy trip – more than eight hours, a long time to keep body and soul together. The Met officer reassured them that the weather to and from the target should be clear, but the assembled crews suspected things were not quite that simple. The last two days had seen strong winds and rain battering most of the country, preventing operations before the night of 5 January. Bomber Command were keen to keep the crews going; perhaps one final push and Germany would capitulate.

In the minds of the men seated on the hard flip-down chairs of the briefing room there was much less optimism. Even wearing their woollen one-piece underwear, the so-called 'Bunny Suit', it was going to be a freezing trip. Those first difficult winter days at RAF Bourn were the bleakest. Not only was the weather against them, but they had to fly long, hard missions, frequently experiencing the loss of fellow airmen, and knowing they still

---

* Stettin is now Szczecin, in western Poland. It belonged to Prussia until 1945.

had many more operations to complete. Some of the glamour of belonging to the Pathfinders had already faded; they sensed they were dead men walking.

At first glance there wasn't much difference between being a normal bomber crewman and a Pathfinder. Apart from a brass RAF eagle worn beneath the left tunic pocket of the Pathfinder crews, their uniforms were identical. The men were ordered to remove the badges before operations, but the Germans often identified the Pathfinders by squadron markings on crashed bombers. Their pay was bolstered by a rise in rank for the duration of their Pathfinder service. Out 'on the town' they had a little more swagger than other crews, feeling that they were part of an elite group.

Tonight, hoping to trick the Germans into believing Berlin would be the target, the bomber stream would turn late into Stettin, and hoped to be heading for home just as the defenders woke up to what was happening. Some crews were inexperienced, coming straight out of training into the Pathfinders. Others, like the Comans crew, had ten or more sorties under their belts. In theory, the best crews of a squadron were invited to apply to join the Pathfinders. Some historians have since speculated that certain squadrons, not being overly keen to lose experienced men, also passed on troublesome or poorly performing crews. Those Pathfinder crews who were not considered experienced enough to drop marking flares carried bomb loads similar to the crews following. The new men were classed as 'supporters', dropping their bombs first onto the flares. The presence of the photoflash, a bright 19lb flare bomb synchronized with an on-board camera, allowed intelligence officers to assess the performance of individual crews in placing markers and bombs.

A bus dropped the Comans crew on the dispersal near Lancaster ND367 'K-King', just after 11 p.m. It was cold, and water droplets were clinging to every surface despite the stiff breeze. Climbing the short crew ladder, they were glad to be inside the aircraft. Ken Cook checked the payload with his torch before he boarded. In the dim light he could make out four massive 2,000lb bombs in the bomb bay. These barrel-shaped demolition bombs looked unsophisticated and lacking in aerodynamic design, but they were the most powerful element of a Lancaster's arsenal.* The Comans crew's role as Pathfinder supporters was to drop on the markers, blasting open buildings to allow incendiaries released by the next wave to take hold. They knew these giants would do more than blow roofs off. Each bomb could demolish a large building, blasting rubble into the streets and preventing rescuers or fire services from reaching the heart of the blaze. Thoughts of the terrible impact of the bombs on the ground, however, were not foremost in the minds of the crew. The bombs presented a terrible danger to them and to their aircraft. There were a dozen ways to die in a Lancaster, but a hit in the bomb bay meant immediate and violent death. One stray shard of flak or a cannon shell would obliterate them. For the crew, these four 2,000lb bombs were not part of their Lancaster, but alien objects whose brooding presence played on their minds.

Jim Comans had not flown this Lancaster before. He wondered what little quirks it might have. All Lancasters drifted to port on take-off – it was part of the gyroscopic effect of the engines – and the greater the load the more pronounced it was. But every aircraft was slightly different, some pulling away more than others from the pilot during manoeuvres. Some of these variations were apparent from the factory, but in many cases battle damage repairs were a contributing factor.

On a night like this one, everyone considered flight engineer Ken Randle to be a lucky devil, since he was still away on marriage

---

* The 'Cookie' was developed to 4,000lb and 8,000lb versions and, at the limit of its practicality, to the 12,000lb, the 'Blockbuster'.

leave. His place on board ND367 was taken by Sergeant E. S. Monaghan. Grim to relate, neither aircraft nor replacement flight engineer would survive to the end of the month. ND367 would crash at Zahrensdorf on the way to Berlin on 21 January, killing Sergeant Cyril Wakely and four of his crew on their first mission together. As for Monaghan, he was lost without trace a week later in Lancaster JB712, on another mission to Berlin. 'Spare bods' were common enough, but their presence unsettled many crews. They were deeply superstitious about any change in their routines – not least when individual crew replacements were necessary.

Not long after Comans had eased the Lancaster off RAF Bourn's damp runway, large cloud banks appeared. On the leg towards the base of Denmark, the cloud blocked their way at 15,000 feet. They flew on, flashes of lightning momentarily transforming the deep mist into an enveloping sheet of light. There was no time to avoid the mass of cloud in front of them, they plunged into the murk, hoping to outclimb the storm. The bomber began to bounce and lunge; St Elmo's fire ran along the aerials and guns, alarming an already nervous crew. George Widdis in the upper turret reported ice forming on his Perspex, blotting out his view. Comans noticed the controls getting heavier as the Lancaster began to ice up. Instinctively he put the nose down, realizing that to continue at this altitude would be folly. Gradually the ice melted, peppering the thin alloy fuselage with small fragments as it did so.

As they broke through into clear air, soft moonlight helped them pick out the coast of Germany. Deep into enemy territory, their final feint east towards Stettin left the rings of searchlights around Hamburg behind them. In the distance, Berlin's defences bristled. At any moment a fighter might break through the darkness. Tension mounted throughout the crew.

'Time to go down I think,' Comans instructed Cook. Leaving

his navigator's plotting table behind the pilot's seat, Ken Randle stood and flipped his seat up, allowing Ken Cook to squeeze through the opening beneath the flight engineer's panel. Down in the orbit of the Perspex nose, Cook was in a new world. Lying on the leather-topped support, he crouched over the bomb sight. Stettin was coming into view, already flares were dropping and the first bombs had started a large fire in the city centre. The main features of the town were clearly visible: docks, railway station and municipal buildings. Fleeting outlines of other bombers swept beneath through Ken's sight as he focused the cross-hairs. There was no time to worry about them. ND367 was flying straight and level as flak drifted up towards them before bursting in angry growls. As Ken pressed the release toggle, he could see the flash of other bombs exploding among the fires beneath.

The Pathfinders' job was done, and the baton now passed to the next wave of arriving Lancasters – there were over three hundred of them in the stream that followed. The Comans crew braced themselves for another battering as they headed home. The wind speed had picked up, with 85mph gusts in the headwind. Too much of this and they would run short of fuel – they had a long journey in front of them. But finally, as the pale winter morning produced thin green strips of light in the eastern sky, they made it into the circuit above RAF Bourn. Other dim Lancaster shapes joined them. They had been invisible for many hours, yet now, within a few minutes, the family was congregating for a reunion. Landing at five minutes past eight, they had been flying for eight hours and eighteen minutes. Most of them were bursting to urinate and had hardly swung out of the side door before they formed an orderly line by the tail. Cigarettes were offered round as the ground crew chatted, relieved to see their airmen safely home.

Over the next forty minutes the other aircraft returned. Sixteen out of eighteen had made it back to Bourn. But what of the two others? The phones in the Ops room remained silent. As the minutes turned to hours, it became obvious that two Lancasters had been lost. The Flack crew were hit near Lüskow on Germany's Baltic coast with Sergeant R. G. Boston the only survivor. Parachuting from the hatch under his bomb aimer's position, Boston later reported, 'When I left my position in aircraft this officer [Flack] was still at controls, this was my last sight of him. German medical officer at Anklam said rest of my crew were dead. Do not know anything of any others, but all members of the crew would have found it extremely difficult to abandon aircraft.'

The Comans crew had flown Flack's aircraft only the day before on a daylight cross-country exercise. It was hard to imagine that this complex piece of machinery, which had performed so well over their two and a half hour flight, was now gone. What had become of aircraft and crew was unknown. They had disappeared seemingly without trace. Everyone fought back thoughts of what the final minutes in a spinning Lancaster must be like.

The second crew missing was Jack Anstee's, their closest colleagues from 9 Squadron. They had served with 97 Squadron for less than a month. Perhaps without Anstee's enthusiasm, the idea of joining the Pathfinders might not have formed so quickly in the Comans crew. Anstee was only twenty-two, and, like Roy Woollford, a Luton lad. The day was a stark reminder that it was unwise to become close to a crew or aircraft. Only after the war would they find out that all but one of the Anstee crew had perished that night. Sergeant C. Cartwright, the flight engineer, was taken prisoner. Their Lancaster JB720 was new and had been with 97 Squadron less than three weeks.

Bomber Command considered the Stettin raid a success. Most crews had reported being able to bomb visually having used the H2S radar system to confirm their position. The weather conditions had turned out to be very different from the pre-raid briefing, with many reporting thick cloud and icing.

The improvement in their accuracy had come about as a result of the interventions of Frederick Lindemann eighteen months earlier in the Butt Report of August 1941. New technology was now arriving at the squadrons on a regular basis, and bringing with it a feeling of impetus. The crews could see the tide of war was turning: how long could the enemy resist the onslaught of Bomber Command, armed with such an array of new devices?

15 February 1944, Berlin

In their preparation for operations, the Comans crew always experienced a strong sense of purpose. For all Harris's desire not to create an elite, the young men of the crew felt that, as Pathfinders, they had reached the top of their game. Soon they too would be dropping marker flares onto targets as leaders, not supporters. If they survived their tour of duty, they also sensed the benefits that lay ahead: greater respect, perhaps even faster promotion. But their key preoccupation was survival; there was no point in winning badges or medals if they ended up dead. Too many of their fellow airmen were failing to return. Every time they landed safely after a mission they felt they had dodged a bullet.

After a month with 97 Squadron, the Comans crew started to carry flares in their bomb load, as they began the task of guiding others in earnest. Early February 1944 turned out to be a troublesome month as heavy winds and lashing rain kept them grounded at RAF Bourn. Perhaps this was no bad thing as the moon was strong for the first week of the month. Several missions were scrubbed even after all the preparation had been made and the Lancasters fuelled and loaded. The anti-climax was often worse than flying the mission itself. On average they sent twenty Lancasters per raid, often losing two of these aircraft. Even for those who made it safely back to base, tragedy was never far away. At the end of January, the Australian Henry 'Jim' Van Raalte returned from Berlin on three engines with the tail of his Lancaster shot to pieces. Inside the aircraft, however, his tail gunner Flight Sergeant Laurie had died a sudden, gruesome death, decapitated by shrapnel. Van Raalte would himself be killed five months later, on 23 June, when his Lancaster ME625 crashed following a mid-air collision.

When airmen were posted missing after a raid, the only comfort for their colleagues was the possibility that they might have escaped the crash of their bomber. It took time, sometimes many weeks, before notifications of prisoners of war were confirmed. If downed airmen were in the evasion network, it could take months before word was heard. In some cases, airmen remained hidden for the duration of the war.

The Comans crew had a two-week respite from operations at the start of February 1944. They had flown continuously since September, completing nineteen missions. The rainy early days of February were not spent in relaxation. When the weather permitted, they flew several cross-country exercises at night. The squadron had 'make and mend' days, organized sports and lectures on 'Evasion and Escape' and 'Photographic interpretation of bomb damage'. There was a sense that something was brewing and, as the crews were pulled together for their final briefing on 13 February, they realized it was to be a 'maximum effort' mission with twenty-four Lancasters from RAF Bourn tasked as part of a massive raid to Berlin. However, even as they stood by their aircraft for an early take-off, the mission was pulled due to bad weather. The next day was no better, but they were ordered to go on the 15th.

This was the largest raid on Berlin to date, with 891 aircraft striking at the industrialized western part of the city. All but one of 97 Squadron's Lancasters returned and reports of their accuracy were good, although they had to bomb through cloud. The

McLean crew went missing, however, shot down by Hauptmann Erhard Peters in his Ju88C near Faaborg in Denmark. Five of the crew died when the Lancaster exploded, scattering sections of wreckage over a wide area. McLean and air bomber Stevens parachuted to captivity.

Erhard Peters had so far claimed twenty-two aircraft destroyed in his career with *Nachtjagdgeschwader* 3.* With masses of bombers appearing over Berlin, his Lichtenstein SN2 radar set was alive with targets. The front of his Ju88C bristled with a complicated array of aerials, which caused his aircraft to make a whistling sound as it flew. Ground controllers steered him to the incoming stream of bombers, giving him instructions through his headphones. As Peters closed on a target his navigator would pick out a bright green dot on his three small round cathode-ray screens. Stalking their prey, they followed the instruments until they could visually make out the shape of a bomber. In the course of a raid, a night fighter might make six or more interceptions. Often, he would be spotted and fired at. Unless he could be reasonably sure of a kill, there was no point pressing home an attack for there were plenty of other targets to choose from. Many bombers were equipped with a tail approach radar device known as Monica, introduced by the RAF in June 1942. A small T-shaped aerial under the rear gunner would detect an aircraft, producing a bleeping sound over the intercom. Although accurate, it did not differentiate between friend or foe, leading to many false alarms in a bomber stream. Detection of a prowling fighter was down to the eyes of the gunners. Unknown to the British bomber crews, from spring 1944 the Germans deployed the Flensburg radar receiver, which allowed night fighters to home in on Monica signals.

---

* A German night-fighter wing formed in September 1941 and often referred to as NJG 3.

Hauptmann Peters knew that his battle was not one-sided. The Lancasters would push bundles of tin foil – 'Window' – through a chute, which would turn his radar set into a fog of tiny targets. And over the past few nights, he had faced the challenging question of which ground controller's voice he could trust. New German-speaking voices were appearing on his radio frequency. Sometimes he had heard arguments, each voice demanding to be heard since *they* were the real controllers. Sitting at radio desks in specially prepared Halifaxes of 100 (Bomber Support Group), bogus controllers mimicked German ground operators with impressive results. Worryingly, it seemed the fake voices were more ordered and controlled than the real ones. But these countermeasures were only an inconvenience. Peters knew that the real threat lurked among the bombers. De Havilland Mosquito IIs equipped with Serrate radar detection devices were stalking the Luftwaffe fighters. Homing into the emissions from the Lichtenstein sets, they would identify and attack the slower two-engined night fighters. Peters' aircraft was fitted with the new SN2 set, which he was told would be harder for the Mosquitos to detect, but it was very new and as yet unproven.

Had Peters continued his career, he would have added many more bombers to his personal score. Ironically, it was the fear of the Mosquito that killed Hauptmann Peters and his crew four days after their attack on McLean. On 19 February a single-engined 'Wild Boar' Luftwaffe fighter mistook Peters' Ju88 for their nemesis and shot him down.

The raid of 15 February 1944 was the Comans crew's eleventh mission to Berlin, and they would fly one more in March. Of sixteen major strikes on the city in the 'Battle of Berlin' (the name given to Bomber Command's sequence of raids on the German capital between November 1943 and March 1944), they flew twelve of them. In doing so, the crew had honed their skills against the most heavily defended target on the planet. Working with navigator Don Bowes, Ken Cook had gained invaluable experience of the H2S radar. With a curtain pulled round them to help block the glow of the instruments, Cook and Bowes succeeded in finding their way to their targets on the foulest of winter nights.

The new technology was allowing RAF bombers to achieve a level of accuracy that would have been unthinkable only two years earlier. For three months, RAF Bomber Command had pounded Berlin without let-up, causing enormous damage and considerable loss of life. The Pathfinders were mastering their techniques and getting their flares onto the targets. However, had Harris's area bombing strategy been working as he predicted it would, by now thousands of civilians should have been on the streets demanding Hitler's resignation; food and water should have been in desperately short supply; a starving and rebellious population should have fled the German capital, overwhelming the Nazis' abilities to feed their armies. The 1930s prophecy of aerial Armageddon had seemed compellingly plausible, but, as in the London Blitz, the complete breakdown of social order failed to materialize. Perhaps Churchill, Lindemann, Portal and Harris had misunderstood the true scale of the Nazis' psychological hold on the German people. Buoyed by the hopes of a troubled nation, Hitler had first charmed and then captured the minds of the majority. He had circumvented the rule of politicians and the law to such an extent that civilians feared to challenge the all-encompassing power of the Nazi state.

Harris's belief that the Allied bombing campaign might tip Germany into rebellion was not without foundation, for the German people had displayed a penchant for civil unrest throughout the 1920s and in the early 1930s. Yet now, when parts of Berlin – once considered one of Europe's most modern and progressive cities – lay a smouldering ruin, there was little sign of civil disobedience. The simple entries in the diary of the teenager Brigitte Eicke appear to sum up Berliners' disregard of the bombers, even after two months of attacks. On 1 February, she records: 'The school had been bombed when we arrived this morning. Waltraud, Melitta and I went back to Gisela's and danced to gramophone records.'

*

The morning after the huge Berlin raid of 15 February, Hitler met with his Chief of Staff, Kurt Zeitzler, not to discuss the bombing, but to consider the situation on the Eastern Front. When Zeitzler reported that the army had requested to fall back from Nikopol, in Ukraine, to straighten their line, Hitler flew into a fury. Launching himself across the table, he attacked the map before collapsing into an armchair. 'If only the generals could finally understand why I cling to this area so much!' he shouted. 'We urgently need Nikopol manganese!' Zeitzler, used to Hitler's outbursts, continued the briefing unperturbed. Eventually Hitler calmed down, but he ordered that the army display an 'iron will', insisting that no further retreats were to be permitted. In so doing, Hitler had signed the death warrant of the Wehrmacht in strategic terms. Although Harris's Berlin offensive was not achieving the breakdown of order and the overthrow of Hitler, it had clearly affected the psychology of the Führer, who was cracking under the strain of his enemies' assaults. The Russians may have been his main preoccupation, but the nightly visits from Allied bombers were a constant reminder to him that before long he would have a Western front to contend with, as well as an Eastern one.

Harris had resisted diluting his area bombing campaign through the winter of 1943/4, but he could not continue his policy without interruption. The poor weather and short days had hampered the USAAF's daylight operations, but as the first signs of spring began to appear, it would be time to throw the full might of the US Eighth Air Force into battle. The desire within Bomber Command to strike at Germany's industries rather than area-bombing Berlin became overwhelming. Harris was dismissive, often describing industry attacks as 'panacea' targets. But even he had to face the reality that his knock-out-blow policy had failed. Bomber Command was returning to a model closer to Lindemann's: attacks on industrial towns to destroy factories and de-house workers. To the bomber crews, the missions were operationally identical, but the strategy was subtly different. Harris did not give up his vision of the knock-out blow, but he believed the destruction of towns would have a domino effect, and that eventually even the Nazis would come to their senses.

Big Week: 20–25 February 1944

With the focus shifting from the wrecked remains of Berlin, the USAAF and RAF combined efforts for Operation Argument, nicknamed 'Big Week', on 20 February 1944. For six days the two air forces hit industrial targets in towns across Germany, including Leipzig, Braunschweig, Gotha and Regensburg. The intensity of the Comans crew's missions picked up pace once again. They had a successful flight to Stuttgart on the night of 20 February. Dropping ten 1,000lb bombs from 20,000 feet, they made it back to Bourn just as the sun was beginning to rise. The Lancasters were landing to plan, with little more than five minutes separating them. As the crews left their aircraft, they became aware that the aircraft of one of their number, Flight Lieutenant Emerson, was still slowly flying the circuit. Some had heard on the radio that ground control was holding him off until the others had landed. He had radioed in an emergency and as the men on the ground peered upwards, they could see that

BERLIN: 21st February 1944. The Unter den Linien by the Bradenburg Gate showing the severe fire destruction. The Reichstag (top right) is damaged by fire.

Bombing reconnaissance photograph of Berlin's Brandenburg Gate, 21 February 1944.

Emerson had a huge gash in the underside of his fuselage. The H2S dome had gone, and in its place a gaping wound, the result of a collision with another bomber over the target. Emerson had done exceptionally well to nurse the stricken bomber home.

Fire vehicles and ambulances stood in position. Men clung to vehicles ready to charge down the runway as Emerson came in. Finally, after more than twenty minutes of preparation, Emerson was given the all-clear to land. A large crowd of ground and aircrew stood watching. Emerson's Lancaster made the slow downwind leg, his flaps and undercarriage down as he made the gentle turn into his final approach. The characteristic shape of the Lancaster's wings formed in line with the runway and his height and speed looked perfect. But 300 yards from the runway the fuselage suddenly snapped in two behind the wing. The bomber plunged to the ground, a fireball lifting immediately from the site of the impact. Aghast, men instinctively ran towards the crash, grabbing on to passing vehicles or seizing bicycles and pedalling frantically towards the rising smoke.

Radio Operator Roy Woollford, 1944. His Pathfinders badge can be seen on his breast pocket.

Comans' wireless operator, Roy Woollford, was one of the first to reach the scene. Although he could clearly see the shape of the fuselage, he was beaten back by the heat. The terrible realization that the men inside were burning before him left him shocked and helpless. Tears of frustration welled up in the onlookers' eyes as firemen finally succeeded in dousing the inferno. There was nothing to be done but recover the charred remains of Emerson and his crew from the smouldering wreck of their Lancaster. Nothing in his war would affect Roy Woollford as much as this tragedy. The bombing of the factory at Luton had placed him in a vulnerable emotional state, but this incident brought him close to breaking point. The gloom around RAF Bourn was profound. Emerson had been only seconds away from safety. Everyone was willing him down, watching every inch of his progress. Even if the fuselage had fractured on the runway, most of the men could have been rescued. It was the cruellest of twists, of the kind that war produces without warning.

Roy Woollford soldiered on. He had been married only a few months and it helped to talk to his wife on the phone. Although four of the crew were now married, they lived apart from their spouses and were not in married quarters. The crew were very supportive of Roy, and he didn't want to let them down. Despite his being in a state of profound shock, his fear of being sidelined as 'LMF' and separated from the crew was enough to keep him going. Whatever happened, he was determined to finish his tour. Physically, however, the strain began to show. Roy's hair, normally thick and curly, began to fall out. Soon, he had very little to poke under his cap. It would grow again after several months, but the memory of that day would remain with him for the rest of his life.

*

By February 1944, Schweinfurt, whose literal meaning is 'swine crossing', had lived up to its name. This northern Bavarian town, home to the biggest ball-bearing plant in Germany and therefore key to wartime production, had been the burial place of the USAAF's initial enthusiasm. Buoyed with confidence at the abilities of their Boeing B-17 to operate in daylight without fighter cover, the USAAF had launched a major attack on Regensburg and Schweinfurt on 17 August 1943. The raid on Schweinfurt, in particular, was a costly disaster. German fighters had swarmed on the bombers, hacking holes in their formation and sending a stream of burning aircraft plummeting to the ground. The force had split to attack Schweinfurt and the Messerschmitt plant at Regensburg. Sixty B-17 bombers were lost and many more damaged irreparably; 552 US airmen were listed as missing in action, of whom half became prisoners of war. Despite these losses, the results of the attack were good. Albert Speer, Reich Minister of Armaments and War Production, calculated that the raid had cost Germany 34 per cent of its ball-bearing production.

Even with this sober lesson learned, the USAAF launched a further attack in October 1943, which resulted in the deaths or capture of 600 American airmen and the loss of sixty bombers. Another seventeen were so badly damaged they had to be scrapped. Allied fighters did not have the range to escort the bombers all the way to targets so deep inside the German Reich. So once again, the gunners faced the fighters alone. This mauling threw the USAAF onto the back foot; they had to admit they did not have air superiority. More damaging to their pride was the irrefutable fact that the B-17, once hailed as their wonder aeroplane, was vulnerable. Speer stockpiled ball bearings, keeping war production moving. For the Germans, Schweinfurt's output was too important to allow production to remain disrupted for long, and a massive effort was put into restoring its factories. Speer also diversified production to keep it out of reach of the bombers, spreading it into all corners of the Reich. From deep, concrete-lined bunkers in the Balkans to wine and cheese storage caves in the Loire Valley, armaments continued to pour forward. German aircraft production increased in 1944, even throughout the debilitating raids and invasion of northern France. That year saw more aircraft manufactured across Germany's empire than the whole of the other war years put together. The only problem was that the Luftwaffe lacked experienced pilots to fly them.

As 'Big Week' got underway, the battle lines had been drawn differently. The Americans now had fighter cover from their P-47 Thunderbolts, P-38 Lightnings, and their new fighter, the P-51 Mustang. Not only would the bombers hit their targets, but the new fighter force would draw in the Luftwaffe for an epic air battle. Losses over the six days within the bomber force were high. The USAAF lost 226 bombers by day, the RAF 131 by night. This represented 6 per cent of the total force deployed in battle. Three hundred and thirty-five German aircraft were downed – 20 per cent of the Luftwaffe's daylight fighters – and one hundred pilots killed. These were unsustainable losses, which left the Germans deeply shaken. Far from succeeding in stopping the Allied bombing onslaught, they saw a future in which their air defences were utterly destroyed. Such fears were well grounded: the new generation of Allied fighter aircraft could outwit most of their Luftwaffe equivalents, even with Germany's most experienced pilots flying them. The battle would hinge on experienced pilots, and the Allies had the upper hand. The RAF had leaned heavily on the training grounds of America, Canada and Australia, knowing that their pilots would be safe from interference there. In Germany, however, a time was coming soon when no inch of their skies would be completely safe for the Luftwaffe trainee pilots.

In a mood of rising confidence, the USAAF changed the colour of its bombers. The practice of painting their upper sides in green-drab, based on the assumption that enemy fighters could observe them from above, was discontinued. Instead, bombers left the production lines in America in bright polished aluminium. The theory behind the new colour scheme was that, henceforth, the enemy would be below them, peering up into a bright sky. The only aircraft above the US bombers would be their own accompanying fighters. However, despite the threat of these US fighters, the Luftwaffe persisted with the high-angle beam attack, particularly against the B-17s.

The experience of the US bomber crewmen was different from that of their RAF colleagues. The Americans expected to meet fighter opposition and, rather than take evasive action, they maintained their course and altitude in formation. Flying with five gunners, the concept of bomber self-defence was etched into every part of the B-17's design. High on the freezing edge of the troposphere, crew wore flak jackets over electrically heated suits. They donned steel helmets when flying over Germany and their movement was further inhibited by the need to keep connected to an oxygen source. Many B-17s had open sides for the waist gunners, giving little shelter from the freezing temperatures. Below the fuselage hung the claustrophobic 'ball turret'. The gunner, generally a small man, would be packed into the turret, which was then winched down into its exposed position under the belly. If the bomber was damaged, the gunner could be trapped inside the turret and, in the event of a wheels-up landing, condemned to an appalling end.

Lines of dull green B-17s formed up on the taxiways of dozens of US airfields in East Anglia. The pitch of their radial engines differed from that of the Merlin-powered Lancasters, producing deep reverberations. One by one they took off, leaving two-minute intervals between each plane. Grabbing each foot of altitude, they circled, gradually gaining height, before splitting into their set formations. Every B-17 formation was similar and the crews knew their slot. Once the squadrons were airborne, they tuned in to 'buncher beacons', ground stations that would help them unite into larger groups of bombers. As they set course for Schweinfurt in February 1944, a cloud of Allied fighters appeared above them. The fight would be just as desperate as in August and October of the previous year, but this time the fighters would make a huge difference. Many men had not taken part in the earlier raids; they were new to the Bomb Groups, men still building towards their thirty-mission target before home leave. Unlike the RAF men, many of these US airmen did not return to fly a second tour and were replaced by a throng of newly trained crews.

The radar in the B-17s was similar to RAF H2S, and was held in a chin position in the nose of the aircraft. As the radar was introduced across the force, the USAAF dropped a waist gunner to make room for a 'Mickey' operator, a bombing navigator with a role similar to Ken Cook's. With the aid of radar, daylight and the Norden bomb sight, the USAAF began to hit their targets with admirable accuracy.

On 24 February, the fires of the American raid were still smouldering as the Comans crew began their bombing run at Schweinfurt. RAF strategy that day was different, too, splitting the main force into separate waves to attack multiple targets. Learning that a feint required more than just a few aircraft, they put 179 trainee bomber crews in the air to simulate a building raid. 97 Squadron was spread between two waves, the first taking off at 18.00 hours, the second at 21.00 hours. The Comans crew, who were in the first section, identified Schweinfurt by the course of the River Main, which passed through the town. The night was clear and Ken Cook could easily make out the key target points from his position in the Lancaster's nose. This was the first time the RAF had flown to this difficult target but flying over Schweinfurt on 24 February 1944 was not like being above Berlin on those heavy, overcast nights in early January, Schweinfurt made life easy for them. A large fire was already burning in the target area and, as the white and red flares fell, they saw two other considerable blazes in the north of the town. They dropped four target indicator flares, five 1,000lb bombs and a 4,000lb 'Cookie'. The glow of the burning town remained visible on the horizon for 150 miles of the return leg.

Almost inevitably, one Lancaster was missing from the two waves. ND497, flown by the Smith crew, had taken off five minutes after the Comans but failed to return. Smith had flown some distance south of Schweinfurt before crashing with the loss of all crew at Vöhringen.

The split-wave raid of the 734 bombers had worked well, exhausting the German night fighters who were forced to land and refuel. In a daring move, the USAAF and RAF were to attack Augsburg the next day. If Schweinfurt rang alarm bells in American minds, Augsburg had similarly grim associations for the British. The RAF had not attacked the Swabian town since Sherwood's heroic day raid of 1942; Augsburg remained a tough call. There was the added incentive that Sherwood had also served with 97 Squadron, and it was a matter of pride to follow in his footsteps even though he now languished in a prisoner-of-war camp. This time, the RAF would be flying after the USAAF had done their work and, just as at Schweinfurt, they would attack in two waves.

The morning sky on 25 February was filled with the rumble of aircraft. Through the scattered clouds high above RAF Bourn, American bombers could be seen toiling upwards to begin their assembly. The eastern horizon shook with noise as 754 B-17s and B-24s took off from their bases in East Anglia. There were so many of them that the assembly areas were spread across much of eastern England. Scores of fighters swarmed together, ready to take up position above the outbound bombers. The Eighth Air Force had come of age. Even before the RAF crews knew where they were going that day, the Americans were heading for Regensburg, Augsburg, Stuttgart and Fürth. They would lose thirty-one bombers with 301 crew killed or captive. In the unwritten rules of the bombing campaign, losses of under 5 per cent of the force sent was considered a success. Worryingly for the Luftwaffe, the Americans lost very few fighters, but destroyed many of theirs.

The Comans crew were once again to be in the first wave, together with thirteen other Lancasters from 97 Squadron. Their route would take them over northern France in a straight line towards Stuttgart, turning south towards Freiburg and seemingly headed for Munich. But a sharp ninety-degree turn brought them to Augsburg. The second wave would arrive from the north after flying over Holland and Germany. It was a boldly confident plan. The day before, the Americans had pinpointed factories and railways, but this raid was to hit hard at the heart of Augsburg.

The Augsburgers knew that a raid would come. They did not know when, but with the newspapers describing the damage done to so many industrial centres across Germany, a destructive attack on their city seemed inevitable. Augsburg was host to the MAN diesel works and a Messerschmitt factory. Nearby camps housed thousands of slave labourers: surely the Allies must know this was an important industrial centre? Air raid shelters were built, slit trenches dug and cellars cleaned in preparation. Across the river in Lechhausen, a baker observed the preparations and in his diary noted down the question that was on the mind of all Augsburgers: 'Will it prove itself, is everything ready when the big blow against Augsburg takes place?'

The city was covered in snow, and the banks of the River Lech clad in sheets of ice. The weather was bright and cloudless, possibly the worst conditions for the defence of the city, as the river was clearly visible as a dark line in the surrounding white-ness. At 13.30 the air raid sirens wailed across the city as the B-17s bore down on the Messerschmitt plant. Those away from the factory site watched the raid with grim curiosity, hearing the crump of bombs as blast waves shook windows. With clear skies the Norden bomb sights worked well, allowing an accurate strike on the plant. The Augsburg Air Defence diary observes: 'The attack was carried out by about 150 machines and was only on the Messerschmitt works, which suffered severe damage and had over 380 dead, including 250 concentration camp prisoners. Of course, there were also deaths and damage in the vicinity of the plant.' The raid was over in less than an hour, but amid the plumes of rising smoke a dread filled the population. What would darkness bring?

In the German control centres they watched the evening raid gathering on radar. Plotters began to pin ribbons to maps. Reports came in of a large force of enemy bombers over Amiens, but was this a feint? As the Allied aircraft headed towards Strasbourg, the controllers had to keep Stuttgart and Munich on alert, but they already suspected the force would turn for Augsburg. They wished they had the fighter resources to harry the enemy all through France, but Hitler had insisted that the strongest night-fighter forces be stationed to defend the Reich. The smaller 'Wild Boar' fighters had landed and refuelled after the day raid, but there was no rest for the pilots.

In Lancaster ND440, Ken Cook watched his aircraft's progress on his H2S radar. Cross-checking their position with Don Bowes next to him, he took several trips down into the nose to verify their location. They had left London behind them and crossed the English coast at Beachy Head, a geographical feature so clear that it could have been invented for aviators. It was a beautiful evening as they crossed the Bay of the Somme south of Étaples. It took them just ten minutes to fly over the whole extent of the Somme battlefield that had taken four years of mud-soaked misery and hundreds of thousands of British, French and Commonwealth lives to win. The thinnest line of the waxing crescent moon could be seen, but it was the darkest night of the month. As they pressed eastwards the faint grey of hoar frost bleached the landscape below, turning whiter minute by minute as the snow-topped ridges of the Ardennes passed on their port side. Southern Germany was enveloped in snow. Even in the darkness, the light it threw up at the bomber stream enabled them to pick out towns, rivers and valleys.

As George Widdis traversed his upper turret, it was hard not to be entranced by the distant lights of Zurich forty-five miles away. Unlike Munich, whose wall of searchlights was clearly visible ahead, in the Swiss city there would be no air raid sirens and no scurrying to shelters. It was 9.30 in the evening and although the Swiss would hear the distant thunder of the Merlin engines, they could sit unworried by their firesides. Above the turret, the vast canopy of stars spread out, but George was looking for movement, a shifting shape against the blackness. The wings dipped as Jim Comans brought Lancaster ND440 onto her last sharp turn to Augsburg. The night was perfect for the Pathfinders and from Ken Cook's position in the nose he could already see the green and red flares piercingly bright in the city centre. He dropped the bombs in the pattern of explosions beneath him as other invisible companions let loose their loads.

Fifteen-year-old Karl Kling and five other students had been drafted into the *Luftwaffenhelfer** to defend the Messerschmitt works. They manned anti-aircraft guns and for the second time that day faced terrifying odds from above. 'We were six students from Krumbach against six hundred bombers,' he later wrote. 'From this hour on, we knew what war is and, for the first time, we feared for our lives.' Most men of fighting age were at the front and, as the camps of slave labourers at Augsburg bore witness, fit German adults suitable to man guns were in short supply.

The destruction of Augsburg city centre was almost total. Large stepped gables of fine buildings had collapsed into the street, blocking all the roads under piles of rubble several feet deep. Huge fires burned out of control as firefighters fought to get water from the frozen River Lech, their hoses freezing on the pumps. Civilians tried to fight the fires with buckets and stirrup pumps. Others tried to extinguish the magnesium-spewing incendiaries that had crashed through their roofs – an impossible task, since 230,000 of these devilishly destructive devices had been dropped by the RAF that night. The second wave of bombers arrived an hour later, but they dropped their bombs less accurately to the east.

Eight hundred people died in the raids that day and night. Perhaps it was Augsburg's historical prosperity that saved it from greater loss. Many of the medieval wooden buildings that formed the character of old towns like Hamburg and Dresden had been

---

* *Luftwaffenhelfer* were 'Air Force assistants' supervised by the Hitler Youth and Luftwaffe. Also commonly known as *Flakhelfer* – flak helpers.

replaced here by tall brick-built buildings. Although the city centre burned ferociously, the uncontrolled firestorm that caused tens of thousands of casualties elsewhere did not take hold in Augsburg. The next day revealed the full extent of the raid. The town's Air Defence diary noted: 'Saturday, February 26, 1944. Weather: Moderately cold, some sun at noon, which could not penetrate the mighty layers of smoke and dust but dulled in the sky with a yellow-red glow.'

That morning, a tide of refugees fled the city to find safety in the countryside. Willy Hassold worked in a rescue centre providing bread and milk to 'thousands and thousands of people, some without shoes, burned, dirty, dog-tired, exhausted and sometimes also wounded'. If the civil unrest that 'Bomber' Harris predicted had failed to materialize, Lindemann's strategy of 'de-housing' and disruption worked very well in the days after the Augsburg raids. Eighty thousand people fled the city, approaching half the population. But many thousands could not leave: slave labourers confined to their cages by armed guards, hoping that perhaps, at last, liberation was on its way. They looked on in grim satisfaction at the Germans' suffering.

Although the RAF lost twenty-three bombers that night, none of them were 97 Squadron aircraft. Most of these aircraft were lost to flak – it seemed few night fighters had been observed. Jim Comans landed back at Bourn at 02.01, after a gruelling seven-hour flight, something that had become a norm through this winter. They were stood down for two days, enough time to have lunch in Cambridge, go to the cinema and hit the local pubs.

As Bomber Command continued to tick off the industrial cities of Germany from their raid list, they took pride in the accuracy of the Pathfinders. At last they could be confident that they were landing their bombs on target. There were signs that new technology was beginning to break through German defences. Ideas for how to achieve pinpoint accuracy were being put forward. Tests revealed that the Lancaster was capable of carrying enormous new bombs, far heavier than anything imagined at Avro's drawing board. But the commanders were choosing to ignore the massive human cost of the strategy they were pursuing. Just as huge casualty numbers were accepted in the First World War, so Bomber Command were prepared to countenance 5 per cent losses per raid. But RAF losses were proportionally much greater, as infantrymen were relieved from front-line duties after days, not weeks. And Bomber Command was not just sacrificing the lives of its highly trained crews, it was exposing those who survived to psychological damage that would last for decades afterwards.

8.

Coningsby

30 March 1944, Nuremberg

A bright moon filled the streets with a clear, soft light. Münchholzhausen, south of the city of Wetzlar, had only a thousand
inhabitants. Nestled in the gentle folds of the fields of Hesse
in central Germany, it would be an unlikely target for the 'terror
flyers'. This quiet village had found itself beneath the flight path
of the bombers before, but no harm had come to it so far. Checking there were no chinks of light from windows or doorways had
become a way of life. The villagers knew the patrolling wardens
of the *Reichsluftschutzbund** would berate them, carelessness could
spell disaster. As the bombers once again pounded their courses
high above them, some felt bold enough to go outside and watch.

On this clear March night the RAF was heading towards
Nuremberg. Vapour trails formed in the crystal-clear sky. The
bombers were more difficult to see, but occasional glints of light
betrayed them. Streaks of coloured light shot horizontally as the
air battle with night fighters started. The watchers had to be

---

* The *Reichsluftschutzbund* ('National Air Raid Protection League') was
a Nazi organization in charge of air raid precautions in residential areas;
the equivalent of Britain's ARP.

careful as spent shell cases and cannon shells could rain down, breaking tiles and embedding themselves in gardens. The children had collections of things they had found. It seemed the bombers often dropped thousands of strips of tinfoil, which would blow around like confetti, littering the fields and getting stuck in bushes and trees. The action was more intense than they had seen on other nights and the watchers were fascinated by the booming noises followed by distant fires as aircraft plummeted to earth.

At 11.43 the night was illuminated by a huge flash. Buildings were silhouetted against the light for a split second. As the echoes of the explosion died away, the silence was broken by barking dogs and the constant drone of the aircraft above. In the fields, 500 metres away from the village, a huge fire was burning. Many villagers were too afraid to come out of their houses, but others ran into the streets immediately to see what had happened.

Some thought bombs had been dropped, but it became clear that a bomber had crashed close by. A series of small explosions and bright lights cascaded into the air. Ammunition cracked from the fire as .303 bullets cooked off in the intense heat. No one could survive this crash, but some felt nervous that there might be men hiding close by who had parachuted clear. By daybreak the intense fire had died down, revealing a deep smouldering gash in a field above the village. The impact had gouged the earth to a depth of ten metres. A mangled propeller perched on the lip of the smoking crater, one of the few recognizable pieces of the bomber. Thousands of burned and blackened metal fragments were scattered over a large area. Throughout the day, villagers of all ages walked out across the field to see what had shaken their houses to their foundations. Standing in small groups, they gazed at the scene of complete destruction in an otherwise untouched piece of land. The field was filled with the stench of burning and aviation fuel and the remains of bodies were being recovered. As it

German military personnel and inquisitive locals explore the crater at the crash site of Flight Lieutenant L. V. Hyde's Lancaster (ND640), Münchholzhausen, central Germany, 31 March 1944.

fell, the tail of the bomber had broken off and landed a kilometre away. There were two bodies inside.

Lancaster ND640, flown by Flight Lieutenant Leonard Hyde DFC, had been caught by the Me 110 of Oblt. Martin Becker. A rising star of the Luftwaffe, Becker claimed seven bombers that night in what emerged as one of the worst raids for the RAF. Becker's eventual haul of fifty-eight kills made him one of the highest-scoring German aces to survive the war. Becker remembered little of the end of ND640; it had all been over in seconds. He had barely needed to use his on-board radar to find the Lancasters. Lining up his gun cross-hairs with the underside of the silhouetted bomber, he had pressed his gun button. A single upward burst of fire had ruptured the Lancaster's fuel tanks. He had to concentrate on getting clear of the flaming meteor above him. He watched in grim satisfaction as the trail of fire dropped steadily towards the ground. There was no time to dwell on his victory – it was just another target successfully picked up by his navigator.

Jim Comans and crew had taken off from RAF Bourn five minutes earlier than Hyde. His Lancaster was almost certainly one of the aircraft the Comans crew saw fall that night. Normally, it was impossible to tell in the darkness who had been shot down, but in tonight's moonlight, identification was more certain. Flight Lieutenant C. S. Chatten reported:

> I saw the light of tracer fire and an aircraft hit and going down on fire. Its markers must have been jettisoned for I saw them burst below. I identified the markers as belonging to those of the aircraft which had taken off just before me and was sure then that it was my friend Len Hyde.

It appeared that ND640 had no bombs on board when it crashed, but the high-impact speed was not survivable. Hyde was an experienced airman and his loss was keenly felt.

His was a fate that could have befallen any of the crews

that took off from RAF Bourn for Nuremberg on that March evening. The crews were witnessing a seminal moment in the history of Bomber Command. A miscalculation had been made – one that exposed the bomber stream to extraordinary dangers. Perhaps the successes of previous raids had made the planners complacent. The Nuremberg operation was a large one, an 'all effort raid' drawing in as many as 779 aircraft. At briefing, crews were aghast to see how straight the course was to Nuremberg. The normal kinks and feints were absent and, with clear weather and a full moon, the crews would be sitting ducks for the German night fighters. A feeling of bewilderment and despair descended on the briefing room. Surely they were not being asked to fly such a direct and risk-laden course? Air Vice Marshal Don Bennett, in command of the Pathfinders, knew the Nuremberg raid could be a disaster. When he had been consulted about the route by Air Vice Marshal Saundby, deputy to Harris, Bennett had proposed a 'dog leg' course to attempt to deceive German defences. This idea was rejected by the other Group commanders, including Cochrane, who believed that extending an already long flight was too dangerous. Bennett recalled his own reaction and those of his squadron leaders and pilots when the plan was revealed: 'It was the nearest I came to mutiny. I had every Squadron Commander in the Pathfinders call me and say "This is crazy, we can't go."' Despite this, orders were obeyed. Bennett's criticisms of the planning of the Nuremberg raid after the war should be read in the light of his power struggle with Ralph Cochrane, commander of 5 Group, over Pathfinder strategy.

As Jim Comans took off from RAF Bourn that evening, he could clearly see other Lancasters of 97 Squadron in the stream. Jeff Pelletier, Cliff Chatten and 'Jim' Van Raalte were just ahead with Wilbur Gee close by. Just behind, Hyde, Ellesmere and Drane rose and began closing up. They flew in one of the brightest of moons they had seen on operations. Looking across, the crew could even read the red code lettering on the sides of the nearby aircraft. The remaining squadron aircraft had left ten minutes before and had disappeared into the distance.

The German fighter attacks began close to the Belgian border and continued remorselessly. The sky was a network of tracer fire, but the gunners Widdis and Bolland struggled to cope with the menace that stalked them. Now and again, the shape of a fighter would appear below, streaking across the path of the bombers, but never clear enough to get a bead on it. At times fighters could be seen a distance away, illuminated by the German flare dropped each side of the stream, but too far to shoot at as they shadowed the bombers. Burning aircraft were clearly visible as they attempted to keep height and course. Other crews knew all too well that they only served to illuminate their path even more clearly for the German defenders. It took some minutes for the burning bombers to disappear from the sky. Some fell away gradually, others blew up suddenly as the fires reached their bomb load. Ken Cook recalls the experience of watching the death throes of aircraft around them: 'We saw them hit, sometimes aircraft alongside would blow up, but there was nothing we could do, we just had to keep flying.'

In all, the RAF lost 106 aircraft that night, resulting in the deaths of 534 airmen and 157 captured. Just as Schweinfurt was scorched into the memory of the USAAF, so Nuremberg would always be remembered by the RAF as its costliest attack in terms of men and aeroplanes. The raid's unwavering course over France meant that German radar operators were able to call their fighters in accurately. The Luftwaffe had 246 fighters in the air that night. The combination of accurate plotting, clear visibility and lack of night-fighter interference condemned hundreds of Allied airmen to certain death. When the bombers reached Nuremberg, they found the target obscured by cloud. The Comans crew's report is typical of many others: '10/10ths cloud, vis good. On run up 6 Wanganuis were seen in a line at right angle to track. On bombing one only remained. No TIs seen on account of cloud.' The results of the raid were mediocre.

Two aircraft of 97 Squadron – Flight Lieutenant L. V. Hyde's and Flight Lieutenant D. H. Rowlands' – did not return from Nuremberg. In both cases, all the crew were lost. Rowlands was new to 97 Squadron, although it was his crew's second tour of duty. Fifteen minutes after Hyde, Rowlands was caught near Ahorn by an Me 110 flown by Major Martin Drewes, who fired a single burst of cannon into the starboard wing of the Lancaster. She fell immediately, exploding on the ground with a huge flash as the full bomb load ignited. One of the members of Rowlands' crew that night was Flight Lieutenant Richard Trevor-Roper, who had been Guy Gibson's rear gunner on the Dam Busters raid.

Pilot Officer Edwards' Lancaster returned to RAF Bourn badly mangled. The aircraft was removed from flying duties for some weeks as repairs were carried out. The reaction to the Nuremberg raid among crews was that of subdued anger. Some pilots made their opinions known to their commanding officer, others complained to each other, but knew that little could be done. They had to hope that the fiasco of Nuremberg was an aberration. It was not just the loss of their comrades that upset them, but also the enormous psychological strain that they had been placed under. Many were already showing the early signs of emotional breakdown. Heavy drinking, depression and nervous tics were commonplace. Men who had joined the squadron with enthusiasm were becoming shadows of their former selves.

*

The Nuremberg raid came at a time of fundamental change in 97 Squadron. Their strength had been reduced to two flights instead of the normal three. 'C' Flight was sent to RAF Downham

Market to form part of a new squadron, 635. Jim Comans became 'A' Flight commander, replacing Charles McKenzie Dunnicliffe, who assumed command of 582, the other new squadron created in the reorganization. Comans had made the transition from a new pilot to a trusted leader. The remaining two flights of 97 Squadron were being moved back to 5 Group from where they originated in March 1943. This meant a move from RAF Bourn in Cambridgeshire to RAF Coningsby in Lincolnshire. Further changes were afoot as the squadron became a pawn in a strategic reorganization hotly contested at Group level. Unknown to the hard-pressed crews, the role and identity of the Pathfinders was being questioned once again. Ralph Cochrane of 5 Group believed that his strategy of getting Pathfinder Mosquitos 'on the deck' to mark the target was paying dividends. His heavy bombers would follow, still with Pathfinders leading the stream, but as a follow-up to the Mosquitos. Don Bennett of 8 Group was dismissive of the proposed strategy. Mosquitos belonged at high level, he maintained. While he believed in the speed and manoeuvrability of the 'Mossie' to loiter and re-mark targets, low altitudes were out of the question. Bennett loved the Mosquito, describing it as ' the greatest little aircraft ever built', but he was dismissive of Cochrane's claims.

In a charged telephone conversation with Air Marshal Harris in March 1944, Bennett asked whether, under the new strategy, losses of Cochrane's Pathfinder Mosquitos would have to be replaced by Mosquitos under his, Bennett's, command. It was a provocative question because, as both men knew, in normal cir-cumstances replacements for lost aircraft came not from other operational units, but from the manufacturers. In effect, Bennett was demanding to know which was more important, 8 Group under him, or 5 Group under Cochrane. A critical aspect of their conversation centred on Berlin. Bennett insisted that low-level marking of a city was very difficult and in this he was

97 Squadron Lancasters flying low over RAF Bottisham, 9 March 1944. 'Beating up' an airfield in this fashion was generally discouraged.

absolutely correct. After all, Bennett had first-hand experience of the dangers of low flying, having attacked the *Tirpitz*, the most heavily defended target in Europe, at low level. Almost inevitably, Bennett's Halifax had been shot down. Although Bennett had Harris's confidence, the strength of his approach on this occasion played against him. Harris informed Bennett in a 'frigid and formal' letter that he had decided to transfer 97 and 83 Squadron to 5 Group together with Mosquitos of 627 Squadron.

Despite Bennett's misgivings, Cochrane had won his argument with some impressively accurate target results. He had ridden high on the success of the Dam Busters raid, and now with 617 Squadron was preparing to use the 12,000lb Tallboy 'earthquake' bomb. A small number of new bomb sights – the Stabilized Automatic Bomb Sight, or SABS – which proved more accurate than the standard Mark XIV, was introduced to the Pathfinders. One of Cochrane's victories was to have the SABS diverted to 617 Squadron ready for his pinpoint Tallboy attacks. 5 Group had also successfully attacked the Gnome & Rhône aircraft factory in Limoges on 8 February 1944 with a low-level marking undertaken by Leonard Cheshire in a Lancaster.

As Cochrane began to gain the upper hand at the Air Ministry, the animosity between him and Bennett became more heated. Bennett claimed that his disagreements were never personal, only professional, but with two men of extraordinary creativity, friction was inevitable. 97 Squadron were to feel the direct effects of the strategic fallout. Two weeks after Nuremberg and after more training flights than raids, news came of the transfer of 97 Squadron to 5 Group. For those on the ground crews who had served with the squadron the longest, the news that they were to be posted to Coningsby heartened them. They were going back to Lincolnshire – 'Bomber County', close to Woodhall Spa – of which pleasant memories of the summer of 1942 still echoed through the squadron.

News that the squadron was on the move came as no huge surprise to the aircrews. Many had already undertaken five or more postings within their training periods. Unlike peacetime professions, there was no sense of permanence in wartime. Even their conditions of service, often listed as 'for the duration', implied that a sudden end to the war would see them rapidly removed to a civilian role again. As the Comans crew had started their operational flying at RAF Bardney in Lincolnshire, they were content to return to the area. The station was closer to Roy Woollford's new wife in Newark, although a little further for Ken Cook to travel home to the Cotswolds. When it came to squadron movements, the Royal Air Force expected rapid relocation. Only three days after receiving movement orders, the hurriedly arranged ground elements left RAF Bourn for Coningsby on 18 April 1944, taking all the tools and spares they could carry in a trail of lorries. The journey along the clogged roads between Cambridgeshire and Lincolnshire was an arduous one. Later that day, twenty-one Lancasters left Bourn for the final time to make the short trip north.

The crews were impressed by what they found at RAF Coningsby. Substantial hangars, brick-built accommodation blocks and an impressive officers' mess greeted them. Compared with the mud-bound huts they had been used to, the pre-war design of RAF Coningsby seemed positively luxurious. But it was also clear from the rows of Nissen huts and small concrete sectional buildings that the plans had been stretched – there were more people on site than had originally been intended. Older hands who knew Coningsby from their sojourn of 1941 still pined for the Petwood Hotel, the officers' mess appropriated for nearby RAF Woodhall Spa. 97 Squadron had moved there in March 1942, enjoying a year of drinks on the terrace and walks in the manicured gardens. Now it was clear that 617 Squadron were firmly in residence at Woodhall, and they were joined there by the Mosquitos of 627 Squadron.

They learned, too, that they were not going to be alone at Coningsby. 83 Squadron were also in residence. Both squadrons were to be known as 'markers', essentially no different from their previous identities as 'Pathfinders' but acting independently for 5 Group. The crews were not greeted as warmly as they might have hoped. Shortly after their arrival, they were summoned to the station cinema, where the base commander Air Commodore Sharpe lectured them on the need to break their ties with 8 Group. The implied criticism was that, as members of 8 Group, they had become sloppy and that 5 Group demanded greater discipline. His order to commence immediate training was resisted by the squadron commanders, who reminded him that some of the men had been on operations the previous night. The resulting tensions at Coningsby took some weeks to subside.

On the day of 97 Squadron's arrival, two pilots were selected to fly with 5 Group to Juvisy, south-east of Paris, to see the new marking techniques. Jim Comans was chosen together with Flight Lieutenant Charles Owen. They were impressed by the increased use of the radio telephone, R/T, in the target area. The master bombers were attentive in their approach, only allowing the main force to bomb when they were completely satisfied the markers were correctly positioned. Monitoring the fall of bombs, they would call in new markers if the raid began to drift.

20 April 1944, Porte de la Chapelle, Paris

Only two days after their arrival, and with little time to settle into RAF Coningsby, the crews were assigned their first mission. The target was an unfamiliar one. After pounding German cities for month after month, this raid was on the railway marshalling yards at Porte de la Chapelle, in northern Paris. The French, even under German occupation, were still considered to be allies, and crews were instructed to take great care during bombing so as to avoid hitting nearby residential housing. The briefing included aerial photographs that showed the complexity of the grid of railway tracks and warehouses. But they also revealed that Porte de la Chapelle was part of the city of Paris, and was interwoven with civilian dwellings.

Group Captain Leonard Cheshire would lead the attack, low marking with his small Mosquito force to bring in the Lancasters of 617 Squadron above. A second wave would then drop their bombs on the markers placed by the Mosquitos. Attacking railways so close to the city was a risky strategy that both Air Marshal Harris and USAAF chief Carl Spaatz resisted, but the emphasis was shifting to the needs of the imminent invasion of German-occupied western Europe – Operation Overlord, the Normandy landings. A pattern of diversionary raids was already being carried out in the Pas-de-Calais to give the impression that the landings would take place there. The Paris attack would appear to be part of the campaign to prepare for a landing in northern France, but, conveniently, would result in the destruction of a transportation hub that could reinforce the German army heading for Normandy.

The Comans crew boarded Lancaster ND740 just after ten o'clock at night. F-Freddie had been with them to Nuremberg, their first flight with her. Their old friend 'K' had gone, downed over Berlin in late March. ND740 was to become 'their' aircraft for the rest of the tour, taking them on a total of eighteen missions. Just over a year old, she had already survived numerous raids, bearing repair scars and the affections of her ground crew.

For April, it was a warm evening; spring was at hand after a chilly start to the month. It was a relief to be able to touch metal without hands freezing. After ground checks, the engines were started as flight engineer Ken Randle kept watch on revs and engine heat. The Lancaster was chuntering into a steady

The Comans crew and ground staff with F-Freddie, Lancaster ND740, which would carry them on eighteen missions. Back row, left to right: Ken Cook, Daniel 'Jock' Bolland, Jim Comans, Ken Randle, Don Bowes, George Widdis and Roy Woollford.

rhythm, the orange instrument panel lights brightening under the aircraft's power. Taxiing out, they were near the front of the queue heading towards the runway. Tail gunner 'Jock' Bolland was accustomed to going everywhere backwards. He had the advantage of seeing the Lancasters forming up behind him, the spinning propellers glimmering in the ground lights. Wing Commander Jimmy Carter in ND739 was immediately behind them as they reached the base of the runway. To the rear of Carter, Squadron Leader Leatherland closed up in the queue ready for take-off. Bolland was always keeping watch in case anyone was slow on the brakes. Other than shouting a warning, there would be little he could do in the event of an accident. His chances of dodging the chop of a propeller were slim. Thankfully, Carter was keeping his distance this evening as the line of loaded Lancasters waddled down the taxiways.

Turning onto the base of the runway, Comans waited for the flash of the controller's light from the operations cabin located halfway down the runway. As he pushed the four throttle levers fully forwards, the engines rose to full power. Comans took his foot off the brakes and from a slow start they gathered pace, rumbling along Coningsby's asphalt on their take-off run. They were the second aircraft of the squadron to leave that night. Nine thousand pounds of bombs strained in ND740's bomb bay – high explosive to rip up railway tracks and destroy rolling stock and buildings. Paris would be a short trip compared to the long freezing night flights to Berlin. If all went to plan, they would be down and ready for an early breakfast in little over four hours.

With clear visibility, the route over a calm Channel to Paris was simple. On time, the nimble Mosquitos had placed their markers on the railway yards just before 97 Squadron dropped the opening salvos on the target. The crews agreed the markers were well placed, and they felt confident their bombs had struck close to the target. Ken Cook released his bombs from 14,400 feet and saw them strike in a knot precisely where he wanted them. However, in the Comans crew's report later, they noted: 'Fires were seen prior to attack to west of aiming point.' Others observed similar off-target hits. The Edwards crew observed, 'fire also possibly ½ mile south of town'. It was the first inkling that not all the aircraft had hit the aiming points. The Air Ministry soon heard bitter complaints of civilian casualties from their French sources. Local properties had been hit hard, killing 641 and injuring 377. The damage was so widespread that some questioned whether the RAF had hit the target at all. However, the marshalling yards were badly disrupted and some of the damage, which was extensive, would not be repaired until after the war. The tragic loss of civilian life in the Porte de la Chapelle raid showed that, despite precautions, bombing was still prone to dramatic inaccuracies.

The controversy was not heard of at squadron level. Over the whole force, six Lancasters had been lost on the raid and the prevailing view was it was inevitable that some bombs would fall free as aircraft were hit by flak and fighters. Squadron Leader Leatherland had not returned to Coningsby. His Lancaster was hit close to the target area by a night fighter and crashed at Piscop, nine miles from Porte de la Chapelle. It is possible that Leatherland was shot down by Hauptmann Fritz Söthe of *Nachtjagdgeschwader* 4, who claimed a Lancaster north of Paris. None of Leatherland's crew survived.

The Comans crew found themselves at the forefront of the new marking strategy. From the start of their operations, they had worked on similar principles, dropping bombs on coloured markers from high altitude. That markers or bombs went astray was an everyday hazard, but, broadly, hitting any part of a target city was legitimate. Now, with the strategy of 5 Group in the spotlight, greater demands for accuracy were placed on them and a whole new system of coordinating the bomber force was put in place. Under the old system, there was limited communication between individual bombers and Pathfinders. In future, the bombers were to be in direct contact with the master bomber, who would stop a raid if it started to swing off target. In practice, this meant that no two raids were the same as each operation was precisely tailored to the nature of the target in question.

⋆

Although the feud between Cochrane and Bennett often seizes the attention of historians, the adoption of lower-level marking techniques was largely due to the influence of Wing Comman-der Leonard Cheshire. A thoughtful and compassionate man, Cheshire possessed a wealth of experience as a bomber pilot. Flying Whitleys and Halifaxes, he had already been awarded the DSO, bar and DFC. He believed that squadron leaders should be personally concerned with every individual under their command. While at 35 Squadron, he tried to prevent battle-fatigued men being labelled 'LMF' and went out of his way to help them. In one case, he even took a man on to his own crew to encourage him. Having seen nearly all of his contemporaries from his training course perish on operations, Cheshire was determined that casualties in the air and, more remarkably, on the ground, should be kept to a minimum.

Cheshire had put himself forward to command the Path-finders in April 1943 but had been rebuffed in favour of Bennett. Six months later, in October 1943, the offer of command of 617 Squadron enabled him to return to operations, where, despite the extreme danger, his heart lay. Relinquishing his rank of Group Captain, Cheshire was called in to give substance to 617, who had lost their way after the unsuccessful raid on the Dortmund–Ems Canal in September 1943. They had lost five of their eight Lancasters, including their new squadron commander,

G. W. Holden. The use of new 12,000lb bombs* proved problematic, their design being too unaerodynamic. Barnes Wallis was near to completing their successor, the Tallboy, a torpedo-shaped bomb capable of considerable ground penetration due to its hardened nose.

Cheshire's first challenge was to overcome the initial hostility towards an outsider coming into 617 Squadron. Cochrane also insisted he undertake a three-week course on the Lancaster, something Cheshire felt was unnecessary. His attitude soon changed once he came face to face with the difficulty of trying to maintain a three-aircraft formation in the dark at treetop level. His second challenge was to prepare the crews to operate with the new Tallboy bomb, which was so big that it required 617 Squadron's Lancasters to be adapted, the bomb bay and its doors being removed completely to allow the bomb to be slung underneath.

The Tallboy brought with it the need for pinpoint accuracy. Barnes Wallis was unequivocal: he needed his bombs within 15 yards of the target from 16,000 feet. Cheshire was taken aback, but Wallis told him, 'If you are going to scatter my bombs all over the countryside, there's no point building them.' Even with the more accurate Stabilized Automatic Bomb Sight, the task of recognizing the target remained difficult. If the target flares were adrift, they bombed the wrong 'pickle barrel' – albeit highly accurately. On 16 December 1943, 617 Squadron bombed the V1 flying bomb site at Abbeville, getting all ten of their Tallboys close to the marker. Unfortunately, the marker was 350 yards short of the target.

Cheshire began to experiment with the idea of low-level marking. He was encouraged in this by Squadron Leader Mickey

---

* These bombs were up-scaled versions of the 4,000 and 8,000lb 'Cookie' – essentially barrel bombs.

Martin, who had participated in the Dam Busters raid and had led the squadron temporarily just before Cheshire's arrival. One of the problems of high-level operations was that the flare would often skip 100 yards or more when it hit the ground. Cheshire and Martin discovered that by diving the Lancaster onto the target and releasing at 5,000 feet, the marker was more likely to stay put. The role of dropping markers from a lower level was best suited to the Mosquito, but at this point Cheshire did not have any. His first raid using the technique had to be approved at the highest level as it would involve the bombing of the Gnome & Rhône aircraft factory at Limoges on 8/9 February 1944. The conditions were demanding. Not one single civilian life was to be lost. Cheshire's first task was to persuade the 500 workers, most of them women, to leave the factory. Cheshire made two low-level passes over the factory ten minutes before the raid at less than 100 feet, which, as he put it, 'seemed to do the trick'. The target markers were laid accurately and the bomber force, supervised by radio communications, proceeded to put the factory out of action.

By the time the Comans crew had made the move across to 5 Group, it was hoped that the enlarged marker force could replicate 617 Squadron's success. Cheshire was based only a stone's throw away from Coningsby at RAF Woodhall Spa and his personable approach meant his advice and support was readily available to the crews of 97 and 83 Squadrons. The Lancasters of these squadrons would not, however, be required to make Cheshire's and Martin's diving attack. Mosquitos would be the first in, placing early markers in key positions. The other Pathfinder squadrons would reinforce the marking on larger targets, circling for secondary tasks if the master bomber felt more marking was necessary. The strategy depended on strong R/T and wireless communications and it was here that parts of the plan broke down.

22 April 1944, Braunschweig

Two days after the attack on Paris, 97 Squadron were on the way to their next target in northern Germany as part of a force of 238 Lancasters and 17 Mosquitos. It was the first time in twenty-one missions as Pathfinders that the Comans crew were not carrying any high explosive bombs, only marker flares. Braunschweig was not as far away as Berlin, but with the need to loiter close to the target the flight would still be over six hours. F-Freddie's tanks were full of fuel so a hit on the underside of the aircraft, near the bomb bay, would still be disastrous. The plane might well not explode immediately, and they would have a few seconds to try to jettison burning flares, but the intensity of the ignition would cut through metal rapidly. If their Lancaster did not explode, they would fall as a blazing star, brilliantly lighting up the bomber stream, a fate they had witnessed before on dozens of occasions.

The crew dismissed such thoughts as they made their way over the North Sea. Approaching Braunschweig and twenty minutes from their target, the 'Flare Leader' decided that visibility was clear enough to bomb visually. This was one of the last clear VHF transmissions the crew heard from him and soon Ken Cook in the Perspex nose was reporting that a thick haze was building. The Flare Leader had changed his mind and ordered emergency illumination by Wanganuis, but not everyone heard him. Jim Comans pressed on, the streaky cloud beneath making aiming very difficult – '6/10th cloud' they would report later. The flak was light and in the absence of blinding searchlights, Ken Cook was able to drop six flares. Jim Comans put the Lancaster into a wide orbit to watch the progress of the raid. Frustratingly, they could see bombs falling well outside the target area. Nothing was heard on any of the frequencies, and it appeared communications had failed. Other 97 Squadron aircraft later reported that the city was completely obscured and chose to use their H2S sets to identify the target.

Even with light flak, staying in the target area was uncomfortable. Every noise seemed amplified as the tension mounted. Jim Comans' voice over the intercom calmly announced they were going around for a second run to reinforce marking. The four men in front were fully engaged in performing the manoeuvre; further back in the fuselage, Woollford, Widdis and Bolland rolled their eyes and muttered to themselves. Homing in on a target flare that seemed to be in the right place, Ken Cook waited until the cross-hairs on his bomb sight converged on the bright green light below. As they came into the run, he had selected the switches that controlled each flare position in the bomb bay. The last few seconds seemed interminable as his thumb remained extended over the hand-held switch. Pressing the button, he released another batch of flares to drop on the target.

'Flares gone,' he called. The lesser weight of the flares meant that the lift in the Lancaster was less perceptible than with a heavy bomb load. Ken Cook's assumptions were correct; the green marker was correctly placed. With the loss of VHF communication, the decision to re-mark the target was a call that Comans had had to make on his own, and it turned out to be a good one. Overall, however, the raid was not a success. The new 5 Group strategy had unravelled because of the problem with communications. Replicating a model that had been successful for a single squadron across a stream of hundreds of bombers would take more time to be effective.

24 April 1944, Munich

The pace of life at RAF Coningsby was manic. Within six days of relocating from RAF Bourn they had been called upon to fly three demanding operations. They were tired, but, being young, were loath to admit it. Falling asleep without warning was commonplace. The pre-raid briefings could take two hours and while some officers injected humour and tried to keep their presentations lively, the monotone delivery of others was sleep-inducing. There had been little time to visit the bar and no chance to get into Lincoln for a night out.

It was pleasant to be outside and, when time allowed, the crew would pedal over to the dispersals to chat with the ground crew. The Lancasters creaked and ticked gently in the sun. Although the crew were very glad of the warmer weather, the narrow metal fuselage heated up quickly, accentuating the smells of canvas, oil and petrol. During daylight training they were in another world of discomfort, still needing to wear their thermals for high-level flight but feeling much too warm on the ground. However, a touch of brightness lightened their spirits. Even the green and brown camouflage of the Lancasters' upper surfaces looked cheerier in the spring light. Around the dispersals, new grass was growing and tiny wild flowers were pushing their way up along the edges of the taxiways. Ground crews worked in light overalls, sleeves rolled up as they peered into engines, checked oil levels and loaded bombs. The sparrows around the hangars cheeped incessantly as they sought out mates for the new season. Spring was breaking out, but would the crew see the summer that followed?

Preparations for the Allied invasion of Europe were gaining momentum. The crews could see in the diversity of targets that the wave of D-Day was preparing to break. More 'no fly' areas, denoting camps and troop concentrations, were marked on their maps. Much of the south coast was off-limits and aircraft straying too close were frequently fired on by trigger-happy gunners. Ships had always been a hazard, but now there seemed to be more white wakes in the seas below. Returning low from a raid in rising light was dangerous if the crew passed too close to an Allied warship. It seemed sailors preferred to fire first and ask questions later. The Germans were also jumpy. Their propaganda broadcasts had often been targeted at the airmen, but now new names and locations were being mentioned, many of them American army units.

Getting F-Freddie airborne for a thirty-minute flight did much to keep their minds focused on the task ahead. Munich would be a long trip and daylight flying to iron out technical problems was a godsend. Coming back into Coningsby's circuit, Comans had to keep a sharp lookout for other aircraft, because there were always plenty of them around. The two squadrons on site and the proximity of the circuit at Woodhall Spa – no more than two miles away – meant that the Lincolnshire skies were crowded. With each of Bomber Command's airfields in the area putting up their aircraft for cross-country or test flights, daylight flying could be just as hazardous as flying by night. A lost training aircraft stumbling through their airspace or even a disorientated American from one of the many airfields further south could spell disaster if it was not spotted. Care was also needed in keeping watch for enemy aircraft. Although attacks in daylight were less common, it was not unheard of for a German fighter to latch on to a bomber in the circuit. Only the day before, an Albemarle training aircraft from 42 OTU had been shot down at Kirton Fen, less than four miles from Coningsby. Training for night flying, the aircraft passed close to the airfield at 04.00 hours when it was hit by an explosion. Its loss was officially attributed to a German intruder, although some rumours suggested it was fired on from Coningsby after failing to identify itself correctly.

Bringing F-Freddie round to its dispersal, the crew left her as ground crew began preparing for the night ahead. Even when it was loaded with flares, the Lancaster would be much lighter than a standard bombed-up aircraft. The mission ahead would be the longest the crew had flown, ten hours. They had enough fuel to loiter over Munich to ensure they were available to the master bomber for re-marking duties. Since night fighters were proving to be such dangerous enemies, the idea of waiting around a target area for an extended period was not a pleasant thought. When the crew had volunteered for the Pathfinders in the headiness of youthful enthusiasm, they imagined they would be first in and first out of the target. 5 Group's method of pathfinding gave them the worst of both worlds: first in and last out. At least by the time they reached Munich, their fuel load would be lighter and make them more manoeuvrable than the heavily laden followers. In the technology arrayed against them, the Germans had also equipped some of their Ju88 fighters with Naxos-Z radar warning receivers, which detected H2S emissions. Although the device proved to be inaccurate, reports of its use trickled through to the crews, further increasing their anxieties.

The raid on Munich was to be a significant step in Leonard Cheshire's plan to close-mark targets. He had asked Harris to give him Mosquitos, but not just attached to the bomber force; Cheshire wanted his own Mosquitos within 617 Squadron. Cheshire admitted that he was nervous accompanying Cochrane to the meeting, a lowly wing commander asking for favours from high command. Operating two types of aircraft within the same squadron was unusual, not least because different aircraft had different requirements when it came to servicing and repairs. And not only did Cheshire want the aircraft to be based at Woodhall Spa, he wanted to fly one of them himself to mark the target. Harris agreed, but in the light of the raid on Porte de la Chapelle he told Cheshire he could only keep the Mosquitos if Munich was a success.

Realizing the raid was important, the squadron navigation officer asked Comans for a seat on the flight, bumping Don Bowes from his navigator's position. Squadron Leader Stevens had already completed his tour with other squadrons, gaining the DFC and bar. Normally, an SNO would not fly on operations; his role was to provide information and on-site training to the operational navigators. Whether Stevens was asked to go on the raid to gain experience of the new marking technique, or whether he leaned on fellow Australian Comans to unofficially hitch a ride, is not known. Whatever the reason for his presence, the new man at the navigation station working alongside Ken Cook should have proved an asset. Unfortunately, the opposite would turn out to be the case.

F-Freddie had twelve cluster flares and a green target indicator on board as it climbed away from Coningsby at 20.50 hours. Ahead, 617 Squadron would start the raid with Leonard Cheshire leading in one of his four borrowed Mosquitos Mark VIs. The speed advantage of the Mosquito over the Lancaster was such that Cheshire took off from Woodhall Spa two hours after the Lancasters. Cheshire was 100mph faster than the bombers, but his calculations were thrown by bad weather. His only option was to take a more direct route, chasing the Lancasters to reach the target on time. Shortening his route meant that he flew over the centre of Augsburg on the way to Munich. Continuous fire rose slowly, flashing in front of him. Light shells, 20mm and 37mm, darted in streams of tracer. Heavy 88mm flak guns produced sudden flashes of flame as altitude-fused shells thumped the air around him. Multiple searchlights tried to pick out his Mosquito. There was nothing to be done but to fly on into the maelstrom. The main force had taken the initiative and were already dropping flares as he approached. Identifying the target, Cheshire pushed down the nose of Mosquito MS993. Diving from 12,000 feet, he dropped his marker at 3,000 feet at 01.41 hours into the teeth of accurate flak. Pulling out, he continued to circle, often making passes as low as 700 feet to assess accuracy. Some might have judged his flying as foolhardy, but Cheshire later said in an interview that his method was to get himself into trouble quickly, then work out what to do.

Jim Comans had arrived at Munich at 01.25, 'topping' the target at 19,500 feet. Ken Cook reported that he couldn't see the yellow target indicator. They were sixteen minutes ahead of Cheshire. As the tension built, they waited. Circling over a target as threatening as Munich was the last thing they wanted to do. A yellow marker finally appeared but Cook and Stevens agreed it was too far south. Turning into their bombing run, they identified the datum point* by H2S at 01.38 and headed into the field of flak. Sitting at his desk behind the cockpit bulkhead, radio operator Roy Woollford was more isolated than the others. He knew for the next few minutes they would fly straight and level, daring the gunners below to pick them off. He listened intently for wireless commands, but his life was out of his hands. They dropped their green target indicator and seven flares just after Cheshire belatedly marked his point. Munich was more than ready for them as flak sailed upwards to their level. They heard Cheshire give the order to bomb over the R/T, then waited to see if they needed to re-mark. But soon they were made aware that their job was done for the night.

Setting course for the return leg, they flew west towards France expecting to make several turns to take them back home. Having an experienced man like Stevens as navigator, Comans should have felt comfortable. As the flight progressed, Comans became aware that there was some discussion as to their position at the table behind him. They seemed to have missed one of their northerly turn points and a nagging doubt began to creep into Comans' mind. Having worked with Don Bowes for so long, he

---

* A marker dropped upwind of the target, enabling crews' aimers to enter a 'false wind' setting into their bomb sight to bring the bombs onto target more accurately.

knew instinctively from the tone of his voice whether or not all was well with their course. But he found it hard to read Stevens' detached voice over the intercom. Was his pause after a question a sign of confidence or of indecision? Stevens appeared to be struggling to answer the question 'are we lost?' It was a dark night with no moon visible. A navigation error now – on such a long trip – could lead to a critical fuel shortage later.

Stevens and Cook pored over the maps on the nav table, but they were unable to provide Comans with any precise instructions. Comans clicked his intercom switch and asked Woollford to look out of the astrodome above the wireless operator's desk. Climbing up, Woollford reported that there were glimmers of dawn light on the horizon, but in the wrong place. Comans cursed under his breath. By the time Stevens had caught up, they were at least 100 miles off course. Turning north, they picked out the Cherbourg peninsula. Not realizing that the German-occupied Channel Islands were heavily fortified, they were bewildered to find they were subjected to heavy flak over Jersey. The gunners below had only one target to aim for. Holes were being punched in ND470 as Comans struggled to get clear, diving and twisting to throw the batteries off target.

Cutting east, Comans ordered that the rest of their flares be jettisoned over the sea as he levelled out at 8,000 feet. F-Freddie was still holding together despite the damage and all four engines sounded steady. It was 6.10 a.m. and they knew that, under normal circumstances, they were due at Coningsby in forty minutes, but there were still eighty miles of Channel to cross before they reached the south coast, and flight engineer Ken Randle was increasingly concerned about their declining fuel reserves. They had lost altitude, and were flying lower now, in choppier air. Even making landfall on the south coast looked improbable, but they had no choice but to press on into the open sea. A forced landing in France would lead to their being taken captive, but to make it inland they would have to fly across the German coastal defence batteries, which would be extremely dangerous. Parachuting out over water would greatly reduce their chances of survival. If they couldn't reach land, their only hope was to ditch the Lancaster and hope they could get into the dinghy before she sank. Jim Comans' memories of his unplanned ditching in the North Sea in September 1943 were not pleasant ones. He knew he might lose some of his crew. It was getting light, too, and they had to hope their course had not attracted the attentions of the German radar operators. As the English coastline formed ahead, Roy Woollford suggested he make a call on the 'Darky' emergency frequency. The crew were relieved to hear the controller reply and vector them to RAF Warmwell close to the Dorset coast.

Calling the approach to Warmwell, Comans heard an American voice reply. As they turned towards the homing beacon, Comans was relieved to see the Drem* airfield lighting guiding him in. This system comprised a series of ten-foot-high posts with lights on the top that enabled long-nosed fighters such as the Spitfire, whose pilots had a restricted view over their nose, to locate the runway. Warmwell was a grass strip, so touching down an aircraft as heavy as the Lancaster required a gentle touch. Comans knew if he was too heavy on the brakes he could skid or tail-loop, yet he knew also that this was probably a much shorter strip than he was accustomed to. Having landed safely, he turned to taxi towards the airfield buildings. He could see now that this was a USAAF fighter base. In the rising light the shape of the twin-boomed P-38 Lightning fighters at the dispersals were unmistakable. Perched on their tricycle undercarriage, they looked powerful and aggressive. A wave of relief swept over the crew. Once again, they had cheated disaster by a narrow margin. The fuel gauges

* The system was developed at RAF Drem, in East Lothian, Scotland.

were touching zero as a jeep came out to guide them across the strip. Jim Comans praised Woollford afterwards, telling him it had been he who had saved them with only a few minutes of fuel left. The Americans welcomed them warmly, gathering curiously around the bomber. It was time for a US-style breakfast, but not before the important phone call was made to Coningsby, informing control that they were safe.

The raid was considered a success. Bomber Command had achieved more hits on the centre of Munich than in all the other day and night raids put together. Leonard Cheshire's tenacity had paid off. Despite flak damage, he brought his force of three Mosquitos safely home. In September 1944, Cheshire was awarded the Victoria Cross. The *London Gazette* cited Cheshire's conduct across his whole operational career, from 1940 to 1944, but special mention was made of the Munich raid:

> He was illuminated from above and below. All guns within range opened fire on him. Diving to 700 feet, he dropped his markers with great precision and began to climb away. So blinding were the searchlights that he almost lost control. He then flew over the city at 1,000 feet to assess the accuracy of his work and direct other aircraft. His own was badly hit by shell fragments but he continued to fly over the target area until he was satisfied that he had done all in his power to ensure success.

Despite holes in their fuselage, the Comans crew in Lancaster ND470 made the flight home from Warmwell next morning. The trip took an hour and demonstrated just how far off course they had been thrown. It was a beautiful sunny morning, with the bright green fields below visible through patchy cloud. It was good to feel the sun breaking into the cockpit, warming the chilly gunners and illuminating the fine dust suspended in the air around their instruments. They hoped to be able to escape to a pub later, but they knew their chances were slim. The crew had become creatures of the night. Following the phases of the moon, they expected to fly on the darkest evenings. Nuremberg had tragically demonstrated that even the light of a half-moon could prove lethal. When they landed at Coningsby, they knew that the ground crew would begin repairing the damage immediately. But first, they would want to know every detail of the flight. Unlike the debriefing officers, the men on the ground had an emotional attachment to their aircraft that equalled the aircrew's. They would work long hours patching holes and replacing equipment so the 'F' would be serviceable the very next day.

26 April 1944, Schweinfurt

After long hours in the air and the need to recover from the stress of Munich, the crews must have hoped for an easier target than Schweinfurt. The operations of 26 April were split into two raids: one was going to Essen in the Ruhr, but 97 Squadron was on the second, to Schweinfurt, further to the south-east. There was nothing good to be said about the target. It was heavily defended from the ground and even with the raid going in further north, the crews felt sure there would be swarms of fighters, too. The briefing room was filled with pale, tired faces, some looking sick, others just afraid. It seemed to the airmen that Bomber Command was doing everything in its power to put their lives in the utmost danger. It was an unspoken thought, for they knew they were part of a much larger war, but they found it hard to resist the rising feeling of helplessness. The writer and journalist James Delingpole suggested in the *Spectator* in 2010 that 'Men fight, not for their country... but for their mates.' In the context of a bomber, this rings true, for not only did a good crew support one another psychologically, but, ultimately, they gave their lives for each other.

For a few, the air battle was overwhelmingly exciting, a high-stakes game of huge risks, but one that fed an adventurous spirit. Many of these men could never settle properly into civilian life when peace came in 1945, because no experience could match the intensity of their wartime operations. When finishing a tour of duty, they became bored and recalcitrant. They had become addicted to the rush of adrenaline that accompanied a dangerous mission. Some turned to alcohol, both to calm nerves and to heighten the emotional effects of flying. A culture of heavy drinking pervaded all parts of their lives as bomber crew.

Schweinfurt may have been a tough target, but had the men of 97 Squadron been able to see into their futures they would have been more optimistic. After losing many men through the protracted Battle of Berlin, they were entering a phase during which only four Lancasters would be lost in 170 sorties over the next six-week period – one of which was in a mid-air collision with another Lancaster.

As the marking force arrived over the target, it seemed that Schweinfurt was living up to their gloomy expectations. The VHF frequency from the Mosquitos was jammed. Heavy breezes threw marking calculations off course as the raid dispersed across the city. Wing Commander Carter of 97 Squadron tried to get flares in the correct target area and supervised his reserve marking force. It was a difficult task. When he observed markers falling in the wrong places, he attempted to drop his own flares to reinforce the target, but saw them fall 1,500 yards south of where he intended. Carter ordered the force to bomb 1,000 yards north of his flares. Ken Cook was confident he had hit the target, reporting that he could see the built-up area visually. Others were more vague, describing a smokescreen and fires burning in scattered areas.

German fighters had latched on to the bomber stream early. Squadron Leader Simpson reported: 'Combat and aircraft losses took place on second half of leg D to E, both sides of track permanently illuminated with fighter flares.' Although 97 Squadron escaped losses on 26 April, other squadrons were hit with constant fighter attacks. The most famous action that night was fought by Flight Sergeant Norman Jackson, a flight engineer on 106 Squadron. Badly mauled by a Focke-Wulf 190, Jackson's Lancaster was on fire. He had been wounded by shell splinters, but still volunteered to climb out onto the wing to attempt to put out an engine fire with a fire extinguisher. Despite his best efforts, he was swept off, trailing a burned parachute, which had opened early. With burns to his hands and face, he landed roughly in a field before crawling to the door of a house to seek help. He spent ten months in a German hospital before being sent to a prisoner-of-war camp. Jackson was awarded the Victoria Cross for his efforts, one of only ten within Bomber Command.

83 Squadron, their neighbours at RAF Coningsby, did not escape losses at Schweinfurt. The Pennington crew in ND400 were shot down by flak. They crashed on the return leg outside the quiet town of Dahn, 118 miles from the target. Only one of the seven crew survived, a depressingly familiar statistic. Bombing accuracy may have improved in the months leading to spring 1944, but there was no improvement in the survivability of a falling Lancaster.

The raid on Schweinfurt, a strategically important target, was deemed a failure. Essen, however, had been a success, so Bomber Command had made something of the night. But even with the promises of increased marking accuracy, the road ahead was far from certain. The American daylight offensive was just beginning to make inroads into Luftwaffe fighter strength. It took several more weeks before the effect of Allied long-range fighters was felt. The Luftwaffe lost 34 per cent of its fighters in February 1944 and faced a huge jump to 56 per cent in March. Nevertheless, aircraft production maintained its fighter force at 1,700 aircraft.

However, the writing was on the wall for the Luftwaffe. Although it was still receiving new aeroplanes, the experienced pilots required to fly them were becoming ever harder to find.

During the early months of 1944, Germany was preparing a new aircraft for combat readiness, the Messerschmitt Me 262. This early jet pioneer came into service too late to play much of a role in the fight against the Allied bombing offensive. A training unit, 262, was formed at Lechfeld, south of Augsburg, on 19 April 1944 to test the new plane. The effect of the Me 262 was not felt until the winter of 1944/5, and only a small number of the aircraft were used as night fighters over Berlin in the closing days of the war.

At last the Comans crew were able to grab a short break, to catch up with letters home and buy tobacco or cigarettes. There was also time to explore some of the airmen's haunts in the district, the Leagate and Abbey Lodge pubs being the most convenient for Coningsby. On days when the crews were stood down, it took some effort to reach the bar through the crush of bodies and the permanent haze of cigarette smoke. During the weeks that followed they also got to know the Blue Bell Inn at Tattershall Thorpe, where the ceiling was covered with the signatures of airmen, and reacquainted themselves with their old haunt from their Bardney days, the Saracen's Head in Lincoln, otherwise known as 'The Snake Pit'. Four of the crew were married, so the dance halls did not have the same attraction, but they enjoyed the single men's stories of romantic intrigue. Ken Cook recalled that the crew had great respect for Jim Comans as a pilot. However, he confesses to not liking him as a man because he had no sense of humour.

Roy Woollford had numbered each raid in his logbook. Schweinfurt was numbered thirty-three. Had he been American, he would have been making his way back to the United States on an ocean liner for two months of leave after his thirtieth mission.

Many did not return to Europe, taking up training duties in the USA to prepare thousands of men for their service as bomber crews. The new chapter in the Comans crew's career may only just have started, with their move to Coningsby, but the pages of a larger story, the D-Day invasion, were about to be turned.

9.

Tour de France

The tiny settlement of Bosc Geffroy, nine miles from Neufchâtel-en-Bray in Normandy, was just waking up. A woman in her fifties walked down the long strip of land at the back of her smallholding. Clutching a bucket of feed, she went to a shed and opened the hatch for her chickens. As they emerged clucking, she emptied her bucket into the shallow wooden trough nearby. This she did every day at around the same time, rarely changing her morning routine. But today she was surprised to hear the noise of an aircraft. In the distance the shape of an Allied fighter appeared out of the haze, then swept across the fields towards her. The woman stood transfixed. Villagers heard the rattle of machine guns as the aircraft swept low overhead. Later, after the undertaker had recovered the woman's body, the village was in a frenzy of speculation. It was rumoured she was a collaborator, or at least on friendly terms with the German occupiers. Had the resistance organized a strike against her? It was a mystery that would reverberate around the farmhouse tables of Bosc Geffroy for the next seventy years.

The presence of the Allied fighter in the area may well have had something to do with developments in Callengeville, less than two miles away from Bosc Geffroy across the fields, where the Germans had built a series of concrete bunkers and a ramp. This was a launch site for the newly developed V1 flying bomb, and low-level Allied reconnaissance flights were showing increasing interest in such facilities, which were beginning to be built across eastern Normandy and the Pas-de-Calais. Whether the fighter mistook the farmer's wife for a German, or if she was indeed the subject of a complex assassination plot, remains a mystery. A few weeks later, Callengeville was to become a target for Allied bombers. As preparations for D-Day intensified, the villagers of these coastal regions of Seine-Maritime wondered what would become of them when the invasion came. Vast waves of bombers swept overhead day and night. Soon it was possible to tell by the dull musical note of the engines whether they were American or British. Normally, the American planes flew by day. Word spread that the bombers were ranging all over France, even down into the south.

As long ago as 1942, the raids on Saint-Nazaire and Dieppe had sharpened Hitler's fears of an Allied invasion of Europe, and he had ordered the construction of an 'Atlantic Wall', a vast line of coastal fortifications stretching from southern France to northern Norway. Along France's Channel coast, the Pas-de-Calais – which the Germans expected to be the location of the Allied invasion – was particularly heavily fortified, as were the port towns of Cherbourg and Saint-Malo. The Germans had filled the fields around the coasts of the Pas-de-Calais, Somme and Seine-Maritime with searchlights and gun batteries. When the bombers flew over, this belt of light lit up the countryside for miles. During the blackout, it was even possible to open the shutters of a house and read a newspaper in the fake moonlight. Over recent months, low-flying Allied aircraft had terrorized farmers and animals alike, the automatic reaction of the former diving to the ground producing a multitude of minor injuries and a torrent of swearing.

Occasional discoveries of parachutes in fields led some to speculate that saboteurs were being spirited in. Others said they belonged to downed airmen who were being sheltered by the resistance. The Germans were constantly vigilant. Large swathes of beach were out of bounds, filled with wire entanglements and giant pieces of metal forming X-shapes. The headlands were fortified with new concrete gun emplacements and trenches snaking through the dunes. The thousands of forced labourers who had been brought in to complete these defences had all left. The nearby villages were now swamped with Wehrmacht and it was unwise to venture close to them without good reason. Some of these soldiers were young boys, others much older men. The coastal garrisons were not manned by prime fighting troops. The edgy Germans set up a multitude of checkpoints, even at locations some miles inland. For the locals, having their belongings searched became part and parcel of everyday life. Baskets on bicycles were favourite subjects of attention, although the prettier the cyclist the easier it was to get through the checkpoint. The gendarmerie were often present as the Germans cracked down on their enemies, fuelling the desire of the resistance to strike back. Throughout northern France a new nervousness was spreading. Radio broadcasts from England carried many code words and French phrases. The Allies were coming and, with Neufchâtel-en-Bray still lying in ruins from the battle of 1940, the locals were under no illusions as to what this might mean. However, most in Normandy believed the invasion would fall further north.

The resistance was growing bolder, although the fear of retribution still constrained their efforts. Churchill's Special Operations Executive, the SOE, helped organize and supply the disparate resistance groups including the Maquis, French guerrilla fighters. Many of them operated further south than the invasion zone, but London increased its influence by dropping agents and supplies. By the spring of 1944 many obeyed direct instructions from London to delay actions until ordered. This did not prevent the resistance from staging small attacks and settling scores. On 22 April, nineteen-year-old Stephen Grady walked into a bar in the French town of Steenwerke close to the Belgian border. Grady was Anglo-French, and his father had been a gardener for the Commonwealth War Graves Commission before the war. Ordering a demi, he asked to see an off-duty German officer who was helping the older woman who owned the bar. When he appeared from the kitchen, wearing an apron, Grady shot him twice in the chest before escaping on a bike.

As well as carrying out direct action, the resistance was supplying the British with target intelligence. Drawn maps of troop positions, factory outlays and the location of garrison buildings frequently made their way into Allied hands.

29 April 1944, Clermont-Ferrand

By the standards of raids on major cities, the planned raid on the Michelin tyre factory at Clermont-Ferrand by a force of fifty-nine Lancasters was a small one. Four Mosquitos were to open the attack, diving to place their markers on the factory roofs. It was unlikely that they would encounter much fighter opposition, although the factory would have some anti-aircraft guns. It was to be a long flight for the bomber crews, over six and a half hours. Bomber Command were also to send seventy-three bombers to a munitions factory in Saint-Médard-en-Jalles, close to Bordeaux. The aristocratic resistance fighter and SOE operative Robert Jean-Marie de La Rochefoucauld later claimed it was he who destroyed the factory with explosives-filled baguettes. This wild story remains unsubstantiated in SOE records, but they used the two bombing raids as cover for twenty RAF aircraft supplying the resistance.

In a report she sent back to London that the Michelin plant at Clermont-Ferrand be targeted by Bomber Command, the SOE agent Pearl Witherington had proposed: 'There is little defence around Clermont-Ferrand and what there is, is mobile. I hate to suggest this bombing of Michelin, but Villiers and I think it would give the management a lesson.'

The implied criticism of the Michelin management suggests the resistance network had penetrated deep into the factory and found an unwillingness to cooperate. Later, Michelin were to claim that staff deliberately adulterated the rubber for tyres going to the German Eastern Front to make them burst in sub-zero temperatures. It was probably true to say that internal sabotage alone would not have dented production to a significant degree in a factory under German supervision. What was required was an air raid that would destroy the machinery on the factory floor – and such a raid would have the added advantage of providing cover for the activities of the resistance network.

At RAF Coningsby, F-Freddie was loaded with a mix of flares and target indicators. She also carried five 1,000lb bombs, each of them chalk-marked 'Fused'. As the last glow of the sun tinged the western horizon, 97 Squadron's fifteen Lancasters set course for southern France. The first quarter moon reminded them of the disaster of Nuremberg a month before, but this evening was very different. German radar operators waited for the bombers to turn into Germany, their course suggesting that Munich would be the target. However, the Lancaster force bore south, away from the Kammhuber Line, the deep string of Freya and Würzburg radar stations extending from Kiel on the Baltic coast to Saint-Dizier, 100 miles south-east of Paris. As the miles stretched away, the Comans crew knew it would be harder for the fighters to find them.

Conditions were perfect over Clermont-Ferrand. The shape of the city was clearly visible on their H2S set. They dropped their flares immediately over the target, illuminating the factory for the diving Mosquitos to place target markers. A Luftwaffe runway, smooth and straight, was caught in the intense brightness, pointing the bombers towards the nearby tyre factory. The twin Gothic steeples of the cathedral were bathed in an eerie light, casting multiple shadows on the buildings nearby. Ken Cook could see the target indicators had dropped on the factory. The Mosquitos had done their job well. They attacked at 8,000 feet, making Ken's job much easier than when they launched high-level attacks on German cities. Jim Comans brought ND740 around again and Ken Cook dropped yellow target indicators. The master bomber gave the instruction to bomb at 01.27 hours. Fires erupted from the factory as the bombs and incendiaries struck home. Thick palls of black smoke rose from the plant as hundreds of tonnes of rubber began to burn. Keeping a lookout for other bombers, Comans brought the Lancaster round for a third pass, this time to drop their 1,000lb bombs. By now the main factory buildings were being swallowed in the glare of the explosions. Percussion waves washed over ND740, booming like giant fists on the underside of the fuselage. There was no fighter opposition. A single light gun was seen to fire from the factory site with flickers of red and white tracer soaring skywards. The Lancasters' gunners sent their own streams of tracers towards the single gun. With its bombs gone, ND740 sailed upwards. At the controls, Comans relished the lighter feel of the aircraft as his thoughts began to turn towards Coningsby and home.

Dawn was creeping in as the Lancasters made the south coast of England. They could see the brown smudge of the London sky to starboard. Factory chimneys streamed plumes of steam and smoke into the chill air over Northampton. A song or two led by George Widdis always helped the inbound flight as the shapes of grey fields formed into hedges and trees. Other bombers were appearing in the rising light. 'Jock' Bolland in the rear turret had watched a couple close by for some time. By their course, he felt certain they were 97 Squadron aircraft and, as they approached Coningsby, he could pick out their large code numbers, OF-L of the Baker crew and OF-Z of Simpson. It was impressive how, after six hours and forty minutes in the air, much of it in pitch darkness, the Lancasters arrived back at the right time. Bob Lasham, another ex-9 Squadron pilot, took off one minute before Comans and landed two minutes afterwards. It was a level of accuracy that the Pathfinders prided themselves on.

All aircraft had returned safely to Coningsby. There were no empty beds to reallocate or lockers to unload. Word came around that they would be stood down for the next day. This was an invitation for a night of heavy drinking, often accompanied by schoolboy antics. Bomb aimer Tom Leake of the Owen crew recalled the sight of a bare footprint in ink on the twenty-foot-high ceiling of the officers' mess. Such wild nights carried the approval of the commanders. Air Marshal Harris, in the introduction to Guy Gibson's book, *Enemy Coast Ahead*, wrote: 'It may well be that the references to "parties" and "drunks" in this book will give rise to criticism… I do not attempt to excuse them, if only because I entirely approve of them.' Harris attempts to soften the admission by saying that the drunks were high-spirited on 'near beer' rather than spirits.* Airmen were partial to every kind of intoxicating liquor and would make up for the lower alcohol content by drinking in prodigious quantities. Often the only barrier to drinking spirits was their shallowness of pockets. Stories of home-brews and moonshines abounded within the RAF, although they were more likely to be found in the far-flung stations of Italy and North Africa than on Lincolnshire bomber bases.

---

* Wartime beer was in fact only marginally weaker than in peacetime. Britain produced 31,472 barrels in 1944, approximately 5,000 more than the Germans.

Among the revelry and high jinks, there were times when air-men overstepped the mark. Canadian air gunners Russell and McBride from the Perkins crew of 97 Squadron were sent to the Aircrew Refresher Centre at RAF Norton near Sheffield, a correction facility, after vandalizing the sergeants' mess at Coningsby in late May 1944. Strangely, this aberration saved their lives. In a twist of fate, the rest of their crew, including a stand-in gunner, were killed in an air accident two weeks later.

1 May 1944, Toulouse

Just as the Alps and neutral Switzerland had fascinated the Comans crew on flights to Munich, so they were intrigued to be flying as far south as Toulouse, less than one hundred miles from the Mediterranean, and only an hour's flight from Spain. They were being exposed to travel in a manner that no other generation before them had ever experienced. A pattern was emerging as 5 Group were sent to selected targets in France based on military importance. Another long flight was inevitable, but, yet again, in clear conditions with little opposition. The raid was to hit the former Dewoitine aircraft plant and a munitions factory nearby. Dewoitine had been swallowed up in the nationalization of small aircraft firms in the late 1930s. Now part of the state-owned aeronautical manufacturer SNCASE, the company hoped that relocation to the South of France would keep them out of the clutches of the Germans following the invasion of May 1940.

The collaborationist French government established after the armistice of 22 June 1940 had nominal administrative authority over the whole of France but in reality had full sovereignty over only the unoccupied southern part of the country, which they ruled from Vichy, a spa town in central France. In November 1942, following the Anglo-American invasion of French North

Africa, German troops occupied southern France militarily to protect its Mediterranean coast from the Allies. This gave the Nazis the opportunity to fully incorporate Vichy factories into their armaments production.

As D-Day approached, the Allies poured their efforts into destroying manufacturing facilities that could reinforce the Wehrmacht's front-line strength, and, in particular, into degrading German tank production. Obliteration of the tank and aircraft engine parts factories at Toulouse became a priority, even though the plants were filled with French workers.

The raid briefing stated that flak was unlikely to be a problem. As it transpired, a flak unit had been relocated to Toulouse from Italy and the marking Mosquitos of 627 Squadron were in for an unpleasant experience. Once the target was illuminated overhead by flares dropped by 97 Squadron, the Mosquitos came in, diving from 3,000 to 500 feet to drop their markers. The initial proposal by Cheshire to Cochrane was that the Mosquitos would dive from 12,000 to 3,000 feet, based on the concern that aircraft operating any lower than this would face unacceptable risks. The Mosquito crews practising over the airfield at Woodhall Spa and the Wainfleet ranges soon decided that diving lower allowed greater accuracy. 627 Squadron pilots competed to drop as close to the target as possible at Wainfleet. Dispensing with the bomb sight, they drew a cross on their windscreen in chinagraph pencil and achieved an accuracy of within five yards. It was a solution as simple as the nails on crossed pieces of wood that 617 Squadron had used to gauge their approach to the towers on the Möhne and Eder Dams during the Dam Busters raid of May 1943. Practice runs over Lincolnshire were one thing, but a real attack, with flak pouring up from the target, was altogether more challenging. Navigator Andy Denholm, flying in a Mosquito with pilot Norman MacKenzie, recalled the scene at Toulouse:

The flak was coming at us from all directions, spiralling around us, when suddenly there was a great crash within the cockpit, and within a second, I could not see Norman for smoke. We were near the bottom of our dive by this time and before I could ask him if he was OK, I could feel that we were pulling out. As we climbed and turned to go round, I put my head into the 'blister' to see where the marker was for accuracy, but it was nowhere to be found.

'Norman, I can't see the marker.'

'We've still got it, I couldn't see for smoke to drop it, we'll have to go round again,' came the reply!

The Comans crew loitered high above, flying in a wide orbit over the target. The munitions factory was producing large explosions and banks of smoke, obscuring the aircraft plant that they were ordered to mark. So it took them several runs to drop more flares. The bombing seemed to be accurate, but since the 97 Squadron Lancasters had to remain over the target for twenty minutes or more, the risks were significant. Squadron Leader Locke, marking the munitions plant, fought off three attacks by an Me 210. Fortunately for his crew, the German attacker was clearly visible against the light of the explosions below. As Locke threw Lancaster ME625 into evasive action, his gunners pounded away at the night fighter until he was eventually shaken off. With his H2S set inoperable and a glycol leak in one engine, Locke cleared the target area after thirty minutes and returned home safely to Coningsby on three engines.

3 May 1944, Mailly-le-Camp

Making two successful raids over France in clear weather with lighter opposition built the confidence of the crews. 97 Squadron had been at RAF Coningsby for only two weeks, but they had

already participated in nine raids. On 3 May they were instructed
to bomb Mailly-le-Camp, a huge Panzer training base seventy
miles east of Paris. The camp had been constructed by the French
before the First World War and was considered to be one of the
most advanced training grounds in France. Its occupation by the
Germans was regarded as another national insult. Most members

*A post-raid photograph of Mailly-le-Camp, showing extensive damage to the
barracks, May 1944.*

of the squadron were led to believe this would be a 'milk run', with little flak or fighter opposition. The problem with this perception was that it ignored the strength of the German fighters and, in retrospect, many have blamed the problems that afflicted the Mailly mission on poor preparation by Bomber Command. Once again, as at Nuremberg in March, there would be a strong moon. However, with the new system of 5 Group marking now in place, it was felt that they could get two waves of bombers – 'Rat 1' and 'Rat 2' – in and out in short order, each wave lasting only six minutes.

The French resistance had been sending information, including details of German troop strengths at Mailly, for several weeks. The main target area was a tight-knit group of barrack blocks first laid down in 1902, and not spaced to withstand aerial

Group Captain Leonard Cheshire drops his marker flare on the Gnome & Rhône aircraft factory, Limoges, 9 February 1944.

attacks. When the 21st Panzer Division withdrew to Mailly from the Eastern Front in April to train and re-equip, London was informed. The camp was placed under surveillance, and it was noted that all troops were ordered to their barrack blocks by midnight under curfew. Leonard Cheshire proposed to lay down his target indicators at 12.01 hours. Supported by his flare markers of 97 and 83 Squadrons, he would illuminate the area for the first wave of bombers to drop high explosives. Since many of the barrack huts were wood-built, the damage was likely to be considerable.

Around ten o'clock in the evening, Jim Comans lifted ND746 'H' from Coningsby as one of nine Lancasters sent by 97 Squadron. It was the only time in recent weeks that they hadn't taken their faithful F-Freddie with them. Although they had flown her two days earlier, records suggest she was in maintenance at the time of the Mailly raid. In the moonlight, the crew could see the mass of Lancasters as they headed towards their first course point at Beachy Head. A massive force of 346 bombers was airborne. As they crossed the Channel at 12,000 feet, the moon reflected off a calm sea. The tops of scattered clouds shone brightly, backlighting the shapes of the bombers as they passed. It was a dangerously beautiful scene. They could see Dieppe dark against the coast to starboard as the force slipped inland close to Criel-sur-Mer. They passed directly over the tiny hamlet of Bosc Geffroy, far below, the immense fleet of British bombers causing late-night glasses of Calvados to vibrate on farmhouse tables. The thirty-mile gap between Dieppe and Abbeville was still well defended, but not in as concentrated a way as the major towns. If they kept away from centres like Amiens and Beauvais, they could slip east of Paris to Mailly without fear of attracting much ground fire. The force began to lose height to their planned 7,000-feet raid altitude as soon as they crossed the French coast. These areas of northern France were beginning to feel very familiar to the crew.

As the marker force pressed in, the main waves would hold fifteen miles away over an assembly point. In ND746, the first sign that things were not going to plan was when Roy Woollford patched through the VHF channel. To their consternation and to the dismay of the whole force, an American swing concert was being broadcast over the frequency. The use of VHF was a recent innovation by 5 Group and no one had thought to inform the Americans. As they closed on the target area, 'Deep In The Heart Of Texas' was blasting out across the airwaves. The Oboe radio signal guiding them to the target was also very poor.

By now, Leonard Cheshire's four Mosquitos from 617 Squadron were also arriving at the target. Perhaps chiding himself over his late arrival at Munich, Cheshire took off just twenty minutes after the bombers. He arrived close to the target eight minutes early and decided to buzz the night-fighter base at Saint-Dizier to give the impression he was a lone intruder, rather than alert Mailly-le-Camp. The other Mosquitos also realized they were ahead of schedule and zigzagged to take more time. Cheshire's activities did little to fool German defences, however. They had already placed sixty night fighters in boxes ahead of the bomber stream. The constant flow of reports coming in from stations in northern France suggested to them that this was not a light feint attack, but a major force.

Bang on time, Cheshire swept in over Mailly and into his diving attack. He dropped his red indicator flares to the east end of the barracks. Happy with the marking, Cheshire called up the main force controller, Laurence Deane, to bring in his first 'Rat 1' wave of 173 Lancasters. Although Deane called his force, it seemed few heard. The Lancasters continued to congregate over yellow indicator flares dropped to the north to mark the holding point. The Luftwaffe pilots also knew what the yellow markers were for and began waves of attacks into the circling bombers. Separated by only 100 feet in altitude, the Lancasters had few options but to continue to mill until they heard the command to bomb.

Jim Comans was over the target as Cheshire dropped his markers and Ken Cook let their illumination flares go. Coming around again, the 97 and 83 Squadron aircraft bombed the markers on time. To their north, they could see the unfolding drama as Lancasters started to drop out of the sky. At one point, five flaming aircraft could be seen falling at the same time. Radio silence was broken and, as Deane later reported, 'The order that RT silence be maintained was now being broken from all quarters, and the gist of the many messages addressed to me, some orderly but many others crudely blunt, was to inquire when they could bomb and get the hell out.'

Sergeant Frank Broughton of the Reynolds crew briefly left his wireless position to look out of the astrodome and saw six aircraft explode around him. He retreated to his desk exclaiming, mostly to himself, that it was 'a bit rough out there'. By this time, the waiting bombers had begun to use their own initiative and bombed Mailly successfully. However, in the delay the second wave, 'Rat 2', had arrived, further congesting the area. The Luftwaffe pilots were in a 'duck shoot' with more clearly illuminated Lancasters than they had ever seen before in one area. One after the other the bombers fell as the sky was criss-crossed with tracer rounds in an enormous air battle.

When deputy controller Neville Sparks finally got a message through to 'Rat 2' to bomb, one pilot likened the charge out of the holding pattern to the start of the Epsom Derby. On the ground, the attack on the barracks had been devastating. As the bombs fell, men took shelter in slit trenches scattered around the site. The blast waves from the 4,000lb 'Cookies' turned buildings to matchwood. Flying metal and timber lacerated anyone who was not under shelter. The trenches began to cave in, leaving men half buried. Those who survived suffered concussion for days afterwards. As the first wave of bombers passed, German NCOs ordered their men out of their shelters and trenches to fight blazes around the camp. When the second wave struck, many of these soldiers were caught in the open. After months of sorties, this was the most direct assault the Comans crew had flown against the Wehrmacht. The strike was one of the most effective made by Bomber Command against a Wehrmacht unit to date. One hundred and fourteen barrack buildings were destroyed, 47 transport sheds, 65 vehicles and 37 tanks, while 218 instructors and soldiers were killed with 156 more wounded.

The departing bomber force was harried all the way to the French coast. Many of the stream decided to drop to treetop height to make it more difficult for the fighters to engage with them. The Augsburg raid of April 1942 had been compromised by daylight, but in the early hours of 4 May 1944 the Lancasters flying at 50 feet against a darkened landscape were scarcely perceptible to the German night fighters. Nonetheless, Bomber Command lost forty-two Lancasters with 258 airmen killed on the night of 3/4 May. On the face of it, a loss rate of over 11 per cent was disastrous, but the damage inflicted on a Panzer Division seemed to outweigh the heavy cost in men and aircraft. Had the destruction of the site at Mailly not been so impressive, it is possible that Cheshire's new marking ideas might have been overshadowed by a 'Nuremberg' of his own. Despite Bennett's dire warnings that 5 Group's Mosquitos would be torn out of the sky, the Mosquito force remained intact. The failing elements on the Mailly raid were the R/T transmissions and the ability of the bombers to clearly hear commands.

On such a costly night for Bomber Command it was perhaps inevitable that – after a happy run of sorties without loss – one of 97 Squadron's nine aircraft would not make it home to Coningsby. The Ellesmere crew in ND706 were shot down by a night fighter on the return leg, crashing at Alainville, south-west of Paris. None of the crew survived. Their navigator, Pilot Officer Stanley Carlyle, had already been awarded the DFM and the crew were in the latter stages of their tour. Stanley had stood in for Don Bowes only three days before on the Comans crew flying to Clermont-Ferrand.

Given the number of aircraft returning with battle damage, it is remarkable that all crew had escaped injury bar one. Flight Sergeant Forrest of the Owen crew had received shrapnel wounds when a cannon shell exploded near his upper turret. His wounds were dressed at Coningsby before he was sent to the RAF Hospital at nearby Rauceby, which had a specialist crash and burns unit.*

The blistering pace of operations was taking its toll. The Comans crew had not properly rested for eight months, with only a few days' leave between leaving 9 Squadron and joining 97 Squadron in December. Since they had joined the Pathfinders, their squadron had lost twenty-three Lancasters – equivalent to the whole squadron strength – in four months. As a result of these losses and the departures of crews who had finished their tour, most of the airmen involved in 97 Squadron's operations had arrived after the Comans crew. Many of those who had completed their tours were now tucked up in relatively safe training roles, but occasionally when they met their former colleagues they voiced their dissatisfaction at no longer being on ops. Such individuals had a love–hate relationship with operational flying: they were unable to take the strain of front-line service, but could not settle into more peaceable roles.

---

* The hospital crash and burns unit included the work of the pioneering plastic surgeon Archibald McIndoe. Some of his early patients formed a drinking club known as the 'Guinea Pig Club', a name affectionately adopted by 649 members by the end of the war.

RAF Coningsby was expanding: work on new buildings and improvements to existing structures on the site continued throughout the spring of 1944. Visits to the smoke-filled base cinema proved popular, and films such as *Angels with Dirty Faces*, starring James Cagney, and *They Got Me Covered*, with Bob Hope and Dorothy Lamour, received regular showings. The squadrons also organized football, cricket and softball matches around the neighbouring airfields. Men at other RAF stations enjoyed putting on shows in their spare time. The airmen at Coningsby, however, seemed less inclined to do so. The entertainments officer reported a 'nil' take-up of his appeal for volunteers with theatrical or singing talents in April 1944.

As well as RAF airmen and WAAFs, hundreds of civilians worked on site at Coningsby. Amid such a hive of activity, emergencies were never far away. Not all of these incidents related to flying. On the day of the Toulouse raid, a civilian, Harry Roberts of the Teesside Bridge and Engineering Works, fell from the roof of a new hangar and was taken to Lincoln Hospital with spinal injuries.

9 May 1944, Annecy

Walking through Annecy's elegant, tree-lined boulevards on a bright spring day, it would be easy to forget there was a war on. For twenty-nine-year-old Maurice Bourgès-Maunoury, the beauty of the city was shrouded in an atmosphere of danger. A former French artillery officer, Bourgès-Maunoury had spent thirteen months in Oflag XVII in Austria before returning to France to work as an engineer. Vichy France, however, was not to his liking and he crossed the Pyrenees to join the Free French forces in 1942 but was captured by the Spanish. To avoid repatriation, he posed as a Canadian, eventually travelling to

London. A man possessed of a considerable intellect as well as the ability to command men, Bourgès-Maunoury came to the attention of the SOE, who trained him as an agent.

Now in Annecy as military delegate of the Rhône-Alpes region, he is neither M. Bourgès-Maunoury or his codename, *Polygon*, but an ordinary French worker with the best forged papers that London can muster. He tries to look relaxed as he sits talking in one of the town's many outdoor cafés, but he feels defenceless. The pistol he carries with him nearly everywhere is concealed in a drawer at his lodgings. In January 1944 the Germans promised to shoot anyone found in possession of a weapon, so it is unwise to walk the city streets armed unless one absolutely has to.

Annecy is perched at the northern end of Lac d'Annecy in the French Alps, fifteen miles south of Geneva. Nicknamed the 'Rome of the Alps' after it became a centre of Catholicism during the sixteenth-century Counter-Reformation, its position close to Switzerland and Italy had always lent itself to intrigue and dubious trading. From the nineteenth century it transformed itself into a tourist resort, the serenity and beauty of its landscapes drawing thousands of travellers from across Europe. The wealthy acquired summer homes here and Annecy expanded into an affluent place of wide streets and fine houses. The outbreak of the Second World War, however, plunged it into a shady world of espionage and crime. Negotiators and middlemen arrived, their business the moving of money and looted goods to Switzerland. A constant stream of strangers passed through the city, many of them Jewish, French and Italian, all of them anxious to get somewhere else. Among the civilian population, downed Allied airmen, German deserters and SOE agents tried to move about inconspicuously. There were talkers and takers; people who would betray others for a bribe and those who would blackmail their so-called 'friends'.

Heavy industry didn't feature strongly in Annecy, but one factory interested the Allies a great deal. In the 1920s Jacques Schmidt built a factory to produce ball bearings for the burgeoning aviation industry. By 1939 the factory was part of the larger SRO company (Schmidt, Roote and Oerlikon) and employed 1,300 staff producing 1.5 million bearings per year. Like Schweinfurt, it played an important part in the Nazi war effort. The RAF had bombed the site twice, the last time in November 1943, but it was clear that little damage had been done. Civilian casualties had been high, causing disquiet among the SOE operatives. *Polygon* had reported back to London that the local population were 'none too pleased' and he undertook to disrupt production through acts of sabotage. These seem to have been carried out soon after the November 1943 air raid, two transformers within the factory being blown up. Reports received via the British agent code-named *Xavier*, aka Lieutenant Colonel Richard Heslop, suggested that the plant would be out of action for at least three months.

By early 1944 the Maquis had grown in size and confidence in the hills above Annecy, using the Glières Plateau some nine miles to the east of the town as an air-drop site. But the size of the group would prove to be its downfall. Some two hundred and fifty men, including French Communists and a group of fifty Spanish loggers and others sought by the authorities, gathered on the plateau. In February, 1,200 Vichy police and militia launched an operation against the Maquisards of Glière. They were soon joined in their assault by 3,000 Wehrmacht troops, who fanned out into the woods with camouflaged ski soldiers leading the attack. The peace of Annecy was shattered by the sounds of battle in the mountains above it, explosions and gunfire echoing through the valleys. The Maquisards were soon crushed, leaving 120 dead scattered on the upper slopes. The remainder fled across the Swiss border. Many injured survivors were tortured to death where they fell.* Regarded by the Germans as guerrilla fighters, they were denied any form of civilian or military justice. The gruesome cruelty of their end was meant to serve as a warning. The Germans also took hostages in Annecy and promised they would be executed should the resistance dare to take retaliatory action.

Amid the terror, news reached London that the SRO factory had recommenced production. 'F' section of the Special Operations Executive concluded the risks to their men of attempting further acts of sabotage were too great, so the job of attacking the factory would be handed back to Bomber Command. The factory was situated within the city itself, next to a railway marshalling yard. Avoiding civilian casualties would be difficult. This was clearly a job for 5 Group and its close marking technique.

In other months, flying thirty-nine Lancasters so deep into France on the night of a full moon would have been considered too dangerous. But the priorities of the coming invasion dictated the timing of the raid. There would only be one more period of moonless nights before the invasion was due. The total flying time of over eight and a half hours would tax the most experienced of crews. However, there were few flak guns in the vicinity and most German night fighters were concentrated well to the north of Annecy.

Squadron Leader Simpson was to lead 97 Squadron's six Lancasters on the night of 9 May 1944. Starting take-off at 21.20 hours, all the bombers were airborne in four minutes. With such clear visibility, sticking together was the best form of defence as they tightened their formation. Most of the Lancasters, including Comans', carried a 4,000lb 'Cookie' alongside the flare load. If the raid was to work as planned, the Mosquitos would have to

* An imposing national monument to the resistance was built on the Glières Plateau and inaugurated on 2 September 1973.

do their job with maximum precision. By the time they reached the target, only two of the four Mosquitos of 627 Squadron had made it, owing to poor weather and technical problems. In Annecy the sirens began to wail at 01.50 hours. Those living around the factory site knew they were in danger. Some fled terrified through the streets as the Pathfinders' flares began to float down above the SRO factory. The piercing lights seemed to make the sky as bright as day. The rumble of bombers was drowned out by the pitch of an aircraft flying at a much lower level, as a Mosquito skimmed the rooftops. A fierce red glow illuminated the streets 100 yards from the factory.

Of the two Mosquitos, only one managed to release its target indicator; the other reported a 'hang-up'. But it was enough. Squadron Leader Simpson knew that the flare was deliberately off the target and called out a false wind speed calculation on the radio, which was entered into the bomb-sight computer of the following Lancasters. Over many raids, the Pathfinders had learned that the target indicator was often extinguished by the explosions of bombs falling on the target. By offset placement, it burned longer and, with the right calculation loaded into the bomb-sight computer, it was possible to still aim on the flare and drop bombs several hundred yards away. And, sure enough, the target erupted into smoke and flames. Ken Cook reported from his nose position that the 'area was a mass of orange flame and it appeared there was an oil fire'. Reports of fires and explosions away from the target continued to come in over the radio, but after fifteen minutes the controller ordered bombing to cease as the target was overwhelmed.

It had been a busy night for Bomber Command. To the north, 414 bombers had struck against coastal gun emplacements in the Pas-de-Calais. The main body of 5 Group, with fifty-six Lancasters and eight Mosquitos, attacked the Gnome & Rhône aircraft factory at Gennevilliers on the outskirts of Paris. The

Annecy group sneaked home without suffering any further losses on the way. Overall, 5 Group had lost only 1.5 per cent of its strength, with all its losses bar one sustained over Paris. The raid on Annecy had been a success, leaving the SRO factory so badly damaged that production was halted permanently. Surviving machinery was sent to a plant near Vienna, its every movement reported to London by the resistance.

22 May 1944, Braunschweig

The crew's target of thirty-five operations as Pathfinders would be their break point. By the end of the third week in May, they had flown twenty-five missions, but the frequency of operations had increased markedly. For most of them, it might well be only another month before they were stood down from ops. Some crew members lagged behind by a few trips. Don Bowes had been replaced a number of times, and Ken Randle had had a three-week break around the start of the year to get married. The French targets involved lengthy flights, but they were proving to be less dangerous than some other missions. However, everyone knew that it only took one incident for their lives to be placed in jeopardy.

After a few days' snatched leave, the crew were back at Coningsby by the morning of 21 May. Although rumours abounded, no one knew the date of D-Day, nor could they work out where it might take place from the targets they were sent to.

Sixteen days before the largest seaborne invasion in history, the men were to fly to Braunschweig in north-central Germany. While the crew had been away, the squadron had flown to Lille and Amiens in northern France, so the sight of a German target at briefing provoked heavy sighs and grunts of displeasure. Lille had proved disappointingly tough. Two squadron Lancasters had been lost, and another aircraft – flown by Flight Lieutenant Walton – was hit by flak at Dunkirk on the return leg, killing Flying Officer Ward, the mid-upper gunner. By now, everyone knew how German fighter units operated and the prospect of going into their territory again dashed hopes of another 'easy' French trip.

Reports from the raid on Braunschweig present a mixed picture. Although the Comans crew noted that the bombing was punctual, they also said it seemed to be ineffective. Once again, reception on the VHF channel was poor, with the result that most of the aircraft of 97 Squadron dropped their bombs on their own initiative. In contrast with the Comans report, another account describes the order to bomb being heard only very late, suggesting that the Mosquitos themselves were not timely in placing their markers. Flak and fighters were heavy. Clear notes of dissatisfaction are palpable through the formality of the post-raid reports: 'Controller not heard', 'Absence of clear instructions', 'No results observed' and 'Picture confused' add up to a description of a raid where everything had become disjointed.

No crew on the raid were tested as much as Flight Lieutenant C. S. Chatten's, flying Lancaster ND746. They were an experienced crew within the squadron, but Braunschweig would push them to the limit. Chatten had seen his friend Len Hyde shot down on the Nuremberg raid, and there must have been times during that night over Braunschweig when he believed his turn had come. On the journey into the target he was attacked by a Ju88, most likely from underneath. Cannon shells ripped through Chatten's Lancaster, completely disintegrating the Perspex nose and wrecking the bombing station. With a 200mph gale blowing through the fuselage, many pilots would have turned for home. However, after shaking off the German fighter, Chatten decided to complete his bombing run. Over Braunschweig he was hit by flak, which destroyed his flying instruments, but he still managed to drop his bombs before turning for home. Taking star readings from the astrodome, his navigator, Flight Lieutenant Campbell, gave Chatten course readings. All Campbell's maps and charts had been blown away through holes in the damaged fuselage. Once again, they were attacked by a fighter and Chatten, by this time no doubt thoroughly browned off with the night's events, turned his Lancaster into the fighter's circuit. This allowed his upper gunner to register hits on the attacker, driving him away. The use of a damaged Lancaster as a fighter was an unusual approach, but Chatten knew that if he allowed the fighter on his tail, attempting a corkscrew in the heavily damaged bomber could be fatal. The drama descended into farce as Chatten approached the English coast. Unable to identify himself, coastal anti-aircraft batteries opened up on him, hitting Chatten's ailing Lancaster twice.

To its crew's relief, ND746's flaps and undercarriage came down normally as they approached RAF Coningsby. They were over an hour later than the others, no doubt inhibited by the drag of the missing nose. Their determination to make it home had been driven by the airmen's inbuilt dislike of resorting to the parachute and of having to divert to strange airfields. Chatten's landing was perfect although the language of the ground crew on seeing the state of ND746 was choice. In recognition of Chatten's adventure, he was awarded an immediate DSO. Flight Lieutenant Jespersen, a Norwegian, was flying on his first operation as a second pilot with Chatten. He required medical attention to pick fine pieces of shrapnel from his arm. The flight engineer, Cyril Baumber, who had received injuries to his face, right hand and left leg, was treated on the taxiway and sent to hospital.

The raid was another unwelcome reminder of how dangerous German targets were. But another chilling incident, even closer to home, demonstrated with tragic consequences the hazards of operating from bomber bases situated close together. Returning from Braunschweig, a twenty-four-year-old Canadian pilot, Flying Officer Wallace Jardine, was approaching RAF Coningsby in Lancaster ND415 when he collided with a Lancaster from 57 Squadron. Jardine and crew had been with 97 Squadron for just over a month and were on their ninth mission. No doubt they were just beginning to wind down from the raid as they orbited, awaiting their turn to land. Lancaster LL967 was in a similar orbit to the returning 97 Squadron aircraft trying to land at RAF East Kirkby, seven miles from Coningsby. Jardine's aircraft appeared out of the gloom and, in a split second, LL967 struck it, slicing the tail off. The crash of Jardine's plane was not survivable. With little altitude, it plunged into the fields near the village of Revesby, causing an immediate explosion of fuel. The black pall of smoke rising from the site was visible for many miles. Such was the intensity of the blaze that four of the seven crew members could not be identified.* LL967, with a badly shaken crew, landed safely at East Kirkby. With airfields so close, it was difficult to ascertain who, if anyone, was to blame. Jardine's Lancaster seems to have strayed a little closer to East Kirkby, but in the suddenness of the accident, height and position were difficult to ascertain. Although a Court of Enquiry was held, accidents of this sort were so commonplace that the incident caused few ripples.

27 May 1944, Morsalines, Normandy coast

Southwick House, a fine white Georgian house some five miles north of Portsmouth, was one of hundreds of properties

---

* Wallace Jardine, Jack Olive, George Wright and Ronald Baker are remembered on the Runnymede Memorial to the missing at Englefield Green, Surrey.

requisitioned for war work. In 1940 the estate owners offered the house as additional sleeping accommodation for pupils at the Royal Navy School of Navigation in Portsmouth Naval Dockyard, but they had no idea the property would be permanently retained. In the late spring of 1944, the house was commandeered as Allied naval headquarters, and became a hub of D-Day planning as the Supreme Allied Commander General Dwight D. Eisenhower and General Bernard Montgomery moved from London to an area closer to the ports from which the invasion force would leave. One wall of a large room was filled with a wooden relief map of the English Channel showing the south coast of England and north coast of France. Secrecy over the proposed landing sites was so tight that the two men sent to Southwick House to assemble the map were not allowed to return home until after D-Day. The map was made by Chad Valley, a Birmingham-based toy manufacturer who had temporarily abandoned their usual commercial activities to produce goods to help the war effort, and whose employees had no idea of the use to which the map was to be put. However, even a casual onlooker would have noticed its geographical emphasis. The map at Southwick House showed no land to the east of Calais, and it was clear that Normandy lay at the centre of its purpose.

Despite many opportunities for the Germans to discover the Allied plans, the cloud of Allied misinformation obscured their proposed landing areas. Field Marshal Erwin Rommel, who commanded the Atlantic Wall, observed attacks against his coastal defences from Calais to Cherbourg. By mid-May 1944, bombers were attacking his defences from Holland to the western reaches of Brittany with near-impunity. There were not enough fighters and anti-aircraft batteries available to seriously challenge the raiders. Rommel remained certain that the Allies would strike the Pas-de-Calais, possibly stretching towards Dieppe, but no further west. He had filled every beach in the area with obstacles, many of them laced with explosives. But his plan to fill the beaches with 50 million mines was behind schedule – so far he had laid only 6 million. The huge concrete gun casemates on the Pas-de-Calais seemed impervious to bombs. Allied and German guns had duelled over the Channel for months and by war's end, together with air raids, the Germans had destroyed 957 houses in Dover with 898 seriously damaged. A further 6,705 were damaged but remained habitable. The loss of Dover as a primary invasion port did not dent D-Day plans. However, with 255 fake landing craft in Dover harbour, the Germans had no reason to suspect it would not be the pivotal port in the coming invasion. Yet there were clues that, had they been followed, would have led Rommel to Normandy.

He visited Morsalines on the upper stretch of eastern coastline of the Cherbourg peninsula on 11 May 1944. Two days earlier an RAF air raid had all but destroyed the six gun emplacements and communications trenches. Many of the men who greeted Rommel that morning had been subjected to a fierce bombardment. Sitting on wooden slatted bench seats, they cowered, with heads down and hands covering their ears, as the explosions shook their positions. After fifteen minutes the raid had gone. Covered in dust, they emerged from their bunkers realizing that the landscape had changed. Huge holes pockmarked the fields. Debris and the dull smell of explosives hung heavy in the air. With power and telephone lines cut, they wondered whether a landing on the beaches 600 metres away was imminent. But they were in no condition to fight; most of the men were stunned and disorientated.

Daylight revealed the extent of the damage. Soon the NCOs were shouting orders as they attempted to clear the debris. The emplacements of the six 155mm guns that had been on site since 1941 had been thrown into confusion. Unlike others, which had been placed in concrete casements, they sat in partially open positions. The bombardment had caused the walls of the emplacements to collapse and had buried some of the guns under huge heaps of sandy soil.

Word that Rommel was to pay them a visit was not received with enthusiasm as the troops had to clean their kit and make sure that their uniforms were flawless. But he didn't stay for long. Staff officers guided him round the scene of destruction before his car drove off in a cloud of dust. Orders were received that the guns were to be pulled back closer to the village of Videcosville, over two miles away. It would be a lot of work, not least because they would have to build new gun emplacements in virgin fields.

On the night of 27 May, the bombers returned. Seven Lancasters from 97 Squadron, including the Comans crew, helped mark the area as Morsalines was bombed again. The guns proved hard to find and the markers were not as concentrated as hoped for. Comans made three runs on the target, each time finding the target indicator obscured. Eventually they managed to drop their bombs, but it seems the controller remained unconvinced they had pinpointed the target. The movement of the guns seems to have thrown Bomber Command for now, but with the site having been bombarded again, there would be little hope of the guns returning to their old homes. A second group from 97 Squadron attacked emplacements further to the east, south of Dieppe at Saint-Valery-en-Caux, which might have steered German thinking away from the Normandy landing zones. In this attack, one of the marking Mosquitos was hit and had to ditch in the sea. In the strategic play and counter-play, perhaps Rommel might have asked himself why Morsalines had been attacked twice in just over two weeks. It was one of the longest serving batteries in the Atlantic Wall. Equipped with captured French guns, it had remained untouched for years. His visit to the area suggested he was concerned that the wide sandy beaches below Cherbourg still looked inviting to the Allies, despite the fortifications.*

The raid on Morsalines marked another milestone for the Comans crew. The strike on the Panzers at Mailly-le-Camp had been their first direct attack on a German army unit. Morsalines, however unsuccessful, was the first they made against a target in support of the forthcoming D-Day landings. This, of course, they could not know at the time.

Four days later the crew were tasked to fly against another complex battery position at Maisy on the western end of what would become the Omaha sector. Maisy was far more sophisticated than Morsalines, with many interconnecting underground bunkers. Its secretive positioning made it a difficult target to find, but on the night of 31 May bad weather also intervened. Flying through 10/10ths cloud, 97 Squadron tried to find Maisy, but without any ground view H2S was too inaccurate. Frustratingly, they knew they were in the right area, but the bunker complex was too far concealed below ground to be picked up from the hazy green images on their H2S screens.

Warm weather had triggered large thunderstorms and lashing rain across Britain. As the force abandoned attempts to bomb Maisy, the weather conditions made the journey back to RAF Coningsby a difficult prospect. Comans, always cautious of fuel levels after two very difficult experiences, decided to jettison their 1,000lb bomb into the sea. Along with the other Lancasters, Comans made for a diversionary airfield. Three and a half hours after take-off, the crew touched down at RAF

---

* Eight days later, poor weather would drive the landing craft further down Utah beach and safely out of range of the guns at Morsalines. As the fleet assembled on D-Day, HMS *Black Prince* continually fired on the battery to suppress them. With less protection than their old site, the German crews had little choice but to shelter in trenches during the bombardment.

Chipping Warden near Banbury. Despite the relief at being on the ground, the sense of disappointment at missing a target was still tangible.

The importance of Maisy as a battery and gun control centre has been the subject of some controversy. It seems that certain invasion maps supplied to troops did not show the site, although its existence was known to Bomber Command. One commander had orders to take it, but did not regard it as a priority. Despite its prime position between Utah and Omaha beaches, Maisy appears to have been ignored, and this 'secret' base remained unresearched for many years after the Second World War.* It has been suggested that, had the bomber force of 31 May found Maisy, perhaps the D-Day casualties on Omaha beach would have been less severe. Whatever the truth or otherwise of such speculation, it is clear that finding the targets remained a complex challenge – and a significant obstacle – for the bombers. 5 Group's techniques had improved accuracy, but the Maisy battery demonstrated once again the principle that if the target could not be seen, it was very difficult to hit.

Through the early days of June, Flight Lieutenant Van Raalte of 97 Squadron was trained to use the new bomb sight, the Semi-Automatic Mark IIA, in his regular Lancaster ME625 – the first such to be fitted to a squadron aircraft. On the evening of 3 June, Van Raalte took off from RAF Coningsby in the company of one other Lancaster from 83 Squadron to act as markers on the wireless listening station located at Ferme d'Urville on the tip of the Cherbourg peninsula. Only two nights before, Bomber Command had hit three sites in the locality but with limited accuracy. Among this force were nine Halifaxes flown by Free

---

* In January 2004 British historian Gary Sterne rediscovered the site after the chance find of a D-Day map in a pair of trousers previously owned by a US soldier.

French crews based at RAF Elvington near York. This was the first time the newly formed 346 '*Guyenne*' Squadron had been used in action. With the invasion so close, their involvement was a risk. If a Free French crew had been shot down, the Germans might have suspected there was some significance attached to their presence.

Van Raalte was returning to support a second raid on the listening station and this time the force destroyed their objective, the Fort de Nacqueville. An Australian who had begun his tour at the same time as the Comans crew, Van Raalte had become a well-known personality at Coningsby. He had suffered crew losses from death, serious injury and battle fatigue. Of his seven original crew, only four remained. With a reputation as a dogged airman, he was held in high regard by the squadron and was an unsurprising choice to be the first to test out the new bomb sight. Sadly, Van Raalte's crew are remembered for a tragic accident that would devastate Coningsby two weeks after the raid on Ferme d'Urville.

Despite the weight of recent raids on coastal positions, there was nothing in the routine of RAF Coningsby to suggest the invasion was only hours away. The Comans crew continued their regular training flights in F-Freddie noting 'NFT' – night flying training – in their logbooks. The arrival of stormy weather on 4 June resulted in their night training being cancelled, but this inconvenience meant there was more time to sit around in the mess and enjoy a drink. They had no inkling that thousands of Allied troops had already boarded their transports and were spending an uncomfortable night bobbing in a rough swell. D-Day had been postponed for twenty-four hours owing to strong winds, heavy seas and low cloud. Despite many clues that the beaches of Normandy would be the site of the Allied invasion, they had successfully kept it a secret.

10.

The Beginning
of the End

The morning of 5 June 1944 began like many others at RAF Coningsby. Squadron Navigational Officer Stevens sauntered down to the planning rooms as usual at seven o'clock. Orders were due in for squadron operations and the busy hours of readying maps and courses for the 1 p.m. crew briefing would soon be under way. Stevens was normally informed the evening before that orders were due in, but that day the orders would be late. With a mug of tea in one hand and a cigarette in the other, he busied himself with meteorological reports until lunchtime. This would be a late briefing, he thought to himself. The orders did not arrive until 1 p.m. An attack on a gun emplacement on the Normandy coast, an all-effort operation with 83 Squadron. This was a heavy raid, not split between targets as in recent days. As Stevens checked the orders for course directions, he became immediately aware that they contained more paragraphs than usual. He quickly scanned the orders, noting a very strict course order. There were convoys to avoid, naval actions to the east and other air operations. Stevens felt a surge of adrenaline; he was sure the instructions added up to only one thing: the invasion was starting.

As Stevens and his team began their work, the guard at RAF Coningsby was doubled. The base moved to the highest security level as additional weapons were issued. No one with the knowledge of the new orders could leave the base. The late briefing began quietly enough, but as more details were revealed the air of excitement mounted. The Squadron Record Book notes: 'Today must be recorded as one of the most eventful days in the Squadron's history.' Wing Commander Jimmy Carter as Squadron Commander was heard to comment, 'Thank God I'm still on Ops and not on an OTU [Operational Training Unit].'

In the euphoria, several officers who had finished their operational tours and had ground roles at Coningsby were keen to go on the raid, Stevens among them. Wing Commander Carter's crew had several members who had already completed a full thirty-mission tour and held senior roles within 97 Squadron. Squadron Signals Officer Albert Chambers and Gunnery Officer Martin Bryan-Smith were both DFC holders. Indeed, Carter's crew that morning had more decorated men on board than any other Allied bomber, with seven of the eight holding DFC or DFM awards. Stevens approached Jim Comans for a flight, just as he had for the raid on Munich in April. Comans, perhaps wary of getting

Don Bowes, the Crew's navigator.

lost again under Stevens, elected to keep Don Bowes as navigator and Ken Cook was 'bumped' to make room for Stevens. The disappointment of not flying on 97's most important mission to date was a blow. All Ken could do was see the Lancasters off at 03.00 hours on Tuesday 6 June, joining the regular crowd of WAAFs and non-flyers to wave them away in the darkness of the small hours.

The target that early morning was the Pointe du Hoc, a heavily fortified gun position that jutted out into the sea between Utah and Omaha invasion beaches. It was a key position in securing the beachheads. After being pounded by the bombers, American forces would storm ashore and take the 100-foot-high coastal promontory.

Thirty minutes before sunrise at 04.45, the German troops in the fortified bunkers and trenches of the Pointe du Hoc heard the rumble of the approaching bombers. Hand-operated air raid sirens were wound, the wailing repeated across the fields, sending men scurrying down into the deeper shelters. Steel helmets were pulled on and their straps tightened. The number of raids on the coast had increased in recent days, confining them to trenches and bunkers time and time again. This time the nervous chatter would be about the rumour that hundreds of ships were appearing as dots on the horizon. The Germans had excelled in building thick-walled concrete bunkers. The bunkers the Germans created on the Western Front during the First World War had surprised the Allies with their size and solidity, but these latest versions surpassed anything built twenty-five years earlier. The white-painted rooms were lit by electricity and supplied with clean air through filtered pumps. A series of steel doors would prevent any attacker making an easy entry. In the stairwells and passages, obscured gun slits guarded the approaches. These were not only bomb shelters, but control bunkers built to withstand land attack and, if necessary, hold out in a siege for some time.

Large bomber formations had passed over the Pointe du Hoc in recent weeks, many of them heading south. The men in the light anti-aircraft gun emplacements around the promontory had the unenviable task of remaining at their posts. Scouring the breaks in the patchy clouds above through binoculars, they searched for the bombers as the noise of engines rose to a crescendo. Suddenly, their world was illuminated by falling flares. The guns began to rattle and clack as handlers darted to retrieve more ammunition from the nearby lockers. The Germans of the Pointe du Hoc had been hit hard in April and their 155mm guns had been withdrawn over a mile inland. Nevertheless, their clear view over the beaches still made this an important defensive position.

With thick clouds covering the target at 9,000 feet, the bomber force was ordered to descend into the clear air below. Once the target indicators had fallen, most crews reported that they had a clear bombing run. The Comans crew, probably inhibited by not having Ken Cook as their bomb aimer, experienced some uncertainty over which indicator to bomb. But eventually they dropped their 13,000lb of high explosive bombs and turned for home in the lightening sky. The Normandy beaches were close targets – the return flight back to Coningsby should take only two hours, most of it in safety.

As the bombs began to fall, the intensity of the raid shook the fortifications to their core. In a wave of huge explosions, bunkers were split open, filling the air with choking debris and dust, burying those sheltering inside and blinding the anti-aircraft gunners. Within minutes the ground was cratered and churned up beyond recognition, as the site was carpeted by 1,000lb bombs. In the deep shelters the ground pulsed under the hammer blows of the bombardment. Where power lines were cut, the men sheltering were plunged into darkness. Their biggest fear was that the stairwells would collapse, entombing them forever. Those positioned further back, towards the village of Saint-Pierre-du-Mont, saw the cliffs erupt in a shower of fireworks. Brilliant flashes lit up the fields, flickering in a continuous angry roar of explosions as the storm fell. Percussion waves rolled across the countryside, shaking doors and windows in a deafening thunderstorm of noise.

Rising to meet the Allied bomber force in his Focke-Wulf 190, Oberleutnant Helmut Eberspächer saw the Lancasters approaching. Their altitude suited his position. They were flying at just half the height that he had seen on some other raids. 'Similar to a shadow theatre, the bombers stood out against the clouds. However, they could not see me against the dark earth,' he later recalled. He attacked and saw three Lancasters fall in a four-minute frenzy of action. One of his victims fell in flames, crashing in a huge fireball below. Wing Commander Jimmy Carter's last message was heard by the raid controller at 5.04 a.m. acknowledging the order to bomb. Shortly after, farm workers near Carentan at the south-eastern base of the Cotentin peninsula saw the flaming Lancaster slam into a marsh and explode.*

Flight Lieutenant Finn Varde Jespersen's Lancaster was also shot down. Flying as a Royal Norwegian Air Force officer, he had only recently joined 97 Squadron and was on his fifth mission. He had been injured by shrapnel on his first mission flying with the Chatten crew to Braunschweig two weeks earlier. All Jespersen's crew members were lost, including his fellow countrymen Christian Münster, Kaare Pedersen, Knut Magnus and John Evensen.

As the Comans crew turned for home, the rising light revealed the mass of invasion vessels making for the Normandy coast – ships of all sizes, leaving white wakes in the choppy seas below. Men were climbing down netting to board landing craft. Loaded boats were already circling in wide arcs, waiting for their moment to head for the beaches. An hour and a half

---

* Carter's aircraft was posted missing, but the crew were never found. The locality of the crash was not confirmed, but the locals knew a bomber had come down in the marsh. Officially, the assumption remained that Carter's aircraft had crashed into the sea. However, in 2012 an archaeological dig on a site identified by locals proved that the crashed plane was Carter's Lancaster, ND739. Personal possessions, including Flight Lieutenant Chambers' signet ring and scraps of uniform, confirmed the find, although no bodies were recovered.

later, at 6.30 a.m., the first waves of assault troops hit Omaha and Utah.

As the Lancasters of 97 Squadron touched down at 07.00 hours at Coningsby, an assault force of US Rangers was scaling the cliffs of the Pointe du Hoc with ropes and ladder obtained from the London Fire Brigade. They reached the headland later than planned after their craft was driven off course by a heavy swell. Having ascended the cliff, they fought the remnants of the surviving garrison who emerged from their tunnels and bunkers. No feature remained the same as on the Rangers' maps, but they soon discovered the gun emplacements. To their surprise, they found telegraph posts mounted instead of guns. However, following the phone lines rearwards, they encountered the 155mm artillery further inland. Sergeants Leonard Lomell and Jack Kuhn led the attack, blowing the guns with thermite grenades and detonating the ammunition dump at 09.00.

As the Lancasters taxied to their dispersals, orders had already been received for the next raid. As the crews finished debriefing and grabbed breakfast, they were disappointed that the BBC news at eight o'clock did not mention the invasion, saying only 'a new phase of the Allied Air Initiative has begun'. Many in Britain knew instinctively that the invasion *was* taking place, even without official acknowledgement. The harbours of the south coast that had been filled with landing craft were now empty. Hundreds of miles north, thirteen-year-old Leslie Price was helping at a farm close to the huge US supply base at Burtonwood in Cheshire. He remembers, 'That morning, dozens of aircraft were taking off and they were all heading south. We knew it could only mean one thing, the invasion had started.'* The BBC made the definitive announcement that D-Day had started at midday. At nine o'clock in the evening, the King broadcast from London.

---

* Leslie Price is the author's father.

His words struck a chord with the many airmen gathered around the radio sets: 'This time, the challenge is not to fight to survive but to fight to win the final victory for the good cause. Once again what is demanded from us all is something more than courage and endurance; we need a revival of spirit, a new un-conquerable resolve.'

The target for the night of 6 June was the rail hub at Argentan, forty miles inland from the inva-sion beaches. Jim Comans had all his regular crew back, giving Ken Cook the chance to fly on D-Day, albeit in the last half-hour of the first day.* Squadron Leader Stevens wanted to fly again even after the loss of Carter and Jesper-sen. This time, however, Comans successfully sidestepped him and Stevens found a place with the Owen crew. Stevens' eagerness to

Flight Lieutenant Charles Owen, with DSO ribbon and Pathfinder badge.

lever himself back into operations – despite the risks involved and inevitable feelings of terror – is perhaps testament to the sheer addictiveness of danger. Some were happy to take roles in training after their quota of operations, others craved further excitement. Henry Jeffery of the ill-fated Carter crew wrote, 'Tout Fini' across his logbook in October 1943. Despite this, he volunteered for a second tour, joining Carter by January. Even as D-Day approached, Jeffery had promised his mother that he would carry out just 'one more flight', yet it appears he had no plan to stop.

---

* Ken Cook, together with all surviving D-Day veterans, was awarded the French Legion of Honour after the seventieth anniversary of the landings in 2014.

Strategically, the use of the heavy bombers to strike railheads was far more successful than attempting to hit targets closer to the beaches. The Allies' use of the lighter and faster bombers such as the A-20 Havoc and the B-26 Marauder in daylight raids proved more effective. As troops moved out of the beach-heads, rocket-equipped Hawker Typhoon fighter bombers were deployed in a 'cab rank' system holding above the battlefield until called down for direct fire support. Overnight, hundreds of aircraft had their wings marked with black and white stripes to clearly identify them to Allied ground forces. Many were crudely painted in haste by brush, using any paint available, even whitewash. The Lancasters of Bomber Command were not painted, much to the relief of the crews, who felt they were conspicuous enough. It was clear their role would remain as night intruders.

The attacks on Argentan had begun on 5 June as American bombers pounded the railway station and yards in daylight. The purpose of the raid of 6 June was to ensure no rail traffic could continue to pass through to the invasion area. During the coming battles the town was left almost completely ruined, a shattered, burned-out shell as the Allies attempted to stop the German 7th Army and 5th Panzer Army from escaping the Falaise Pocket during August 1944. That night the weather over Argentan was not perfect, with 4,000 feet of cloud between the tops and the base. The Comans crew located their target by Gee and dropped their bombs as planned. Since operations in Normandy were less than four hours in duration, it was possible for crew to fly two attacks per day if necessary. But the crew were tired. Apart from some snatched naps in the afternoon, they had not slept properly for nearly forty-eight hours. When thick cloud proved difficult on the return leg, Jim Comans decided to head into their old station at RAF Bourn.

Many aircraft were forced to make diversionary landings on

the evening of 6 June because of poor weather. The USAAF had also flown many missions that day. Flight Lieutenant Johnnie Colburn of 388th Bombardment Group had only begun his operational career two days earlier. Flying from RAF Knettishall in Suffolk, he and his B-17 crew found themselves in the lead group of bombers in the early morning coastal attacks on 6 June. Having a clear view of the invasion fleet, they were amazed at its size. As they ran into their target, they spotted C-47 transport aircraft towing gliders beneath them and concluded they much preferred their viewpoint of the battle unfolding below. The poor weather delayed their second mission of the day, but taking off at 17.20 hours they headed for Pont-l'Évêque, a town east of the invasion zone. Diverted to Flers, forty miles behind the beachheads, they were forced to break their formation into smaller sections because of the worsening weather. Colburn, however, eventually became detached from the group. Making landfall near Dover much later in the evening, he suddenly found another B-17 flying directly towards him. Taking evasive action, the rogue B-17 passed only a few feet above Colburn's aircraft. Lost in failing light and poor weather, the two planes had clearly struggled to cope with unfamiliar conditions. Much of their training had been completed in daylight in good weather. The two American crews were lucky to emerge from the episode unscathed.

The Comans crew were an hour into their night flight before Colburn found RAF Tuddenham at 00.30. Home to 90 Squadron Lancasters, the base was busy with its own operations as the visitor approached. With next to no fuel and a high approach, Colburn touched the B-17 down halfway along the runway before locking his wheels and coming to a halt in the gravel run-off.

RAF Bourn may have been familiar to the Comans crew, but it was no longer in their family of airfields. 8 Group Mosquitos were hurrying in and out, in weather that was worsening by the hour. When they arrived back at Coningsby the next day, having made the forty-minute hop, they were relieved to find they weren't tasked for operations and could get some sleep. No operations were carried out from Coningsby on 7 June because of the poor weather conditions.

D-Day had seen 97 Squadron contribute to attacks on a number of key targets, but the day had also brought tragedy in the loss of their Squadron Commander, E. J. Carter. He had taken command at RAF Bourn on 7 January 1944 only days after the Comans crew arrived to begin their time with the Pathfinders. But against the melancholy backdrop of Carter's death, operations had to continue. The Lancasters of 97 Squadron, in common with all bomber squadrons, were given a series of supporting attacks to accomplish in the coming days.

★

Eisenhower was concerned that the night of 7/8 June was unsuitable for raids. However, he was satisfied that his troops had enjoyed close fighter support through the day. Clearing land near Colleville-sur-Mer, close to Omaha beach, the US Army created the Allies' first airstrip on French soil on 8 June and began ferrying wounded soldiers back to Britain. During the day, Hitler had taken personal command of the defence of Normandy. After hearing from his commanders that there had been little or no Luftwaffe support for their troops, Hitler ordered that his air force be thrown into the battle. 'Even if it means the end of the Luftwaffe,' he barked. It was an order that the Luftwaffe's supreme commander, Hermann Goering, did little to fulfil. Addicted to amphetamines, Goering had lost all direction, leaving nearly all operational matters to his staff. Luftwaffe strength in France had been reduced, at Hitler's command, in order to defend Germany's cities from Allied bombers. Already stretched on the Eastern Front and by Bomber Command's operations over the

Reich, the Luftwaffe now faced having to fight on a third front, in Normandy.

Radio operator Roy Woollford numbered his operational missions in his logbook, circling the number in black fountain pen. Whether the numbers were added as a final calculation or were written as each mission was completed is unclear, but they feel like a countdown. Woollford was not one of the men who would rush towards a second tour. The operation to Argentan was numbered '43'. In theory, the crew had only two more operations before the end of their tour, but they were to fly three. Orders were coming in for daily raids, so they all knew it was a matter of days rather than weeks now to the end of their tour. On the night of 8 June they flew to Rennes to destroy a rail bridge, noting the flak was heavy.

They didn't fly the next night, but others did, the Giddings crew failing to return. On only their fourth operation with 97 Squadron, they were hit by flak and finished by a fighter over Étampes, south of Paris. Nineteen-year-old Arthur 'Taffy' Pritchard, the only Welshman in an Australian crew, bailed out at low altitude and landed heavily in a field. He broke his ankle, but still managed to hobble to a road. It was past midnight as he tried to flag down cars, not caring if they were French or German, but no one would stop. Seeing a village a mile away he made for it, finding a bar that was still open. He knew no French other than the word 'Champagne' and, pulling a franc note from his emergency money, tried to order a drink. But there were Germans present in the bar, and several Frenchmen bundled him quickly out of the back door.

Pritchard was sheltered by the resistance, but not before enduring an arduous interrogation. The few English speakers available had never met anyone from Felinheli in Gwynedd and struggled to understand his Welsh accent. The resistance feared he was a German spy, and he was hidden away in a hole beneath an outside tap before his identity was confirmed with London. After two months in hiding, he returned to Britain, but was devastated to learn that only one other member of the crew had survived as a prisoner of war.

13 June 1944, Caen

Of the many targets chosen by the Allies in Normandy, the city of Caen remains one of the most contentious. The city was taken in July 1944 but was reduced almost entirely to rubble. Like Ypres in the First World War, Caen had the misfortune to be a strategic waypoint for both armies. The Germans were determined to bar Montgomery's way, and 'Monty' knew the city had to fall before the invasion force could move on. By the end of the battle, 20,000 French civilians were dead and bombers and artillery had obliterated nearly every building. The controversy over whether the Allies should have bypassed the city and held it under siege until the garrison surrendered endures to this day.

Jim Comans, from an Australian newspaper clipping.

The Comans crew attacked Caen alongside seven other 97 Squadron Lancasters in the early hours of 13 June. The aim was to destroy the bridges and block the roads through the city. Before road bypasses had been built, the heart of a city like Caen was the main thoroughfare. Adjacent to the bridges, a large railhead filled the southern bank of the Orne River. With German forces building in the area, the first task was to deny them Caen as a hub. For the unfortunate inhabitants, the raid on Caen did not go smoothly. Markers were inaccurate or obscured and the Comans crew reported loitering for three-quarters of an hour for re-marking. Many of the bombs fell on houses packed close to the city centre before the raid controller instructed the bombers to cease.

On the eve of their last operation together, the crew knew they were taking part in an operation of profound historical importance. They knew, too, that the critical nature of the events taking place around them would obscure their own considerable achievements. But there was deep satisfaction to be had from the fact that they had managed to survive. And soon they would be able to give full release to their feelings of rising elation: they intended to drink the bar dry when they were finished. Their target for the night of 15 June was in the Vienne département north of Poitiers. The ammunition facility at Châtellerault would be the crew's last raid together. Without opposition, the Mosquitos dropped their markers squarely on target. Jim Comans' post flight report ended with a flourish: 'The illuminating was excellent, marking prompt, the aiming point kept marked throughout attack and bombing concentrated. Good H2S picture. Model attack.' The only fly in the ointment was that the Comans crew had to divert to RAF Upwood, south of Peterborough, on their return, denying them their triumphal breakfast at Coningsby.

The next day they made their final flight together, the short thirty-minute hop home. Most of the crew – Bolland, Woollford, Cook, Widdis and Comans – had hit their magical thirty-five missions and had completed together. It was an emotional moment, as they knew they had survived the most perilous time of their lives. Flight engineer Ken Randle had a few ops to make up on other crews, as did navigator Don Bowes. Ken Cook wrote the words 'Completion of 2nd Tour' in red ink in his logbook and tallied his hours: he had amassed a total of 556 hours and 35 minutes flying time, 356 of these at night. Jim Comans signed the logbook as 'Officer Commanding A Flight'. It was also time to say goodbye to ND740. F-Freddie had carried them safely for seventeen missions, more than any other Lancaster they had flown. She had been new when they first took her on in late March 1944 and they had given her a first air test with 97 Squadron. In less than three months they had spent 131 hours with her, and she bore the scars to prove it: there were scuffs and chips to the paint inside her, and she had been patched and mended on several occasions to repair flak damage. ND740's matt paint may have dulled, but she was still meticulously kept by the ground crew.

ND740 was one of 600 Lancasters built at Avro's plant at Chadderton near Oldham under contract 1807. After the Comans crew had disbanded, she carried on in service through July and August 1944 with numerous crews. During this period, she remained a 'spare' aircraft, unallocated to one crew, although C. S. Chatten flew her the most. Her adventures were far from over, however. On 17 August, Squadron Leader Parkes took her on a mining operation off Stettin and fought a pitched battle with flak ships. 'We were engaged the whole time by flak ships and our three turrets were firing continuously. Tracer seen going in to 2 flak ships and about 3 searchlights and they went out of action. The other searchlights were sweeping at sea level.' ND740 returned safely to Coningsby with her wireless aerial shot away. It was the last time she flew operationally with 97 Squadron. Transferred to 83 Squadron, she was recoded to OL-H (from OF-F), but her time there was cut short. On 11 September 1944 she took off for Darmstadt with Wing Commander Jesse Walker at the helm but was shot down over Germany before reaching the target. Four of the crew, all experienced men and DFM or DFC holders, including Walker, perished, and the other three were taken prisoner.

For the men who had finished their tour, it was time to take some leave and begin to make plans. There were wives to consider, but their immediate futures would be dictated by the RAF. Within days, new posting orders would arrive, transferring them to training squadrons that they hoped would not be too far afield. For a crew that had flown continuously together for thirteen months, the final break was approaching.

11.

Separate Ways

On Tuesday 13 June, exactly a week after the D-Day landings had commenced, the air raid alarms sounded over London. The fire picket at Woolwich's Royal Military Repository pulled on their battle dress trousers, shirts, socks and gym shoes and made their way across to the fire station ready to man their Scammel pump trailer. They were in no great hurry – apart from lone intruders trying to photograph the docks, no bombs had dropped on London since January 1944. Most of them were young men who had barely entered their teens when the war started. On D-Day they had watched transfixed as wave after wave of aircraft cut through the dim light of morning, heading for Normandy. Since that day, when the sky was full of thousands of aircraft, the mornings had become quieter again. It was 4.30 a.m. and the light was building after a night when it had barely grown dark. Normally there would be at least ten minutes from the sounding of the alarm to any sign of a raider. This morning, while some were still crossing the parade ground, the sounds of light ack-ack began to stutter a mile south towards Bexley. To a man, they stopped and stared towards the noise. Searchlights had latched on to something low in the crossbeams. An aircraft was powering towards central London, much faster than any they had seen before.

Other searchlights flicked across the path of the raider as all the 40mm Bofors guns within range began pounding. Above the sound of gunfire, the men at Woolwich could clearly hear a peculiar sound, like a stuttering blowtorch. As the aircraft raced over the city, the men saw that its tail was ablaze with a short brilliant flame. 'They've hit the bastard,' someone shouted, and a spontaneous cheer rose. But at the same moment they realized they were watching something very new. The noise coming from the aircraft could only be some sort of jet. Suddenly, among the banging and popping of anti-aircraft fire, the engine fell silent and the flames went out. They waited to hear a crash. The best part of a minute seemed to pass before they heard the deep muffled explosion ring out across the city. In that time they were aware of the clatter of pieces of shrapnel from the guns falling on the roofs and yards around them. Sprinting to a corrugated iron open store to take cover, they saw a dark pall of smoke mushrooming against the morning sky. As the all-clear signal sounded, they made their way back to their quarters, unsure as to what they had seen.

The first of Hitler's new *Vergeltungswaffen* ('vengeance weapons') had fallen on London. It was part of a wave of ten V1s, most of which had fallen short – some of them not even making it very far from their launch ramp in the Pas-de-Calais. The single V1 to reach London struck Grove Road, Mile End, killing six people. It was the first strike in an onslaught by these early cruise missiles that was to kill 6,184 and injure a further 17,981 across the summer and early autumn of 1944.

Within minutes of Jim Comans touching down at RAF Upwood after their final raid on Châtellerault on 15 June, the Germans began the first concerted V1 attack on England, launching 244 of the weapons from northern France. The unfortunate C. S. Chatten of 97 Squadron, who had been hit badly on several previous occasions, caught flak damage from the coastal defences as he stumbled into the airspace of the V1 attacks. He would land safely later, but he was baffled as to why he had been fired on. Later in the day, as the Comans crew enjoyed their celebration back at RAF Coningsby, evening newspapers published stories of the new attacks by 'pilotless planes'. On 18 June 1944, a V1 hit the Guards Chapel at Wellington Barracks, not far from Buckingham Palace, during the morning service, killing 121 soldiers and civilians. It was the worst single loss of life caused by any single V1 raid on London. Concerned at the alarm spreading through the capital, the cabinet instructed the press that from now on the V1s were to be referred to as 'Flying Bombs' and not 'Pilot-less planes', but many referred to them as 'buzz bombs' or 'doodlebugs', from the characteristic sound they made in flight.

*

A week after Comans' last flight with 97 Squadron, a tragedy struck that left a lasting impression on the whole station. As with the events of Black Thursday in December 1943, the incidents that affected the crews most were those that took place on their own doorstep. When men did not return from operations, a hope remained that they had evaded capture and remained hidden. But standing by the graveside of an airman in a local cemetery had a terrible finality about it, compounded further if the event leading to their death was an accident. The tragedy of one summer afternoon still resonates through the 97 Squadron (Straits Settlement) Squadron Association seventy-five years later. On 22 June 1944, several squadron aircraft took part in daylight formation flying. With the gradual destruction of the Luftwaffe and the anticipated need to support Allied ground forces, it was likely that the Lancasters would be pressed into daylight raids. On these long, bright days of high summer, aircraft flying in spaced formations were more vulnerable to attack by fighters. The flying that afternoon passed without incident, but the Group

Exercise planned for that evening was cancelled. The RAF Coningsby diarist writing in the station book commented sardonically, 'One gets the impression that these "Exercises" are laid on and cancelled at such late hours to prevent the aircrews ever having an evening out of camp to themselves.'

The next afternoon, Friday 23 June, the crews were in mischievous mood. Spotting Flight Lieutenant Ted Perkins' small Fiat car, they manhandled it onto the roof of an air raid shelter. It was still perched there as the six Lancasters took off to practise formation flying. Separated into two vics of three, the formation turned south, heading across the wide expanses of the Fens. In Bill Gee's lead Lancaster, the view from the tail turret was unusual. Inglis, the gunner, was not used to seeing other aircraft so close, particularly in daylight. It was a fine June afternoon, with a gentle haze softening the horizon. The sun glinted on the spinners and tops of the canopies, creating rings of light in the blur of the propellers. The wingtips of the Lancasters behind seemed very close, breaking only in the space directly behind Inglis's tail turret. Inglis knew them well, Jim Van Raalte and Ted Perkins, both seasoned men with experience of many raids. The gunner could see their faces clearly – at lower altitude there was no need to wear their oxygen masks. Beside each pilot the flight engineers peered cautiously forward while keeping watch on the instruments. The speed and power of the bombers flying so close together produced a feeling of exhilaration. The ground below seemed to move faster under the beat of the Merlin engines.

As the formation approached Crowland, on the southern edge of Lincolnshire, villagers were just beginning to drift away from a summer fete. It was four o'clock in the afternoon as the six Lancasters approached across the fields. As the lead vic began a gentle turn, Jim Van Raalte's Lancaster got caught in Gee's slipstream. Within seconds, it began to bounce viciously, sailing upwards, before slipping sideways and plunging down on top of

ND981, flown by Perkins. The impact sliced through Perkins' tail section and destroyed Van Raalte's nose. Both aircraft spiralled to the ground out of control and exploded in huge fireballs near the village. Miraculously, wireless operator Joe Coman managed to parachute from the severed tail section, the only survivor of the Perkins crew. He landed so close to the wreck that he required treatment for burns to his hands, but he was otherwise uninjured. There was nothing that could be done for the rest of the crew as rescuers were driven back. Local man William Smedley recalled, 'I was at a Red Cross fete at the time. We were ordered to sit behind a heap for a quarter of an hour while the bullets exploded.'

All those on Van Raalte's Lancaster perished as it plunged into a dyke near Cloot Farm. The impact ripped the aircraft apart and buried the engines in the ground. Performing a wide turn, the four remaining Lancasters eased apart and circled the scene. Each crew could see the situation was desperate. They had hoped to see the waving figures of their friends beside their wrecked aircraft, but the black smoke rising from the twisted debris left no room for hope. The incident left a deep impression not only on the crews, but also in the local community. That night, the men of the formation flew to Limoges, the long flight giving plenty of opportunity for them to reflect on what they had seen. Percy Cannings of the Reid crew had been in the aircraft just behind the collision and narrowly missed disaster. 'We were very lucky that our aircraft didn't get caught up in the slipstream and get taken out ourselves… we had to go out on operations the same night. It's something you had to be prepared for.'

★

The members of the Comans crew began parting company very soon after their last operational flight. Leave was normally granted for those completing their tour of missions before they embarked on their next posting. In some cases, men would travel from their place of leave to the new posting without returning to their original unit. First to be posted on 1 July 1944 was Roy Woollford, to 17 Operation Training Unit (OTU) at RAF Silverstone,* near Towcester, to fly on Wellingtons, and George Widdis to 24 OTU at RAF Honeybourne, near Evesham, which trained Canadian crews – also on Wellingtons. Of the other non-commissioned men, rear gunner 'Jock' Bolland left on 22 July for the Aircrew Allocation Centre (ACAC) at RAF Brackla in Nairnshire – a sympathetic posting back to his native Scotland. The only remaining non-commissioned man was engineer Ken Randle, who was short of mission numbers and joined Bob Lasham's crew until the end of July. He would be posted on 12 August to 1661 HCU at RAF Winthorpe, near Newark, where the crew had trained just prior to joining 9 Squadron.

Of the officers, Jim Comans left Coningsby for 1661 HCU on 12 July, a month before Randle, and Ken Cook left on 15 July to join 49 Squadron as a navigation officer at RAF Fiskerton, just outside Lincoln. Like Ken Randle, Don Bowes had to continue operations to see his tour out. All the newly posted men of the crew were on non-operational training posts. It was possible, had they wished, to volunteer to return to operations, but these requests were not always granted. However, it seemed no one had a burning desire to embark on operations again, perhaps not surprising considering all the stress they had endured. Ken Cook summed up the feelings of the crew in an interview with the author: 'By that time we'd had enough.'

In recognition of their tour of duty, Jim Comans, Don Bowes and Ken Cook received the Distinguished Flying Cross (DFC) at the end of June 1944. Comans' citation read 'For skill and fortitude in the face of the enemy'. He subsequently received a

---

* Now Silverstone racing circuit.

bar to his DFC in October 1944. Roy Woollford, who held the rank of warrant officer, also qualified for the DFC, which he was awarded in September. Other non-commissioned ranks were normally awarded the Distinguished Flying Medal (DFM). Of the rest of the crew, Daniel Bolland and Ken Randle received the DFM in September 1944. George Widdis was to follow in October, his DFM citation reading:

> Flight Sergeant Widdis is one of the best air gunners in the squadron and his enthusiasm and keenness to operate against the enemy has been an inspiration to the whole squadron. His work has been of a high standard throughout his tour and his unremitting search has played a great part in the safety of the aircraft and crew on their numerous operational flights.

Although Jim Comans recognized some of the old Lancasters when he arrived at 1661 HCU at Winthorpe, it must have seemed a lifetime since he and his new crew had gone through the course there. The faithful Mark I aircraft had been the first Lancasters to see operational duty and had endured numerous hard landings, stalls and near misses in an eventful life at 1661 HCU.

They were slightly less powerful than the operational Mark IIIs but still had the classic – and endearing – handling characteristics of the Lancaster, particularly as these training models were often flying unladen. Training pilots

Roy Woollford's Distinguished Flying Cross. Crew members Comans, Bowes, and Cook also received the DFC. Widdis, Bolland and Randle received the Distinguished Flying Medal. Ken Cook was awarded the Légion d'honneur, France's highest award for bravery, in 2014.

to fly the Lancaster was still a challenge. Many trainee crews still had insufficient experience of four-engined aircraft. Most instructors agreed that, at times, an inexperienced RAF pilot could represent as much of a danger as a Luftwaffe fighter ace. The many thousands of air accidents that took place are grim evidence of the sheer riskiness of Second World War flying, no element of which was safe. On 22 October 1944 Stirling LJ586 of 1661 HCU suffered severe icing and plummeted from 17,500 to 3,000 feet before the captain ordered the crew to bail out. Air gunner Eric Bailey's parachute failed to open properly because of the low altitude and he fell to his death. The pilot survived the crash-landing at Blandford in Dorset.

*

Don Bowes knew he still had mission numbers to make up before he could take a break. The daily routine of meeting up with the crew had finished. As a spare navigator, Bowes had to rely on his circle of associates in the mess to get good positions for future flights. In these circumstances, few relished making up numbers on new crews. Some, fresh out of training, could prove to be a liability; everyone knew new men were likely to make more mistakes in the early part of their career. After hearing familiar voices over the intercom on so many flights, it was going to be hard to get used to others.

Fortunately for Bowes, Flight Lieutenant Charles Owen was keen to jettison Squadron Leader Stevens as navigator on his crew. Stevens had attached himself to the Owen crew after D-Day, and although as captain of the aircraft Owen had authority over Stevens, it was not proving a happy match. Stevens had completed his operational tour and was a rank higher than Owen, holding the position of squadron navigation officer. Normally a man in his position would not be required to fly operations.

No account involving Charles Blundell Owen would be

complete without some words on his background and character. Owen was one of a small number of airmen who relished flying to the extent that he would continue to place himself in extreme danger rather than rest. This should not imply that he was cavalier in any way in his attitude to flight safety – he was considered an outstanding pilot.

Born to English parents in Barcelona in 1923, Owen attended Malvern College, leaving school in 1940 at seventeen to work in the Supermarine factory at Southampton. In September 1940 Owen was badly injured in an air raid on the factory and spent that winter in hospital. When he was discharged he was old enough to join the RAF and undertook flying training, qualifying as an instructor, a role he performed for the first year of his flying career before joining 97 Squadron. He was still only twenty when he began flying operations and experienced Black Thursday at Bourn in December 1943.

Don Bowes was probably drawn to Owen by his confident approach. Owen had no time for what he saw as unnecessary rules, nor for the stuffiness of certain officers in matters of class. In some quarters, the belief persisted that officers should always be drawn from the public schools, but although Owen fitted this criterion he did not agree with it. Suspicions were often voiced that some promotions were awarded on the basis of social background rather than true ability. As in the First World War, casualties had greatly depleted the ranks of pre-war officers, some of whom treated flying as a great adventure to be fitted in between drinks parties and rounds of polo. The Royal Air Force that developed over the course of the Second World War was a rather different service in its make-up, both socially and geographically: men like Don Bowes came from working-class backgrounds and spoke with regional accents. For some of the old officer class, their presence in this select flying club was a temporary aberration. Commonwealth officers, particularly

Australians like Comans, who had no truck with old-fashioned English snobbery, did much to dispel such attitudes.

Charles Owen had only a few flights remaining before completing his second tour on Lancasters at forty-five missions. He had reached the end of his first tour, at thirty missions, with the Annecy raid on 9 May. But rather than take the opportunity to rest, he had decided to press on immediately with the second tour. It was a decision that proved too much for his navigator, Flying Officer Bill Shires, who opted to leave the crew at this point, thereby creating a vacancy that was filled by various temporary navigators, including Stevens. As with all characters who thrilled to a life of severe danger, Owen's personality was complex. He was a heavy drinker but showed no signs of alcohol dependency at this point.* His confidence could make him appear rude in his dealings with his fellow airmen, a characteristic that made him immensely popular with some but heartily disliked by others.

Although books and films produced after the war perpetuate the notion of bomber crews as close-knit groups, in reality relationships within crews were extremely varied in nature. The Comans crew had a close working relationship during operations, but they never became best friends and would not keep in close contact once their tour was over. In some crews the bond was weaker. Bill Shires of the Owen crew recalls an incident in which the rear gunner, F. B. Thomas, was injured when their Lancaster crash-landed at RAF Tangmere in Sussex after a raid on Berlin. The stricken gunner was taken away to hospital, but following his departure no one asked after him or attempted to discover his subsequent whereabouts. Arguably, indifference to the suffering of others could be part of an airman's psychological defensive mechanism, but there were clearly occasions when crews simply did not gel. When contrasting characters clashed,

* Owen was to suffer with alcoholism after he left the RAF.

belonging to a crew became something to be endured rather than enjoyed.

Don Bowes first flew with Owen to Gelsenkirchen on 21/22 June 1944, five days after the Comans crew disbanded. The 123 Lancasters and 9 Mosquitos hit an oil production plant and reduced its production by 20 per cent. Bomber Command was demonstrating that it still had spare capacity to hit targets of secondary importance after the invasion. But within days, the Lancasters would be required to engage with the new and deadly threat represented by the V1 flying bombs. The 1,870lb warhead carried by the 'doodlebugs' was less than half the weight of an RAF 'Cookie', but the destruction it could cause was considerable. The Allies had known of the flying bombs' existence for months through reports from the resistance of their manufacture. Photo reconnaissance had also revealed curious structures at various locations in the Pas-de-Calais that did not appear to relate directly to coastal defence. The Nazis' extensive use of forced labour meant that there were plenty of people who were better disposed to the Allies than the Germans and who had first-hand knowledge of these sites. Even in the most secure labour camps, inmates found ways of smuggling out information. More specific data was gleaned from radio intercepts provided by the many signals intelligence collecting stations – 'Y' Stations – spread across Britain. When the information they had gathered was fed back to the codebreakers at Bletchley Park in Buckinghamshire, it was possible to build a picture of the sites and their likely operating status. Even before the first V1 had been fired off its ramp by a rocket charge, the RAF and USAAF had attacked launch sites and factories where flying bombs were being produced. The V1 launch sites – prominent concrete structures surrounded by command bunkers – had been spotted in aerial photographs as they were being built, even though most of them were in forested locations.

The Allies relied on low-level reconnaissance Spitfires equipped with lateral cameras to pick out targets in northern France. Many V1 sites were concealed in woodland with the ramp constructed on an outer edge, making target identification more difficult than factories and marshalling yards. On Don Bowes' second flight with the Owen crew to a V1 launch site at Prouville in the Somme *département* they were unable to identify their target accurately. Picked out by German searchlights, Owen had to abandon his first run. They heard the Mosquito markers being called in, but nothing seemed to happen. After a delay, flares were dropped on an adjacent wood and, in the confusion, the bombing was inaccurate. It was also apparent that there were German fighters in the area. The Baker crew in ND501 were attacked by three Ju88s, but gunners Jones and Clark claimed two destroyed and a third damaged. The confusion was captured in Owen's diary, writing in his typical jocular style, '… fighters arrived at the same time as we did and we all orbited together. Very matey but a little hectic. We departed hurriedly after our second flare run and left the rest of the boys to enjoy themselves.'

The inefficiency of high-level raids on V1 launch sites was noted and the heavy bombers were soon moved to striking railheads, manufacturing sites and storage areas in the battle against the *Vergeltungswaffen*. The Mosquito would prove to be more effective in launching low-level raids on the launch sites.

Charles Owen's final flight in a Lancaster in operations (which was also Don Bowes' last) took place on 12 July 1944. This was also the first time that Owen had acted as 'Master Bomber', a raid controller who circled the target to direct the marking of the target and call in the subsequent waves of bombers. It was an important, albeit daunting, role that had been performed by leaders in Lancasters and Halifaxes, but now also increasingly in Mosquitos. The target on 12 July was Culmont-Chalindrey, an important railway junction on the Paris–Mulhouse railway. Owen's diary records the proceedings with enthusiasm:

> My last trip on Lancs and my first as a pukka Master Bomber, having only done Deputy before. Tricky target to find, but Nigel did his stuff with the box and our flares were spot on. Got the attack going smartly on my aiming point, but heard Ted Porter mucking about with his 20 mins after we'd left the target. First-class prang, but rather disappointing at the time as we were using long-delay fuses. Arrived back at dawn in pouring rain, low cloud and shocking visibility. Managed to creep in more by luck than good judgement, feeling rather relieved. Rest of the squadron diverted, so we got two eggs each for breakfast.

★

The Culmont-Chalindrey raid marked the end of Don Bowes' tour, the last member of the Comans crew still flying on operations. There was no necessity for Don to continue, but it seems Owen's influence and passion for flying had persuaded Don to join him on an adventure in Mosquitos. Owen's future as a master bomber would depend on his having a good navigator, and he believed he had found one in the man from the north-east.

Three days later, on 15 July, Bowes was formally transferred to '5 Group Headquarters', but in practice he stayed at RAF Coningsby to fly with '54 Base Flight', a pool of aircraft used by an elite group of master bombers who marked targets and provided illumination for 5 Group operations. 54 Base Flight was not part of a specified squadron. It consisted principally of Mosquitos, though it also contained at least one P-38 Lightning of the USAAF. Leonard Cheshire had secured his first Mosquitos for 617 Squadron, but it appears subsequent allocations served with 54 Base Flight at Coningsby. This small group took on the most hazardous tasks of the master bomber, even having their own allocated simulator for training.

On 31 March 1944 Leonard Cheshire had entertained a USAAF delegation visiting Coningsby and Woodhall Spa that included Generals Carl Spaatz and Jimmy Doolittle. They were very taken with Cheshire, who was just beginning to develop the new 5 Group marking technique. Cheshire found the Americans far more forthcoming than RAF top brass and civil servants at the Air Ministry, whose deliberations tended to err on the side of caution. Spaatz and Doolittle left Lincolnshire with the promise 'whatever you need, just ask'. When he was building resources for the force that would become 54 Base Flight, Cheshire remembered the generals' offer. In late June, finding no Mosquitos available owing to the demands of other raids, Cheshire asked the Americans for a P-51 Mustang for a mission to destroy a VI bunker at Sirecourt in the Pas-de-Calais. The Americans responded quickly, sending the aircraft requested. The P-51 had barely been prepared before Cheshire took off from Woodhall Spa on a sortie without any pre-training. He had not flown a single seat aircraft for some time.

Often flying through a hail of fire that threatened to knock them out of the air, master bombers had to be able to shut down their senses to personal danger, whether real or imagined. Clear thinking and a certain cool doggedness marked the men who made the grade. With these attributes came eccentricities, ill temper, heavy drinking and a penchant for chasing women. In the two-man team, an essential part of the navigator's role was to act as a foil to the wilder elements of the master bomber. While the pilot would pitch his Mosquito into the teeth of a storm, the navigator was quietly working out how best to get out of it.

Owen's and Bowes' first sortie in a Mosquito was on 19 July 1944, flying against a V1 site at Thiverny, north of Paris. Utilizing caves and tunnels, the Germans stored and assembled the

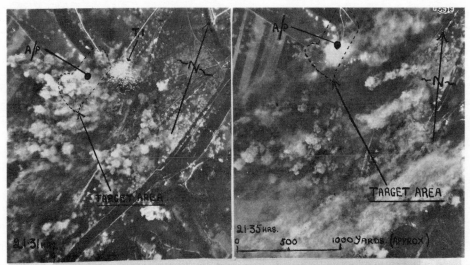

No. 22 THIVERNY (France).
Daylight attack on 19th July,1944 showing T.I. at "H + 1"
and concentration of bombing 4 minutes later.
(5 & 8 Groups)   Confidential

*Charles Owen's and Don Bowes' first Mosquito sortie, an attack on the V1
storage facility at Thiverny, 19 July 1944.*

V1s at several locations. 617 Squadron had attacked a nearby V1
site at Saint-Leu-d'Esserent on 4 July, dropping eleven 12,000lb
Tallboy bombs. The long summer evenings allowed the Thiverny
raid to be launched in daylight, using conventional bombs to
block the cave entrances.

Owen's description of his flight fairly bristles with enthusiasm:

First trip in Mossie, and my first daylight op. Took off an
hour after the Lancs and caught them up at the French coast
much to the joy of Don, who'd had enough of sitting behind
the curtain in a Lanc and twiddling knobs. France looked very
peaceful in the afternoon sun, and I even caught a glimpse of
Paris in the distance. Heavy flak at the target, but the Lancs
caught while we watched. Left the Lancs at the coast and
beetled back to base flat out. Arrived at dusk and beat up the

mess, much to the consternation of the gang at the bar. Decide
that a Mossie is definitely a safe way of going to war.

Charles Owen enjoyed a friendship with Guy Gibson, leader
of the Dam Busters raid in 1943. Moving into the role of Base
Air Staff Officer of 54 Base Flight, Gibson arrived at Coningsby
on 4 August 1944. He had held a deputy position at nearby East
Kirkby, so he was a familiar face in the mess. Gibson's celebrity
had proved to be an obstacle in his dealings with ordinary airmen, many of whom – while still maintaining an admiration for
his skills – found him rude and superior. Awarded the VC for
his assault on the Ruhr dams, Gibson had undertaken public
relations tours, including one to America. He was considered
too valuable to undertake operations again, but he chafed at the
restriction. Even before his appointment to Coningsby, he had
hitched a ride on a 630 Squadron Lancaster and terrorized the
crew by insisting they make several passes of the target so he could
observe results. After D-Day, Gibson had appealed personally
to Harris to allow him to fly again. His request was grudgingly
accepted on condition that he fly only where he could bale out
over Allied-occupied territory, a near-impossible condition to
guarantee. During his enforced grounding in the first half of
1944, Gibson had written *Enemy Coast Ahead*, a memoir of his
experiences in Bomber Command. Commentators agree that
Gibson himself wrote the book rather than a ghost writer, but
that he received some editorial help. It appears this help was
provided by Charles Owen, who read the manuscript in the
summer of 1944 before Gibson submitted it to his publishers.

Owen and Bowes continued flying operationally until October 1944. It is clear from Owen's diary, in which Bowes makes
frequent appearances, that the navigator was enjoying his time
on Mosquitos. Describing their attack on another V1 storage
facility, at L'Isle-Adam, Owen writes:

Another daylight stooge to France, but more amusing than last time. Had to mark the target myself in a hurry and went down to 100ft. Luckily no defences opened up and we got away with it. Quite a lot of flak from Rouen on return, and we followed a Lanc down and saw it belly-land in a field. Went down to have a look and saw the pilot climb out and wave. Came home across France at 0 feet and saw some very surprised Huns when we nipped over a big chateau near the coast. Quite an amusing trip, and Don very pleased.

It was a light-hearted form of writing, its style not dissimilar to Guy Gibson's, transmuting life-threatening danger into breezy adventure. In the boozy chatter of the bar, there's little doubt that pilots would have described their exploits in similarly blasé terms. But there are only so many times that a pilot – even one as skilled as Gibson – can fly by the seat of his pants. And on 19 September Gibson's luck was finally to run out.

Guy Gibson had fitted in only a few flights during his time at Coningsby. He was not, despite his wealth of experience, a master bomber, but he was determined to go on a scheduled raid to Bremen. During the day, however, it was decided that the reserve targets of Rheydt and Mönchengladbach would be hit instead. The news at briefing that Gibson would be raid controller was greeted with some consternation. Although Gibson had arguably been the

Wing Commander Guy Gibson, VC, photographed in 1944.

first master bomber in his actions during the Dams raid, he had not completed the rigorous training and assessment that others had undertaken before promotion to the role. That night's raid involved a complicated plan and the crews were unsure how Gibson would perform. Perhaps, also, there was something about Gibson's stubbornness on that day that sent warning signals around Coningsby. Don Bowes was told, possibly by Owen, not to go to the mess as 'Gibbo was stooging around looking for a navigator'. It was a warning that Don heeded, thereby ensuring he would not play the fatal role of supporting actor in the tragic drama of a national hero's final flight. Finding no navigator immediately available, Gibson asked Station Navigational Officer Jim Warwick to accompany him. Gibson had only flown the Mosquito on a small number of occasions and Warwick had no experience at all.

There were no suitable Mosquitos at Coningsby, so Gibson and Warwick were driven the short distance to Woodhall Spa. Gibson found a reserve Mosquito of 627 Squadron waiting, KB213, but he rejected it and commandeered KB267, which was already standing to in readiness for the operation – much to the irritation of its scheduled crew. Writing in *Aeroplane Monthly* in the 1970s, Charles Owen related that he had briefed Gibson on the route in and out of the target as Owen had been controller on a similar raid to Mönchengladbach on 10 September. Owen accompanied Gibson and Warwick to Woodhall Spa, but as Gibson was strapping into Mosquito KB267, he made it clear he wanted to fly home the direct route over Holland at low level, rather than over France. Owen disagreed forcefully with Gibson and told him he thought this was unwise. But despite Owen's remonstrations, Gibson would not be moved. Quite apart from the more hazardous nature of the Dutch route, the alternative route over France had more Allied occupied zones – so Gibson was blatantly disregarding a key proviso of his permission to fly.

The argument with Owen, one of his best friends, was a further indication of Gibson's state of mind that evening.

The raid did not go as planned and there was much confusion over marking. Gibson's primary red flare failed to drop. It is likely he loitered in the target area until 22.00 hours. His Mosquito crashed at Steenbergen in the southern Netherlands at 22.30. Witnesses reported seeing a light in the cockpit shortly before KB267 dived into the ground, killing both men. The controversy surrounding Gibson and Warwick's deaths has spawned a number of plausible explanations, including the possibility that neither man was fully familiar with the fuel tank switches and that they may unwittingly have themselves caused the engines to fail. Speculation as to whether their aircraft was damaged over the target has never been backed up by solid evidence. In 2011, reports circulated that rear gunner Sergeant Bernard McCormack of 61 Squadron believed he had accidentally shot down Gibson over Steenbergen when he was approached by what he believed was a Ju88. Although McCormack had died in 1992, his confession to his wife seems to tally with records of the time, including that of another Lancaster crew who witnessed the action and saw a red flare burning at the crash site.

With little left of Mosquito KB267 and few human remains, the Germans initially believed only one person had been in the Mosquito at the time of the crash, leading to the conclusion the other crew member may have bailed out. Jim Warwick was identified by his dog tag but Gibson was only identified by a sock tag after the gruesome discovery of a third hand had prompted further investigation. The local deputy mayor, Mr Herbers, insisted that the men be given a proper funeral and a horse-drawn hearse was hired from nearby Halsteren. A cross was erected over the grave with Jim Warwick's full rank and name. At this point, they did not know the rank of the other man, simply inscribing the name 'Guy Gibson' underneath. Later, when Gibson's identity was confirmed, a new cross was erected detailing his rank and decorations. Owen notes in his 1970s article, 'We were used to losing friends in those days, but his [Gibson's] loss hit us very hard.'

Don Bowes, the last member of the Comans crew to finish operational flying, had flown almost constantly for over a year. On 5 October 1944, he flew his last mission. It took him and Charles Owen to Wilhelmshaven in a P-38 Lightning, still carrying American code 423517 rather than an RAF one:

Last trip of the war for Don and I, and a pleasant daylight stooge across the North Sea. I was doing Deputy to Johnnie Simpson, so I could sit back and enjoy myself. Good trip out in sunny weather, and very quiet except for flak from Heligoland. Target was covered by 10/10 cloud, but a good deal of flak. I went up to 25,000ft and watched Johnnie being shot at down at 12,000ft. Saw plenty of our Mustang escort but no Huns. Good thing. Came home at 26,000ft in bright sunlight and not a cloud in the sky. Very peaceful except for a V2 shooting up from Holland, leaving a long jagged white trail. First time I'd seen one. Came in very fast and beat up the aerodrome before landing... Johnnie came in in the Mossie, ten minutes later. It was his last trip too, so we adjourned to the bar before lunch and celebrated suitably. Recollection of subsequent session somewhat hazy. Good show.

★

Pedalling along the B1308 towards Lincoln in August 1944, Ken Cook mused on how much his life had changed in the last few weeks. Not long ago he was risking his life at 20,000 feet dodging flak and fighters and now his greatest threat was from the constant stream of traffic heading in and out of the city. It was often a wet journey, dodging puddles and trying to avoid being run over, but for the first time since his wedding he was living the settled life of a married man. After leaving Coningsby, he had spent his leave back in Gloucestershire with Muriel, adjusting to his life ahead and making plans. As he finished his tour with 97 Squadron, he learned that he had been awarded the DFC and that he would be posted to RAF Fiskerton, to the east of Lincoln, as radar navigation officer. There was no chance of finding married quarters on the station. As with most of Britain's rapidly constructed wartime airfields, accommodation at Fiskerton was in rows of Nissen huts. But Lincoln was only five miles away, and by the end of the summer, Ken had found a house to rent in the city.

Some training postings were situated well away from front-line squadrons, but Ken was still close to the action with 49 Squadron. They were not Pathfinders, but part of the regular bomber force attached to 5 Group. Ken's task was to train newly arrived crews on H2S and keep navigators and air bombers abreast of new technology. He would still fly the Lancaster regularly, mostly by day and not operationally. Normally, as 49 Squadron took off for its night mission and the roar of the ascending Lancasters sounded over Lincoln, Ken would be home by the fire with Muriel. He exchanged the occasional letter with his former colleagues on the Comans crew and was able to catch up with their news. Ken and Muriel's first taste of married bliss was interrupted in September, when the RAF moved 49 Squadron from RAF Fiskerton to RAF Fulbeck, east of Newark. Ken was now fifteen miles away from Lincoln, not an easy commute. Nevertheless, by the end of year he and Muriel were expecting their first child.

In autumn 1944, Allied bomber losses increased again as the Luftwaffe fielded more fighters. The jet-powered Me 262, powered by the Junkers Jumo 004 turbojet engine and with a speed superior to any Allied fighter, proved particularly difficult to counter in the air. Hitler's insistence that V weapon development took priority had brought the Me 262 to the battlefield too late. Of 1,430 built, only 200 were operational at any time, but they were highly effective in the air. The Luftwaffe claimed 542 aircraft were destroyed by the Me 262, many of them on the Eastern Front. The cause of the improvement in German fortunes was partly Harris's reluctance to press the Allied advantage with continued attacks on the oil refineries across the Reich. The attacks had eased, allowing German oil production to rise again, from 18,000 tonnes in October to 39,000 tonnes in November. Air Chief Marshal Harris had always considered the oil war a distraction from the real task of crushing Germany. As the USAAF began to face limited daylight in the autumn of 1944, Bomber Command's night force was not used to maintain pressure on German oil supplies.

In the remaining nine months of war that Ken Cook spent with 49 Squadron, twenty-eight Lancasters were lost, only marginally fewer than 97 Squadron lost in the dark winter of 1943/4. Of the sixteen crews Ken flew with in H2S training, four were lost on operations. Pilots Derrick Talbot, Roussel Stark, Roger Cluer and Edwin Maul all died with their crews. When Maul's plane exploded on 21 November 1944 on a raid to the Mittelland Canal at Gravenhorst, there was speculation that he, or the other 49 Squadron Lancaster lost nearby, had been hit by bombs falling from above.

Ken's relationships with the crews of 49 Squadron were different from those with his former crew members of 97 Squadron in his operational days. In his training role, he got to know the crews more intimately, flew with them and engaged with their gossip and banter. Ken's world was no longer confined to the horizons of a single crew and the relief from extreme danger was refreshing. His role did not remove all the hazards of being an airman – new crews were led by relatively inexperienced pilots. On several occasions after encountering bumpy landings, Ken recalls he heard gripes from crews about their captain; 'He can fly it but he can't bloody land it' was a common complaint.

*

A particular source of fascination for the men involved with the Lancaster was the constant flow of technological innovation. In December 1944 Ken Cook took part in a LORAN (Long Range Navigation) training course. The system, developed by the Americans, used lower radio wave frequencies than Gee. LORAN's signals reflected off the ionosphere at night, giving direction over the horizon. Rumbling along in a specially equipped Halifax, Ken had no idea that this device would form the backbone of air navigation right through to the 1980s. For the first time since operations, Ken ventured out into the dark skies of Europe, travelling a course from Fulbeck via Dungeness to Saint-Quentin, then across to Lyons, and returning via Saint-Quentin and Beachy Head. Their course was tucked safely behind the lines, in Allied-occupied territory, but they still ran the risk of an encounter with a German fighter. Little did they suspect at the time that the German army was massing its forces 100 miles to the east of their route. Two weeks later, Field Marshal Gerd von Rundstedt's forces would rush the snow-covered Ardennes in an attempt to cut the Allied armies in two and race for the coast.

The introduction of LORAN also meant that the days of the bomb aimer crouched in a Perspex observation position were numbered. Developers were convinced that eventually bombs could be delivered by guidance systems. While the RAF strove for greater accuracy with specialized bombs, the Americans worked on a weapon so powerful that the location of the epicentre was of secondary importance. The first atom bomb test, 'Trinity', which would take place in the New Mexico desert in July 1945, was only seven months away. As the secretive work of the Manhattan Project continued, its developers realized that hitting the 'pickle barrel' had taken on a new meaning. But positioning bombs without direct human supervision was still some years away. Although London had been shocked by the Germans' deployment of flying bombs, investigators found the V1's navigational equipment to be crude. A device cut the fuel and locked the elevators and rudder into a dive once it had reached the end of a timed flight. Once it was in flight, a simple autopilot system of on-board gyroscopes corrected the V1's straight-line path.

From September 1944, attacks on Britain with V2 rockets – the first long-range guided ballistic missile – changed strategic thinking almost overnight. The V2's inertial navigational system was far more sophisticated than the V1's and was capable of calculating and correcting the rocket's course in-flight. Although the V2 did not possess the ability to perform course changes once the rocket booster stage was over, it was obvious that this further development was not far away. The V2 and later ballistic missiles were almost impossible to defend against once they had been launched. On Charles Owen's and Don Bowes' last flight in their P38 Lightning on 5 October they saw the streak of vapour in the sky from a launched V2 over Holland, but there was nothing they could do. It is hardly surprising that Wernher von Braun and his V2 weapons team were warmly welcomed into the American fold after their surrender in May 1945. Any embarrassment felt at the USA's speedy co-option of the services of a Nazi scientist would be mitigated by the revelation that von Braun had been viewed with suspicion by the German authorities. He had even been detained by the Gestapo for two weeks in March 1944 over allegations that he had engaged in defeatist conversations. Although his weapons had been aimed primarily at civilian targets, expediency dictated that neither he nor any member of his development team faced any charges.

As Europe entered 1945, thousands in Britain followed the war via radio broadcasts and wall maps produced by newspapers. These adorned the walls of many homes, small flags showing the extent of the Allied advance. After the excitement of the D-Day landings, the eastward progress of the Allied front was eagerly tracked. When Paris was liberated in August 1944, it seemed the Allied advance was unstoppable. As Montgomery's forces struck north, the launch of Operation Market Garden gave rise to hopes that the whole of the Netherlands would soon be liberated, and an invasion route opened into northern Germany. But the failure at Arnhem brought a pause, and the small flags on the wall did not move as quickly. The men of Bomber Command knew where the lines were drawn better than most. If your aircraft got into trouble, knowing where the front line lay could be the difference between life and death.

On 17 January 1945 the Soviets captured the piles of rubble that had once formed the elegant streets of Warsaw. It was a hollow victory. In August 1944 the Polish resistance had launched the Warsaw uprising against the Germans, who were beginning to withdraw from Poland. But the Soviets halted their advance outside the city, allowing the Germans to regroup and crush the uprising in October, killing thousands of civilians and razing the city to the ground. The failure of the Soviets to intervene was deeply cynical: among those eliminated by the Nazis were many who might have opposed Stalin's post-war strategy of suppressing and occupying Poland. Eventually, when the Poles had fought to their last, it took the Soviets only three days to dislodge the Germans from the wrecked city. Ten days later, on 27 January 1945, the 322nd Rifle Division of the Red Army entered a concentration camp south of Katowice. The name of the place was Auschwitz, and the horrors the Soviet soldiers found there were beyond human understanding.

On 10 February 1945, Ken Cook climbed aboard Lancaster G 'George' piloted by Flying Officer Frierer. Ken was flying as a set operator on the new model of H2S, the Mark IId, which was being trialled in 49 Squadron for the first time. It was increasingly clear that the role of radar navigator would, eventually, permanently supersede that of the bomb aimer. Ken Cook was to find himself at the forefront of a change of technological direction within the RAF. At the end of the war, thousands of pilots, navigators and gunners found that the RAF had no further need of their services. However, the development of new technology in aircraft and weapons guidance meant there were opportunities in the RAF for men like Cook who had not only used radar in action, but had excelled in their Pathfinder role.

As each new version of H2S came into service, it was often the Pathfinders who were the first to receive the latest models. They already had Mark IIIA, a model that promised roll stabilization,* but its broader dissemination across the service had been delayed. The Mark IId was the stop-gap version for the worker bees of Bomber Command, 49 Squadron among them. The problems lay with manufacturers, and in particular with the gramophone companies that were responsible for producing a significant portion of the equipment. Avro also failed to provide the engineering backup required to adapt Lancasters for the new system. The renowned physicist Bernard Lovell, part of the H2S team in the Telecommunications Research Establishment (TRE), was aghast at the delays: '... we had overloaded the firms, peoples' brains and probably ourselves. The delays were appalling – it seemed the whole country had stopped working. ... In January 1945 instead of having a whole command equipped with the best roll stabilised S band equipment, Bomber Command was forced to undertake ad hoc squadron modifications.'

On 13 February, three days after Ken Cook's trialling of the Mark IId, Lancasters from 49 Squadron formed part of the vast fleet of 772 RAF bombers launched against Dresden in two waves. The raid caused huge firestorms that engulfed the beautiful

---

* The scanning system was kept level in relation to the ground by means of a mechanical *stabilizer*.

city known as 'Florence on the Elbe'. The following two days saw daylight attacks by the USAAF, which further devastated Dresden. The city, especially once it was ablaze, was such a clear target that there had not been any need for H2S to guide the bombers. To the crews, it was an attack similar to dozens they had carried out over the last two years, but the clear conditions, low defences and accurate targeting combined to make the Dresden raid a deadly masterclass in the art of saturation bombing. They had little clue that Dresden would be their war-defining raid, and the single most controversial Allied bombing attack after the dropping of the atom bombs on Hiroshima and Nagasaki. The Germans released falsified casualty figures in March 1945 declaring that 200,000 had died, but later studies found between 18,000 and 25,000 lives had been lost.

*

As the Soviets powered eastwards towards Berlin, Eisenhower's Allied forces, having entered Germany from the west, were massing on the western bank of the Rhine. When troops of the 9th Armored Division of the US First Army found the Ludendorff Bridge at Remagen intact on 7 March 1945, they poured across it, a full two weeks and more ahead of Montgomery's planned northern crossing of the Rhine, Operation Plunder. Once American troops had broken out of the Remagen bridgehead on 25 March, the flags on those wall maps around Britain could not keep up with the advance. As the remnants of Hitler's once great army of the west were encircled in the Ruhr Pocket, the end was in sight. The news that 317,000 men had surrendered on 18 April 1945 brought gasps of astonishment at RAF Fulbeck. Of those who surrendered, only 75,000 were adequately armed; some of the many thousands of older men and boys who made up a large part of this defeated army didn't have a pistol to share between them.

The men of 49 Squadron now knew for certain that the war in Europe would soon be over. Their feelings of euphoria were tempered only by the realization that more men were going to die before the fighting finally stopped. Ken Cook watched the Lancasters depart for raid after raid. The rate of losses had decreased significantly but, with the end so close, it was particularly hard to bear when planes failed to return. On 4 April, as the Allies tightened their grip on the Ruhr Pocket, 49 Squadron hit the barracks at Nordhausen, not knowing they were part of the Mittelbau-Dora concentration camp. On the bombing run, Lancaster ME308 flown by the Fischer crew suddenly broke in two and plummeted to the ground. It was initially believed that ME308 had been hit by bombs from above, but Dennis Over, a rear gunner from 227 Squadron, who were flying ahead of Fischer, witnessed what actually happened. Over recalled:

> I was looking directly at the aircraft, it was flying straight and level and suddenly snapped in two. It was 500 yards low on my starboard quarter. The two halves plunged vertically to the ground, no parachutes deployed, no fire or explosion. The forward part descended at an angle, the aft part dropped vertically. The aircraft broke up in a clear space between two clouds, we were both in that clear area for about ten seconds. As we were still two minutes to target, no aircraft were bombing at the time.

Whether ME308 suffered a flak hit or suffered structural failure is unknown.

Four days later, on 8 April, two more Lancasters were lost on a raid to an oil refinery at Lutzkendorf, the last casualties of 49 Squadron in action. All fourteen crew members were killed, the Cluer crew of Lancaster PB374 disappearing without trace. The Soviets had now reached the outskirts of Berlin and, as the final battle raged, 49 Squadron were ordered to move from

Fulbeck to RAF Syerston. It wasn't far, little over fifteen miles by road and a very short westward hop for the Lancasters. RAF Syerston had been under construction before the war began and boasted better standards of accommodation than Fulbeck, so the move had its advantages, despite its inconvenience.

On the morning of 22 April lines of lorries were loaded with ground equipment, kit bags and every sort of appendage a squadron carried. Ken Cook packed up his things and, having lugged his kit bags to the transports, was waiting to leave. It was a beautiful spring Sunday and the move had the feel of a school outing. Soon the familiar hum of the Merlin engines filled the airfield. Every Lancaster was moving, engines were revved with great enthusiasm as waving hands appeared at open cockpit windows. The procession turned for the runway and soon began taking off. It was a tradition that departing aircraft would turn and give a final low-level fly-past. Quentin Snow, Australian mid-upper gunner on the Wright crew, described the scene:

> The wing commander took off first and set the pattern by doing a long sweeping turn, screaming over the aerodrome at about 50 feet. Four or five more followed him. We took off and had started the long sweep around when we could see the aircraft in front of us was in trouble. His turn was much too tight and he wasn't doing anything about it, and very slowly losing height. It was apparent that something had fouled and jammed the control cables that ran along the inside of the fuselage. It could have been a bicycle or kit bag, but we were never to find out.

At 10 a.m. 5015 Works Flight were holding their last pay parade in preparation to leave. They were mostly WAAFs and standing as they were behind a two-storey workshop did not see Flying Officer George Elkington's Lancaster PB463 approaching. Unable to maintain height, Elkington's aircraft struck the workshop and demolished it before hitting the parachute drying hangar and pyrotechnics store underneath. In an instant, the Lancaster exploded, engulfing the WAAFs on parade. Those who were not killed instantly jumped into a concrete duct that carried a small canal nearby to escape the flames. Ken Cook was the other side of the buildings as the explosion rocked the airfield.

A witness, Eric Read, experienced the full horror of the accident:

> I had just left Flying Control and saw the whole thing as if in slow motion – the aircraft was 'shooting up' Fulbeck and was very low; it came from my right (heading north) and as the pilot pulled up, the tail hit the MT shed, bringing the aircraft down onto a large group of ground personnel. The clothing store was demolished along with the private car belonging to S/Ldr Brydon. The fire crew was there in seconds but to no avail; I was asked to give evidence at the court of enquiry; it was all very sad and a long time ago, but some of the shocking images still remain in my memory.

Fearing sabotage, all the Lancasters already in flight were ordered to land immediately. But with no evidence of foul play found, 49 Squadron continued their movement later that day. Fifteen members of 5015 Works Flight died as a result of the accident, some immediately, others from their injuries in the days that followed. A further four had been seriously injured. All six crew of PB463 were killed. The mid-upper gunner, Flight Sergeant Logan, was not with the crew that day and therefore had his closest escape of his war. The body of the pilot, Flying Officer George Elkington, was not found until sometime after the accident. It had been catapulted through a roof and into a mattress store.

In the immediate aftermath of the tragedy, everyone tried to carry on as before, and the feeling that the 'war goes on' remained undiminished. One crewman concentrated his thoughts on their new home at Syerston: 'The immediate task was to locate all the amenities on the new base – the initial verdict was grub at the Mess very good and ultra clean after Fulbeck – the Station dance was wizard and there are some wizard WAAFs here! By 23.00hrs that night, 49 Squadron had well and truly arrived and were settled in.' Perhaps his breezy words were the signs of a man trying to put a brave face on things. For some of those who witnessed the events of 22 April, the trauma would remain with them for a lifetime.

⋆

Britain's street lights came on again in April 1945. On the day of Hitler's suicide, 30 April, the clock face of Big Ben was lit for the first time in more than five years. Even before the formal ending of the war in Europe on 8 May, VE Day, many bomber squadrons were involved in Operation Exodus, the Allied operation to bring home tens of thousands of liberated prisoners of war. The crews of 49 Squadron were not used to having so much company in their Lancasters. Many of those repatriated were RAF personnel who had last flown in a Lancaster in unhappier times. There were no seats fitted and the men sat on their kit bags, which contained what few items they had. For the crew, dealing with grateful but nervous passengers made a huge change from the draining and emotionally charged night sorties of wartime. The musty smell of the prisoners of war lingered in the aircraft after they had gone and the task of cleaning up after airsick travellers was unpleasant. The Lancaster was never designed for passengers. Packing men into the cramped fuselage was a challenge, but their charges were immensely grateful for the lift home. In Operation Exodus the crews knew they had reached the end of their war in Europe. They flew in daylight, unmolested in skies that had until recently proved so deadly.

49 Squadron Navigators at RAF Fiskerton, May 1945. Ken Cook is fourth from the left in the front row.

VE Day saw riotous celebrations on many bomber bases. In the Far East, half a world away, the war still had three months to run, but in the flat green fields of the bomber counties it had run its course. At 1661 Heavy Conversion Unit at RAF Winthorpe, Jim Comans joined the men in a station parade at 10 a.m. followed by a short thanksgiving service. Their thirty-two Lancasters were parked up ready to recommence training, and there were still men engaged on their training course, but everything had changed in the few weeks leading up to this day. The Japanese still needed to be subdued, but men like Jim Comans sensed it was time to go home.

12.

Into the Jet Age

12 June 1958, RAF Tangmere

The large Perspex canopy was pushed fully back on its runners as Ken Cook placed his feet into the D-shaped crew steps in the fuselage of the Meteor NF14. Climbing up, his hands caught the lip of the open cockpit; pulling himself high enough to swing a leg in, he caught his balance before settling carefully down into the navigator's position. Unlike the Mosquitos he had flown in after the war, he sat behind the pilot rather than next to him. As he got in, he had been careful not to snag the straps of his bright yellow lifejacket. A ground crewman handed Ken his helmet. The 'bone dome', a crash helmet, was a recent addition to aircrew's equipment. Compared with canvas or leather headgear, it tended to feel top heavy. But this was progress, for in the high 'G' turns of a jet, its aircrew often banged their heads on the canopy sides. Strapped into the narrow cockpit, there wasn't much room to move, a common feature of military aircraft where a man was considered a piece of operating equipment rather than a passenger.

The Meteor did not have an ejector seat. In many ways the NF14 was behind the times – some of the single-seat Meteors had been equipped with this terrifying contraption. If the NF14 got into trouble the two crew would have to climb out into an airstream of up to 600mph, a feat almost impossible and made more hazardous by the high tail behind them.

Everything inside the cockpit was painted black. In the sun, both pilot and navigator tended to roast in the tight-fitting cockpit, but it was only 06.45 and cooler this morning. The navigation and radar equipment sat in a rack in front of Ken. Much of it looked similar to the early models developed during the Second World War. By the end of the war, Ken's role had altered as radar technology changed his role from 'bomb aimer' to 'radar navigator'. He spent less time visually observing through the Lancaster's Perspex nose and more time using instruments on the enlarged navigation table behind the pilot. In his post-war RAF career, his knowledge of radar had enabled him to move with ease from bomber to night fighter operations.

The NF14 Meteor was a jet night fighter with an improbably long and rather ugly nose. The neat slope of the early Meteor

Wing Commander Ken Cook standing beside the Meteor NF14 jet fighter in 1958, when he was in command of 153 Squadron.

A Meteor NF14 of 153 Squadron in flight. Ken Cook is in the rear seat.

had been removed and the stretched replacement carried a radar dish internally. Aircrews had reason to be cautious around the Meteor. Although she flew well, at slower speeds she had a reputation as a killer. The placement of the engines in the middle of the wings produced asymmetric effects, particularly if one engine wound up at a different speed from the other. An engine failure turned a speeding thoroughbred into a stubborn mule and it required skill as well as strength to prevent the aircraft from stalling. These failings meant that the RAF paid a heavy price in crew casualties: of 3,545 Meteors built in Britain, 890 were lost in accidents, killing 436 crew. It is notable that both senior RAF officers and society in general seemed so desensitized by high wartime casualties that they tolerated peacetime losses that can only be described as horrendous. Nonetheless, the Meteor was considered an outstanding success and became the RAF's most prolific fighter of the post-war years. An aeroplane born in the heat of the Second World War proved adaptable and flexible enough to hold its own in the new strategic context of the Cold War.

153 Squadron were preparing for a transit flight for their month's detachment to Cyprus. They had made the short hop from their home base, RAF Waterbeach in Cambridgeshire, to RAF Tangmere, in Sussex, the day before. That day they would make the exciting journey to Akrotiri with refuelling stops at Orange-Caritat, in the South of France, and Rome. The exercise wasn't long enough to make it worthwhile for wives and families to accompany the crews to Cyprus, so for Ken and his colleagues this would be a month spent in their own company, flying in the perfect blue skies above Nicosia and Akrotiri. It would also be the swansong for 153 Squadron's Meteors as they prepared to convert to the more powerful Gloster Javelins.

As the whine of the jet engines grew louder, Ken looked across the flight line at the other Meteors running up. Most of the young aircrew were single men. Ken, as their Commanding Officer, was an old man of thirty-five. Many of them had been in junior school when Ken was flying sorties in the winter skies of 1943/4. The brakes came off and the Meteors began to move to form a queue at the base of the runway. Unlike the propeller-driven aircraft of Ken's early years of flying, which gently vibrated every part of the aeroplane, taxiing in a Meteor was a serene experience. At take-off the difference was even more marked. As the tone of the two Rolls-Royce Derwent 9 engines rose to a crescendo, Ken felt a surge of energy pushing his back into the seat. Even with the large under-belly fuel tank and wing drop-tanks full to capacity, the Meteor showed itself keen to fly. The jet was airborne almost as soon as the nose wheel left the ground, climbing steadily and seemingly effortlessly as the summer sunlight glinted on the faces of the instruments. Unlike in the Lancaster, there were no anxious moments when one wondered if the aeroplane would succeed in leaving the runway.

RAF Waterbeach was Ken's last RAF posting in which he would fly regularly. Wing Commander Cook was flight commander of 153 Squadron – an unusual state of affairs, since commanders of flying units were normally pilots rather than navigators. In the thirteen years since the end of the war Ken had followed a steady career path in the RAF. He had returned to 97 and 83 Squadrons at RAF Coningsby in October 1945, when the war was over and the diminishing bomber squadrons were marking time after the Japanese surrender. Lancasters had given way to Avro Lincolns, an improved version with more powerful engines. Ken became No. 1 Group Radar Navigation Officer. He joined the famous 617 Squadron at RAF Binbrook, yet another Lincolnshire station, in June 1947, and crossed the Atlantic with them to make a victory tour of the USA and Canada. There was little suggestion at this stage that bomber crews were anything other than war heroes worthy of admiration.

Avro Lincoln bombers of 617 Squadron over Toronto, during the goodwill tour of the USA and Canada, 1947.

Ken continued with his training roles in radar navigation and served on the Vickers Wellington until April 1949. He accepted a permanent peacetime commission and, after further navigational training, made the change to fighters, joining 23 Squadron at RAF Coltishall in Norfolk. The de Havilland Mosquito was different from anything Ken had flown in before. He had grown accustomed to the radar navigator's desk, which, as equipment improved, had been pushed further down the fuselage into the dark recesses behind the wireless operator. Now, he was sitting in the bright daylight of the Mosquito cockpit, with a clear view all round. It was a novel and giddying experience. The power of the aircraft felt very close at hand, in a way that the heavy bombers could not match. The propellers seemed to flick by inches from the cockpit, but the crew rarely felt uncomfortable. They were thrilled by the power of an aircraft made from balsa and plywood that was keeping company with the new jets. The aircraft of the Second World War were now in their twilight years, and would soon be superseded by a stream of new designs. By 1951 the Avro Lancaster's immediate replacement, the Avro Lincoln, already looked old-fashioned as the English Electric Canberra, a jet-powered medium bomber, entered service. The high-altitude Vickers Valiant, the RAF's first 'V' bomber – powered by four Rolls-Royce Avon turbo jets mounted in the wing – flew for the first time that year and entered service in 1955.

Although Ken's career had progressed steadily in the post-war RAF, his home life was shaken by tragedy. Muriel gave birth to their second son, David, in Doncaster, but succumbed to influenza a few days later, on 10 March 1947. Ken's family in Gloucestershire played a big part in ensuring the young boys, Brian and David, were looked after in the sad months that followed their mother's death.

Ken would not remain a widower for long. Perhaps his instinct for survival, honed in the course of a dangerous flying career, told him he could not live without the comfort of loving companionship. In April 1948 he married nineteen-year-old Sonia Middleton, who worked at the hotel her uncle owned in Grimsby. She took on the boys as her own, a brave choice given her age. Subsequently Ken and Sonia would have three more children, Julia, Marilyn and Jonathan. The two older boys had been so young at the time of their mother's death that they did not realize Sonia was not their birth mother for many years afterwards.

⋆

Other former crew members stayed on in the post-war RAF. Don Bowes had finished his war as a navigation officer at 207 Squadron at RAF Spilsby in Lincolnshire. He met Margaret Sanders at a dance at the Cooperative Hall in Castleford, their hometown, in 1946. She described him as a 'suave young man in an RAF uniform' who asked her to dance. It appears that Don, who had little difficulty in acquiring girlfriends in wartime, was immediately besotted. He served another four years in the RAF before leaving the service in February 1950. He was assessed as 'Class A' for the RAF Reserve, which meant he could be called back at any time as a navigator. During this period, the Admiralty, War Office and Air Ministry all maintained an emergency reserve of men in the event of a crisis. Most of those who left the forces were listed in the reserves as the Cold War threatened a further conflict.* Don and Margaret married in January 1951 and settled in Townville, an area of Castleford. After a spell selling vacuum cleaners, Don followed Margaret into

---

* Alongside those Second World War veterans who remained in the services through the 1940s and 1950s, National Service, an extension of wartime conscription, was introduced in 1948, requiring all men reaching eighteen years of age to serve two years in the armed forces.

Three weddings (from top): Don and Margaret Bowes, January 1951; Ken and Joan Randle, with the Crew in attendance (Ken Cook is on the right in the front row), January 1944; Roy and Phyllis Woollford, May 1944.

teacher training and became a mathematics teacher.

Jim Comans made the long sea journey home to Sydney to resume his legal career in 1946. Unlike the other members of the crew, he had established himself in a profession before the war. Others took their chance on 'civvie street' in a 'demob suit' to find employment where they could. Thousands of young men had joined the forces before their training or apprenticeships were over and, unsurprisingly, many thousands chose to stay on in the armed forces. For the married men of the crew, seeking to settle down and establish a family was a priority.

Roy Woollford had married Phyllis Brewer in the spring of 1944 and was looking forward to their future together. Posted to 17 OTU RAF Turweston in Buckinghamshire in July 1944, Roy had spent the rest of his time in the RAF in a training role with radio operators. At the end of the war he flew in decommissioned Vickers Wellingtons up the A1 on their final journey to be scrapped in Blyth.

From there the aluminium was taken to Sheffield to be smelted down to feed the demand for pots and pans and sheet metal for prefabricated houses. As the aircraft he had spent many hours in were put out to pasture, so it was time for Roy, too, to leave the RAF. Memories of the long hours sitting in the darkness of the Lancaster fuselage never left him; but nor, it would seem, did memories of the songs that the crew sang to relieve tension on the return legs of operations. In the decades afterwards, Roy's interest in music led him to join an amateur operatic society and perform in shows such as *The King and I* and *Oklahoma!*. He was also a fan of Bing Crosby and teamed up with a friend, Dick Bradbury, as a singing duo.

Roy maintained an interest in aviation and on 6 September 1952 took his seven-year-old son, Russell, to the Farnborough Air Show. They arrived late, to learn that the de Havilland DH110 had disintegrated in flight minutes earlier, killing test pilot John Derry and test observer Anthony Richards. The two Rolls-Royce Avon engines ripped from within the aircraft wing, plunged from the sky into the crowd, killing twenty-nine and injuring sixty. Remarkably, once the ambulances had left the site and wreckage had been removed from the runway, the air show continued, with test pilot Neville Duke flying his Hawker Hunter through the sound barrier. The ingrained stoicism of the wartime generation had revealed itself once again. No matter what happened, 'the show must go on', although on this occasion it seems, in retrospect, extraordinarily insensitive to the memory of those who had been killed not to have abandoned the air show with immediate effect.

Radio operator Roy Woollford also talked only briefly to his family of his time in Bomber Command. Of all the crew, he appears to have suffered the most in terms of early trauma, although this was not apparent in later life. He was very proud of his Distinguished Flying Cross and kept letters and photographs with it. In his later years he became involved in the 97 Squadron Association and met Ken Cook again at a reunion, but the crew never reunited as a group.

The experience of being part of a bomber crew left an indelible mark on all those involved. Some spoke freely of their experiences, but others chose to say nothing, even to their families. Some were embarrassed at the dashing portrayals of airmen in films produced by Pinewood Studios, remembering a far tougher and coarser life of hard drinking and bad language. Others just wanted to get on with their lives and saw little value in exploring the past. The crew's navigator, Don Bowes, said very little to his wife and family about his wartime experiences. He passed away in February 1989 and only in recent years have his daughter Hilary and her husband, Michael, embarked on the task of piecing together his history. His logbook was missing, but he had left a large collection of photographs, many of which were informal pictures of his time in training. Don had also collected a significant number of post-raid target photographs that had been used to assess damage done and to gauge the accuracy of the bombing. He was a man who liked to look to the future and did not spend much time reminiscing. Hilary remembers there was always music on in the house and that her father was always busy with some project or other.

George Widdis returned to Canada and Jim Comans to Australia, but the presence of so many men from the Commonwealth in the armed forces led many in Britain to consider emigrating after the end of the war. Rear gunner 'Jock' Bolland married Margaret Fraser in 1952 and they had four children, each of them born at two-year intervals, thereafter. In 1963 he and his family emigrated to Australia on the Assisted Package Migration Scheme. Setting sail on the SS *Oriana* to Sydney, the family eventually settled in Queensland to start a new life.

By the 1980s, Ken Cook's son David was also living in

Australia. During one visit, Ken and Sonia met up with Jim and Joyce Comans in Sydney for a meal. By this time Jim had built a reputation for representing sporting interests in New South Wales, particularly in the field of horse racing and rugby league. He was a committee member of the Australian Jockey Club and served as chairman of the New South Wales Rugby League Judiciary from 1980 to 1986. His efforts to rid rugby league of violence led to his reputation as a 'hanging judge', as the judiciary handed out career-ending suspensions. Premiership player Bob Cooper, for one, was banned for fifteen months after a brawl and Comans was uncompromising, telling him during the hearing, 'Acts such as these must be obliterated from the game, and I'll begin by obliterating you.' Perhaps Jim's experience as a fifteen-year-old playing against the heavy-handed adult teams of the 1930s Premier League hung heavy in his memory. Inevitably, he made enemies, not least for his part in rewriting the laws of the game, outlawing some of the more extreme tackles. He was forced out of office in 1986, but the effects of his disciplinarian approach still attract polarized opinions. Roy Masters' book *Bad Boys*, published in 2006, includes a review of the case and an interview with Cooper as he watches video footage of the 1982 fight that ended his career. There was no doubt about Cooper's culpability in the incident, but the book portrays the dryness of Comans' character with Australian forthrightness. Masters writes of a 'parchment-faced Comans, a man with the pulse rate of a fish' and describes the audio recording of the hearing as revealing Comans to be 'ponderous, his mind moving at the speed of cold honey. Yet when he delivered his verdict, it was so clinical and concise. It appeared as if it had been written in advance.'

On Ken Cook's next visit to Australia, he tried to meet Comans once more, but found his approach rebuffed. They were never to meet again. Comans' reluctance to meet may have had something to do with anxieties arising from his controversial public profile, but another shadow seems to have emerged. Although there is no written evidence for it, rumours circulating within the Air Force community in Australia and Britain suggested that Comans had exaggerated his wartime service. An historical tribute written for Darlinghurst School after Jim's passing in 1992 states that Comans undertook 'over 100 separate bombing missions over Germany and occupied France'. If this statistic is correct, it would place him in the league of the select few like Group Captain Leonard Cheshire (who flew 103 missions and was awarded the Victoria Cross). However, such rumours should not rob Jim Comans of the very considerable credit he is due for his forty-six operational sorties. As Darlinghurst historian Scott Coleman writes, he 'is remembered as a tough, fair, brave and good bloke'.

Ken Cook meets Princess Alexandra (first cousin of Queen Elizabeth II) at a reception in Tehran, 1975.

Following his departure from the Royal Air Force in 1967, Ken Cook worked with a London firm of solicitors, before becoming a management consultant with an American business consultancy firm, Wofac, who specialized in time and motion studies. He later joined British Road Services as their Midlands manager. His career took him to Iran to look after BRS interests there and he was subsequently promoted to be a director as one of the team that brought the BRS group into the private sector.

In retirement Ken was able to reacquaint himself with many former comrades within the 97 Squadron (Straits Settlement)

Association. The young men who had once roamed the dark skies of Germany to help free Europe from Nazism's grip were now grandfathers with whitening hair and increasingly unsteady of gait. The medals that adorned their dress blazers bore witness to their wartime service, yet they were painfully aware of those who had been robbed of the opportunity to grow old with them.

Gradually, as the years passed, their numbers thinned. More and more, these yearly reunions were attended by sons and daughters as the Association members themselves became too frail to travel. They remain all too aware of the controversy that still swirls around the bombing campaign, which threatens to consign the sacrifices of an entire generation of airmen to a footnote in history. But these proud children of fathers who risked their lives in the flak-torn skies of mid-1940s Europe will not allow the heroism of the crews of Bomber Command to go unrecognized.

EPILOGUE

The Writing of History

No account of a Lancaster crew can avoid mention of the wartime strategy that placed the airmen in the skies over the Reich. Many hundreds of books have been written that examine their experiences and also pore over every element of Allied and German strategy in the Second World War. Further reading beyond *The Crew* is to be strongly encouraged. But the

Avro Lancaster PA474 of the Battle of Britain Memorial Flight at Coningsby, May 2018.

author feels he owes it to veterans like Ken Cook to explore further, albeit briefly, the policy decisions that led to the bombing raids. Undoubtedly, mistakes were made in selecting individual targets and arguments abound as to which German towns and cities were strategic in their importance. It would be unbalanced to suggest every action of Bomber Command was thoroughly prepared, or that the efficacy of every raid was correctly assessed. Equally, it is not possible to dismiss the bombing of civilian targets as wholly inappropriate. Although such actions seem abhorrent to the modern mind, the destruction of German cities can be directly linked to the need to defeat the Wehrmacht and Luftwaffe in the field and in the skies. The argument that the bombing campaign speeded the end of the war and alleviated the suffering of millions cannot be disregarded, however horrifying the outcome of specific raids.

It is difficult fully to comprehend the complexity and evil of a war that killed 70–85 million people – approximately 3 per cent of the world's population. Numerous politicians and military decision-makers played key roles in the turmoil and cruelty of the war years, but in our desire to simplify our understanding of events we tend to concentrate on key personalities like Hitler, Churchill, Stalin and Roosevelt. In the drama of the bombing campaign, Air Chief Marshal 'Bomber' Harris is traditionally allotted the central role – a role that, for some, was a morally dubious one. However, he was not alone in directing policy. Many who championed Harris' views moved silently into the shadows after the war, distancing themselves from the mounting controversy.

This generation of Second World War military leaders has passed away, leaving us with some written memoirs and a small group of old men who, in their youth, carried out the orders of their superiors. The opinions of the veterans, often far simpler than those who have sought to explain the conflict, carry a forthright honesty. In interviews for this book, Ken Cook was asked what he thought about the bombing of German cities at the time. He replied: 'They started it. When we saw what the Germans had done to London and Coventry, we thought they deserved everything they got.'

★

On 1 December 1943, Richard Stokes, Labour MP for Ipswich, pressed Sir Archibald Sinclair, Secretary of State for Air, on whether the RAF was engaged in indiscriminate bombing. Harris's saturation bombing of Berlin was by now in full flow, and the newspapers carried frequent reports of night-time raids on the German capital. Although Bomber Command had clearly widened its scope of operations after the Area Bombing Directive of February 1942, MPs were unclear about what this meant in practice.

Stokes asked, 'Am I to understand that the policy has changed, and that now the objectives of Bomber Command are not specific military targets but large areas, and would it be true to say that probably the minimum area of a target now is 16 square miles?' It was a provocative question that cut to the heart of bombing strategy. Were attacks on German cities intended to weaken Germany militarily, or was this a deliberate targeting of the civilian population to spread fear? Sinclair, a former army officer of the First War (who had been under Churchill's command) and a Liberal in the all-party coalition government of 1940, would not rise to the bait.

'Berlin is the centre of 12 Strategic railways; it is the second largest inland port in Europe; it is connected with the whole canal system of Germany; and in that city are the A.E.G., Siemens, Daimler, Benz, Focke-Wulf, Heinkel and Dornier establishments; and if I were allowed to choose only one target in Germany, the target I should choose would be Berlin.'

Stokes, sensing Sinclair was being defensive, pressed him further. 'Does not my right hon. Friend admit by his answer that the Government are now resorting to indiscriminate bombing, including residential areas?' There was a stirring on the seats in the Commons, and some muttering. To some, it seemed impertinent that anyone would question the strategy of Bomber Command when the House itself was sitting in temporary accommodation amid streets ruined by the assaults of Germany's own air force. Sinclair stood to reply, 'The hon. Gentleman is incorrigible. I have mentioned a series of vitally important military objectives.'

Other Members of Parliament came to Sinclair's defence, asking questions that were supportive of his position. Many considered Stokes's questions to be those of a nuisance backbencher, but he had voiced the concerns of an increasing number of politicians.

In the early years of the war the House had opposed the bombing of civilians, condemning Germany for the brutality of its assaults on Britain's cities during the Blitz, but when the RAF – and later the USAAF – began to deploy a similar strategy, it did not debate the matter. Stokes's intervention also echoed concerns raised earlier in the war about the accuracy of RAF bombing. His mentioning of the figure of '16 square miles' suggested the target designated was so broad that bombers were bombing without proper target acquisition. But this was to ignore the assiduous efforts of the Pathfinders to improve the marking of targets and thereby to enhance the accuracy of the bombs delivered.

The unfortunate truth was that a bomb falling four miles off target from 20,000 feet was a common occurrence. And, once fires started outside the target area, it was all too easy for bomber crews to mistake them for the original target – a phenomenon known as 'creepback' – thereby further compromising the accuracy of the raid. In his questioning, the honourable member for Ipswich failed to discriminate between bomber accuracy and target designation. Had he chosen to question Operation Gomorrah, the multiple attacks on Hamburg of July 1943, which, as the name implied, was an attempt to completely destroy a city, he would have made his point better.

Parliament had raised the subject of bombing strategy during an earlier conflict, the Spanish Civil War of 1936 to 1939. The bombing of the Basque town of Guernica on 26 April 1937 caused a flurry of questions in Parliament, but the British government was slow to respond to the indignation of members. In the confusion of war the government wanted to establish the facts accurately, not least to confirm the reports that German aircraft and pilots had carried out the attack. Some of the delay was doubtless born of a desire to avoid confrontation with Germany. It was not until June 1938 that the House debated Franco's bombing of open cities, those designated for non-combatants in the Spanish Civil War. On this occasion, condemnation of the bombing of civilians had been unequivocal. However, the experience of the Blitz – the Luftwaffe's bombing campaign against Britain's cities from September 1940 to May 1941 – changed public opinion, pressuring politicians to respond in kind. Willie Gallacher, the Communist member for West Fife, raised concerns over the tone of a *Daily Mail* column of 20 March 1941. He complained that suggestions that a 'Bomb Berlin' fund be set up was inappropriate and sought confirmation that the Air Ministry did not have one. However, with the demand for retribution against Germany mounting, there were few who felt the newspaper's approach was extreme.

On 9 February 1944, two months after Stokes's question in the Commons and a year before the bombing of Dresden, George Bell, Bishop of Chichester, raised the issue of area bombing in the House of Lords. Bell had consistently opposed the bombing of civilians. He had made his views known as early as November 1939, supporting the Committee for the Abolition of Night

Bombing set up by 'Corder' Catchpool, a Quaker pacifist who had been imprisoned as a conscientious objector during the First World War. This group changed its name to the Bombing Restriction Committee in 1942. In 1944 the writer and feminist Vera Brittain, one of the committee's founder members, published *Seed of Chaos*, an impassioned plea to cease saturation bombing of civilian targets. 'We must decide whether we want the government to continue to carry out through Bomber Command a policy of murder and massacre in our name. Has any nation the right to make its young men the instruments of such a policy?' Despite these impassioned pleas, the voices of dissent were very much in the minority. A war-weary Britain believed that the obliteration of Germany was a necessity.

George Bell's speech in 1944 was more nuanced than Stokes's parliamentary question of 1943. He explored the subject in greater detail but was still uncompromising in his conclusions. He began, 'I would humbly claim to be one of the most convinced and consistent Anti-Nazis in Great Britain. But I desire to challenge the Government on the policy which directs the bombing of enemy towns on the present scale, especially with reference to civilians, non-combatants, and non-military and non-industrial objectives.' He made it clear that his intention was not to condemn aircrews: 'no criticism is intended of the pilots, the gunners, and the aircrews who, in circumstances of tremendous danger, with supreme courage and skill, carry out the simple duty of obeying their superiors' orders.' Bell went on to describe, as he saw it, the slide towards indiscriminate bombing, and to emphasize the previously accepted legal position: 'It is still true, nevertheless, that there are recognized limits to what is permissible. The Hague Regulations of 1907 are explicit. The right of belligerents to adopt means of injuring the enemy is not unlimited.'

In contrast to the cut and thrust of the Commons, the response of their Lordships was polite and respectful, but the dominant opinion voiced was that if the area bombing strategy was the surest and swiftest way to defeat Hitler, then it was right to pursue it. The majority of parliamentarians felt that since they were engaged in all-out war, Bomber Command's actions were justified. In the light of the Axis's destruction of dozens of towns and cities from the Baltic to the Mediterranean, Bell's argument against area bombing was unlikely to make much headway. Quite apart from their appalling treatment of Jews and other minority groups, the Nazis' bombing of British cities had spawned a widespread – and vengeful – feeling that the Germans deserved a retribution of biblical proportions. It was no accident that Harris in 1942 had quoted a phrase from Chapter 8 of the Old Testament book of Hosea in justifying the onslaught he was about to unleash: 'The Nazis entered this war under the rather childish delusion that they were going to bomb everyone else and nobody was going to bomb them. At Rotterdam, London, Warsaw and half a hundred other places, they put their rather naive theory into operation. They sowed the wind, and now they are going to reap the whirlwind.' The invocation of scripture implied that the RAF was doing God's will, a view not at odds with public opinion. Britain required revenge for the dead of London, Liverpool, Manchester and Coventry. In the heat of a desperate war, the imperative of crushing Germany's civilians as an industrial force outweighed other arguments, yet there was a need to place these actions in a moral framework.

That Hitler had taken on the mantle of a Pharaoh in the persecution of the Jews was not lost on churchmen and theologians. George Bell's compassionate approach was fuelled by news filtering out of Germany. He was an ardent supporter of the *Bekennende Kirche*, the Confessing Church, a movement that stood against the pro-Nazi *Deutsche Evangelische Kirche* (known in English as the Protestant Reich Church). Bell was moved by stories of civilian suffering coming through his ecumenical contacts in Switzerland. In May 1942 he met with pastor and theologian Dietrich Bonhoeffer, a founder member of the Confessing Church. Bonhoeffer had joined the Abwehr, the German military intelligence service, but was a double agent. His post allowed him to travel to Norway, Sweden, Denmark and Switzerland, enabling him to act as a courier for the German resistance movement. Bonhoeffer had crossed the dangerous line from moral disagreement with the state to actively opposing it. It was a decision that was to cost him his life. Bonhoeffer was arrested in 1943 and following the July Plot of 1944* was accused of being associated with those who had conspired to kill Hitler. In the dying days of Nazi rule, he was executed on the morning of 9 April 1945. Admiral Canaris, former head of the Abwehr, and his deputy General Oster were executed alongside him.

Despite the interventions of men like George Bell, the role of the civilian in Germany's ability to wage war was not in dispute at the Air Ministry. Many German civilians became unwitting collaborators in their army's success through the industrialization of war production. Supply chains that equipped armies for war had become increasingly sophisticated. Traditionally, invading armies looted their supplies from the territory they took, but this proved insufficient to maintain the larger European armies of the eighteenth and nineteenth centuries. The *Grande Armée* with which Napoleon invaded Russia in 1812 required a huge supply train for a force of some 480,000 troops. One hundred years later, the First World War proved it was possible to use railways, horses and motor vehicles to maintain millions of men in the field with supply lines that stretched back to the combatant nations' largest factories as well as their smallest towns

---

* On 20 July 1944, Claus von Stauffenberg and other conspirators attempted to assassinate Adolf Hitler inside his Wolf's Lair field headquarters near Rastenburg, East Prussia, with a briefcase bomb.

and villages. Whether it was ammunition, vegetables, or buttons for jackets, civilian populations were able to provide for their soldiers without leaving home.

In the Second World War, the ability to transport vast supplies of food became the deciding factor not only in the performance of armies, but in the survival of the civilian populations who supported them. In an agreement of 1 January 1945, America pledged to supply the Soviet Union with more than a million tons of flour and sugar, along with 520,000 tons of canned meat and 440,000 tons of fat and butter. It was a small percentage of the USSR's needs, but it helped propel the Soviet armies forward against Berlin. From a Soviet perspective, the destruction of Germany's cities as supply and transport hubs was essential to winning the war. It was inconceivable that German cities should remain untouched while the Soviet army lost hundreds of thousands of men fighting against a comparatively well-fed German army.

That civilians would be drawn into the conflict and subjected to the same rigours as combatants was an inevitable corollary of the way the Second World War was fought. Hitler knew that the bombing of cities would lead to retaliation, but believed he could keep the Reich safe through an invincible Luftwaffe. His aerial attacks on Warsaw on 1 September 1939 and Rotterdam on 14 May 1940 were against an enemy that did not have the capacity to strike back. These events proved to the Allies that Hitler had no compunction in targeting civilians. The pre-war prophesies of H. G. Wells and Giulio Douhet seemed to be fulfilling themselves – the next war would be won by attacking civilian populations.

The first Luftwaffe bombs fell on London on 24 August 1940 during the Battle of Britain. Believing Hitler had deliberately targeted Londoners, Churchill ordered an attack on Berlin the next evening. Two more raids followed, causing limited damage but denting Hitler's pride. Hermann Goering had promised the Führer that Berlin was unreachable by the enemy. In a spiralling fit of rage that overshadowed much of Hitler's decision-making, he ordered Goering to undertake a bombing campaign on London. Throughout the 1940s the overwhelming opinion in Britain was that as Hitler had started the bombing, Germany deserved what befell it. By war's end, the moral horror of the concentration camps had been laid bare by Edward Ward at Buchenwald on 1 April 1945 and Richard Dimbleby at Belsen on 19 April. Their profoundly shocking radio broadcasts further reinforced the view that Germany's inhumanity provided ample justification for the bombing of their cities.

This view remained largely unchallenged during the 1940s, but politicians, recognizing the controversial nature of the policies, began to distance themselves from their decisions. Just as Allied strategy had moved seamlessly from declared military targets to city-wide bombing, the shift away from it was gradual as the war was won. Chief among the movers was Churchill, who believed Dresden was the tipping point in the usefulness of area bombing as a strategy. In a telegram of 28 March 1945 to General Ismay, chair of the Chiefs of Staff Committee, he wrote:

> It seems to me that the moment has come when the question
> of bombing of German cities simply for the sake of increasing
> the terror, though under other pretexts, should be reviewed.
> Otherwise we shall come into control of an utterly ruined land.
> We shall not, for instance, be able to get housing materials
> out of Germany for our own needs because some temporary
> provision would have to be made for the Germans themselves.
> The destruction of Dresden remains a serious query against the
> conduct of Allied bombing. I am of the opinion that military
> objectives must henceforth be more strictly studied in our own
> interests rather than that of the enemy.

Charles Portal, Chief of the Air Staff, was taken aback by the tone of the memo and asked Churchill to amend it, which he duly did with the concluding lines, 'we must see to it that our attacks do not do more harm to ourselves in the long run than they do to the enemy's immediate war effort'.

Many commentators have seized on Churchill's words as proof of his own doubts about the morality of area bombing. In their study of 2016, 'Winston Churchill and the Bombing of German Cities, 1940–1945', Peter Lee and Colin McHattie argue that the memo was the opening shot of a sustained campaign by Churchill to bolster his popularity by distancing himself from the bombing war. However, whatever Churchill decided subsequently, his unaltered memo can be read as a pragmatic intervention. His words suggest he believed the Allies had exhausted city attacks as a useful strategy, rather than that he was querying the morality of the entire bombing campaign.

As the new post-war world order emerged, the vanquished Germany – in the form of its Allied-occupied western areas – would need to become a friend and ally of the West. This realignment would lead the Allies to re-examine the suffering of Germany and adopt a more compassionate reading of history. If Cold War spending on nuclear weapons was to be justified, it was the Marxist-Leninist Soviets, still exerting a totalitarian grip on their empire, who had to be stigmatized as the barbarians at the gate. In the spirit of reconciliation that was applied to Germany, many perpetrators of Nazi terror would escape justice in the rush to stabilize a divided nation.

Almost as soon as the fighting stopped in Europe, the Western Allies and the Soviets began to square up against each other. The Soviets occupied a significant portion of Central and Eastern Europe, and it was apparent they had no intention of withdrawing. With between 7 and 11 million displaced people scattered throughout Europe, the task of building the peace seemed to far outweigh the need to dispense justice. In facing the Soviet threat, it was argued, old enemies needed to work together.

By the time Winston Churchill stood to make a speech at Westminster College in Fulton, Missouri, on 5 March 1946, the boundaries of the new world order were already set. Churchill saw the threat of war with the Soviet Union but believed it could be avoided:

> I repulse the idea that a new war is inevitable; still more that it is imminent. It is because I am sure that our fortunes are still in our own hands and that we hold the power to save the future, that I feel the duty to speak out now that I have the occasion and the opportunity to do so. I do not believe that Soviet Russia desires war. What they desire is the fruits of war and the indefinite expansion of their power and doctrines.

The Soviet Union had lost 26.6 million of its citizens by military action, disease or starvation. The Wehrmacht and SS had slaughtered tens of thousands of Russians as they advanced in 1941, destroying towns and villages with precision. Stalin was in little mood to consider the liberties of the German people or the countries that had supported her. His primary focus was on receiving reparations, $10 billion tentatively promised at the Allied leaders' conference at Yalta in February 1945. By the Potsdam Conference of July 1945, Stalin believed Churchill and Truman were rowing back on their promises, not least in giving him joint control over the Ruhr, Germany's economic powerhouse. The long-serving Soviet foreign minister Andrei Gromyko recalled Stalin saying, 'The USSR is being cheated... The British and Americans were not behaving as real allies. They want to force us to accept their plans on questions affecting Europe and the world. Well, that's not going to happen!'

After thirty years of nuclear stand-off, the Europe of the 1970s was a profoundly different place from that of the 1930s. The

West Germans who won football World Cups and produced Volkswagens were undoubted friends of the Allies. They had joined NATO in 1955 and acquiesced to the stationing of hundreds of thousands of troops on their soil. With the growing popularity of foreign travel, millions had the chance to meet ordinary Germans and were left in no doubt whatsoever that they were remarkably similar in their attitudes to Britons and Americans. It seemed that the Nazis had melted almost invisibly into European society, with only a few hard-line right-wingers trying to relive their glories in South America. In the dialogue of the 1970s, Germany's willingness to accept responsibility for genocide was coupled with an expectation that the Western Allies would admit their faults also. The most obviously morally dubious aspect of Allied strategy was their bombing campaign against German cities. While America felt no obligation to apologize for its bombing of Japan, citing the maniacal resistance of Japanese people to invasion, Britain began to wring its hands over the suffering of cities like Hamburg and Dresden. In trying to defeat the evil of Nazism, had they allowed themselves to commit crimes of the kind they held Germany accountable for? It was as if the transformation of Germany from a society responsible for committing the most unimaginable acts of terror into a reasonable free-thinking country had happened so quickly that it had wrongfooted the British.

National hero status is often the product of political expediency. Battle of Britain pilots, for example, remained in pole position as the ultimate Second World War heroes of popular perception, while the courageous sailors who had the unenviable task of manning the convoy routes to the ports of northern Russia were considerably less fêted. The Atlantic Star was awarded in 1945 to all those who had participated in the Battle of the Atlantic, but the lion's share of public gratitude was lavished on those who had kept Britain supplied on the American routes. It was not until 2012 that the Queen approved the Arctic Star for those who had undertaken the dangerous sailings to Russia. In other words, the veterans who had helped 'Uncle Joe' Stalin had to wait until after the Cold War was over to be recognized. Britain's relationship with the reunified Germany, a partner and friend in the European Union and other international organizations, has made the honouring of bomber crews more difficult. The airmen of Bomber Command have long requested a campaign medal for their efforts, but to date their pleas remain unanswered.

★

The blackened tower is all that remains of St Nikolai Church, Hamburg. Completed in 1874, the building was for two years the tallest building in the world. Designed by English architect George Gilbert Scott in the Gothic Revival style, the 86-metre-long nave was damaged badly on 28 July 1943 and was finally demolished in 1951. The crypt contains a museum that explains Operation Gomorrah. With displays covering Warsaw, Coventry and Rotterdam, the display's creators conclude, 'the fuse for the firestorm was lit in Germany'. St Nikolai serves as Hamburg's primary memorial and speeches made here act as a barometer of German thinking. Henning Voscherau, Mayor of Hamburg from 1988 to 1997, asked the question, 'If the Allies had not had the courage and determination to answer Nazi violence with violence in order to stop the Germans running amok, would liberation, renewal, a democratic future have been possible?' By 2003 the mood had changed, Mayor Ole von Beust choosing to make no mention of the Nazis as he described Operation Gomorrah as a 'breach of civilization'. Von Beust's words were spoken just a year after the publication of the historian Jörg Friedrich's book *Der Brand* (translated into English as *The Fire*, 2006), a study of the Allied bombing campaign, which placed the German dead of Hamburg and Dresden as equal victims of the atrocities of war, alongside the victims of Nazism. Graphic in its descriptions – and photographs – of the effects of bombing, the book caused a sensation in Germany, treating as it did a subject that had hitherto been considered taboo. Although widely criticized for his use of the term 'final solution' in respect of Allied bombing strategy, Friedrich's reflections, while provocative, constitute a serious contribution to the historiography of the bombing war. Perhaps if any criticism can be levelled at modern interpretations, it is that in the detailed examination of one aspect of war the wider context is all too easily forgotten. The Second World War was a catalogue of intense horror, in which strategic and moral decisions were made by a relatively small number of people. It should not be regarded as surprising that in the mayhem these leaders were not able fully to manage the consequences of their decisions.

When proposals to build a Bomber Command memorial in Green Park, London, were approved in 2010, Helma Orosz, the Mayor of Dresden, criticized the plans, saying they would 'not be part of the culture of reconciliation' and that 'the emotions of the people of Dresden are running high, it is against our culture of remembrance'. By the time the memorial was finished in 2012, the hostility in German quarters had calmed a little, as the inscription 'We remember those of all countries who died in 39–45' was approved. Designed by architect Liam O'Connor, the colonnaded structure houses seven figures in bronze. Dressed in the equipment of a bomber crew, they stand, one of them with his hand shielding his eyes, looking into the sky for a returning aircraft.

The opening of the memorial by Her Majesty the Queen on 28 June 2012 was one of the last events attended by significant numbers of former aircrew. Many, now in their late eighties, were happy that their efforts had at last been formally recognized. Ken Cook was there, together with 5,000 former crewmen and

Ken Cook, aged 79, attends a reunion at RAF Wyton.

their families. Walking sticks, Zimmer frames and wheelchairs were much in evidence, many veterans sheltering from the summer sun under umbrellas. Dark suits laden with medals bore testament to their actions sixty-seven years before. There was a sense of great pride but also sadness for the 55,573 men who failed to return. It was the swansong of the fliers of RAF Bomber Command, a group of men who had suffered appalling casualties and yet, despite all the hardships they experienced, had completed their missions. They are also representatives of a generation that has proved – even after the most catastrophic of wars – that the bitterest of enemies can become friends.

Appendix: Operations listed in Ken Cook's Logbook

	Date	Target	Notes	Lanc
9 Sqn	**1943**			
	2 Oct	Munich		B
	3 Oct	Kassel	Attacked at Minden E/A stb inner shot up	B
	7 Oct	Stuttgart	Diverted Boscombe Down	G
	18 Oct	Hanover		G
	22 Oct	Kassel	Diverted Winthorpe	C
	3 Nov	Dusseldorf		C
	18 Nov	Berlin	stb inner U/S landed East Kirkby	H
	22 Nov	Berlin		C
	23 Nov	Berlin		B
	26 Nov	Berlin	Diverted Leconfield	B
	16 Dec	Berlin		G
97 Sqn	**1944**			OF-
	1 Jan	Berlin	Supporter PFF 4 Engines cut glide landed Granston	L
	5 Jan	Stettin	Supporter	K
	20 Jan	Berlin	Marker visual	L
	21 Jan	Magdeburg	PFF supporter	L
	27 Jan	Berlin	PFF marker, landed Hunsdon	K
	28 Jan	Berlin	PFF marker	K
	30 Jan	Berlin	PFF supporter	K
	15 Feb	Berlin	V. Heavy attack. Marker PFF	K
	19 Feb	Leipzig	Marker PFF	K
	20 Feb	Stuttgart	Support PFF	K
	24 Feb	Schweinfurt	Marker PFF	K
	25 Feb	Augsburg	Marker PFF. 360 photo 1 mile from aiming point	K
	1 Mar	Stuttgart		D
	15 Mar	Stuttgart		K
	18 Mar	Frankfurt		K
	22 Mar	Frankfurt		H
	24 Mar	Berlin	Landed Warmwell out of petrol	S
	26 Mar	Essen		G
	30 Mar	Nuremberg		F
	20 Apr	La Chapelle	Paris	F
	22 Apr	Brunswick		F
	24 Apr	Munich		F
	26 Apr	Schweinfurt		F
	29 Apr	Clermont Ferrand		F
	1 May	Toulouse	Aiming point. Good attack	F
	3 May	Mailly le Camp	Aiming point. Good attack. Heavy fighter opposition	H
	9 May	Annecy		F
	22 May	Brunswick	Bombing scattered	F
	24 May	Eindhoven	Recalled abortive	F
	27 May	Morsalines	Attacked from 7000 feet	F
	31 May	Maisy	Diverted Chipping Warden	F
	6 Jun	Argentan	Landed at Bourn	F
	8 Jun	Rennes		F
	12 Jun	Caen		F
	15 Jun	Châtellerault	Landed at Upwood	F
	16 Jun		**Completed Second Tour**	**Hours**

Day 230.20
Night 371.34

Total Ops Hours   **275.35**

A Note on Sources

The Crew is the product of many wet Cumbrian winter days spent on detailed research into the activities of Bomber Command. The task of piecing together the lives of the crew was a challenge that required me to pore over logbooks, squadron records and a host of other sources, both printed and online, including newspaper articles and websites. The internet proved invaluable, providing largely untroubled access to records that would have otherwise been viewable only in paper archives. In acknowledging my sources, I must first give credit to the many devoted individuals who have uploaded thousands of pages of information onto websites. As well as the official record keepers, a host of amateurs, many of them family members of bomber crewmen, have shared their personal stories. It is thanks to their efforts and their attention to detail that I have been able to reconstruct events that took place more than seventy-five years ago, and create the narrative of *The Crew*.

Central to the book is the testimony of Wing Commander Ken Cook, who shared his recollections through a series of interviews conducted in 2018 and 2019. With the passage of time, Ken's memories are not always as clear as they once were and the author has spent many hours corroborating facts from secondary sources. This research was greatly helped by members of Ken's family who took the time to trawl through family records and the many hundreds of photographs in their possession. I am indebted to Anthony and Julia D'Auvergne Oake who opened their homes to me during my visits to Ken. Their help and enthusiasm allowed for a much greater interrogation of Ken's memory than might otherwise have been possible.

The relatives of other crew members have also been enormously helpful. Visits, telephone calls and emails all generated a large quantity of fascinating material. Their input enabled me to find the human stories behind the bald statements of the official squadron records. Tales of wartime exploits, told and retold around family dinner tables, often not only added colour but also supported both Ken's version of events *and* the official version. Hearing the same story from two different sources allowed me to verify its accuracy. In cases where items of information – often of a personal nature – could not be fully verified, I have generally chosen to retain them, since they tend to carry the authentic flavour of genuine, lived experience. Tellingly, I sometimes found that thoughts and feelings expressed by one crew member were echoed in the published accounts of their fellow airmen.

In the disciplined environment of the wartime Royal Air Force, in which all Lancaster aircrews were required to carry out the same checks and follow the same routines before take-off, we can plausibly imagine what the airmen said and did as they prepared to take to the air. Once they took off into the gathering gloom of the evening, however, a thousand different scenarios could play out.

I would like to make particular mention of Hilary Lee and her husband, Michael, whose memories and family albums yielded much crucial information concerning Hilary's father, Don Bowes, the crew's navigator. Michael has written a family history, 'Don and Marg', which was invaluable in tracing the steps of Don's wartime journey and beyond. Russell Woollford, the son of the crew's radio operator Roy Woollford, opened up his family records and gave me access to Roy's logbook. Although

Roy passed down only a few stories, they proved to be very accurate in content.

I devoted a great deal of time to examining official records, the key resources being the Royal Air Force Operational Record Books (ORBs), held at the National Archives in Kew. These were created to provide a complete record of RAF units on a day-to-day basis. The ORBs describe aircraft movements and flying crews rostered, but give few additional details. For the purposes of *The Crew*, I chose to use copies of the Operational Record Books held on Squadron Association websites, in particular those of 9 and 97 Squadron Associations. The author is indebted to the work of association members in transcribing these.

Thanks are also due to the dedicated volunteers of Coningsby Aviation Heritage Centre for their help in providing access to their records – in particular to the RAF Coningsby Station Record Book. I am acutely aware that the photographing and digitizing of these records are the result of many hours of painstaking work.

Official records were reliant on a small number of men to check their accuracy, and inevitably they contain small factual errors. Airmen's names are sometimes spelled incorrectly and target names, often unfamiliar to those who were entering the information, are not infrequently misspelt. Aircraft identities are another source of errors. While airframe numbering (ND740, ND692, etc.) remained unchanged throughout a plane's operational life, the squadron letter codes were often changed. Thus F-Freddie might become G-George, and so on. Once an error is introduced at source, it tends to be repeated in other publications and websites. I trust that I have provided an accurate rendering of names and numbers, but I realize that some details may have slipped through the net.

Other published accounts of the Second World War bombing offensive have been referenced and detailed in the Bibliography. In referring to websites, I am very aware of the temporary nature of some of these sources: webpages can move, change or simply disappear from time to time. All of the webpages mentioned in this Note on Sources were accessed in 2018 and early 2019. The author apologizes in advance if any of the links have become inactive in the interim.

Prologue

I came to the interviews with Ken Cook with the knowledge that many servicemen greatly underplay their experiences. Some, including certain other members of this crew, said very little, if anything, to their relatives. Their recounted memories are shards of information spread over decades rather than a cohesive narrative. Ken's willingness to share his experiences more freely than some of his fellow fliers has been a great benefit to historians.

Although Ken takes great pride in his wartime service, there is not the slightest suggestion of pretension. He counts himself as being lucky, a word he often repeated during our conversations. The word is well chosen. The Bomber Command statistic of 55,573 killed in action produces a percentage loss rate of 44.4 per cent. A further 8,403 were wounded and 9,838 taken prisoner, which means that chance of something unpleasant happening to an airman on an operation was as high as 59 per cent. Bomber Command also lost over 3,000 men to training accidents throughout the war, which are not included in the quoted casualty figures. A young man volunteering to fly on bomber crews faced a daunting prospect.

Prelude

My first encounter with the ring of defensive forts around Liège in Belgium took place during an early Sunday morning stroll in July 1980, when I stumbled unexpectedly upon the deserted

Fort de Flémalle near Seraing. I was amazed at its subterranean structure, and the blasted concrete that spoke of its bombardment in the First World War. The entrance gateway, located in a defensive cutting, was peppered with gunshots. Flémalle has been preserved as a museum, but Fort Fléron, despite its place in the history of aerial bombardment, is buried under a municipal park and surrounded by housing.

Overshadowed by the later events of the First World War, the role of Belgium's forts was short-lived. The twelve forts around Liège were central to Belgium's defence but fell to specially designed siege guns, made by Krupps, in the early part of August 1914. Some of the forts, including Flémalle and Fléron, were attacked again by the Luftwaffe in 1940. Interest in the forts has revived in recent years with a number of informative websites provided by local people.

One: Uncertain Years: 1919–1939

The accessibility of online material from Australia proved immensely helpful in tracing the early life of Jim Comans. The influenza outbreak of 1919 was particularly well covered in the local press. The National Archive of Australia's digitized newspapers enabled me to find references to Comans, particularly in school and sporting reports. Reports featuring the Marist Brothers High School in Darlinghurst were not uncommon, particularly activities at the end of their academic year. The MB Darlinghurst Old Boys' Union were helpful in providing background information, including a tribute to Jim Comans by the union's historian, Scott Coleman, which can be read on their website (see page 392).

The BBC's 'People's War' project was particularly useful for the period around the outbreak of the Second World War. Comprising 47,000 eyewitness accounts written by people who lived through the war, the 'People's War' archive paints a fascinating and informative picture of the everyday lives of men and women in wartime. I used the archive to corroborate other accounts of events, including the bombing of Luton in August 1940.

Two: The Adventure

Accounts and photographs of RAF airmen in training seem more plentiful than those of them in regular squadron service. Many airmen's memoirs are available online, but they also can be found in the archives of independent aviation museums such as my local Solway Aviation Museum at Carlisle Airport. Don Bowes' photographic collection has numerous images of his time in Canada: informal shots of groups of men smiling widely or spending carefree days at the beach. Bowes was one of four crew members, the others being Comans, Cook and Widdis, who received their training outside the United Kingdom. A sense of adventure shines through many of the photographs taken of training in North America. Men were keen to send home pictures that showed the places where they were based and the company they were keeping. Regulations on personal photography seem to have been less restrictive in the USA and Canada. In wartime Britain security was much tighter and photographic processing more expensive.

Not only are there fewer photographs of operational flying than of training, but written references to it in airmen's personal diaries seem less common than in those of other servicemen. This comparative lack of material creates a sense that the airmen's thoughts were fully occupied by their life and death struggles. Servicemen seem to have been far happier talking to their relatives about training than about operational flying.

It is even more difficult to find personal accounts of the crew's German opponents. Few experienced Luftwaffe aircrew survived the war, and those who did were reluctant to tell their stories. Men like Günther Rall who both survived the war and were willing to talk of their experiences are in short supply.

Three: Lancaster

In writing about the Lancaster I was able to draw on my years of preservation work on historic aircraft as a museum volunteer. Complete Lancasters are a rarity, and, strangely, there are no examples extant that were built by Avro. I am grateful to the Imperial War Museum at Duxford in Cambridgeshire for an informal guided tour of their airframe KB899 some years ago. There are plenty of good photographs of the internal workings of the Lancaster, but to gain a real sense of the physical reality of the aircraft nothing can beat the experience of actually walking up the fuselage and clambering over the wing spar to the cockpit. I was struck by the clear view from the latter, but also by the frightening thinness of the Perspex windows. When I thought of the flying white-hot shards of flak the Lancaster was exposed to, I realized just how vulnerable the pilot was. Seeing the physical spaces that each crew member occupied inside the aircraft, I felt better able to understand the operational memories of former airmen.

As I was listening to Ken Cook, therefore, I had the advantage of knowing what his surroundings looked like. My experience of not only studying aircraft controls and instruments over many years, but also of handling them and – in some cases – of refitting similar equipment, greatly helped the visualization process. The aluminium construction of the Lancaster followed a pattern common to many aircraft I had worked on, including the Lancaster's amazing grandchild, the Avro Vulcan, which is one of the residents at Solway Aviation Museum. In the pursuit of a hobby, I realized I had retained a huge amount of technical information that had not been learned in the conventional sense.

In the writing of *The Crew*, I came to understand that the mind retains far more information when it is enjoying itself than it does through formal learning.

But it was still necessary to do further research, particularly on the workings of the innovative technology the Lancaster carried: H2S radar, Gee and Oboe navigation guides and LORAN (Long Range Navigation system) to name but a few. Bernard Lovell's *Echoes of War: The Story of H2S Radar* (CLC Press, 1991) is particularly informative on the development of H2S. Lovell's account serves as both an historical account and personal memoir of a renowned physicist.

Because the Lancaster proved to be such a spectacularly successful bomber, a great deal of written material is available to historians. Air Ministry Specification P13/3, which gave rise to the unsuccessful Avro Manchester bomber, is a useful guide to understanding the thinking of pre-war planners. Most books concentrate on the exploits and memories of aircrews rather than the design of the aeroplane. However, Leo McKinstry's book *Lancaster: The Second World War's Greatest Bomber* (John Murray, 2010) describes both the elements of the design process and the operational service of the bomber. No mention of the Lancaster in print would be complete without mention of the work of Mike Garbett and Brian Goulding, whose hugely successful *The Lancaster at War* series (Ian Allen, 1971–84) combined photographs, technical data and personal accounts by airmen, which – even after thirty years – were still relatively fresh. Comparing these earlier accounts with later memories enabled me to corroborate certain points of detail.

In considering the Augsburg raid of April 1942 it was instructive to see and hear media reports of the time. The release of media archives from sources like the BBC sound archives and Pathé Collection film clips allows a better understanding both of the nature of wartime news reporting and public perception of the RAF. *Heroes of Augsburg* (1942) and *Lancaster Bombers – First Pictures* (1942) are both viewable on YouTube.

Four: Bardney

This chapter is heavily reliant on official records – in particular the Operational Record Book of 9 Squadron. However, the basic information provided by these sources told me very little of the men's actual experiences. I pieced together the account of Flight Lieutenant Leonard Hadland's ditching in Lancaster ED648 from a variety of sources. Technical information on how the dinghy was used can be found in the Lancaster Pilot's notes (AP2062A – Pilot's and Flight Engineer's Notes for Lancaster I, III and X, Paragraph 63), a booklet given to pilots and reproduced widely for today's enthusiasts. RAF Search and Rescue records also provided a detailed breakdown of the type, speed and port operations of their craft.

I began my investigations into particular raids undertaken by the crew in the Squadron ORB, noting the names and numbers of the aircraft involved. Since raids often involved many hundreds of aircraft, I was able to piece together a narrative of the night in question – the weather, the intensity of the German defences, the losses suffered by the RAF – by referring to records of individual aircraft participating in the raid. The testimonies of other aircrews about particular raids, written after the war, were another very helpful source. For those airmen unlucky enough to be shot down, the precise details of the experience remained etched on their minds with particular clarity.

Five: Bourn: The Road to Black Thursday

Before writing about the airfield at Bourn in Cambridgeshire, I spent several hours walking the deserted runways and hardstands to understand the site fully. My thanks to the Rural Flying Corps for granting me permission to visit this private site. The club still fly from Bourn, using a grass strip close to one of the broad taxiways of the old airfield. With industry and new housing developments nibbling at its edges, it is uncertain how long Bourn will remain recognizable as a Second World War airfield. What is striking about any bomber airfield is the immensity of the concrete laid. Over the decades, their surfaces have become potholed and riven with cracks, but they still provide impressive evidence of the scope and energy of Britain's war effort.

The RFC maintains a small display about RAF Bourn. The staff talked to me about the visits of the former servicemen whose slowly fading photographs adorn their noticeboard. Once regular visitors, they have stopped coming now, a poignant reflection of the gradual passing of the generation who fought in the Second World War. Local knowledge is invaluable in the quest to understand a site. The RFC were able to point out where hangars once stood and accommodation long since gone was once located. Even the control tower, or Watch Office as it was then known, has been demolished.

A short trip over to the site of RAF Gransden Lodge, a close neighbour of Bourn, proved equally revealing. Lancasters of 97 Squadron, desperately short of fuel, tried to land here – as well as at RAF Bourn – during the dense fog of Black Thursday, 16 December 1943. The runways at Gransden Lodge have long since gone. In their place swaying crops fill the landscape, giving little clue as to the site's wartime purpose. Despite this, a thriving glider school uses a grass strip in the line of an old runway. Small towing aircraft are used to pull the gliders, but the school also uses a winch that produces a characteristic singing noise as the glider soars upwards on the cable. Here, outside the flying area, the brick Watch Office remains, forlorn and derelict in a patch of rough grass, a silent testimony to the bombers that once graced these fields. Close by I stopped a dog walker from the nearby village who told me about some of the history of the area and recounted stories of the airfield – I must apologize for not recording his name at the time.

In the account of Black Thursday, I quote the diary of Charles Owen, a pilot of note and – to judge from his writing – a man of carefree disposition. Owen's diary entries are also quoted in Chapter Eleven: Separate Ways, particularly in reference to the crew's navigator, Don Bowes, whom he flew with in Mosquitos. Owen's diary is held at the Imperial War Museum. I spoke on the phone with Charles Owen's son, Oliver Owen, who kindly forwarded me a full copy of his father's diary and granted me permission to use extracts. Oliver's memories of his father were not of a dashing airman, however, but of a man in the grip of alcoholism. Oliver's candid article in the *Guardian* in November 2008 (see Websites, page 395) explains the complex personality of a man who served his country with distinction in wartime, but who subsequently struggled with life after his service in the RAF was over. Oliver Owen wrote: 'He died in the summer of 1984, a few days after my 20th birthday. He was only 61, but looked very much older, due to a long battle with alcohol. In fact it was no battle at all, just one-way traffic with booze very much in the driving seat.'

Memories of Black Thursday are well documented on the RAF Pathfinders website. Relatives of those who died on 16 December 1943 continue to make efforts to reconstruct the events of that night, thereby adding to our understanding of the tragedy.

Six: Berlin

Ken Cook flew forty-five completed missions, and it is unsurprising that his memories of certain individual raids are sometimes less than entirely clear. The Berlin mission of 1/2 January, the crew's first as Pathfinders, belongs in this category. The Comans crew flew to Berlin on twelve occasions, one of which was aborted when they experienced a faulty engine. The observations of the target noted in the crew's post-raid intelligence debriefing could only have come from Ken Cook, as he was the only crew member with a clear view.

Although the Berlin raid is not considered remarkable in terms of Bomber Command records, numerous sources detail the crashes of individual bombers that evening, the men who flew them and, in the cases of fatalities, where they are buried. Throughout this book, I am indebted to the work of the Commonwealth War Graves Commission in the provision of detailed casualty records.

In interviews, Ken was surprisingly phlegmatic about the Comans crew's nerve-wracking return to RAF Gransden Lodge with all engines stopped. He remembered the experience, the heart-stopping realization that this was a serious situation, but little else. What caused the engines to stop seemed to be a lack of fuel, but the direct cause evaded us for some time. However, Ken eventually recalled that the flight engineer was a stranger (Steven Smith) rather than their regular F/E Ken Randle. He also recalled Smith had problems with the fuel system. The completion of the story came from members of Ken's family, who remembered Ken had told them how the flight engineer had accidentally closed the fuel cocks in the minutes prior to landing.

Seven: Pathfinders

Churchill's friendship with Lindemann (later Viscount Cherwell) is a key element in the foundation of the Pathfinders. However, space did not permit a fuller examination of Lindemann, although I would recommend *Prof: The Life of Frederick Lindemann, by Adrian Fort* (Pimlico, 2004). Another fascinating, if rather more troubled, character is Ernst 'Putzi' Hanfstaengl, Hitler's foreign press chief, whose attempts to introduce Hitler to Churchill have captured the imaginations of historians. *Hitler's Piano Player*, by Peter J. Conradi (Carroll & Graf, 2004), is an interesting biography of Hanfstaengl.

The Butt Report of August 1941 is accessible through the National Archives at the Public Record Office (AIR 14/1218) and provides a clear summary of bombing results in the period 1940 to 1941. The foundation of the Pathfinders as 8 Group under Don Bennett has been a subject of keen discussion by historians, not least because of Bennett's stormy relationship with 5 Group commander Ralph Cochrane. In seeking to understand the personalities of the men in high command, it was instructive to watch interviews with Bennett and Leonard Cheshire that are available on YouTube (the web links can be found in the Website section, pages 394 and 395). The interviews were conducted in the 1980s and are of poorer technical quality than we would expect today, but they make for fascinating viewing. Martyn Chorlton's *The RAF Pathfinders: Bomber Command's Elite Squadrons* (Countryside Books, 2012) provides an excellent overview of the formation and operations of the Pathfinder force.

Eight: Coningsby

It has been interesting to note an increase in German sources of information about wartime events. Residents of the village of Münchholzhausen have featured the crash of Lancaster ND640 in local publications and on their website. Their curiosity is not an isolated case and although opinion in Germany may be divided as to whether the bomber crews were 'terror fliers', liberators from Nazism or both, the compassion displayed for the RAF victims of crashes is heart-warming.

97 Squadron's move from Bourn to Coningsby is well documented in official records. The Squadron's Operational Record Book is enhanced by RAF Coningsby Station Record Book, which is kept by the Coningsby Aviation Heritage Centre, based at the modern RAF station. As well as listing squadron movements, the squadron records also include reports on casualties, injuries and those admitted to hospital. Within these valuable volumes of typewritten pages are reports on sporting events, cinema showings and social events at the station. Taken together, these important sets of records provide a rounded picture of life at RAF Coningsby, which, together with nearby Woodhall Spa, provided significant operational leadership in the remaining months of the war.

Ken Cook's logbook for 24 April 1944 lists Munich as their target, along with a note saying 'short of petrol, landed at Warmwell'. It is a typical example of the brevity of logbook entries. No further explanation is given and Ken could not remember much about the flight. Fortunately, Roy Woollford, the crew's wireless operator, had recounted what happened in greater detail to his son, Russell. The crew's accidental flight over the Channel Islands illustrates another facet of Second World War history that space did not permit a fuller exposition. I visited Guernsey in 2017 and was struck by the level of German fortification of this small island, which was equipped with a number of anti-aircraft batteries. A trawled-up propeller of a crashed aircraft on the harbourside at St Peter Port bears witness to the effectiveness of these defences. The Comans crew's discomfort was caused not by a lucky hit from an isolated gun, but by the batteries of a well-fortified group of German-occupied islands.

Nine: Tour de France

The story about the village of Bosc Geffroy with which I open this chapter was told to me during a visit to Normandy in the

1990s. I was working on a British-owned holiday home in the village, and was invited to a local farmhouse for an evening meal with my employers. Fortunately, some of the teenage members of the farmer's family had a grasp of English and we enjoyed a convivial evening with our hosts. The conversation turned to the war and to stories of local life under the German occupation, and it was then that I heard the story of the woman attacked early one morning by a lone Allied aircraft. I revisited the area in the summer of 2019 and explored a preserved V1 site in the woods at Val Ygot, near Ardouval.

The crew's participation in some famous raids – much studied and much narrated – meant there was a particular wealth of sources of information for these episodes. The attack on the barracks at Mailly-le-Camp is celebrated as a moment of enlightenment in pathfinding as Leonard Cheshire proved his low-level marking could cause severe damage to a German military unit. Jack Currie's *Battle Under the Moon* (Crecy, 1995) paints a detailed picture of the events of 3/4 May 1944 with personal accounts like those of Ron Storey of 166 Squadron and 49 Squadron's Ron Eeles (referenced in the Website section, page 394) giving some useful insights. I found some very detailed information on participating aircraft and losses on the *RAF Commands* website forum.

Ten: The Beginning of the End

In dovetailing details of the crew's experiences of D-Day with the broader story of the events of 6 June 1944, I found John Keegan's *Six Armies in Normandy* (Jonathan Cape, 1982) and Stephen Ambrose's *D-Day* (Simon & Schuster, 1994) especially helpful.

Ken Cook's memories of this momentous day are now a little vague and it may be that his flight to Argentan on the evening of 6 June was similar to many that preceded it. It was dark and the target was completely obscured, and their flight home was hampered by poor weather. The ORBs become more significant a source when Ken's memories are weaker. As brief as the ORBs are in individual crew entries, they become a little more conversational in their writing style over the period of D-Day and the days immediately thereafter. Other crew entries paint a fuller picture of the Argentan raid. For example, Pilot Officer Gee's report contains the phrase, 'Heard Controller saying some bombs dropped carelessly.' The Comans crew entry for the raid ends as follows: 'Satisfactory trip, though obliged to land at Bourn because of 10/10ths cloud at 10,000. Haze made it impossible to assess result of raid.'

The author has benefited from visits to the D-Day beaches and particularly the *Le Grand Bunker* museum at Ouistreham, which provided a fascinating insight into the construction and equipping of German bunkers. A visit to sites on Guernsey – in particular the *Pleinmont* naval observation tower – shed informative light on the fortifications of the Atlantic Wall.

Eleven: Separate Ways

As the crew end their operational flying careers, I lose direct contact with them in official records. For understandable reasons, the RAF logged combat information in far greater detail than it did the more mundane details of its training operations. However, day-to-day records were kept by training units such as 1661 HCU at RAF Winthorpe, where Jim Comans was posted as an instructor. Unlike Comans, however, Ken Cook was posted – as squadron navigation officer – to another operational squadron (49 Squadron) rather than to a training establishment. I was therefore able to compare Ken's entries in his logbook for the crews he flew with in training, with the 49 Squadron ORB, and track those who were subsequently lost on operations.

Charles Owen's diary allowed me to keep track of Don Bowes'

flying days alongside Owen after the Comans crew disbanded. The tone of Owen's diary is very similar to that of Guy Gibson's book *Enemy Coast Ahead* (1946), almost certainly reflecting the style of speech these men adopted.

Because of the high levels of operational casualties, air accidents on home soil tended to be downplayed. The disaster at RAF Fulbeck in April 1945 seems to have been largely forgotten, but an account of the tragedy can be read on the 49 Squadron Association website (see link in Websites section, page 396). Despite the absence of certain details from the website account, such as the ranks or roles of some named eyewitnesses, it offers an accurate and compelling picture of the events of the day.

Twelve: The Jet Age

Much of the detail in the early part of this chapter is based on Ken Cook's logbook. For the post-war era of flying, more photographs are available and they are generally of better quality than the earlier ones. The RAF seems not to have regarded its official photographs with the same security consciousness as it did during wartime and they were shared freely among servicemen. As with the Lancaster, my experience of working with museum examples greatly aided my understanding of the early jets that Ken flew in. After spending many hours working on the Meteor NF-14 (built in 1953) at Solway Aviation Museum, I have come to appreciate its robust construction. Despite being an aircraft of the new jet age, many of its features descend directly from aircraft of the Second World War era. Navigation equipment first installed on Lancaster and Halifax bombers can be found on much later aircraft like the English Electric Canberra and Avro Vulcan, which can also be seen at the museum. H2S radar was last used in the Falklands War of 1982 by 'Black Buck' mission Vulcans, forty years after they first flew.

Unlike today's digital age, where most of us leave a clear trail of footprints in the virtual world, it is easy to forget the generations of our recent past. I am reminded almost daily that their world was one of typed documents and handwritten letters. The postal service handled most transactions and even a telegram would be transcribed to paper and delivered by hand. The lives of the crew are documented in files held at the National Archives, in small photographs and family albums, and in the minds of their loved ones who remember brief conversations about their war experiences. Sometimes a man might receive a brief mention in a newspaper, an award, or a retirement interview.

After the war, the majority of the Comans crew disappear into the anonymity of everyday life. Jim Comans emerges again in Australian media reports in connection with his sporting interests decades later. But for some of the others the trail goes cold, and finding them again after seventy years has proved an impossible task. Daniel Bolland, who emigrated to Australia with his family, proved untraceable. After George Widdis's mention in the *London Gazette* for his DFM in 1944, he too disappears into obscurity back in Canada. Online genealogy research sites have proved useful in sketching a broad outline of the men's lives after the war: who they married, the children they had, and – sadly – their passing.

Epilogue: The Writing of History

In attempting to condense a vast body of material and opinion into an Epilogue, I realize I run the risk of simplifying the complex issues surrounding the bombing war. But I am indebted to the following outstanding books on the subject for their insights and clear analysis: *The Bombing War*, by Richard Overy (Allen Lane, 2013), *Bomber Command*, by Max Hastings (Michael Joseph, 1979), *The End: Hitler's Germany 1944–45*, by Ian Kershaw (Allen

Lane, 2011), *Berlin – The Downfall: 1945*, by Antony Beevor (Viking, 2002) and *Savage Continent: Europe in the Aftermath of World War II*, by Keith Lowe (Viking, 2012). I would strongly recommend any of these books to readers who wish to explore further the strategic and ethical issues surrounding the Allied area bombing campaign.

Online sources

General Research

9 Squadron
   http://www.9sqn.co.uk/research

97 Squadron
   http://www.97squadronassociation.co.uk/operations.html

Prelude

Fort de Fléron.
   http://www.saive.be/Histoire/martyrePdH_1914/saive_martyre_
      fleron-1914.htm
   https://translate.google.com/translate?hl=en&sl=fr&u=http://users.
      skynet.be/jchoet/fort/fleron.htm&prev=search

Hauptmann Rudolph Kleinschmidt.
   hauptmann-kleinschmidt-zeppelin-z-vi/

Destruction of Leuven University Library.
   http://www.ww1.manchester.ac.uk/destruction-of-the-university-
      of-leuven-library/

Kagohl 3.
   https://www.military-history.org/articles/strategic-bombing-gothas-
      over-london.htm
   The Command of the Air, translation, full text. https://permanent.
      access.gpo.gov/airforcehistory/www.airforcehistory.hq.af.mil/
      Publications/fulltext/command_of_the_air.pdf

One: Uncertain Years: 1919–1939

Eveleigh Railway Workshops Strike.
https://carriageworks.com.au/journal/1917-the-great-strike/

Spanish influenza.
https://www.nationalgeographic.com/archaeology-and-history/
magazine/2018/03-04/history-spanish-flu-pandemic/

Byron Bay Record.
https://trove.nla.gov.au/newspaper/page/11992388

Marist Brothers High School in Darlinghurst.
https://www.mbhsdarlinghurst.org/WW2_Honour_Roll.htm

Two: The Adventure

Bombing of Luton. Fred Morrad's testimony.
https://www.bbc.co.uk/news/uk-england-beds-bucks-herts-
34083126

Lord's Cricket Ground.
https://www.stjohnswoodmemories.org.uk/content/amenities/
clubs-societies/lords-cricket-ground/royal_air_force_in_st_
johns_wood_in_the_2nd_world_war

Albany Field.
https://tailendcharlietedchurch.wordpress.com/raf-stations/77-
squadron-elvington/oor-wullie/dave-clark-pilot/albany-field/
http://www.no-50-and-no-61-squadrons-association.co.uk/
veterans-album/f-lt-a-e-stone-dfc-afc/

Avro Anson. Patricia Bay.
https://aviation-safety.net/wikibase/144917

Chapter Three: Lancaster

Henschel factory.
http://www.alanhamby.com/factory1.shtml

Churchill illness.
https://www.rcpe.ac.uk/sites/default/files/jrcpe_47_3_vale.pdf

Chapter Four: Bardney

Airfield.
   http://www.bcar.org.uk/bardney-history
   http://www.controltowers.co.uk/B/Bardney.htm
   https://community.lincolnshire.gov.uk/bardneyvillagehistory/sec-
      tion.asp?catId=22918

9 Squadron
   http://www.historyofwar.org/air/units/RAF/9_wwII.html

Hadland crash.
   http://www.bcar.org.uk/1943-incident-logs

Chapter Five: Bourn: The Road to Black Thursday

Bomber airfields.
   https://www.telegraph.co.uk/history/raf-bomber-command/9361471/
      Every-RAF-Bomber-Command-base-in-England-mapped.html

Black Thursday.
   https://raf-pathfinders.com/black-thursday/

Tom Leake interview. 97 Squadron Association.
   http://www.97squadronassociation.co.uk/tomvid.html

Six: Berlin

Anti-handling devices.
   http://www.rafbdassociation.com/early-days.html

Elsan toilet.
   https://tailendcharlietedchurch.wordpress.com/halifax-bomber/
      halifax-aircrew/caught-short-aloft/

Mr Fox.
   https://www.forces.net/news/toy-fox-only-remaining-member-
      dambuster-crew

Gerda Kernchen.
   https://www.elinorflorence.com/blog/berlin-bombing

Seven: Pathfinders

Churchill in 1932.
  https://winstonchurchill.hillsdale.edu/churchill-wilderness-years-
  meeting-hitler-1932

Correspondence between Stalin and Churchill.
  https://www.marxists.org/reference/archive/stalin/works/
  correspondence/01/42.htm

University of Cambridge. Churchill at war.
  https://www.cam.ac.uk/ChurchillAtWar

Mailly-le-Camp.
  http://www.rafcommands.com/archive/09529.php

Ron Storey.
  https://www.bbc.co.uk/history/ww2peopleswar/stories/04/
  a4292804.shtml

Ron Eeles.
  http://www.49squadron.co.uk/assets/pdf/ron_eeles.pdf

Brigitte Eike.
  https://www.spiegel.de/international/zeitgeist/wwii-diary-shows-
  surprisingly-ordinary-life-of-berlin-teenager-a-901355.html

Eight: Coningsby

Don Bennett interview.
  https://www.youtube.com/watch?v=UjHoUwNJ6O4

Leonard Cheshire interviews.
  https://www.youtube.com/watch?v=Q8j9w6VsZKo
  https://www.youtube.com/watch?v=_JihH2VSiqU

Leonard Cheshire Victoria Cross citation.
  London Gazette, 5 September 1944.https://www.thegazette.co.uk/
  London/issue/36693/supplement/4175

Delingpole, *Spectator*, 9 June 2010.
  https://www.spectator.co.uk/2010/06/men-fight-for-their-mates-it-
  is-the-secret-of-why-they-so-love-war/

Nine: Tour de France

627 Squadron Association.
   http://www.627squadron.co.uk/afs-bookpartII-Toulouse-Raid.htm

Percy Cannings
   https://johnknifton.com/2016/03/15/john-david-fletcher-part-two/

Oliver Owen, *Guardian.*
   https://www.theguardian.com/lifeandstyle/2008/nov/30/war-raf-
   hero-oliver-owen

Ten: The Beginning of the End

Pointe du Hoc
   https://armyhistory.org/rudders-rangers-and-the-boys-of-pointe-
   du-hoc-the-u-s-army-rangers-mission-in-the-early-morning-
   hours-of-6-june-1944/
   https://www.dday-overlord.com/en/d-day/beaches/pointe-du-hoc
   https://www.independent.co.uk/news/world/world-history/d-
   day-deadliest-battle-avoided-normandy-omaha-beach-discov-
   ery-a8943416.html

Carter's Lancaster.
   https://www.telegraph.co.uk/news/newstopics/howabout-
   that/9578931/Lost-Lancaster-crew-identified-after-68-years-by-
   wireless-operators-wedding-ring.html
   https://www.mirror.co.uk/news/real-life-stories/lancaster-bomber-
   found-in-normandy-68-1355246

Helmut Eberspächer.
   https://www.tracesofwar.com/persons/22676/
   Ebersp%C3%A4cher-Helmut.htm

Eleven: Separate Ways

Fulbeck tragedy.
   http://www.49squadron.co.uk/assets/pdf/the_fulbeck_tragedy.pdf

Epilogue

Richard Stokes. *Hansard*.
https://api.parliament.uk/historic-hansard/commons/1943/dec/01/
bombing-policy#S5CV0395P0_19431201_HOC_35.

George Bell. *Hansard*.
https://api.parliament.uk/historic-hansard/lords/1944/feb/09/
bombing-policy

Transcript of Churchill's memo.
http://www.nationalarchives.gov.uk/education/heroesvillains/tran-
script/g1cs3s3t.htm
Peter Lee and Colin McHattie, 'Winston Churchill and the Bombing of German Cities, 1940–1945'. https://www.
ingentaconnect.com/contentone/gws/gws/2016/
00000013/00000001/art00005?crawler=true
Melvyn P. Leffler, 'The Struggle for Germany and the Origins of
the Cold War', 2006.
https://www.ghi-dc.org/fileadmin/user_upload/GHI_Washington/
PDFs/Occasional_Papers/The_Struggle_for_Germany.pdf

Hamburg.
https://www.spectator.co.uk/2015/05/the-carpet-bombing-of-ham-
burg-killed-40000-people-it-also-did-good/

Dresden, Helma Orosz.
https://www.telegraph.co.uk/history/raf-bomber-
command/7985917/Dresden-mayor-to-lobby-against-building-
of-Bomber-Command-memorial.html

Bibliography

Air Ministry, *The Rise and Fall of the German Air Force* (London: The Air Ministry, 1948).

Ambrose, Stephen, *D-Day* (London: Simon & Schuster, 1994).

Barker, Ralph, *Strike Hard, Strike Sure* (London: Pan 1965).

Beevor Antony, *The Spanish Civil War* (London, Orbis 1982).

Beevor, Antony, *Berlin – The Downfall: 1945* (London: Viking, 2002).

Beevor, Antony, *Ardennes* (London, Viking 2015).

Bending, Kevin, *Achieve Your Aim* (Bognor Regis: Woodfield Publishing, 2007).

Brickhill, Paul, *The Dam Busters* (London: Evans Brothers, 1951).

Chorlton, Martyn, *The RAF Pathfinders* (Newbury: Countryside Books, 2012).

Churchill, Winston, *The Gathering Storm* (London: Cassell, 1948).

Conradi, Peter J, *Hitler's Piano Player* (London: Carroll & Graf 2004).

Currie, Jack, *Battle Under the Moon: The RAF Raid on Mailly-le-Camp, May 1944* (Manchester: Crecy, 1995).

Feast, Sean, *Master Bombers* (London: Grubb Street, 2008).

Friedrich, Jörg, *Der Brand* (translated, New York: Columbia University Press, 2006).

Ford, Roger, *Steel From The Sky* (London: Cassell, 2004).

Fort, Adrian, *Prof: The Life and Times of Frederick Lindemann* (London: Pimlico, 2004).

Garbett, Mike and Goulding, Brian, *Lancaster at War*, 1st, 2nd and 3rd edns (London: Ian Allen, 1971–84).

Grady, Stephen, *Gardens of Stone* (London: Hodder & Stoughton, 2013).

Gibson, Guy, *Enemy Coast Ahead – Uncensored* (Manchester: Crecy, 2003).

Grey, Jennie, *Fire by Night* (London: Grub Street, 2000).

Hampton, James, *Selected for Aircrew* (London: Air Research Publications, 1993).

Harris, Arthur, *Bomber Offensive* (London: Collins, 1947).

Hastings, Max, *Bomber Command* (London: Michael Joseph, 1979).

Hastings, Max, *Catastrophe* (London: William Collins, 2013).

Johnson, Boris, *The Churchill Factor* (London: Hodder & Stoughton, 2014).

Keegan, John, *Six Armies in Normandy* (London: Jonathan Cape, 1982).

Kershaw, Ian, *The End: Hitler's Germany 1944–45* (London: Allen Lane, 2011).

Kirby, Robert, *The Avro Manchester – The Legend behind the Lancaster* (Stroud: Fonthill Media, 2017).

Knott, Richard, *A Black Night for Bomber Command* (Barnsley: Pen & Sword, 2007).

Lee, Michael, *Marg and Don* (privately published, 2018).

Levine, Joshua, *Forgotten Voices of the Blitz and the Battle for Britain* (London: Ebury Press, 2006).

Lovell, Bernard, *Echoes of War* (Boca Raton: CRC Press, 1991).

Lowe, Keith, *Savage Continent: Europe in the Aftermath of World War II* (London: Viking, 2012)

McKay, Sinclair, *The Secret Life of Bletchley Park* (London: Aurum Press, 2010).

McKinstry, Leo, *Spitfire* (London: John Murray, 2007).

McKinstry, Leo, *Lancaster: The Second World War's Greatest Bomber* (London: John Murray, 2010).

McLoughlin, Roy, *Living With The Enemy* (Jersey: Starlight Publishing, 1995).

Masters, Roy, *Bad Boys* (Sydney: Random House Australia, 2006).

Middlebrook, Martin and Everitt, Chris, *The Bomber Command War Diaries* (Leicester: Midland, 1996).

Moorhead, Caroline, *Village of Secrets* (London: Vintage, 2015).

Overy, Richard, *The Bombing War* (London: Allen Lane, 2013).

Price, David, *A Bomber Crew Mystery* (Barnsley: Pen & Sword, 2014).

Robson, Martin, *The Lancaster Bomber* (London: Conway, 2012).

Uhl, Matthias and Eberle, Henrik, *The Hitler Book* (Washington D.C.: Public Affairs US, 2006).

von Boeselager, Philipp, *Valkyrie* (London: Weidenfeld & Nicolson, 2009).

von Kardorff, Ursula, *Diary of a Nightmare: Berlin 1942–1945* (New York: John Day Co., 1966).

Wrench, John Evelyn, *Struggle 1914–1920* (London: Ivor Nicholson & Watson, 1935).

Wilson, Kevin, *Bomber Boys* (London: Cassell 2005).

Acknowledgements

Special thanks are extended to:

Wing Commander Ken Cook
Anthony and Julia D'Auvergne Oake
Brian Cook
Russell Woollford
Michael and Hilary Lee
Oliver Owen
Andrew Copley
Ryan Tomlinson
9 Squadron Association
97 (Straits Settlement) Squadron Association
49 Squadron Association

Their assistance and attention to detail have been invaluable in the research for this book. The author also acknowledges the wealth of information provided by others, too many to name, whose contribution formed a small but essential part of this story.

I also wish to thank my agent, Charlie Viney (The Viney Agency), for his support through this project, my editor, Richard Milbank, and all the staff at Head of Zeus who have made this book possible.

Index